Y0-BEF-275

Global City Challenges

Global City Challenges

Debating a Concept, Improving the Practice

Edited by

Michele Acuto
Senior Lecturer, University College London, UK

Wendy Steele
ARC Fellow, Griffith University, Australia

palgrave
macmillan

First published 2013 by
PALGRAVE MACMILLAN

Palgrave Macmillan in the UK is an imprint of Macmillan Publishers Limited, registered in England, company number 785998, of Houndmills, Basingstoke, Hampshire RG21 6XS.

Palgrave Macmillan in the US is a division of St Martin's Press LLC, 175 Fifth Avenue, New York, NY 10010.

Palgrave Macmillan is the global academic imprint of the above companies and has companies and representatives throughout the world.

Palgrave® and Macmillan® are registered trademarks in the United States, the United Kingdom, Europe and other countries.

ISBN 978–1–137–28686–4

This book is printed on paper suitable for recycling and made from fully managed and sustained forest sources. Logging, pulping and manufacturing processes are expected to conform to the environmental regulations of the country of origin.

A catalogue record for this book is available from the British Library.

A catalog record for this book is available from the Library of Congress.

Contents

Figures and Tables

Figures

Tables

Contributors

Michele Acuto is Senior Lecturer in the Department of Science, Technology, Engineering and Public Policy (STEaPP), University College London, UK, and Stephen Barter Fellow of the Oxford Programme for the Future of Cities at the University of Oxford, UK. He is the editor of *Negotiating Relief* (2013) and author of *The Urban Link* (2013).

David Bassens is Assistant Professor at the Free University of Brussels, Belgium (Cosmopolis research group) and has been a researcher at the Social and Economic Geography research group at Ghent University, Belgium, since October 2007. Since 2008, he has been employed on a four-year FWO-project entitled *Globalization Revisited: The Relationship between Global Commodity Chains and Urban Networks*. David focuses on 'alternative' world city networks and newly arising lines of research on urbanization and globalization in non-core regions of the world economy and Gulf cities in particular. Since 2008, he has been a member of the editorial board of *AGORA Magazine*, a Dutch–Belgian journal on socio-spatial issues and a research fellow of the Globalization and World Cities (GaWC) Research Network.

Kerwin Datu is a PhD Researcher in the Department of Geography and the Environment, London School of Economics (LSE), UK, and the editor-in-chief of *The Global Urbanist* – an online magazine analysing urban development issues worldwide. Originally trained in architecture, a field in which he worked in Sydney, Paris and London over nine years, he completed an MSc in Urbanisation and Development at the LSE in 2009, which inspired the magazine. He is now completing a PhD in Economic Geography at the LSE, focused on the role of global and regional city networks in economic development.

Ben Derudder is Professor of Human Geography in the Department of Geography, Ghent University, Belgium, and Associate Director of the GaWC Research Network. He is also a Marie Curie Fellow in the School of Geography and Environmental Science, Monash University, Australia. His research focuses on the conceptualization and empirical analysis of transnational urban networks. He has published in key geography and urban studies journals and written and co-edited books on world city network formation, including *Cities in Globalization* (2007), *Global Urban Analysis* (2011) and the *International Handbook of Globalization and World Cities* (2012).

Howard Dick is Professorial Fellow in the Department of Management & Marketing, Faculty of Business and Economics, University of Melbourne, Australia, where he has taught since 1998. He was previously senior lecturer in Asian Economic History, in the Department of Business Development & Corporate History (formerly Economic History), University of Melbourne, Australia, and senior lecturer in the Department of Economics, University of Newcastle, Australia, between 1976 and 1998, after completing his PhD in the Research School of Pacific Studies of the Australian National University. He is the author of *Surabaya, City of Work* (2002) and has written several articles, chapters and books in collaboration with Peter Rimmer.

Mark Graham is Research Fellow in the University of Oxford's Internet Institute, where he focuses on Internet and information geographies, and the overlaps between ICTs and economic development. Mark's work on the geographies of the Internet examines how people and places are ever more defined by, and made visible through, not only their traditional physical locations and properties, but also their virtual attributes and digital shadows. He is currently involved in a multi-year project funded by an ESRC-DFID grant to study the effects of broadband use and access in Kenya and Rwanda, asking who benefits (and who doesn't) from improved connectivity. Mark's previous work in this area focused on similar questions within the context of the Thai silk industry. He has also recently set up a commodity chain tracing project (Wikichains.org) that will allow people to harness the power of user-generated content to uncover the hidden production practices, environmental effects and economic geographies behind everyday items.

Sheila Hones is Professor in the Department of Area Studies, Graduate School of Arts and Sciences, University of Tokyo, Japan. She holds a BA (University of Manchester, UK) in English/American Literature, an MA (Clark University, USA) in American literature and a PhD (Boston University, USA) in interdisciplinary American studies. Within American studies, her main research interests have to do with the integration of literary studies and cultural geography. Recent publications include articles in *American Quarterly, ACME, Comparative American Studies, Cultural Geographies, Environment and Planning: A, Geography Compass, and Social and Cultural Geography.*

Michael Hoyler is Senior Lecturer in Human Geography at Loughborough University, UK, and Associate Director of the GaWC Research Network. His research interests are in urban, economic and social geography with a focus on the transformation of European cities and metropolitan regions in contemporary globalization. He has published widely in the field of urban studies. Recent co-edited books include *Global Urban Analysis* (2011) and the *International Handbook of Globalization and World Cities* (2012).

Roger Keil is Professor and Director in the City Institute at York University, USA, where he heads a seven-year international Major Collaborative Research Initiative on 'Global Suburbanisms: Governance, Land and Infrastructure in the 21st Century'. He was co-editor of the *International Journal of Urban and Regional Research* (IJURR), co-editor of *The Global City Reader* (with Neil Brenner, 2006) and of *Networked Disease: Emerging Infections in the Global City* (with S. Harris Ali, 2008) and is a co-founder of the International Network for Urban Research and Action (INURA).

Oli Mould is Lecturer in Human Geography in the Department of Geography, Royal Holloway (University of London), UK, and was previously Lecturer in the School of Environment and Life Sciences, University of Salford, UK. His primary research interests lie at the intersection of contemporary economic process, human creativity and urban life. This leads to studies of the creative and media industries, urban subcultural creativity and theories of economic geography. His recent work has focused on the recent surge in 'creative city' urban policies including cultural quarters, media cities and urban interventions. His studies have focused on a number of cities including London, Tel Aviv, Istanbul and Sydney.

David Murakami-Wood is Associate Professor and Canada Research Chair (Tier 2) in Surveillance Studies at the Department of Sociology, Queen's University, Canada. He was previously Reader in Surveillance Studies in the Global Urban Research Unit at Newcastle University, UK, where he is now Visiting Fellow. He has been Visiting Professor in the Postgraduate Program in Urban Management at the Pontifical Catholic University of Parana, Curitiba, Brazil and Visiting Fellow in the School of Social Sciences at Waseda University, Tokyo, Japan. He is the Editor-in-Chief of *Surveillance & Society*.

Christof Parnreiter is Professor of Economic Geography at the University of Hamburg, Germany, and Associate Director of the Globalization and World Cities research network. He holds a PhD in Economic History from the University of Vienna, Austria, and has been a Fellow at the Globalization Project at the University of Chicago, USA. He has published extensively on global city formation, Mexico City and, more generally, on the economic geography heritage of the global city paradigm.

Peter Rimmer is Emeritus Professor in the School of Culture, History and Language at the Australian National University, where he works on a project entitled *Global + Local Logistics: Asian-Pacific Rim Perspectives*. He was previously editor of *Australian Geographical Studies*, Hanjin chair of Global

Logistics at Inha University, Korea, consultant to a number of Australian federal and state governments, as well as to the World Bank, Asian Development Bank and Transport Planning and Research Institute, the Ministry of Transport of the People's Republic of China. He is also distinguished fellow in the Institute of Australian Geographers and member of Korean Maritime Institute Global Advisory Board (KGAB). He is the author of *Cities, Transport and Communications: The Integration of Southeast Asia since 1950* (2003) and *The City in Southeast Asia* (2009).

Glen Searle is Associate Professor in the School of Geography, Planning and Environmental Management, University of Queensland (UQ), Australia, Chief Editor of *Urban Policy and Research* and a Fellow of the Planning Institute of Australia. He joined UQ in 2009 after a previous appointment at the University of Technology Sydney as Director of the Planning Program, and policy positions with the New South Wales departments of Decentralization and Development, Treasury and Planning, and with the UK Department of the Environment.

Wendy Steele is a Senior Research Fellow co-located in the Urban Research Program and Climate Change Response Program at Griffith University, Australia. In 2009 she was awarded the Peter Harrison Memorial PhD Prize for research and scholarship in Australian urban studies administered by the Fenner School of Environment and Society and the Endowment for Excellence at the Australian National University. In 2011 she was awarded a three-year Australian Research Council grant (DECRA) which examines the security discourses framing the governance critical infrastructure (i.e. food, energy, water, transport, housing) in Australian cities. She is currently on the international editorial board for the journal *Urban Policy and Research*.

Peter J. Taylor is Professor of Human Geography in the Faculty of Engineering and Environment at Northumbria University, UK, as well as founder and Director of the GaWC Research Network based at the University of Loughborough, UK, where he was Professor between 1995 and 2010. He was previously in the Department of Geography at Newcastle University, UK, from 1968 to 1995 and has held nine visiting appointments in North America and Europe. A Fellow of the British Academy, he has honorary doctorates from Oulu and Ghent Universities. He is author of over 450 publications including 60 that have been translated into one or more of 23 languages. He is author and editor of over 30 books, including *World City Network* (2004), *Global Urban Analysis* (2011) and *Extraordinary Cities* (2013).

Vanessa Watson is Professor in the City and Regional Planning Programme and Deputy Director of the School of Architecture, Planning and Geomatics,

University of Cape Town, South Africa. She writes on planning theory and practices in Africa, is an editor of *Planning Theory* and is on the editorial boards of *Planning Practice and Research, Journal of Planning Education and Research* and *Progress in Planning*. She also represents the Association of African Planning Schools on the Global Planning Education Association Network.

1
Introduction

Michele Acuto and Wendy Steele

'Global city' is one of the most successful terms that emerged from urban studies. Originally the focus of planning research concerned with the changing impact of urban settlement on our societies, as in Peter Hall's *The World Cities* (1966), the discussion of the globalization of major cities extended in the 1970s and 1980s to a survey of the networked imprint of these places on humanity. What was theorized by scholars like John Friedmann (1986) as a hypothesis on how cities influence the new international division of labour as promoted by the growing clout of neoliberalism on world affairs was to become in the following years a complex research programme with a variety of ramifications. Critical in this expansion was the work of Saskia Sassen, who popularized the term 'global city' (1991), first employed by David Heenan (1977), and promoted Friedmann's plea to link global flows with local social developments. Likewise, of key importance was the Globalization and World Cities network (GaWC) founded by Peter Taylor, who pushed for a formalization of the network analysis of how major cities are intertwined with the global economy as well as with each other. Having emerged as a dominant discussion in urban studies through the mid-1990s, the global city paradigm has progressively expanded in the past two decades to extend beyond geographical and urbanist research and has become an attractive area of research of direct appeal to scholars across most of the social sciences. While we will see in closer detail in the next two chapters how this has been the case, it is crucial to understand here two key features. The increasing interest in the 'global city' has, firstly, promoted scholarly divergences and cross-disciplinary translations while, secondly, it has at the same time trickled into the practices and rhetoric that uphold urbanist *practices*, not only academia, in these very cities.

The contested identity, and emerging pull, of the 'global city'

Popularity rarely translates into universal definitional convergence, and 'global city' is no exception to this. As with several other popular terms in urban studies and geography, like 'scale' or 'space', there persists a vast variety of interpretations of what the 'global' city might be. Early urban studies such as those of Hall (1966) put a mostly qualitative emphasis on how these cities represent places where most of the regional and international business is conducted. This was progressively developed into a (mostly quantitative) discussion of the networked interconnection of major centres via Friedmann's research hypothesis (Friedmann and Wolff, 1982) as well as Peter Taylor (2004b) and GaWC's key role in formalizing the analysis of the 'world city network' of commerce, services and mobility that connects metropolises worldwide. At the same time, Sassen (1991) advocated how the focus on the 'global' city as a hub of command and control functions of those advanced producer services that are core to the neoliberal economy needed a conjunct analysis of how this economic order was shaping the social order of these cities. While many focused on how 'global' or 'world' cities (a definitional discrepancy discussed here in Chapters 2 and 3) are pivotal elements of contemporary world affairs, empirical and methodological divergences progressively developed into a variety of sub-disciplinary stances. If at the outset terminology and strands of global city research were used in a fairly interchangeable way (see, for instance, Brenner, 1998), the late 1990s saw a progressive demarcation in approaches and orientations. Moreover, the global city phenomenon itself grew in popularity and multi-disciplinary application. As Ben Derudder (2006) highlighted in more than a few occasions, the scholarship on metropolises and globalization today remains characterized by conceptual confusion and alternative understandings of what these cities really are. Certainly, as the growing interest in fields beyond urban studies testifies, global cities are seen today as more than simply economic pivots. Likewise, this picture is further complicated by the fact that the global city is nowadays challenged on social equality bases by those who advocate for an urbanist scholarship conscious of the 'uneven development' (Smith, 1990) embedded in the contemporary economic system. So, if on the one hand global city theorists themselves have acknowledged the dual social effects of neoliberal globalization that are polarizing class divisions and splintering the human geography of these cities (Sassen, 2001; Massey, 2007; Hamnett, 2012), on the other hand other geographers and urbanists like Jenny Robinson have pointed at the unequal division that the global city creates in theoretical terms as much as in practical realities with those cities that are perceived as 'off the map' (2002) that the networked pictures of the 1990s analyses have charted. Confronted then by both internal divergences as much as cross-cutting critiques, the 'global city' presents us today with substantial scholarly challenges. Yet, the importance of this phenomenon and its contradictions do not stop at the academia.

Global city-thinking has, in the past years, had a very real pull on society at large. Global cities seem in fact an unavoidable fact of everyday world affairs. For instance, to reach the United States from the Asia-Pacific region, one could in theory fly through any settlement on the Western coast of North America but, as thousands do on a daily basis, people mostly choose Los Angeles as their entry port: tacitly, and most certainly not because of some international covenant, individuals commit themselves to specific networks controlled by this North American hub, which in turn gains prominence as a central place in the geography of regional and global mobility. Global cities have in this sense developed a mutually constitutive relationship with the processes of globalization that uphold them. As Sassen and Taylor illustrated, and at odds with much of the hyper-globalist stances that burgeoned in social science in the early 1990s (Omahe, 1990), contemporary globalization trends have not annihilated the relevance of place and location. On the contrary, as Sassen's scholarship has demonstrated, the territorial revolution brought about by the age of information technology (IT) and the emergence of a finance-dominated world economy is paradoxically characterized by the increasing centralization of very localized processes that underpin cross-border flows, de-nationalization and the creation of new global orders. Global cities become sites of concentration of those command and control functions necessary to such dispersal of de-territorialized operations, which rely on the local production of a vast range of correlated highly specialized services, telecommunication infrastructures and industrial complexes. These functions, as we will see in Chapter 2 by Christof Parnreiter, are not just limited to economic activities but rather extend through countless sectors stretching through cultural, political and even religious fields. This is because, as Manuel Castells (1996, 384) explained, the 'spaces of flows' that sustain today's 'network society' need specific hubs and nodes, 'informational cities' as he calls them, that act as 'spaces of places' functioning as 'information-based, value production complexes where corporate headquarters and advanced financial firms can find both the suppliers and the highly skilled specialized labor they require'. Positioned at the crossroads of countless worldwide networks, and blessed with the attractiveness of globalizing infrastructures, marketplace of goods, services and ideas, these cities have developed a form of 'gravity' which pulls people to choose them (more or less consciously) as privileged global hubs for their strategic positioning in the networked geography of twenty-first century relations.

The pull of the 'global city' as both an idea and a condition of interconnectedness to global processes (Allen, 2010; Acuto, 2011) has developed solid ramifications in the practice of urbanists, local government officials and corporate entities worldwide. In bidding for the 2020 Olympics, for instance, Istanbul self-declared itself as 'a global city of inspiration for thousands of years' while Tel Aviv has recently inaugurated a Global City Strategy 'dedicated to elevating the city's global positioning'.[1] Istanbul and Tel Aviv are not isolated cases: from the antipodean shores of Melbourne and Sydney to the heart of the old colonial empires of London and Rotterdam, or the emerging geographies of Asia and Latin America as epitomized by Shanghai and Rio de Janeiro, countless metropolises have embraced the idea of the 'global city' as strategy and a desirable evolution of their positioning in world affairs. Importantly, this trend has paved the way for a renewed understanding of what makes a city truly 'global' and thus of an increasing widening of the appreciation of global city markers. Cities themselves have become widely proficient in this matter: Tel Aviv's strategy, for instance, is geared not only to attracting international business but also to boosting the city's reputation as a 'hotbed of creativity by internationally promoting the city's other major cultural assets, including dance, design, cuisine, architecture and music'. This appreciation is not just echoed but further enhanced by the encounter of public and private, a connection that has offered a very fertile ground for global city-speak to thrive. Amongst the many cases, for instance, the Chicago Council on Global Affairs issued in 2011 a memorandum for the city's future by calling specifically on the new mayoralty to 'define an explicit global city strategy' that would recognize how 'the city's future, like its past, will rest on achieving broad global excellence across many different sectors and not on a single "big bet" in the development of any one new industry or capability'.[2]

Global cities, then, have sought to locate themselves prominently within international geographies not by just posturing on the map as exotic locations but rather by speaking the language of those globalization processes they aim to stand in the midst of and master. Being 'globalized' is, in current global city-speak, maintaining a modern edge that is reflected in prominent urban developments capable of situating the city in the dominant flows of information, representations and trends that characterize globalization. Crucial to the recognizability of today's globalizing metropolises is then their ability to mirror and enhance dominant 'signs of modernity' (King, 2004, 5) and urban development recipes put in place by globally recognized hubs like New York, not just by replicating them, but also by hybridizing them to produce the city's unique image on a global scale. In this process, as Sharon Zukin (1992) pointed out and as we will see in the chapters 9 and 10, respectively by Kerwin Datu and Oli Mould, culture is more and more the business of cities as metropolises morph into cultural products to be consumed. Global cities have become central marketplaces in the symbolic economy of images, trends, fashion and skill sets that is burgeoning in our age besides commerce, global trade and international finance (Florida, 2005). By organizing their urban texture with international hubs and cultural hallmarks, many cities have devised strategic policies to maintain their 'grip' on global audiences, while enhancing their attractiveness as central places of the world system. Yet by doing this, cities also partake in the structuration of transnational processes and in the reproduction of dominant flows and cultures, thus organizing the geography of world affairs while at the same time being highly dependent on it. By sustaining this dependency, global city policies have pushed many metropolises to become providers for much wider publics than their local constituencies. They serve their urban community, those who travel through them, but also national economies and, in many cases, other governments and non-state actors, in an intricate web of transnational and cross-regional relations. The global city scholarship has slowly realized this impact, but, to date, there remains a lack of reflection on the state of affairs of this academic phenomenon, and of its relationship with urbanist practices, as well as a poor comprehension of the avenues for productive scholarly exchanges beyond economic-centric considerations – still the dominant game in town when it comes to theorizing global cities.

Challenging the 'global' city

The global city has for long now presented a wide array of scholarly challenges. As an entity characterized by both worldwide connectivity as much as complex localized social processes, it has in the 1990s tested the conventional limits of the social sciences and called for an approach to the globalization of today's metropolises that is wary of state-centrism, excessive localism and hyper-globalist explanations. Freed from the constraints of methodological territorialism, and empowered with a geographical understanding of the networked spaces making the global city a truly 'global' entity, the urban theorist needs to come to grips with the intricacies of almost endless horizons. When we move to consider these urban settlements as places in a complex entanglement of global flows, we are, in fact, prompted to consider the city as a place inextricably linked to places beyond, a situated context in a very fluid human geography that is ceaselessly remade and recast. If these considerations amount to a potentially very progressive approach to what global cities mean for the contemporary conditions of humanity, then this intricate nature also presents us with a variety of analytical and normative challenges.

First we begin with the prominent position occupied by economic-centric thinking in global city research. This has raised growing concerns in the recent years, as the chapters 9 and 11 by Oli Mould and Michele Acuto point out, but presents us with the analytical dilemma of going beyond 'economicism' (Bourdieu, 1985) while not dismissing the prominent positioning of global economic processes in the production of the global city. Similarly, the demand for alternative analytics of the global city (Bunnell and Maringanti, 2010) and for innovative disciplinary approaches is necessarily confronted by the challenges of duplication of the substantial work already undertaken by global city researchers since at least the 1970s. At the same time, we need to be wary of not allowing for the scholarship to spin into meta-theoretical speculation of poor relevance to the actual practices of urbanism *in* these cities.

These issues have been coupled, as Parnreiter argues more at length in the following chapter, with a set of scholarly critiques of the global city phenomenon that have emerged in urban studies in the past two decades. To begin with, as also noted above, the growing dominance of this frame as a way of thinking of cities and globalization has in the eyes of many placed the 'global city' into a wrongful hegemonic position in urban research (Robinson, 2002). Rather, many like Brenda Yeoh (1999) have argued, as even global city author Anthony King pointed out (1990, 82), that every city is 'global' to some extent and that instead of focusing on the privileged sites of globalization processes we would be better off studying the pervasiveness of globalization and local distinctiveness of cities. Related to this, and as voiced by Peter Taylor (2004, 33), the global city literature seems to many as characterized by 'theoretical sophistication and empirical poverty', with evident limits on the sophistication of the methodological tools available to global city researchers to put the now long-lived urban theory debate on this phenomenon into actual analytical practice. As such, some of the more recent scholarship has been criticized for being affected by a 'categorizing imperative' (Robinson, 2002, 536) and a compulsive focus on measurement for the sake of ranking rather than a more critical stance on the multifaceted influence of these cities on world affairs. Importantly, this emerging critical scholarship has often called for multidisciplinary analysis (Amin and Graham, 1997) and for a move beyond the 'metrocentricity' that has selectively brought 'to light certain features of urban worlds while leaving others very much in the dark' and that has promoted an often uncritical and poorly reflexive replication of the dominant global city paradigm (Bunnell and Maringanti, 2010, 416) – calls that we believe have yet to be answered systematically.

Investigating the 'dimensions' of the global city

There is a wonderful juxtaposition, for example, when contrasting the everyday ordinariness of Michel De Certeau's poetic urban wanderer – the *wandersmanner* – with the master images, starchitecture, power and hypermobility typically associated with representations of 'global' cities as centres of global capital accumulation, command and control. As De Certeau goes:

> The ordinary practitioners of the city live 'down below', below the threshold at which visibility begins ... they are walkers whose bodies follow the thicks and thins of an urban 'text' they write without being able to read it. These practices make use of spaces that cannot be seen ... it is though the practices organizing a bustling city were characterized by their blindness. The networks of these moving, intersecting writings compose a manifold story that has neither author nor spectator, shaped out of fragments of trajectories and alterations of spaces ....
>
> (De Certeau, 1984, 128)

Besides the challenging visuality and critical normative potential of this image, this brief juxtaposition of De Certeausian wandering with the 'globalized' rhetoric illustrated above prompts us to take an alternative pathway to produce a reflexive and multidisciplinary response to the emerging critique of the global city paradigm. Instead of seeking a 'new' theory of the global city, we aim here to collect a sample of alternative ways of seeing the 'global' and the 'city' that can hopefully promote both reflexivity in the existing scholarship and a renewed view of the multiple dimensions of this phenomenon that has practical relevance for these ordinary practitioners of the city.

This book has therefore emerged from our concern with the present paucity of multidisciplinary discussions of the idea of the 'global city' and what we perceive as a need for a more critical consideration of the practical challenges both faced and inspired by this scholarship. Represented by an almost unanimous reference to Sassen's two editions of *The Global City* (1991, 2001) or to the alternative 'world city' formulation of this hypothesis by Friedmann and Taylor, the idea of the 'global city' has for long been uncritically referenced. More recently, a set of inquiries such as Doreen Massey's *World City* (2007) or Jennifer Robinson's *The Ordinary City* (2006) has sought to provide more balanced investigations, or indeed postcolonial re-appraisals, of this phenomenon. This calls for a critical re-theorization of global cities and the implications for urban research, policy and practice. Specifically this involves a critical rejoinder to the global city research by actively juxtaposing the established concept of the 'global city' with new perspectives that emphasize emergent analytical and practical insights, opportunities and challenges. The key objectives driving the book have therefore been threefold:

1. To *re-cast the ambit of what constitutes global city scholarship* through the integration of an extensive set of new disciplinary dimensions to which the concept of 'global city' can speak;
2. To *promote the establishment of cross-disciplinary conversations* and novel research collaborations including (but not limited to) perspectives that incorporate the cultural, historical, postcolonial, virtual, architectural, literary and political dimensions of global cities; and
3. To *highlight the need for both conceptual and applied research* that not solely relies on theory but also draws on urban communities of practice in global cities such as New York, Shanghai and London, or emerging metropolises like Dubai, Singapore and Sydney.

In order to tackle these theoretical and practical challenges, the book is organized in three analytical steps. First, two introductory chapters by Christof Parnreiter and by Ben Derudder, Michael Hoyler and Peter Taylor provide a reflection on the current status of the idea of the 'global city'. Reviewing the state of the art of this scholarship, and offering an overview of the concurrent 'world city' research agenda, these theoretical reflections set up the context and problematization for the following multidisciplinary inquiry. Second, nine thematic chapters tackle these metropolises in a specific dimension of the global city phenomenon, offering cultural, economic, planning, architectural, historical, postcolonial, virtual, literary and geopolitical critiques from several social scientific standpoints. Each chapter's short case study, paired with a main theoretical section, offers direct illustration of the analytical challenges both raised and faced by each disciplinary standpoint when confronted with the 'global city' idea. Third, the book looks back at the scholarship overviews and the specific dimensions of the global city phenomenon, in order to further animate the interdisciplinary debate on these metropolises and their investigation in urban studies. Along with a conclusion geared at a holistic reading of the various viewpoints presented in the thematic sections, this part is rounded off by a 'reverse' inquiry that takes a specific case study as starting point, rather than testing ground as in the previous thematic sections, to investigate the practical connection between the multiple dimensions of the global city through an emerging metropolis such as Sydney. Linking different analytical standpoints, case studies for long-lived as much as emerging global cities, and reflections on the connection between theory and practice, this preliminary investigation of the state of global city urbanism is aimed at highlighting the implications of this complex scholarly landscape for the actual practice of urbanism in these very cities.

Outline of the book

Ultimately focused on promoting an even greater multidisciplinary discussion of the global city phenomenon, *Global City Challenges* was conceived as a collaboration geared towards providing a practice-oriented review of this scholarship that is critical and case-based. While not seeking to be absolutely comprehensive on all possible dimensions of the global city, we have attempted in this book to gather both traditional ways of seeing the global city and innovative or less trodden research pathways such as culture, the virtual world or literature. A campaign for multidisciplinary inquiry into the global city, however, needs to start from the ground currently available to urbanists tackling the complex reality of these metropolises. In the second chapter of the collection, Christof Parnreiter then provides us with a summary of the current state of the art of global city research by surveying the emergence of this literature as a key voice in contemporary urban studies. The chapter provides an introduction not only to the field of study then investigated in the following issue-specific chapters but also to the key questions that this scholarship has raised in the past few decades. In particular, the chapter discusses the development of two twin and often interconnected strands of research: that of the 'global city' agenda inaugurated by Saskia

Sassen and grown in popularity across a number of qualitative urbanist studies, as well as that of the 'world city' that has its roots in the early 1900s, the 1960s discussions of Peter Hall, and the 'world city hypothesis' by John Friedmann, which is today widely regarded across a variety of quantitative approaches. This parallel viewpoint is then further unpacked by the following chapter, by Ben Derudder, Michael Hoyler and Peter Taylor, who look back at the experience of the GaWC and the last two decades of quantitative investigation of world city networks. As the chapter points out, the world city scholarship has been prey to simplifications. The refined Interlocking World City Network Model (IWCNM) developed by GaWC, for instance, has often clashed with the 'list-mania' now so common amongst popular discussions of global/world cities. Mostly driven by ranking understandings of the global city phenomenon, this misinterpretation has for the most part overlooked the inherent relationality and the deeper networked ramifications that urban studies have generally implied when it comes to locating global cities on the world map.

These introductions are then followed by another thematic chapter on the planning dimension of the global city. Offering a renewed understanding of a traditional avenue for global city research similar to planning, the fourth chapter by David Bassens tackles economic and financial dimensions. In particular, Bassens aims to understand how the dynamics of global cities as nodes on global financial and economic circuits confront the contemporary crisis-rife and rapidly shifting global economy. As he points out, current structural changes in the global financial architecture urge us to 'contemporize' the role of financial institutions and affiliated financial elites in global city formation. An increasingly pressing issue that emerges from this viewpoint is whether and how the rise of emerging economies in the 'Global South' (also unpacked later in Watson's chapter) can be linked to the rise of emerging global cities in their territories. Here, changing geographical articulation of global finance results in the rise of 'emerging' world cities, involving an increased dealing with geo-historical particularities that shape the integration of these cities into global financial circuits. Global Islamic finance, which is flourishing in the Gulf region, is a case in point. This 'decentring' trend, however, is not necessarily changing the centrality of 'mainstay' global cities as command-and-control centres over such emerging markets, making Islamic finance highly susceptible to processes of mimicry vis-à-vis 'mainstream' finance as practiced in and from these global cities. Witnessing such processes in Islamic markets, the chapter challenges Islamic finance's discursive construction as an 'alternative' financial model. In hindsight, then, it concludes with the observation that the growth of cities such as Dubai remains indeed very much dependent on its entangled financial connections to the global cities shortlist.

Following this trend towards an expanded contextualization of the global city, Peter Rimmer and Howard Dick prompt us to then look into the historical trajectories that, they argue, 'global city' taxonomies often tend to ignore. This chapter presents a conceptual framework to trace key phases of convergence and divergence in urban development, highlighting differences in economies (market or command), governance and sustainability that have made cities 'global'. As Rimmer and Dick argue, a historical perspective allows us to appreciate how shifts in the locus of wealth and power are related to technological changes in the modes of both production and consumption along with the connecting means of transport and telecommunications and, not least, the means of war. The authors round off the chapter by applying this viewpoint to the case study of Shanghai, which began as a walled city, became a treaty port and international metropolis, went into eclipse for several decades after the Communist revolution and then re-emerged as a global city.

If planning, economics and history have for the most part been part of the heart of the traditional global and world city paradigms, Vanessa Watson prompts us in Chapter 6 to appreciate how the postcolonial perspective has equally provided an important source of critique of global city scholarship. Watson's chapter, then, illustrates why the 'global city' scholarship deserves postcolonial critique like those moved by Jennifer Robinson (2002) and why these provide a productive dialectic with more established voices such as those echoed in the previous three chapters. Watson illustrates how this scholarship has had the (possibly unintended) effect of encouraging non-global cities to aspire to 'global' status by mimicking the plans and projects of 'global' cities. Global cities are assumed to have a particular appearance: modern buildings and efficient and car-oriented movement systems, with all signs of informality, dirt and chaos removed. Many cities have adopted technocratic and modernist city plans (usually accompanied by vision statements declaring as aspiration to become 'world class cities') which exclude the poor, in the belief that this will somehow allow them to 'catch up with the West'. Watson then takes the case of Cape Town, and particularly the ways in which planning has been an expression of a colonial and postcolonial relationship. Through Cape Town, Watson highlights the assumption that we can learn from cities in the global periphery as much as from global cities, focusing on the interface between central and peripheral nations, as well as on the issues this relationship raises for understanding the geopolitics of knowledge.

A further insight into how both global cities and alternative disciplinary views intersect with the geographies (and geopolitics) of knowledge is that presented by Sheila Hones in Chapter 7. Hones prompts us to connect emerging lines of theory and practice in literary geography with work on the global city, suggesting some of the ways in which contemporary literary geography can function as a useful resource for students, researchers and practitioners of urban studies. The scope of literary geography has undergone considerable expansion in recent years, and now, in addition to its traditional focus on fictional setting and description, also includes studies of the ways in which literary texts participate in the production of particular locations and geographical knowledge generally, as well as studies of the geographies of inspiration and creativity, the spatial aspects of collaboration and co-authorship, the literary space of intertextuality, geographies of production and dissemination, and geographies of reading and reception. This expanded and even more interdisciplinary definition of the geographies of fiction provides a productive context for a literary approach to the study of global cities. Taking New York as its case-study city, Hones concentrates on Colum McCann's novel *Let the Great World Spin* (2009). Through this case study Hones considers the creative processes through which McCann acquired his knowledge of the global city and its globalizing history, then looking at the novel as a version of New York in the period 1970–2006, and finally turning to a discussion of the city-based geographies that have enabled the novel's current status as a critically acclaimed bestseller and the transnationally networked geographies of its reader response.

Further reinforcing the necessity to engage with these alternative geographies, Mark Graham reminds us in Chapter 8 that while cities have always been socio-cultural palimpsests, this feature has recently begun to take on an entirely new dimension. Cities are being represented on the Internet by millions of writers, photographers, cartographers and artists. Graham's chapter, then, traces the history and geography of virtual places in relation to global cities. As he argues, virtual dimensions to places are not a simple mirror of their physical counterparts but instead characterized by both black holes of information and hubs of rich description and detail. This chapter explores how the virtual layers of cities are constructed, ordered and ultimately brought into being into the global city. By drawing on a case study of Wikipedia articles in Arabic, English and Hebrew about the city of Jerusalem, Graham concludes that the virtual palimpsests that now form an integral part of global cities both influence and are influenced by older, offline patterns and processes of voice, representation and power.

Literary and virtual geographies of the global city, then, bring us to the inevitable confrontation of the traditional global city scholarship with the role of culture. Offering an overview of this key societal realm, Oli Mould explores the way in which the cultural dimensions of global cities have been created, forged, utilized and manipulated. Specifically, this chapter will discuss two main themes of how culture elucidates the complexity of the contemporary global cities – top-down and bottom-up. Cultural provisions in the form of major artistic or sporting events, creative industries, architecture or planned sites of cultural consumption (such as Media Cities or Cultural Quarters) have recently been used to promote and vitalize cities. From the importance of the creative class to the regenerative qualities of the Olympic Games, culture plays a critical role in how urban governance affects the 'feel' and general quality of life of a global city. However, parallel to the 'high-end' cultural provisions are the small-scale, community-based cultural activities. Relying on the case of Copenhagen, Mould illustrates how, whether it's urban subcultures (such as parkour, skateboarding and urban exploration) or local artistic groups performing intervention in the built environment (through flash-mobing or guerrilla art), there exists an alternative cultural provisioning that can complement, but is often marginalized by global cities. Mould's chapter, then, ultimately highlights the inevitable challenges faced by the global city in ameliorating the wide range of cultural provisions without alienating particular groups of people.

Mould's overview of the social-physical interconnection of the 'cultural' dimension of the global city takes us to a further realm that, historically, has been crucial to the development of these metropolises: architecture. Kerwin Datu's Chapter 10, then, reminds us how the discourses surrounding the architecture of global cities is often as spectacular as the architecture itself, resounding with terms like the 'Bilbao effect', the 'icon' and the 'starchitect'. Architectural works and architectural criticism are both highly polemical and normative, obscuring a scholarly understanding of why the architecture of the global city emerges in this way. Such an explanation must be traced to the specifics of the consumption, the production and the market-making of architectural services in the context of globalization. Datu's chapter, then, notes how architecture is shaped by how it is consumed by global city constituencies, by how it is produced by professionals coordinating across global distances and how all such groups must make markets meet at the global scale, attracting suppliers, generating demand and closing deals. As Datu demonstrates through the case of Singapore, the iconizing tendency of global city architecture has a great and yet terrifying capacity to sweep away many of the issues posed by specific locations, such as the historic and social value of existing urban fabric, the homogenization of the new architectural environments being produced throughout the world's cities and the ethical problems of working with local authoritarian regimes.

These concerns about the built environment, which echo the challenges highlighted by Watson on planning and by Mould on culture, are further unpacked in the following chapter where Michele Acuto focuses on the burgeoning literature of the intersection between politics and global cities. This chapter aims at providing an introduction to such evolving literature. Acuto illustrates then how global cities are strategic contexts to appreciate present geopolitical realignments, presenting the reader with the questions revolving around the govern*ment* to govern*ance* shifts, citizen participation via social movements and business lobby, as well as the dominance of neoliberalism. However, these more familiar elements of the global city need to be coupled, argues Acuto, with the uncharted geopolitics *of* global cities as both objects of and actors in global governance, therefore illustrating their growing centrality vis-à-vis emerging transnational issues for world politics. Chapter 12, then, underscores the international role of mayors, the challenges of 'city diplomacy' and the expanding pervasiveness of city-based policymaking networks by relying on a snapshot of the complex positioning of London in the contemporary geopolitical scenario, considering what multi-scalar political structures underpin its global primacy as well as what transnational political tests are faced, and created, by the British capital's environmental politics.

Continuing on the theme of unpacking the socio-political impact of the global city, David Murakami-Wood's last thematic chapter considers the urban dimensions of security and insecurity, specifically in relation to the contemporary urban condition represented by the term 'global' or 'world city network'. In order to make sense of the intricate socio-spatial changes impacting this dimension, Murakami-Wood takes a biopolitical approach to security/life and focuses on the way in which global circuits of security knowledge are deployed to govern insecure populations and marginalized people in the global city, the new urban outcasts (Wacquant, 2008) or the 'precariat'. These global circuits of security knowledge are illustrated with the case of Rio de Janeiro, offering an insight into how global cities are rarely simply receivers of security knowledge but, whether successful or not, have become sources of new security knowledge that continues to circulate in the global city network.

Building on this wide variety of disciplinary standpoints, Chapter 13 steps into a case study, that of Sydney, to offer a view of the global city scholarship and its variegated dimensions as they can be interpreted by practitioners in the field. In this chapter Glen Searle shows how Sydney's particular socio-cultural and political-institutional practices cause these to be produced by, or reflected in, these different dimensions of globalization. As he notes, global city spaces have been produced that replicate similar ones elsewhere, that are distinctive and that mix the local and global. The processes of generating and accommodating Sydney's global activities have produced challenges that reflect problems both common to global cities in general as well as some that are more specific. Socio-economic polarization has been accentuated by globalization and its high-income jobs on the one hand and inflows of Asian immigrants on the other, with concentrations of poorer Asian and other households in lower amenity areas that belie virtual representations of global Sydney. Yet, an increasingly politicized public sector that is called to account by a relatively narrow cross-section of the media and the wider populace has meant that the problems of global Sydney have not always generated required solutions with the necessary political support, providing an impetus towards more pro-active government responses to Sydney's global city issues. Taking this practice-oriented view as a starting point to draw home some lessons from the whole book, the last chapter of the collection then pushes us to take into account the mix of 'glocal' (Swyngedouw, 1997) construction of the global city and therefore the demand for greater multidisciplinary attention to the global–local dialectics in place when investigating these cities. As Acuto and Steele note in this final overview, it is crucial not only to unpack the processes of globalization shaping these metropolises in a more holistic way than much global city research offers, but it is also essential not to dismiss the agency *of* the global city as a locality that does not disappear under the strains of globalization. Global cities act and react to the many challenges noted above, and eventually test our tolerance of multi-disciplinarity and eclecticism. So, as we challenge it beyond its traditional boundaries, the global city will inevitably challenge us back, a trial we as editors judged worth taking for the sake of greater cross-disciplinary engagements and for an urbanist scholarship more open to the variety of practices on the ground of these metropolises.

Notes

1. See respectively, Owen Gibson, '2020 Olympics: Istanbul says it would host "open and affordable" Games', *The Guardian* 8 January 2013, available at http://www.guardian.co.uk/sport/2013/jan/08/istanbul-olympic-games-2020 and *Tel Aviv Global City Strategy*, available at http://www.tel-aviv.gov.il/eng/GlobalCity/Pages/GlobalCityLoby.aspx?tm=24.
2. Chicago Council on Global Affairs, *Capturing Chicago's Global Opportunity*, memorandum of the Global Chicago Advisory Committee, 18 January 2011, available at http://www.thechicagocouncil.org/UserFiles/File/Globalmidwest/Capturing%20Chicago's%20Global%20Opportunity.pdf.

2
The Global City Tradition

Christof Parnreiter

> The key indicator of global city status is whether a city contains the capabilities for servicing, managing, and financing the global operations of firms and markets.
>
> [...]
>
> The question is whether coordination and specialized servicing of global firms and markets is taking place.
>
> (Sassen, 2001, 359, 361)

Introduction

For an opening chapter of a book titled *Global City Challenges*, it seems to be appropriate to begin with a terminological clarification. Today, many authors use the terms 'global' and 'world city' either interchangeably or, if they opt for one of the two terms, do not provide a rationale for their choice. Both implys that no significant conceptual differences are being attached to the terms. This view has been challenged by Derudder (2006, 2034) who claims that 'world' and 'global city', as employed by Friedmann and Sassen, refer to 'very different analytical frameworks', namely the spatial distribution of economic power more generally in the case of Friedmann and the geography of the production of the inputs that constitute the capability for global economic control in the case of Sassen. Though I agree that there are important differences between the concepts of Friedmann and Sassen (most significantly Sassen's exclusive focus on producer service firms and hence her disregard of multi- or transnational corporations), I disagree with Derudder's notion that the two have 'very different' (ibid.) takes on the role of cities in economic globalization. In fact, I see Friedmann's world cities closer to Sassen's global cities than to earlier notions of world cities as capitals of empires or as the top of the global power hierarchy, because both are, as I shall argue, concerned with networked cities engaged in the articulation and governance of cross-border economic activities.

Acknowledging, however, the heterogeneous terminology in the literature, in this chapter I will adopt the respective language of the authors I refer to. Where I allude to the general debate, I stick to 'global cities'.

A second preliminary remark refers to the intellectual milieu out of which global city research was developed. Just as mainstream accounts of economic development have been traditionally framed in a national perspective, cities' economic roles and their relations to other cities have mostly been studied through analyses of national urban systems. In both economics and urban studies, however, such 'methodological nationalism' (Wimmer and Glick Schiller, 2002), which (implicitly) thought of and constituted the nation state as the 'natural' container of social processes, has been undermined since the 1970s. On the one hand, the rise of what was then called multinational enterprises (Dunning, 1971) and the recognition that they were establishing a 'new international division of labor' (Fröbel et al., 1977; Cohen, 1981) led to questioning of 'the modern system of territorial states as the primary locus of world power' (Arrighi, 1994, 81). On the other hand, in urban studies a paradigm shift occurred, which has been strongly inspired by emerging world-system analysis. It put cities in a global rather than a national perspective and prompted thereby 'the rise of a new "urban political economy" approach' (Smith, 2003, 113), whose main contention was to 'view cities of the capitalist world-economy as participating in a single interactive spatial system' (Chase Dunn, 1985, 269). While a first thread of this literature began to study patterns of dependent urbanization in the 'Third World', such as rapid demographic growth, high urban primacy or the persistence of a large informal economy in a global rather than a national context, others investigated 'First World' cities in global perspective. The urban crisis and restructuring in the 1970s and 1980s have encouraged a number of studies to relate economic, social, spatial and political transformations in core cities to the demise of Fordism, austerity programmes and the strive for making cities fit for global competition.

Eventually, these intellectual currents stimulated the development of global city research. In this chapter, I will deal first with the paradigm's origins to then summarize what for me constitutes its central claims. Third, I will introduce the major strands of the global city literature as well as some of the major criticisms. Based on these overviews, I will then critically assess the contributions the global city literature – and its critics – have made to the debate. My contention is that much of the literature has actually failed to deal with the key arguments as developed by Friedmann and Sassen, for which reason global city research still faces the evidential crisis for which it has been criticized right from the beginning. To overcome this flaw, in the last section I propose a return to the economic geography spirit inherent in the early global city studies and, in particular, to focus on agency in economic articulation and governance.

The origins

After Hall (1966) had re-introduced the term 'world city' half a century after Geddes (1915) had coined it[1], Heenan (1977) is said to be the first to use the term 'global city'. Positing that 'global cities are evolving in response to fundamental changes in the world's industrial system', he argued that 'these regional requirements as well as the changing configurations of multinational corporations are creating a need for global cities' (ibid., 82). Yet, it was Hymer (1972) who 'initiated the "economic turn"' (Beaverstock et al. 2000, 125) in world city research, because it was he who elaborated in more depth on the relationship between major cities, their arrangement in a hierarchical order and the organizational structure of multinational corporations. In the hierarchical division of labour between geographical regions they produce, they 'would tend to centralize high-level decision-making occupations in a few key cities in the advanced countries, surrounded by a number of regional subcapitals, and confine the rest of the world to lower levels of activity and income ... the basic relationship between different countries would be one of superior and subordinate, head office and branch plant' (Hymer, 1972, 114). This quote not only shows the innovation made by Hymer – to draw attention to the role of specific cities in the making of uneven globalization[2] – but also reveals that he had not yet fully embraced these cities' functions. Firstly, Hymer conceived of the suggested global hierarchy of cities as the geographical expression of the uneven structure of the world economy, rather than its organizing structure: The 'geographical specialization' that the highest business activities are concentrated in the world's major cities, while lesser cities deal with day-to-day operations, will come, according to Hymer (1972, 124; emphasis added), 'to *reflect* the hierarchy of corporate decision making'. Secondly, Hymer (ibid.) associated some cities' status as 'major centers of high-level strategic planning' with their respective countries' position in the world economy ('a few key cities in the advanced countries'), while Sassen later proposed that global cities were (partially) detaching from their national backgrounds and that the network of global cities would cut across the traditional national North–South divide.

The economic turn in world city research was consolidated by Robert Cohen (1981), whose main merit was to expand upon the relationship between (a) the making of a new international division of labour; (b) the organizational changes this 'going global' has implied for the corporations, mainly their growing needs for externally provided corporate services; and (c) 'the emergence of a series of global cities' (ibid., 288). Cohen thus saw the functions of global cities not mainly in the traditional aspect of housing the corporations' headquarters. Rather, he stressed that cities become global cities 'because they are key centers of corporate related services and part of the international network of financial centers' (ibid., 293). Moreover, Cohen linked this corporate service sector – and thus global city-ness – explicitly to economic governance. Because service firms 'help companies to develop their overseas operations' and to 'obtain profits even in a disorderly world', the places where these service firms are located 'serve as international centers for business decision-making and corporate strategy formulation. In a broader sense, these places have emerged as cities for the coordination and control of the NIDL' (ibid., 290, 300).[3] A second innovation was that Cohen saw global city-ness not exclusively resulting from the strength of a national economy, because 'international boundaries become blurred by the increasingly global nature of corporations' (ibid., 308). Whether a city would develop global city functions depends on corporate strategies – cities with nationally oriented corporations and cities which do not receive large numbers of corporate offices and service firms will hardly become prominent global cities. What, thus, shapes the 'new hierarchy of world cities' (ibid., 307) is the specific geography in which corporate activities and services have internationalized.

The global city paradigm according to Friedmann and Sassen

As we have seen, Heenan, Hymer and Cohen have established the global city paradigm as an economic geography perspective on how and from where globalization processes are organized and governed. To explore and to theorize the geography of management and control in the 'new' world economy has been the principal interest of Friedmann and Sassen's seminal contributions, too. As the latter has put it in the second edition of 'The global city' (Sassen, 2001, 347f): 'A key purpose of the model is to conceive of economic globalization not just as capital flows, but as the work of coordinating, managing, and servicing these flows. [...] The global city network is the operational scaffolding of [...] the global economy.'

Accordingly, Friedmann and Wolff (1982, 309) defined 'the spatial articulation of the emerging world system of production and markets through a global network of cities' as their prime concern and contended that management and power in the world economy were increasingly centralized in a certain number of cities – the 'world cities'. These were seen as 'the "basing points" in the spatial organization and articulation of production and markets' (Friedmann, 1986, 71) with the task to 'articulate larger regional, national, and international economies' (Friedmann, 1995, 22). In addition to this articulation function, Friedmann (1986, 73) pointed to the 'control functions of world cities', which he assumed to be reflected in the clustering of corporate headquarters, international finance, transport and communication infrastructure for global business, high-level business services, and the production and dissemination of information and cultural artefacts. Friedmann and Wolff (1982, 310) also emphasized that world cities were '(t)ightly interconnected with each other through decision-making and finance', thereby constituting 'a worldwide system of control over production and market expansion' – a notion that clearly hints at what later should be conceptualized as the 'interlocking world city network' (Taylor, 2004b).

Though Sassen opted for a different terminology – global instead of world city – she shared Friedmann's concern with the articulation and governance functions of global cities. '[M]y use of the notion of global city functions [is] to identify a particular case, that of a city which fulfilled a fairly limited and highly specialized set of functions in the management and servicing of the global economy' (Sassen, 2001, 351). Sassen's basic contention is that global cities are places 'from where the world economy is managed and serviced' (Sassen, 1988, 126f), as well as 'highly concentrated command points in the organization of the world economy' (Sassen, 1991, 3). Yet, Sassen's interest does not lie in formal command power (as expressed, for example, in the number of corporate headquarters in a city). Rather, building on the service literature, she argues that management and coordination functions of global firms have become so complex that their headquarters increasingly have outsourced them to specialized service firms. From that follows a double argument which in my reading constitutes the conceptual core of Sassen's line of reasoning.

Firstly, she claims that producer service firms accommodate a demand that emerges from the organizational needs of companies with global operations, because the 'capabilities for global operation, coordination, and control [...] need to be produced'. Producer services are therefore needed to connect the globally dispersed activities of a firm, and they also contribute to their governance, whereby governance is understood as a 'kind of embedded governance – embedded in the lawyering, the accounting and the investment choices of the firm' (Sassen, 2010b, 158).

Secondly, Sassen asserts that producer services are subject to agglomeration economies. They concentrate in global cities because of their dense, knowledge-rich and technology-enabled environments. The overall centrality in the world economy that these cities achieve stems, thus, from their function as 'a space for the production of organizational commodities needed by firms and markets to operate globally and to shift national wealth to global circuits, and [...] this entails command functions that are distributed across those operations' (Sassen, 2010b, 158). On the other hand, Sassen also sees the tendency towards a polarization of labour markets and incomes in the cities where producer services cluster, what gave rise to the debate on the social structures of global cities (see below).

Sassen also alludes, though without going into detail, to cross-border relations as a characteristic feature of global cities, because the offices maintained by producer service firms in different cities operate in a division of labour. Consequently, relationships between global cities are characterized by a division of functions rather than by simple competition: There is, in

Sassen's (2002, 31) words, 'no such entity as a single global city as there could be a single capital of an empire; the category "global city" only makes sense as a component of a global network of strategic sites'.

In sum, the global city paradigm as put forward by Friedmann and Sassen consists of four interrelated claims: Firstly, global cities are clusters for producer service firms, which are key agents for the servicing and controlling of cross-border operations of firms. Therefore, global cities are, secondly, centres for the management of the world economy, and, thirdly, also centres for its governance. Fourthly, producer service firms are organized in a cross-border division of labour and operate in a worldwide network of cities. It is important to note that for Sassen, who describes herself as a 'political economist interested in the spatial organization of the economy and in the spatial correlates of economic power' (Sassen, 1998, 182), the notions of articulation and governance functions of global cities are embedded into a critical inquiry into 'questions of power and inequality' (Sassen, 2001, 351). It is her key contention that global cities represent the most distinctive of these spatial correlates of economic power – they are, in a nutshell, a 'spatialization of inequality' (Sassen, 1998, 182). I stress on this because it is striking how far much of the literature, which has been published since Sassen's *The global city* (Sassen, 1991), has veered away from such a critical engagement with the geographies of the world economy. Most contributions to the global city literature have either focused on specific urban phenomena related to global city formation or dealt with the cross-border connections of global cities. Both approaches will be introduced in the following sections. Given, however, that these bodies of literature are huge, it is far beyond the limits of this chapter to summarize, let alone to discuss all contributions. I will therefore limit myself to briefly present some important and/or typical studies.

The urban studies approach to global cities

One of the most extensive threads in global city literatures is the urban studies approach. Within it, one of the main topics is the reorganization of urban economies and societies, with particular attention being paid to the ascent of producer services and the polarization of labour markets and incomes. These notions are, on the one hand, based on the 'Dual Cities' debate (Mollenkopf and Castells, 1991; Fainstein et al., 1992), and, on the other, directly derived from Friedmann's and Sassen's work. While the former contends that '[w]orld city formation brings into focus the major contradictions of industrial capitalism – among them spatial and class polarization' (Friedmann, 1986, 76), the latter posits that because in global cities large-scale manufacturing is being replaced as the key economic sector by producer services, economic and social structures tend towards polarization. While the leading sectors employ an extraordinarily high-earning workforce, they also create demand for low-paid, low-skilled service workers. Moreover,

Sassen sees a renaissance of small-scale, sweatshop manufacturing in global cities, relying mainly on immigrant labour.

This polarization thesis has been strongly debated. In sum, there is a tendency to agree with the diagnosis but to disagree with the explanations. Fainstein (2001), for example, confirms in an assessment of the evidence for New York, London, Tokyo, Paris and Randstad increasing inequality. Yet, she attributes this less to a shrinking of the middle class than to 'very large increases in both individual earnings and household incomes at the top' (ibid., 292) nurtured by returns from financial markets. Since the latter are subject to fluctuations, growing inequality is not necessarily a structural feature of global cities. Fainstein also qualifies Sassen's claim that increased demand for low-paid workers in some services and in sweatshop manufacturing increases poverty, arguing that 'exclusion from the labor force is the principal cause of poverty.... Moreover, the severity of poverty is largely a consequence of public policy' (ibid., 291). More recently, Timberlake et al. (2012) have examined the hypothesized positive association between global city formation and social polarization for 57 US cities. The authors obtained mixed results, finding, on the one hand, little evidence that centrality in the global city network is generally associated with higher levels of income or occupational polarization. On the other hand, they also discover that centrality in the global city network is associated with higher levels of GINI inequality, and that its concrete impact on income polarization is related to levels of immigration. This finding replicates a study by Hamnett (1994), who argued that Sassen's polarization claim might hold true only for large-scale immigration cities like New York and Los Angeles. More recently, Hamnett (2012, 365) reaches an even more sceptical conclusion: '[T]he evidence... suggests that, within Western developed countries outside the USA, there has not been a general process of occupational class polarization.' For London, Massey (2007) does not reject the notion of growing inequalities, but she attributes them not to global city formation, but, more generally, to the 'politico-economic strategy of neoliberalism', which has 'found its most acute expression in the capital' (ibid., 55).

Another important issue in the urban studies strand of the global city literature is socio-spatial reordering. According to Sassen (1996, 208f), global city formation has brought about 'a new architecture of centrality that represented and housed new forms of economic power – that is, the hyperspace of international business; witness the corporate towers, corporate hotels, and world-class airports that have constituted a new geography of the built environment of centrality'. While many studies generally relate globalization processes to the emergence of a new spatial order in cities, global city researchers have emphasized the relationship between the expansion of advanced producer services, the internationalization of real estate markets, major changes in the built environment induced by the spread of (mainly) high-rise office complexes and the making of new spatial orders (e.g. Fainstein, 2001). Lizieri (most recently in 2012) has pointed out that in global cities such as London global ownership of offices has increased drastically since the 1980s, mainly because the distinction between the funding of real estate development, ownership of real estate as an investment and occupation of property has become blurred. There is also a growing number of studies on the relationships between global city formation and spatial transformations in cities in the 'global South' (e.g. Haila, 2000; Ciccolella and Mignaqui, 2002; Beavon, 2005), though allusions to global city research are by and large limited to the absorption of a specific terminology. An exception is a study of Mexico City and Johannesburg, which shows that the increasing demand for prime office space caused by the expansion of the producer service sector in the course of global city formation has led to the production on new Central Business Districts (Parnreiter et al., 2013).

Thirdly, increased and more diversified immigration to global cities has also received considerable attention. On the one hand, labour mobility of professionals has been studied not only as a critical factor for producer service firms to serve clients and to accumulate financial capital but also as an important means providing connectivity for the world city network (e.g. Beaverstock, 1996, 2002; Shen, 2010). In regards to low-skilled immigration, Sassen's claim that occupational polarization drives ever-more workers to the peripheral labour markets in the very centres of the world economy, Samers (2002, 391) has criticized the 'unreliable evidence' both for this assertion and for the supposed expansion of the informal economy or sweatshops in global cities. In fact, Waal (2012) examining immigration into Dutch cities found no evidence that increasing immigration was related to growth in neither producer nor in low-paid services. Investigating into London's labour market, Datta et al. (2012), however, provide evidence for a growth of the low-wage economy as well as for its increasing reliance on immigrant workers. In a cross-country study, Benton-Short et al. (2005) found that some of the top global cities yield very high in the 'Urban Immigrant Index', namely New York, London and, to a lesser extent, Paris, while other high-immigration cities (Toronto, Dubai, Amsterdam) are not particularly important global cities.

A final topic is the interplay between global city formation and a city's 'cultural reorganisation' (Zukin, 1992, 200). Zukin argues that 'material and symbolic reconstruction' (ibid., 217) are intertwined processes, which lead to 'creating the city as a landscape of power' (ibid., 200). Thus, the remaking of global cities' centres through huge real-estate projects is not only a matter of providing infrastructures for global business but also one of the creation of hegemonic images: 'Seeing the landscape of the City is believing in its mission' (ibid.). The very incarnation of such landscapes of power is the high-rise office tower – what looks like New York City suggests to be like New York City, even in secondary global cities such as Vienna (Grubbauer, 2011). Accordingly, Yeoh (2005, 946) speaks of a necessity to 'imagineering' the global city. This term is borrowed from Paul (2004), who for his part has taken it from Walt Disney Studios, where it was coined to describe the company's method of 'combining imagination with engineering to create the reality of dreams' (quoted in Paul, 2004, 574). Investing in such imagineering of the global city is, according to Yeoh, particularly necessary in post-colonial cities (as in South-east Asia), where not only the social, ethnic, class and gender polarizations resulting from global city formation have been masked, but also the tension between the governors' 'affirming national identity' and their feeding 'the "mobilizing myth" of becoming a global city' (Yeoh, 2005, 952, 946).

The network approach: Cross-border connections of global cities

A second major strand of the global city literature is concerned with identifying and measuring inter-global city connections. This interest emerged as a response to the criticisms of the empirical basis of global city research, which surfaced quickly after Friedmann's (1986) 'World City Hypothesis'. Korff (1987, 483, 491), for example, argued that 'world city analysis depends on aggregated statistical data which tend to be unreliable', for which reason the selection of world cities 'involves a high degree of chance and a low degree of reasoning'. In a similar vein, Smith and Timberlake (1995, 292) noted that Friedmann's 'writing is full of references to how world cities relate to places in their national and regional hinterlands, to the world economy and to each other.... However, there is little direct evidence on such linkages provided in his work.' Short et al. (1996) also referred to the difficulty to corroborate the notion of a hierarchy of world cities, denoting the lack of good comparative data as the 'dirty little secret of world cities research'. In a similar vein, Taylor (1997, 323) spoke of 'empirically deficient theoretical ideas' and, therefore, of the need for 'fresh empirical grounding' for the idea of a world city hierarchy.

Interest in quantitative assessments of flows between global cities was as widespread as the concern for a specification of their ranking. As Smith and Timberlake (1995, 292) put it: From the 'several important assumptions [Friedmnann] makes about world cities,... the most relevant to our discussion is that world cities can be located in a global hierarchy on the basis off being geographical nexus of economic power'. They then go on to suggest that 'formal network analysis provides an elegant and rigorous way to operationalize theoretical conceptions about the world economy and global city' (ibid., 295). This double bias towards measuring connections between global cities and towards their arrangement in a global hierarchy has been the backdrop against which Peter Taylor began his work 'to counter the dearth of data on inter-city relations' (Taylor, 2004, ix). As everybody knows, the search for an appropriate approach to create the missing data on inter-city relations resulted in the development of the 'interlocking world city network model' (IWCNM), which was first presented in 2001 (Taylor, 2001) and which has since then dominated much of the empirical research on global cities. The IWCNM was, in brief, devised to assess the way in which world cities are connected to one another through the flows between the offices of advanced producer services. These firms are, thus, seen as the key agents in network making – they are 'inter-locking' cities through their global office location practices (for an introduction into the IWCNM, see Derudder et al. in this volume).

(Big) data sets to measure cross-border networks of cities are analysed in three further fields of research. Firstly, some authors have applied the IWCNM to study further inter-firm networks (e.g. Verhetsel and Sel, 2009). Secondly, there is much literature on inter-city connections established through air travel and telecommunication infrastructures (e.g. Rimmer, 1998; Townsend, 2001; Graham, 2002; Matsumoto, 2004; Choi et al., 2006; Neal, 2010). The third strand of the literature deals with the intra-firm networks of TNCs, analysing ownership linkages in order to identify links between headquarter and subsidiary cities (e.g. Alderson and Beckfield, 2004, 2007; Rozenblat and Pumain, 2007; Wall, 2009; Alderson et al. 2010). Many of these studies reach the conclusion that economic power is increasingly concentrated in a few cities (New York, Paris, Tokyo, London). Finally, some studies have used a qualitative approach to examine city-to-city connections established through the labour mobility of professionals (see above). Moreover, Faulconbridge (e.g. 2006, 2008) contends in his studies of advertising, headhunting and law firms that local and global learning networks of producer service firms are mutually interwoven and complementary at scales ranging from the local to the world city network.

Major critiques of global city research

After having exposed the main strands of the global city literature, in this section I will introduce some of the major criticisms raised. As already indicated, global city researchers have been confronted with the critique of not disposing of reliable data to buttress the theoretical claims right from the beginning. Thanks to the various applications of the IWCNM, this problem has been partially solved, though some researchers (e.g. Parnreiter, 2010; Beaverstock, 2011) insist that an evidential crisis continues to undermine the strength of the global city argument and the forthcoming issue of Tijdschrift voor economische en sociale geografie (2014) on the IWCNM.

Another line of critique developed in the late 1990s, probably as a reaction to the increasingly hegemonic position of global city research in the field of urban studies. This critique is best summarized under the question: 'global or globalizing cities'? This is, of course, more than a matter of semantics. A common notion in these criticisms is that global city research 'adheres to a rigidly dualistic categorization of the urban world as comprised of global and non-global cities' (McCann, 2004, 2316). Accordingly, the proponents of 'globalizing cities' suggest a shift of attention from the study of certain – 'privileged' – cities' role in globalization to 'how "global" economic processes affect all cities' (Öncü and Weyland, 1997; Yeoh, 1999; Marcuse and Kempen, 2000; Robinson, 2006, 102; see also Watson in this volume). Yet, favouring 'globalizing' over 'global cities' implies more than the common-sensical insight that there is no such thing as a 'non-global' city standing outside the world economy. The proponents of 'globalizing cities' employ the term deliberately to level out the global city argument that some cities matter more to the world economy than others. This notion is discarded because it 'privilege[s] the experience of some cities over those of others' (Robinson, 2006, 93), and because it shows a 'Euro-American bias [...], which sets up certain Western cities [...] as norms against which others then come to be judged' (Massey, 2007, 35; cf. King, 1990; Olds and Yeung, 2004; Shatkin, 2007). Global city research is, thus, seen as being indifferent to the various ways in which cities in poorer countries can be connected to the world economy, for which reason 'millions of people and hundreds of cities are dropped off the map of much research in urban studies' (Robinson, 2002, 535). To counter this – allegedly – white academic elitism an alternative perspective is called for: 'Rather than viewing global cities as central expressions of the global accumulation of capital, all cities can then be viewed in the fullness of their particular linkages with the worlds outside their boundaries' (Smith, 1998, 486; emphasis in original).

A third major critique has recently been summarized as the 'political deficit' (Ancien, 2011, 2477) and 'stateless economism' (Therborn, 2011, 282) of the global city paradigm. One aspect of this questioning of global city researchers' treatment of the state is the critique that the importance of state politics and of national economies for global city formation has been neglected or downplayed. For example, some researchers have pointed out for the case of Tokyo that Japan's 'state-centred developmental capitalism' (cf. Machimura, 1992; Hill and Kim, 2000; Fujita, 2003) has played a decisive role in the rise to one of the world's most central global cities, while Tokyo's recent decline in world city connectivity (Taylor, 2011) is the result of the waning strength of this developmental state (Therborn, 2011). Another aspect of the 'political deficit' critique emerges from the debate on globalization as the 'politics of rescaling' (Swyngedouw, 2000). Brenner (1998, 2) argues that the global city paradigm's 'analytical privileging of the global/local dualism' has 'deflected attention away from the crucial role of the state scale in the currently unfolding transformation of world capitalism'. Instead of following a narrative of state decline, deterritorialization and spaces of flows, Brenner (ibid.) suggests conceptualizing global city formation as one process within the ongoing reconfiguration of state territoriality: 'Global city formation is linked both to the globalization of

capital and to the regionalization/localization of state territorial organization.... States are being re-scaled and reterritorialized in conjunction with
the process of global city formation, and the resultant transformed configurations of state territorial organization operate simultaneously as agents and
sites of the globalization process' (ibid., 3, 8). Referring to Harvey's (1989b)
'entrepreneurial cities', Brenner continues to argue that this downscaling
'of state territorial organization enhances the role of urban-regional scales
in promoting capital accumulation. This re-scaling of state territorial power
toward the regional and local levels can be viewed as a state-directed attempt
to propel cities and regions upwards in the urban hierarchy' (ibid., 19).

Fourthly, some researchers have taken issue with the notion of the centralization of economic command and control in global cities. For Jones (2002,
348) this idea 'of centralised "global management" where the world economy is run from a few key urban centres is an over-simplistic myth'. He
criticizes, firstly, the global city paradigm's assumption that power and
control are contained in the offices of key economic branches located
in global cities. According to Jones (ibid., 337), these offices – and thus
these cities – are nothing more than an 'arbitrary physical context' for
key decision-making: To 'understand the nature of transnational corporate
power and control, building theories around a spatially centred epistemol-
ogy of place/location is unproductive' (ibid.). Secondly, Jones argues that
power and control are not centralized but spatially diffused, 'spread between
a decentralized network of social actors across the transnational context of
producer service TNCs' (ibid.). From the first two points results Jones' third
claim, namely that theorizing corporate control requires a focus on those
'social practices of business activity' (ibid., 349) that constitute transnational
corporate power.

Jones' critique can be connected to two further criticisms, which, however, take absolutely opposite positions. On the one hand, Smith (2011;
Smith and Doel, 2011) further sharpens the 'myth-argument', maintaining
that the notion of strategic control and command is nothing other than a
'neo-Marxist myth' (Smith, 2011). Drawing on some of the social studies
of finance literature, Smith (ibid.) not only rejects 'any idea of the global
economy being controlled, let alone commanded' but also 'dispel[s] the
illusion that the world economy is a structured totality' (Smith and Doel,
2011, 36). Accordingly, Smith (2011) considers the global city paradigm in
toto as 'inadequate envisioning of the global economy'. On the other hand,
Jones' call for examining the social practices of command and control has
been reiterated by Beaverstock and Parnreiter, who both insist that research
into the agencies in global city formation and in the world city network
is the chief task (see below). In the next section, I will critically assess the
two major strands of the global city literature presented above as well as the
major criticisms. Particular emphasis will be paid to the question whether
and to what extent these studies have provided evidence to substantiate the

key claims made by Friedmann and Sassen. For that purpose, I will start with a brief outline of the methodological implications arising from Friedmann's and Sassen's lines of reasoning.

A critical assessment of the global city literature so far

A starting point to empirically corroborate the global city concept is to verify the clustering of producer services in a specific city. To do so requires, on the one hand, the compilation of attribute data on the size, growth dynamics and compositions of the producer service sector, and, on the other, to locate headquarters and affiliates of globalized producer service firms, because it is these firms that are supposed to have the highest capability for servicing, managing and controlling the global operations of firms. Yet, attribute data are insufficient to comprehensively assess global city formation because the existence of a large and globalized producer service sector per se does not tell us whether a specific city is de facto a center for the management and the governance of cross-border economic activities. What is necessary, then, is to confirm the trading of these services, that is, to corroborate demand and to identify the producer service firms' clients. This implies the creation of relational data informing about connections between the suppliers of producer services and client firms. Moreover, it is imperative to examine whether and how these service flows contribute to the articulation and governance of the client firms' cross-border activities. Finally, it is also important to measure and to map the intra-producer service firms and inter-city networks and to specify the divisions of labour between offices and cities.

Considering these empirical challenges, we now can scrutinize the contributions made by the global city literature. The urban studies approach has considerably deepened our knowledge of economic, spatial and social dynamics in individual cities. There is, for example, ample consensus that massive interventions into the built environment happen in order to produce the new spaces of economic centrality. On the other side, the question whether global city formation leads to polarization is still highly contested. Yet, despite providing rich information on urban transformations, the overall contribution of this approach to our understanding of the role of global cities in the world economy remains limited. Most of the studies have not dealt with and therefore not provided evidence for the key conceptual claims of Friedmann and Sassen, which are centred on, I repeat, economic rather than on urban geography issues. While debates on polarization or immigration are, without any doubt, of the essence of contemporary urban analysis, they are not a primary source of knowledge as regards the geographies of economic command and control. There is, however, one indeed important exception, namely the investigations into the dynamics and compositions of the producer service sectors in various cities. These studies have created an extended and refined knowledge about a critical economic sector and its geography, what eventually can serve as a basis for further investigations into the articulation and governance functions of producer service firms in global cities.

As regards the network approach, the IWCNM and other quantitative approaches have significantly enhanced our knowledge of cross-border connections of global cities. Though the 'world according to GaWC' (GaWC, 2012) remains an assumption (neither Taylor nor his colleagues have ever claimed to dispose of 'hard' data on 'real' flows between global cities), the numerous studies which were conducted applying the IWCNM allow for an unrivalled empirical account of the world city network and of its transformations in the last decade. Nevertheless, it is also true that the IWCNM's solely focus on inter-world city relations bypasses the theoretical core of the global city paradigm: If the notion of articulation and governance functions of global cities is taken seriously, then attention should be drawn to the multiple ramifications on which the word city network is built upon, and which link global cities (and, thus, producer service firms) to the countless non-global, but yet globalized cities,[4] towns and other localities, where firms are producing for global markets (Parnreiter, 2010, 2013).[5] Because such an assessment of supplier–client relations is currently the paramount strategic empirical task, I consider the IWCNM only of limited help to further substantiate the theoretical claims made by Friedmann and Sassen.

In addition to the urban studies and the network approach there is, however, a third, much smaller strand of the literature which contends with the articulation and governance functions of global cities. One of the first studies in this spirit was Meyer's (1991) analysis of London as a pivot of international finance, in which he discusses strategies of business intermediaries in London in order to maintain control and coordination 'of the nonlocal exchange of commodities and capital' (ibid., 98). London as a 'hinge' between the global and the European markets has also been analysed by several GaWC-related authors (e.g. Hoyler and Pain, 2002; Faulconbridge, 2004; Beaverstock et al., 2005). Focusing in particular on London's relationship to Frankfurt, these studies show that while London-based producer service firms gain access to continental European markets through the 'gateway city' Frankfurt, at the same time they promote 'a shift in Frankfurt's connections to global markets' (Hoyler and Pain, 2002, 83). For Latin America, gateway functions of global cities have been analysed by Brown et al. (2000), who show that Miami is the city through which Central America is connected to the world economy, by Rossi and Taylor (2005), who confirm São Paulo's position as the leading, though not only gateway into the Brazilian economy, and by myself. Mexico City has developed since the country's integration into NAFTA into a critical node in the many global commodity chains originating in, running through or ending in Mexico. Nevertheless, while articulation functions performed in Mexico City are indispensable for the functioning of these commodity chains, both the geographical reach and the depth of control functions exercised by Mexico City-based producer service firms seem to be limited (Parnreiter, 2010, 2012). Finally, Vind and Fold (2010) and Hanssens et al. (2012) have reinforced the economic geography spirit by scrutinizing the role of Ho Chi Minh City and Ghent in specific global commodity chains. Yet, none of these studies offers a detailed insight into the articulation, let alone the governance functions of global cities.

Finally, I will very briefly address some of the major criticisms. As regards Smith' post-structuralist questioning of the epistemological foundations of the global city paradigm, it is fair to say that he disregards a whole body of literature on the governance of global commodity chains and of transnational corporations, which proves that the idea of command and control is, in fact, more than a 'myth'. Concerning the alleged 'political deficit' (Ancien, 2011, 2477) of global city research, my take is that both arguments – that the fate of national economies is important for global city formation and that the latter has also be considered in relation to the rescaling of state territoriality – are correct. Think, for example, on the rapid rise of Shanghai's and Beijing's connectivity values in the world city network (Taylor et al., 2011), which reflects the growth of the Chinese export economy: the more production is to be articulated with the world market, the more important are the nodes from where this articulation is achieved. Yet, Shanghai's and Beijing's rise also mirrors the re-scaling of political authority within China, where 'state-owned' means in many cases not controlled by the national government, but also by province, city or county governments.

As regards the 'global or globalizing cities' debate, my contention is that most, if not all authors contributing to it misinterpret the global city paradigm as an urban studies concept – a misconception that they share, ironically, with many followers of Friedmann's and Sassen's ideas. Frequent complaints about the global city paradigm's inadequacy for grasping the fullness of urban development (particularly, but not exclusively in poorer countries) show that the critics miss the key theoretical points of the global city paradigm. Though I agree that the diversity of cities is not assessed by Friedmann, Sassen or Taylor, it is important to be accurate about the argument. The global city paradigm does not intend to deal with the complexities of urban economies or city life, nor is it about the general connectedness of cities to the world economy. Rather, global city research is concerned with the geography of a very specific input into global commodity chains, namely the means by which their organization and control is made effective. Thus, the 'privileging' of producer services stems from an economic geography perspective rather than from urban studies.[6] From this follows that most cities around the world are indeed no direct subject for global city studies, because no core activities necessary for running and controlling global commodity chains are located there. Thus, the 'dropping-off' (Robinson, 2002, 535) of hundreds of cities results from uneven development itself, which produces cores and peripheries, and that is why the suggested shift to 'how "global" economic processes affect all cities' (Robinson, 2006, 102) would obscure the fact that there are places, wherefrom rule-makers operate, and places, where most, if not all people are confined to be rule-keepers. For me, it is one of the main merits of the global city paradigm that it provides insights into the geography of the making of power asymmetries, rather than blurring them through a discourse of 'all are global(ized)'. Cd. Juárez on the Mexican-U.S. border, for example, has been, as a maquiladora-town, thoroughly shaped by its function as a production site in the chains of the automotive, computer and electronic industries, and it is therefore likely to be more 'global' than Mexico City or New York, which also count with and cater to a domestic markets. Nevertheless, Cd. Juárez – or firms there – has virtually no hand in the governance of these chains, while Mexico City is involved to some and New York to a high degree – a power distinction not at least important to the residents in these cities (Parnreiter, 2010).

The in my understanding most important critique – and the one that can bring global city research a step forward – refers to the lacking focus on agency. I agree with Jones (2002), who calls for examinations of the 'social practices of business activity' (ibid., 349), as well as with Beaverstock (2011, 216) who has recently called for '(m)ore informed research on current agency and agents' because 'a reluctance of the key proponents of the model [the IWCNM]...to focus their energy on researching agency in the networks' has driven global city research into a 'theoretical impasse'. In this chapter's last section I will present a possible way out of the theoretical impasse. The main contention here is that verifying the – hitherto only supposed – flows between a global city's producer service firms and their clients, and scrutinizing the management and control activities embedded within them, is, paramount.

Concluding remarks

In a discussion of the global city literature I have maintained that so far only few researchers have seriously engaged with the economic geography perspective on articulation and governance functions of global cities, which constitutes, at least in my reading, the theoretical core of the global city paradigm. Though the notion that global cities function as organizing nodes and as command points of the world economy is widely accepted, little is still known, more than 20 years after Sassen's (1991) 'The global city', about the actual practices of management and control exercised in global cities. This lack of evidence undermines the strength of the global city argument. Moreover, it is used by radical opponents of the paradigm, who reject the whole concept because of its critical inquiry into the agencies and geographies of the making of uneven development, to claim that strategic economic command and control are just a 'neo-Marxist myth'

(Smith, 2011). Though I share the argument that '(o)ne cannot infer interaction, coordination, command, control, domination and subordination from the mere existence of office networks' (Smith and Doel, 2011, 27), I contain that the lack of information on how certain firms in certain cities 'accomplish strategic control of distanciated economic activities on a global scale' (ibid., 26) is an empirical rather than a conceptual problem. Where global city researchers have endeavoured to investigate mechanism of economic command and control, they have found it (Parnreiter, 2013).

Sassen's work provides some suggestions as to how to operationalize this issue. She notes that a city must have 'significant exports of producer services' (Sassen, 2001, 359; emphasis added) in order to realize the management and control functions. Such exports could be accomplished in trade between producer service firms, and also in intra-firm trade in this sector, as suggested by the IWCNM. However, in my reading of 'The global city', the gist of Sassen's argument is that producer service firms in global cities export to other firms, namely those with global operations along commodity chains. From a bank's initial lending of capital to initiate production, to the use of an advertising agency's services to facilitate final consumption, the provision of producer services through global cities is essential in linking and governing dispersed production and consumption sites. Producer services are, thus, key activities in commodity chains, essential to their successful operation, and that is why the global city, from which they are provided, constitutes the 'service sector nexus' (Rabach and Kim 1994) in all kind of commodity chains (Brown et al., 2010; Parnreiter, 2010). Yet, such service flows from producer service firms in global cities to companies operating in manufacturing, agricultural or service commodity chains have barely received attention (for exceptions see Parnreiter [2010], Parnreiter et al. [2010] and Hanssens et al. [2012]), and neither global city research nor other globalization literatures have systematically sought to explore how producer services are means for the management and the control of global operations of firms. Against the backdrop of this disillusioning résumé, we have to return to the beginnings in order to revitalize global city research. Remember that Sassen (1991, 6; original emphasis) opened 'The global city' with a call for studying agencies:

> I am seeking to displace the focus of attention from the familiar issues of the power of large corporations . . . or supracorporate concentration of power through interlocking directorates or organizations, such as the IMF. I want to focus on an aspect that has received less attention, which could be referred to as the *practice* of global control: the work of producing and reproducing the organization and management of a global production system and a global marketplace of finance. My focus is not on power, but on production: the production of those inputs that constitute the capability for global control.

Notes

1. In fact, Berry and Pred (1961) had already earlier anticipated the articulation-function of global cities teased out later by Friedmann and Sassen. Discussing the literature on central places in the United States they argue that "there is evidence that the various metropolitan apexes of regional hierarchies are linked into a completely interdependent metropolitan system, each part of which provides some specialised activity for the whole". They then go on to suggest that the "country however, (is) linked via the metropolitan system into higher levels of functional organisation, culminating in a world economy, by "world cities" " (Berry & Pred, 1961, p.7). I thank Michiel van Meeteren for drawing my attention to Berry and Pred's early use of "world cities".
2. In fact, some years before Hymer, André Gunder Frank suggested in his conceptualization of the 'development of underdevelopment' something near it. Frank delineated the Latin American city as a bridgehead for the interests of the dominant centers of the world economy, arguing that: '(j)ust as the colonial and national capital (…) become the satellite of the Iberian (and later of other) metropoles of the world economic system, this satellite immediately becomes a colonial and then a national metropolis with respect to the productive sectors and population of the interior. (…) Thus, a whole chain of constellations of metropoles and satellites relates all parts of the whole system from its metropolitan center in Europe or the United States to the farthest outpost in the Latin American countryside. (…) we find that each of the satellites (…) serves as an instrument to suck capital or economic surplus out of its own satellites and to channel part of this surplus to the world metropolis of which all are satellites' (Frank, 1969, 6).
3. NIDL = new international division of labour.
4. I use 'globalized cities' here to denote all those cities, which have no command and control functions, but which as sites of material production, nevertheless critical places for globalization.
5. See also the empirical part in Derudder et al.'s paper in this volume, in which they show that Hong Kong, Shanghai and Beijing are not only the best connected chinese cities in the world city network, but also have above-average national connections.
6. This said, it is fair to add that some of the critics have expanded their criticisms beyond global city research to generally disapprove a tendency in Anglophone urban and regional research to deal mainly with large financial centers and associated professional networks (Bunnell and Maringanti, 2010). I agree with this criticism, given that in the field of urban and regional studies the rationale given by global city research for specializing on specific cities (what some criticize as 'privileging') does not apply.

3
The Network Dimension

Ben Derudder, Michael Hoyler and Peter J. Taylor

Introduction

There is now a considerable literature on the role of cities as key nodes in an increasingly globalized economy. One expression of this can be found in recent large edited volumes such as this one: for instance, Scott (2001), Brenner and Keil (2006), Taylor et al. (2007, 2011, 2013) and Derudder et al. (2012) have mustered over 300 chapters between them but still represent only the tip of this particular iceberg. Within this literature, the research in the context of the Globalization and World Cities (GaWC, http://www.lboro.ac.uk/gawc) research network has pioneered a *relational* approach to understanding cities in globalization as a 'world city network' (WCN). One area of focus has been the formal analysis of inter-city relations of cities based on a precise specification of the WCN as an 'interlocking network' (e.g. Taylor, 2001; Taylor et al., 2011). In the initial specification of this model and in much of the subsequent empirical WCN research, it is put forward that globalized producer services firms are the key 'network makers': drawing on the work of Sassen (1991) and Castells (1996), it is posited that these firms 'interlock' cities through their global, city-centred location strategies.

The purpose of this chapter is to provide a critical roundup of the research inspired by the 'interlocking world city network model' (IWCNM). To this end, we review the position of the WCN approach within the broader literature on 'world cities' and 'global cities', and present an overview of the analytical possibilities it offers. To this end, we present an IWCNM-based assessment of the position of Chinese cities in transnational urban networks in 2010. Although much of the chapter is purposefully empirical, our most important objective is conceptual: we aim to show that although the IWCNM is often equated with one of its many possible empirical outcomes, that is a 'global hierarchy of cities' (e.g. Bunnell and Sidaway, 2012), producing such a ranking is neither the purpose nor the fundamental outcome of the model. Rather, the IWCNM's key objective is to reveal one of the functional and spatial backbones of the transnational urban networks in which cities are entangled. In this chapter, we clarify and illustrate this vantage point as to facilitate a critical appraisal of the possibilities and limitations of the WCN approach beyond the ranking clichés.

The remainder of this chapter is organized in four main sections. First, we introduce the overall rationale of the WCN approach by framing it in the evidential crisis that has long plagued the global/world city literature. Second, we discuss the WCN's general specification, its key underlying assumptions and some connectivity measures that can be derived from this specification. The third section shows how the model is operationalized through a discussion of the source data, and an overview of the key features of the connectivity of Chinese cities in transnational networks. And fourth and finally, we discuss the analytical possibilities and limitations of this approach, thereby paying attention to some of the critiques that have been raised over the years.

The IWCNM approach: Addressing an evidential crisis

Although this is not the place to reiterate or debate the history and legacy of the 'world city' and 'global city' concepts, it is useful to remember that neither Friedmann (1982 with Wolff; 1986) nor Sassen (1991, 2001) devoted much attention to a methodical analysis of how and why cities could qualify. It is therefore no surprise that critiques of the narrow empirical basis of the world/global city concepts are basically as old as the literature itself. For instance, quickly after the publication of Friedmann's (1986) paper, Korff (1987, 491) argued that the identification of world cities 'involves a high degree of chance and a low degree of reasoning'. A decade later, Short et al. (1996, 698) observed that this situation had not really changed, as the privileged position of cities such as London, New York and Tokyo was 'more often asserted than clearly demonstrated'.

In parallel to the unanswered question of which cities could be designated as global/world cities, the wider and *more relevant* issue of how cities could be convincingly arrayed in an overarching 'hierarchy' or 'system' also became debated. Smith and Timberlake (1995, 292), for example, noted that although Friedmann's writing is full of references to how world cities relate to each other, the actual evidence presented is simply an amalgamation of commonsensical criteria at the level of individual cities. A case in point is Short et al.'s (1996) 'world city ranking', which is based on a combination of five straightforward indicators, that is the presence of (i) major financial institutions, (ii) corporation headquarters, (iii) telecommunications and (iv) transportation infrastructures and (v) global cultural events. Although most would find Short et al.'s (1996) ranking credible, it is flawed because it essentially remains the result of informed speculation that does not reveal how cities *relate* to each other, and thereupon constitute an overarching 'system' or 'hierarchy'. More generally, this problem relates to the fact that information on transnational *relations* between cities is usually not publicly available (Taylor, 1997).

Taken together, by the end of the 1990s there was a growing feeling that the global/world cities research was held back by the lack of evidence on the transnational *connections* of cities. This evidential crisis has since then been averted through two separate and distinctive meta-solutions (Derudder, 2006): (i) arraying primary data on worldwide corporate organization in such a way that cities' connections can be conjectured from these data (e.g. Alderson and Beckfield, 2004; Rozenblat and Pumain, 2007; Wall and van der Knaap, 2011), and (ii) using secondary data describing the global infrastructures connecting cities (e.g. Smith and Timberlake, 2001; Malecki, 2002; Tranos, 2011).[1]

The IWCNM specification is clearly part of the first solution to the evidential crisis. The starting point by Taylor (2001, 181) was that the world/global city 'system' was above all in need of a formal network specification, as '[w]ithout it there can be no detailed study of its operation – its nodes, their connections and how they constitute an integrated whole'.[2] Combining a series of techniques borrowed from social network analysis with the insights of Sassen (1991) regarding the rise of integrated producer services economies in major cities, the WCN was specified as an inter-locking network with three levels: a network level (the global economy), a nodal level (cities) and a critical sub-nodal level (firms providing the producer services). In the IWCNM, it is assumed that network formation takes place at the sub-nodal level: based on their attempts to provide a seamless service to their clients across the world, financial and business service firms have created global networks of offices in cities around the world. Each office network represents a firm's urban strategy for servicing global capital, and the IWCNM fundamentally projects a city's overall position by estimating the aggregated geographical patterns of flows within the office networks of such firms. As a consequence, in addition to a formal specification of how, in the words of Smith and Timberlake (1995, 292), 'world cities relate to each other', the IWCNM also has the distinct advantage of providing a clear indication of the data required: information on the office networks of producer services is needed. From this vantage point, the IWCNM can be seen as an answer to the empiricism and vagueness that were rife in this global/world city literature until the late 1990s. In the next section, we present the IWCNM specification, its key assumptions and how this general specification gives way to detailed measures of cities' position in transnational urban networks.

The IWCNM: Specification

The formal mathematical specification of the IWCNM begins with a city-by-firm matrix V_{ij}, where v_{ij} represents the 'service value' of city i to firm j. This service value is a standardized measurement of the importance of a city within a firm's office network, which depends on the size and functions of a firm's office(s) in a city (see below for the actual operationalization, which results in a six-point scale of values ranging from zero to five).

The basic measure in the IWCNM suit of measures is the city-dyad connectivity CDC_{a-i} between cities a and i, which is defined as follows:

$$CDC_{a-i} = \sum_i v_{ai} \cdot v_{ij} \qquad \text{(where } a \neq i) \qquad (1)$$

CDC_{a-i} measures the potential working flows between any two cities within the WCN. It is based upon the assumption that the more important an office, the more working flows it generates; therefore, flows between two cities with many large offices will be appreciably greater than flows between two cities with fewer large offices (for alternative specifications see Neal, 2014).

Equation (1) shows that the IWCNM is essentially defined by the very simple notion of an interaction model. The thought upon which this builds is thus to answer the following question: if someone walked into the London office of a major advanced producer service firm, what level of service could he/she expect for his/her business needs in city X? One would expect first-class service for dealings in New York since almost all such firms in London also have an office in New York. But what if advice is needed for new work in Melbourne, Accra or Hamburg? Undoubtedly the chances of there being an office in these cities will be less than for New York, and the degree of service offered would likely be much less than in New York. Similarly there will be differences between these cities with respect to the likely intra-firm service available. The IWCNM provides a way of answering such questions quantitatively on a firm-by-firm basis. Of course, all global service firms' networks are different in terms of their geographies and operations: they are idiosyncratic, depending on a firm's geographical origin, its agglomeration history, its clientele, its business model and so on. As a consequence, this method of deriving inter-city relations depends upon aggregating a large number of office networks to iron out the idiosyncratic, which in turn implies that results for cities housing only a small number of firms are unlikely to be robust.

Based on Equation (1), another basic measure can be calculated – the global network connectivity (GNC_a) of city, which is simply an aggregation of all its connections across the network:

$$GNC_a = \sum_i CDC_{a-i} \qquad \text{(where } a \neq i) \qquad (2)$$

Equations (1) and (2) are the backbone of the GaWC approach towards measuring world city *network* formation. Tables 3.1 and 3.2 show the workings of the model. Table 3.1 presents a (fictional) example of a city-by-firm

Table 3.1 City-by-firm matrix and summed service values

V_{ij}	PWC	Deloitte	BNP Paribas	E&Y	LeBoeuf & Dewey	Barclays	Sum service values
New York	5	4	4	2	5	4	24
London	3	5	3	3	3	5	22
Paris	0	2	5	0	4	4	15
Tokyo	2	3	2	1	0	0	8
Beijing	2	2	3	0	0	1	8

Table 3.2 Dyad connectivity and global network connectivity

CDC_{a-i}	New York	London	Paris	Tokyo	Beijing	GNC
New York	0	88	64	32	34	218
London	88	0	57	30	30	205
Paris	64	57	0	16	23	160
Tokyo	32	30	16	0	16	94
Beijing	34	30	23	16	0	103

matrix V_{ij} consisting of 5 cities and 6 firms, while Table 3.2 shows the CDC_{a-i} and GNC_a measures derived from this dataset. To aid in showing that the IWCNM is more than merely counting the presence of firms, Table 3.1 also features the sum of a city's service values across all firms. The Tokyo/Beijing contrast is a clear case in point: although both cities harbour a similar mixture of firms (3/2/2/1/0/0), their overall connectivity GNC_a is different: Beijing is deemed more connected, in particular because its Barclays office produces major intercity connections CDC_{a-i}. This also implies that the Paris–Tokyo connection is less strong than the Paris–Beijing connection.

Equations (1) and (2) encapsulate the IWCNM approach in general terms. However, over the years we have developed a number of more refined measures to tease out the geographies underlying a city's connections. This need for more refined measures is clear: although the Beijing/Tokyo contrast in Tables 3.1 and 3.2 show the opportunities offered by the IWCNM, it can be seen that a refined appraisal of a city's connections is hampered by the fact that CDC_{a-i} largely 'follows' GNC_a: all cities are relatively well connected to London, and all cities relatively poorly connected to Tokyo (Neal, 2013). As a consequence, we developed a number of measures dealing with this problem. In this chapter, we focus on two alternatives.

A first alternative is to extract the *relative* strength of inter-city connections by calculating the concentration of two cities' potential working flows. This city-dyad relative connectivity (CDR_{a-i}) is calculated by dividing a city-dyad's connectedness relative to the two individual city's overall connectivity as indicated by the product of their global network connectivities:

$$CDR_{a-i} = CDC_{a-i}/(GNC_a . GNC_i) \quad \text{(where } a \neq i) \tag{3}$$

High values indicate many firms choosing to locate offices, often important offices, in both cities, suggesting extra business being conducted through this particular city-dyad; such city-dyads are relatively over-connected, we can think of these connections as 'punching above their weight' in the IWCNM.

A second alternative is to focus on particular *components* of a city's connections, that is the *relative* importance of its relations with a specific subset of cities. This subset may be 'hierarchical' (e.g. major cities across the globe), 'regional' (e.g. Pacific-Asian cities) or functional (e.g. Commonwealth cities) depending on the research question at hand. By way of example, in this chapter we focus on two straightforward possibilities: (1) the relative strength of a city's connections with the ten most connected cities (i.e. the 'globalism' of its connectivity), and (2) the relative strength of a city's connections with other cities in the same country (i.e. the 'localism' of its connectivity).

These measures can be calculated as follows:

$$Globalism_a = r_{a-TOP10} = 100^* \left(\frac{\sum\limits_{i=TOP10} r_{a-i}}{\sum\limits_{i=all\ cities} r_{a-i}} - \frac{\sum\limits_{i=TOP10} GNC_i}{\sum\limits_{i=all\ cities} GNC_i} \right) \tag{4}$$

$$Localism_a = r_{a-country} = 100^* \left(\frac{\sum\limits_{i=country} r_{a-i}}{\sum\limits_{i=all\ cities} r_{a-i}} - \frac{\sum\limits_{i=country} GNC_i}{\sum\limits_{i=all\ cities} GNC_i} \right) \tag{5}$$

The results of these measures are to be interpreted as follows: a positive value implies that city a has *stronger* connections with the top ten cities than expected; a negative value implies that city a has *weaker* connections with the top ten cities than expected; the larger the value, the stronger this tendency. As a consequence, a value 'close' to zero implies that city a has connections with the top ten cities that are neither particularly strong nor weak based on what can be expected from the involved cities' overall connectivities. Note that this is a *relative* measure that is therefore in principle *independent* from a city's overall connectivity GNC_a. Localism scores can be interpreted along similar lines. In the next section, we show how these measures are operationalized, thereby focusing on the results for Chinese cities in 2010.

The IWCNM: Operationalization

The data requirements for operationalizing calculating of equations (1) through (5) are straightforward: information on advanced producer firms' networks is needed, that is which cities they have offices in, and differences in importance of these offices for their business needs. The operationalization and subsequent results described here are for the latest data collection, carried out in 2010.

Information was collected on the location strategies of major firms in a number of key service sectors: financial services, accountancy, advertising, law and management consultancy. In our research, firms were chosen by their ranking in lists of the largest firms in each sector. For financial services, the top 75 banking, insurance and diversified finance firms were identified as ranked in the Forbes composite index (www.forbes.com), which combines rankings for sales, profits, assets and market value. For the four other producer services sectors we included the top 25 firms as follows: for accountancy the ranking by revenues by www.worldaccountingintelligence.com; for advertising agencies the revenue ranking of 'marketing organizations' by Advertising Age (www.adage.com/); for law the Chambers Global list of corporate law firms (www.chambersandpartners.com/global); and for management consultancy firms the Vault Management & Strategy Consulting Survey, which ranks firms in terms of their 'prestige' (www.vault.com). These lists were the latest rankings available at the planning of the research in 2009 and tended to be based on 2008 data due to the usual time-lag in reporting such data. Substitute firms were identified for each sector (ranking just below the top 75 and 25) to cover for situations where a firm had disappeared (e.g. been taken over) in the two years before the actual data collection. There is, of course, no 'objective' way to choose the exact number of firms to be included per sector; our choice to include more financial services firms is based on recent trends towards financialization in the global economy and the crucial role this entails for such firms (Pike and Pollard, 2010).

A few of the larger firms have branches in many hundreds, even thousands, of cities and towns. The data collection has been restricted to the more important cities for two reasons. The first is analytical: the more cities are being included, the sparser the final matrix will become with almost no offices present in the smaller cities and towns. The second is theoretical: the interest is in the more important inter-city relations, ultimately the WCN. Nevertheless, it is also important not to omit any possible significant node so that a relatively large number of cities need to be selected. Additionally, it is necessary to ensure that all continents are reasonably represented. The selection of cities is thus based on a number of overlapping criteria, whereby the selection is in part based on cities identified in previous GaWC research with additional cities based upon city size (all cities with populations over two million) and function (all capital cities of states with populations over a million) – 526 cities across the settled world were thus selected.

Assigning service values v_{ij} for the 175 firms' use of the 526 cities focused on two features of a firm's office(s) in a city as shown on their corporate websites: first, the size of office (e.g. number of practitioners) and, second, their extra-locational functions (e.g. regional headquarters). The resulting multifarious compilation of information on firms was codified into service values ranging from zero to five as follows. The city housing a firm's headquarters scored five; a city with no office of that firm scored zero. A typical office of the firm resulted in a city scoring two; reasons for moving away from this score were (i) with something missing (e.g. no partners in a law office), the score reduced to one, (ii) with particularly large offices the score was raised to three and (iii) with important extra-territorial functions (e.g. regional headquarters) a score of four was recorded. All such assessments were made firm by firm. The end result is 526 cities × 175 firms matrix of 92,050 service values ranging between zero and five, which can be used as the input to the IWCNM as summarized in equations (1) through (5).

Chinese cities in the world city network in 2010

To provide an overview of the kind of insights regarding cities' *connections* that this approach can provide, here we describe the results for Chines cities. First, there are the most basic calculations: CDC_{a-i} and GNC_a as measures of the overall strength of a city's connections in the WCN.[3] Table 3.3 presents an overview of the 20 largest CDC_{a-i} and GNC_a values for Chinese cities in 2010. The table shows that Hong Kong, Beijing and Shanghai are playing in their own league as these cities have far bigger connectivities than the other Chinese cities. Beyond this clear-cut top three, only Taipei as a special case and Guangzhou/Shenzhen are reasonably well connected in the office networks of global advanced producer services (APS) firms. Other major cities such as Nanjing and Chengdu, but perhaps especially Chongqing and Wuhan are far less connected in the WCN in spite of their size and unmistakeable economic importance within the Chinese space-economy (Ni, 2012).

A clearer example of what can be gleaned from the IWCNM can be obtained by calculating (1) the relative strength of inter-city connections CDR_{a-I} as well as (2) the overall patterning of these connections as measured through 'Globalism' and 'Localism' scores. Table 3.4, in turn, shows the Globalism and Localism scores for the 20 most connected Chinese cities (the table also features these cities' GNC to facilitate comparisons). Table 3.5 shows the five most important connections of six Chinese cities: Beijing and Shanghai as Mainland China's major cities; Hong Kong and Taipei as

Table 3.3 Largest values of CDC_{a-i} and GNC_a for Chinese cities in 2010

	City-dyad		CDC_{a-i}	City	GNC_a
1	London	Hong Kong	75.0	Hong Kong	73.0
2	New York	Hong Kong	69.0	Shanghai	62.7
3	Shanghai	London	62.1	Beijing	58.4
4	Shanghai	New York	58.7	Taipei	41.7
5	Beijing	London	55.6	Guangzhou	34.1
6	Beijing	New York	52.3	Shenzhen	25.8
7	Hong Kong	Singapore	51.6	Tianjin	16.8
8	Hong Kong	Shanghai	47.5	Kaohsiung	14.3
9	Hong Kong	Paris	47.2	Nanjing	13.5
10	Hong Kong	Tokyo	44.9	Chengdu	13.1
11	Beijing	Hong Kong	43.9	Hangzhou	12.5
12	Shanghai	Singapore	41.1	Qingdao	12.3
13	Shanghai	Paris	40.4	Dalian	12.0
14	Hong Kong	Dubai	39.8	Macao	10.9
15	Hong Kong	Chicago	39.7	Chongqing	8.9
16	Hong Kong	Sydney	39.2	Xi'an	8.7
17	Beijing	Singapore	38.8	Suzhou	8.6
18	Shanghai	Tokyo	38.4	Wuhan	8.0
19	Shanghai	Beijing	38.0	Xiamen	7.5
20	Hong Kong	Milan	37.0	Ningbo	7.5

Table 3.4 GNC, globalism and localism of the 20 most connected Chinese cities in the WCN in 2010

Rank	City	GNC	City	Globalism	City	Localism
1	Hong Kong	73.0	Hong Kong	3.11	Wuhan	10.02
2	Shanghai	62.7	Shanghai	2.87	Xiamen	9.17
3	Beijing	58.4	Beijing	2.68	Chongqing	8.92
4	Taipei	41.7	Taipei	1.72	Suzhou	7.98
5	Guangzhou	34.1	Guangzhou	1.05	Xi'An	7.25
6	Shenzhen	25.8	Wuhan	1.04	Ningbo	6.88
7	Tianjin	16.8	Tianjin	0.28	Qingdao	6.76
8	Kaohsiung	14.3	Dalian	−0.3	Dalian	6.52
9	Nanjing	13.5	Chengdu	−0.6	Chengdu	6.5
10	Chengdu	13.1	Xiamen	−0.65	Tianjin	6.19
11	Hangzhou	12.5	Suzhou	−0.68	Hangzhou	6.13
12	Qingdao	12.3	Shenzhen	−0.69	Nanjing	5.84
13	Dalian	12.0	Qingdao	−0.76	Shenzhen	4.59
14	Macao	10.9	Nanjing	−0.79	Guangzhou	3.57
15	Chongqing	8.9	Chongqing	−0.98	Beijing	3.34
16	Xi'an	8.7	Macao	−1.05	Macao	3.17
17	Suzhou	8.6	Hangzhou	−1.11	Shanghai	3.01
18	Wuhan	8.0	Xi'An	−1.44	Hong Kong	2.48
19	Xiamen	7.5	Kaohsiung	−1.73	Kaohsiung	1.42
20	Ningbo	7.5	Ningbo	−2.24	Taipei	1.37

Table 3.5   The five most important relative connections of six Chinese cities

Rank	Hong Kong	Shanghai	Beijing	Taipei	Ningbo	Xiamen
1	Palo Alto	Hong Kong	Palo Alto	Bangkok	Hangzhou	Qingdao
2	Singapore	Beijing	Shanghai	Palo Alto	Dalian	Dalian
3	Shanghai	New York	Hong Kong	Kuala Lumpur	Nanjing	Chengdu
4	Beijing	London	Tianjin	Singapore	Qingdao	Tianjin
5	London	Tianjin	Singapore	Sydney	Chengdu	Hangzhou

well-connected cities with a distinctive position *viz*. Mainland China; and Ningbo and Xiamen as cities with relatively limited connectivities.

The most important finding contained in Tables 3.4 and 3.5 is that although CDR, Globalism and Localism measures are *relative* in that these have no direct relation with overall connectivities, these rankings are nonetheless clearly interrelated with GNC: Hong Kong, Shanghai and Beijing stand out not only because of their sheer overall connectivity in comparison to other Chinese cities but also because of the strength of their connections with the world's leading cities. However, even though the connections of Hong Kong, Shanghai and Beijing are relatively more directed towards other major cities, there is still an important regional and national dimension to them: the three leading Chinese cities have (1) above-average national connections, (2) are strongly inter-connected (in all three cases, the other two cities rank in the top 5), while (3) the remaining major connections also have a regional dimension (e.g. major business connections with Singapore or Tianjin). In addition to the particular nature of connectivity profiles of this leading 'triad', Taiwanese cities (Taipei and Kaohsiung) also have idiosyncratic profiles combining small levels of Localism with strong regional connections beyond China.

For the remaining Chinese cities, the relation between globalism and GNC is slightly less clear-cut, although it is notable that overall only seven cities feature above-average connections with the world's ten most connected cities. In the case of the Guangzhou/Shenzhen pair, Guangzhou seems much strongly connected to key cities in the global economy than Shenzhen in terms of its business service connections. Meanwhile, Wuhan features relatively strong connections with the world's major cities in spite of having a rather smallish GNC_a overall. The Localism scores of these Chinese cities are (roughly) inversely related to their Globalism. This is also shown by the major connections of the least-connected Chinese cities (Ningbo and Xiamen), which are consistent with other Chinese cities. This shows that within China's main cities myriad (emerging) global connections, there continues to be a distinctively Chinese layer of inter-city networking.

Discussion

Rather than presenting a set of results per se, the purpose of this chapter has been to provide a critical roundup of the research inspired by GaWC's 'interlocking world city network model' (IWCNM). Our brief summary of the connectivity profiles of major Chinese cities in the WCN offers a useful backdrop to review the purpose and possibilities of the approach, as well as addressing some of the critiques raised against this research agenda.

First, it should be clear that the ultimate objective of the IWCNM is not to produce a 'global ranking of cities'. Although such a ranking can be produced and often serves as a useful introduction to an analysis of connectivity in the WCN, it is neither a goal in itself nor the privileged way of conveying results. Above all, the interest is in revealing one of the ways in which the functional and spatial outline of the transnational urban networks in which cities are enmeshed. The GaWC approach provides one specific method to approximate these networks, and analyses can be tailored to specific research interests. In addition, empirical results are not necessarily end products in and by themselves, but part of a wider research agenda in which there can be a complementary relation between quantitative and qualitative research. A good example of this can be found in a recent paper by Lai (2012). Lai's paper reports on intensive research using qualitative data on how Shanghai, Beijing and Hong Kong relate to each other in the context of the global and Chinese space-economy. Drawing on previous quantitative results to set the scene, Lai analyses the reasons for the absolute and relative strength of the relations between China's major cities. Based on her research, she traces this intensity to the presence of 'dual-headquarter strategies' and 'parallel markets' in response to the different 'functions' of these cities in linking China up with the global economy. As Lai's (2012; see also Wójcik, 2011) research clearly shows, IWCNM-inspired research should be seen not as 'opposing' qualitative research, but as part of a much wider, critical-realist methodology where extensive research may provide formative input to intensive research that takes the research agenda further (see Sayer, 2002).

Second, one recurring pattern in our analyses is the variegated mix of hierarchical and regional tendencies. In this chapter, we, for instance, show that Hong Kong, Shanghai and Beijing are not only more strongly connected in the WCN as a whole, but also that their connections with other major cities are relatively stronger. At the same time, less-connected cities such as Ningbo and Xiamen are characterized by relatively stronger 'local' connections. In addition, inter-city relations are also influenced by geopolitical patterns, for example Taipei's strong connections with non-Chinese cities in Asia-Pacific. Taken together, the IWCNM approach to WCNs does not necessarily reflect or even advance a 'globalist' perspective on inter-city relations, as we identify multiple scales of city-network formation (global, regional and national) (see Taylor et al., 2013).

Although the mathematical specification of the IWCNM in and by itself has only recently come under closer scrutiny (e.g. Neal, 2013), its (1) operationalization through a focus on producer services firms and (2) the way in which results are sometimes presented have been criticized over the years. Two major areas of critique stand out.

First, in addition to post-structuralist readings that dismiss measurement per se as the 'categories of "world" or "global" city are [...] more and more meaningless' (RG Smith, 2003, 578), there have also been a number of post-colonial critiques lamenting the narrow empirical focus on producer services. It is asserted that this results in a 'biased' reading that neglects myriad processes and cities. The most trenchant critique along these lines has been by Robinson (2002, 536), who complains that 'millions of people and hundreds of cities are dropped off the map'. This exclusion is from two 'maps': (1) the geographical map as most cities in the 'South' are missing, which is in turn related to (2) the conceptual map as myriad types of con-nections between cities are not considered (see also MP Smith, 2001; Bunnell and Maringanti, 2010; Watson, this volume).

Second, critics have often focused on one of the most straightforward presentations of the empirical operationalization of the IWCNM, that is the GNC rankings and – although this initially stemmed from another research project – the associated identification of 'levels' of world cities (i.e. alpha/beta/gamma). For instance, when Bunnell and Sidaway (2012, xvi) state that in 'the world/global cities literature [...] the assumption of hier-archical relations continues to present alpha [or, most recently, alpha++] cities as the leading edge of urban innovation, dynamism, and aspiration', it is clear that they single out a very particular portion of the GaWC research agenda to address the research presented here and even the literature as a whole.

There is, of course, some truth in both critiques: (1) most IWCNM opera-tionalizations do indeed focus on a narrow set of economic processes, while (2) in Taylor et al. (2013) the citation 'success' of these rankings has been dubbed the 'alpha-beta-gamma misgiving'. Nonetheless, we feel such cri-tiques sometimes misunderstand what the research and therefore the results are all about.

First, the critique of the 'missing' cities/processes tends to confuse the encompassing concept of 'cities in globalization' with the initial purpose of 'world city research', revealing how and from which cities globalized cap-italism is being (re)produced. We agree with Parnreiter's (2010, this volume) observation that it is precisely the focus on advanced producer services that allows grasping the fundamental difference between the role of cities in engendering globalization and the impacts of globalization on cities. At its core, WCN research is a city network-centred approach towards highlight-ing uneven development, and critiques of these analyses not being 'globally encompassing' ignore this core idea.

In addition, although in much of the empirical research drawing on the IWCNM the focus is on producer services firms, it is useful to point out that this model can be used for investigating 'other' WCNs. Thus there have been analyses based on the networks of 'non-economic actors' (e.g. NGOs as in Taylor, 2004a), while regionally more relevant definitions of key network makers have also been applied (e.g. Bassens et al., 2010a, on the importance of Islamic financial services in connecting the Gulf region to the WCN). As such, critiques of the IWCNM and its particular operationalization though producer services should be disconnected.

Second, most of the critics of the 'alpha/beta/gamma misgiving' are active in the blogosphere, where they tend to evaluate the research in terms of how it fits with their personal horizons.[4] These accounts are above all part of a contemporary 'list-mania', where the ranking is all that matters. Of course, ill-informed discussion in the blogosphere is an easy target, but peer-reviewed knowledge is by no means immune from the basic assumptions underpinning list-mania, in that results are used without much regard for the underlying rationale, let alone the more refined and labour-intensive nature of how results are produced. Specifically, in this chapter, we have tried to show that although empirical analyses based on the IWCNM are characterized by myriad assumptions that can and should be critically scrutinized, *there is a clear conceptual rationale that underlies its specification, measurement, analysis and objectives.* As a corollary, the 'meaning' of the empirical results produced through the IWCNM differs greatly from those put together by consultancy firms such as AT Kearney's Global Cities Index.[5] In the latter case, all kinds of 'commonsensical' variables (and processes) are aggregated to develop city rankings to satisfy the needs of list-mania. The fact that these lists may or may not converge with some of the GaWC findings is simply irrelevant, as the overall rationale and purpose are miles apart. In this chapter, we have emphasized this by focusing on what has always been the key purpose of the IWCNM: advancing and exploring the idea of the importance of the external relations of major cities.

Notes

1. It can be noted that we continue to see the publication of rankings that suffer from a 'high degree of chance and low degree of reasoning' as they are based on commonsensical combinations of different measures of cities' 'importance'. Key examples include the rankings of consultancy firms such as Knight Frank's 'Prime Global Cities Index' (http://my.knightfrank.com/research-reports/prime-global-cities-index.aspx), AT Kearney's and Foreign Policy's 'Global Cities Index' (http://www.atkearney.com/gbpc/global-cities-index), PWC's 'Cities of Opportunity' (http://www.pwc.com/us/en/cities-of-opportunity/index.jhtml) and Mori's Global Power City Index (http://www.mori-m-foundation.or.jp/english/index.shtml).

2. In GaWC research, the term 'network' is favoured over 'system': the idea of a system comes with baggage that implies a series of processes such as 'feedback loops' and 'tendencies toward equilibrium' that are not part of the (simple) model. As consequence, from this point onwards we will consistently use the term 'network'.

3. Note that for pedagogic and comparative reasons, measures of CDC_{a-i} and GNC_a will in practice be presented as percentages of the largest values, as this makes results independent from the number of firms and cities in the analysis.

4. For example, the discussion on the ranking of US cities at http://www.city-data.com/forum/city-vs-city/1382110-world-city-rankings-according-gawc-2010-a.html.

5. http://www.atkearney.com/gbpc/global-cities-index.

4
The Economic and Financial Dimensions

David Bassens

Introduction

This chapter[1] discusses the relationship between established measurements of service-related world city formation on the one hand and world city functions under global capitalism on the other. A common approach with regard to the former is to measure centrality in office networks of firms that produce advanced producer services (APS) such as finance, accountancy and auditing, advertising, law, and management consultancy (Taylor, 2004b). world city functions, on the other hand, have been associated with command and control (Friedmann, 1986) or the production of central functions in a global economy (Sassen, 1991). While both dimensions have been discussed somewhat autonomously in this volume (see Derudder et al. on measuring world city formation and Parnreiter on how to interpret world city functions), this chapter's argument is that high connectivity or centrality through the former not necessarily entails a fundamental position in the latter. To reinvigorate the debate on this fundamental cog in conceptualizing world city formation, it is useful to draw on Taylor's (2000) notion of 'monopolization through regionalization'. Taylor explains how under conditions of contemporary globalization world cities[2] are the sites where a 'monopoly of place' (in the words of Scott, 1997) or in Taylor's words 'monopoly by regionalization' can emerge: 'In services such as finance, accountancy and corporate law, practitioners are not just servicing "global capital"; they are creating new products based upon their unique knowledge collectivities. In other words, they do not aim to operate in a price-setting market, but rather develop multiple monopolies of quality knowledge products to reap appropriately large profits' (Taylor, 2000, 10).

While this is a fundamental insight, it also poses the challenge to explore other forms of monopoly that are associated with other notions of space. The above notion of regionalization monopoly mainly draws on what Harvey (1973, 13) would call an *absolute* and *relative* conception of space. Absolute space refers to space as 'a thing in itself' with certain (place-based) properties; relative space implies that space should be understood as a relationship between objects which exists only because objects exist and relate to each other. To understand world city formation in emerging markets it is helpful to reground the absolute and relative spatial framework of Sassen/Friedman/Taylor in *relational* theories about capitalism and its constant struggle to accommodate inherent crises through spatial fixes (Harvey, 1982, 1989b). The chapter therefore hinges on Harvey's (1973, 13) concept of relational space, which denotes space 'as being contained in objects in the sense that an object can be said to exist only insofar as it contains and represents within itself relationships to other objects'. The object of analysis then becomes the nature of this relationship and the mutual representation that exists between a 'world city' and all 'significant others' in the network of world cities. In fact, this means taking seriously the recommendation by Derudder et al. in this volume to complement GaWC-heuristics with a more in-depth analysis of specific city-dyads. However, such an analysis simultaneously problematizes the 'neutral' reading of interurban 'work flows' that underpins the GaWC model. Zooming in on the network inevitably raises the question of *what* that work may entail in specific instances and *how* it relates to power (a)symmetries in terms of the position of world cities as 'places' in world city networks. In this light it will become clear that, in addition to 'monopoly through regionalization', world city formation also emerges out of other monopolies of the finance-dominated service complex, such as monopoly through multi-location activity and (financial) innovation. The case of Dubai will illustrate that world city formation is not singularly related to functions of governance in the sphere of production. The chapter does not challenge Parnreiter's assertion (in this volume) that governance should be studied through the linkages between the APS complex and global commodity chains. Rather, the Dubai case illustrates that another equally challenging research agenda lies ahead in understanding the APS-complex: not in a 'productionist' logic, where questions about coordination of global production are at stake, but under conditions of financialization, where the question becomes a matter of how the APS complex works relationally across world cities to earn monopoly fees for functions that relate to the endogenous workings of global finance.

The value of such a move towards a relational understanding of word city formation is emblematically illustrated by the case of 'world city' Dubai: even though assessments of APS-connectivity capture Dubai's rapid growth in service-related centrality, such measurements are less apt to clarify why and how cities like Dubai pop up as 'world cities' in places where 'tangible' production is completely absent (besides the rapid construction of these cities themselves). Of course, judging by its commanding skyline there seems little doubt that the city-state of Dubai truly is a world city. Moreover, Dubai has been growing rapidly as a hub for international sea-trade and related services (Jacobs and Hall, 2007) and airline travel (O'Connell, 2006), and has become a major destination for luxury tourism. Dubai not only looks like an important place; it also ranks high on a variety of 'world city lists'. The Globalization and World City (GaWC) methodology measures the degree to which cities are connected by the office networks of global APS firms. Here it was ranked 9th among 525 cities (GaWC, 2011), a big leap forward compared to its 2008 ranking, which was then only 29th (Taylor, 2011). Dubai ranks even higher on financial centers listings: it ranked 29th of 75 on the Global Financial Centre Index. This index is produced by the London-based consultancy group Z/Yen and surveys financial center competitiveness by a combination of instrumental factors such as infrastructure and market access and competitiveness evaluations by financial elites – reasons enough to conclude that Dubai counts as a world city, even though mostly a 'financial' one.

Moving beyond these absolute and relative measurements of world cityness, however, the chapter will argue that the growth of Dubai and some other financial world cities in emerging markets can only be explained as a temporary fix for overaccumulation. This happens through the production of world cities as emerging markets in themselves – a process which is crucially mediated by institutions operating from the 'capitals of capital' in the world. In this case predominantly the City of London. The implication thereof is that the growth of APS complexes should not self-evidently be read as the shifting or decentralization of command-and-control functions from a limited number of world cities in the 1980s (New York–London–Tokyo) to a broader array of cities. Instead, it involves a growing dispersal of circuits of surplus value generation (Lee, 2002, 2006) that are increasingly linked to financial 'innovations' resulting from processes of financialization. This entails both the financialization of production and, mostly since the last decade, financialization feeding on itself (Sassen, 2010a; Engelen et al., 2011). This means that the growth of Dubai is fundamentally entangled and dependent on the decisions made in the capitals of capital, even though Dubai might be a fundamental site to tap excess oil income or enter 'alternative' circuits of value such as those of Islamic 'interest-free' finance. To make my point, this chapter first reviews some of the main contributions to economic theories of world/global cities, before outlining some challenges to this framework given in by the lessons of the recent financial crisis in the second section. The third section, then, brings up the case of Dubai, and reviews its growth as an alleged 'world city' from the variety of frameworks reviewed in the previous sections. The chapter concludes with recommendations for further reading.

Economic/financial geographies of the city

While it has been asserted by some that world cities cannot be read in economic terms alone (Robinson, 2006; Massey, 2007), it is the economic dimension that has sparked much of the existing world/global city research. Critics from comparative urbanism and post-colonial theory have argued that the existing body of research ignores myriads of other non-economic (inter)urban processes that shape urbanity in cities beyond the world/global city shortlist (see also Watson in this volume). While this is irrefutably true, it is good to recall a recent comment by Saskia Sassen (2010b, 159) clarifying that 'the larger global city and world city analyses are not urban theories: their aim is, rather, to explain a new phase of global capitalism, its strategic spaces and its exclusions. [...] The issue here is not a theory of the city. It is a theory of how the new empire functions.' With this in mind, I focus on three key contributors to the study of contemporary financial capitalism, which Sassen calls 'empire', through the development of world/global city research over the last three decades, namely the work of John Friedmann, Saskia Sassen herself and Peter Taylor.

John Friedmann's (1986) early work on world cities mainly emerged as a way of theorizing and analysing transformation in the world economy in a shift from Fordism to more flexible forms of accumulation that were by then crystallized, and in which cities clearly were playing a fundamental role. John Friedmann was inspired by the work of Manuel Castells (1972) and David Harvey (1973) as they had theorized the link between urbanization and the historical movement of industrial capitalism. In his 'world city hypothesis' (Friedmann, 1986) he takes up this agenda and tries to connect the study of cities to evolutions in the global economy. For Friedmann world cities research is the study of the spatial organization of a 'new international division of labor' (NIDL). The NIDL in itself was a result of reorganizations in industrial capitalism as it tried to 'solve' the crisis of Fordism in much of the high-income countries by shifting and hence globalizing production to low-income countries, a process which was hence crucially mediated by Euro-American multinational enterprises (MNEs). In this context of globalized production, and I focus on three of his seven theses that are fundamental to my argument, Friedmann (1986, 71) observes that 'key cities throughout the world are used by global capital as "basing points" in the spatial organization and articulation of production and markets' (Thesis 2). As basing point for global capital, these world cities also function as places through which global control functions are exerted, especially via a number of rapidly expanding sectors, such as corporate headquarters, international finance, global transport and communications, and a range of business services (Thesis 3). World cities, besides being 'command-and-control' centers for global capital, also form the sites where capital is concentrated and accumulated (Thesis 4). As the Dubai example will show, much of this accumulation can be absorbed in the built form itself.

A second major contribution to the field came from the sociologist Saskia Sassen. In her book *The Global City*, Sassen (1991) looks afresh to the functional centrality of cities in the world economy, and she does so by focusing upon the attraction of APS firms to major cities that offer knowledge-rich and technology-enabled environments (see Bassens et al., 2010a). In the 1980s and 1990s, many such service firms followed their global corporate clients to become important MNEs in their own right, albeit that these firms tend to be more susceptible to the agglomeration economies enabled by central city locations. This susceptibility relates to the production process of these services, which involves a lot of face-to-face communication because of the necessity of multiple simultaneous inputs and feedbacks. Based on this insight, Sassen argues that the particular characteristics of the production process in these sectors explain the centralization of management and servicing functions that has fuelled the economic boom of the early and mid-1980s in a number of major cities across the globe. A major implication of Sassen's work is that the study of cities in the context of a globalizing economy should focus on 'the *practice* of global control: the work of producing and reproducing the organization and management of a global production system and a global market-place for finance' (Sassen, 1995, 63–64, her emphasis). Her theoretical framework can therefore be summarized as a continuously unfolding process in which territorial dispersal of production at a variety of scales raises demand for centrally produced internationalized business service firms in general and financial services in particular.

Third, Peter Taylor and his colleagues in the GaWC research network have formulated an operational definition of Sassen's widely acclaimed conceptualization of world city formation (Beaverstock et al., 1999). GaWC treats world cities as post-industrial production sites where innovations in corporate services and finance are produced that have been integral to contemporary globalization. As Taylor (2000, 9) explains, there is something particular to world cities in that they constitute 'dynamic spatial knowledge complexes which combine a particular mix of skills and information which cannot be easily replicated elsewhere thus avoiding direct competition'. Taylor here deepens Sassen's empirical observations about the necessary (but not sufficient) conditions of knowledge-rich environments to APS complexes, by drawing on what he calls 'Braudel's provocation' that capitalism is inherently anti-market (Braudel, 1982, 1984). In Braudel's view capitalists will always strive to obtain a monopoly position to maximize surplus value accumulation. As he states, 'long-term successful capitalists are inherently generalist in nature; they are neither financial, nor merchant, nor industrial, nor agrarian, but any and all, depending on the size of the profits available' (Taylor, 2000, 7). Under global capitalism, a dominant way of surplus accumulation is via APS services; world cities, therefore, are defined based on the presence of internationalized clusters of these firms. It became Taylor's and GaWC's research project to study the geographies of their 'monopoly through regionalization' through their *locus* of world cities (Taylor, 2004).

In sum, the Friedmann–Sassen–Taylor framework discusses in increasing empirical and theoretical detail the centrality of (world/global) cities in the spatial organization of global capitalism. For Friedmann, 'world cities' embodied basing points of capital and the power to command-and-control it brought along; Sassen's 'global cities' are about the production of central functions embodied in knowledge-rich APS complexes, which are the emanation from the need for new forms of centralization in global financial markets and global production networks; Taylor, in turn, further specifies the place-based opportunities for monopoly generation that 'world cities' provide for current forms of APS-dominated capitalism.

Relational geographies of financial surplus value generation

While the above framework has immensely enriched thinking on urban-centered growth under conditions of contemporary globalization, the ongoing global financial crisis poses a big challenge as to how world/global city research relates *to the growing role of finance and the ongoing process of financialization* (Leyshon and Thrift, 1997; Pike and Pollard, 2010; French et al., 2011). In this context, it is relevant to note that a dominant view in the world/global city framework places APS complexes in an industrial capitalist and productionist framework. Multiple contributions to a recent issue in *Global Networks* (2010), for instance, aim to theorize and empirically substantiate the relationship between APS in world cities and global commodity chains. For Brown et al. (2010), APS serve as crucial inputs along various points of the global commodity chain, while for Parnreiter (2010) APS are a crucial input for control over or governance of the chain. The fundamental argument is then that APS functions allow for increased flexibility in production and marketing processes of, in particular, manufacturing TNCs.

This singular productionist reading is crucially challenged by three prominent and interrelated processes: First, the globalization of financial markets and growth of trading in secondary markets (enabled by revolutions in ICT and competitive deregulations of national jurisdictions), which has been detached from the spatial logics of direct control over production (Clark and Wojcík, 2007). Second, the deepening financialization, or subjection to the impulses of equity and debt markets, of large chunks of industrial production, since at least the 1980s. This has been associated with the rise of shareholder value-capitalism (i.e. the obsession to please shareholders in the short-term versus goals of long-term growth) and the associated need to instil investor confidence for firms that finance through the capital market (Froud et al., 2006). This has produced a tremendous change in the productive, organizational and managerial practices of firms and has necessitated the use of a range of APS to maintain profit levels and (keep on) satisfying investors. Third, and finally, the growing financialization of financial institutions (Engelen et al., 2011), which have made them susceptible to the short-term whims of financial markets themselves. This incentivizes the seeking of innovative ways to make a profit, either through regulatory arbitrage or the speeding-up of financial innovations, in which they can briefly maintain a competitive edge. These 'innovations' imply an ever-more complex structuring of existing financial products in developed markets (Wainwright, 2009; Engelen et al., 2010; Aalbers et al., 2011), but can also imply the innovation, but more often adaptation, of existing products in 'new' emerging markets or the 'creation' of emerging markets altogether (Sidaway and Pryke, 2000; Lai, 2006).

The challenge posed by financialization is to be more precise about the various urban 'economies' APS firms envisage that are associated with the world city network in general, and the forms of monopoly that are associated with world city formation in particular. Here I think it is useful to stress the fact that besides the 'place-based' 'regionalization' monopoly Taylor (2000, 9) mentions, two other concepts Taylor distils from economic literature, namely monopoly through 'innovation' and monopolies of 'large multi-location companies' are fundamental building blocks of a relational theory of world city formation. Taylor's concept of monopoly through 'innovation' can be traced back to Schumpeter's (1934) theories of innovation, while monopolies of 'large multi-location companies' can be conceived as a specific form of economies of scale, namely 'economies of overview' (Johannisson, 1990), which are achieved through the 'demarcation of an action frame where overview facilitates the identification and subsequent exploitation of opportunities'.

world city formation that acknowledges these other forms of monopoly, however, can only be fully grasped through the notion of capitalist crises of overaccumulation (Harvey, 1982, 1989). For Harvey and others (notably French regulationists, see Aglietta, 2000; Boyer and Saillard, 2002) the crisis of Fordism in high-income countries of the 1970s led to a regime of flexible accumulation. This was evident in the organization of production that accompanied the new international division of labour, but also led to a shift to services and finance as a *temporal fix* to the crisis of overaccumulation (i.e. excess capital looking for profitable investments that could no longer be absorbed by growth in production) (Harvey, 1982; Arrighi, 1994). Out of the crisis of Fordism in the 1970s grew the 'innovation' of the expansion of capital in the form of more and more intricate forms of credit in these countries, which was embodied in the rise of New York and London as deregulated financial centres during the 1980s. Importantly, these 'world cities' started serving as a destination for speculative investments in the built form itself, a recurrent process which Harvey calls a *spatial fix* to the problem of overaccumulation (Harvey, 1978). In these 'world cities' monopoly through innovation became a crucial element: within the day-to-day practice of the highly competitive global finance sector innovation, which entails finding niche markets where a monopoly can be temporarily defended (Engelen et al., 2010). At first, then, innovation monopolies in 'developed' markets sufficed to temporarily fix the problem of overaccumulation.

From the 1990s onward, however, when the initial financial innovations in developed markets became less profitable, this temporal and spatial
fix was increasingly sought in emerging markets (see e.g. Sidaway and
Bryson, 2002). The opportunities for such temporal fixes at other locations
obviously depended on existing geo-historical linkages between a world city
and a range of untapped markets, as was and is the case of London and
the Middle East and many other areas of the Commonwealth (King, 1990;
Beaverstock et al., 2003). The need for gateway functions that organize and
channel the investment of excess capital in the high-income countries into
emerging markets explains the emergence of financial centres in their spatial
proximity. Such a globalization of finance in general and growing activities in emerging markets in particular made that innovation monopolies
also hinged on 'monopolies through activities at multiple locations'. This
form of monopoly is what is at stake in much of the activity of financial-
ized productive or financial institutions today, either as a source of profit for
themselves or as a service they can offer to their clients. Productive multinational enterprises are renowned for their utilization of regulatory arbitrage,
for instance by reporting income and profits where taxes are low, either
in offshore centres (from Bahrain to the Bahamas) or onshore light-touch
jurisdictions (such as Ireland or the Netherlands). Financial profit-making
strategies are crucially supported by the 'services' of investment banks and
law firms who structure such ways of tax evasion. But even more generally,
financing in developed and emerging markets alike happens through complicated legal structures linking up various jurisdictions that aim to make
the products attractive for investors and minimize the financing cost for the
client. The crucial point is that the production of such financial innovations
happens in a number of world cities at the same time (the client can be based
in the Gulf Region, while the listing happens in London), so that multiple
world cities enter into the creation of the innovation. In sum, both examples illustrate that there is more to world city formation than the place-based
opportunities for monopoly formation; rather, relational forms of monopoly
such as innovation and multi-locational activity are at least as fundamental
to grasp dynamics of world cities.

At some points in time, emerging markets themselves generate
overaccumulation – a situation which produces the need for financial innovation to sustain accumulation. This can be the result of overaccumulation
in manufacturing (e.g. in China), but the extreme of which is the excess
capital that is produced by the extraction of raw materials as is happening in
the oil-rich Gulf region. The result is a growing amount of capital seeking a
profit, which can either be transformed into credit or can be absorbed in the
built form. The response to such overaccumulation issues can have significant implications for the command-and-control that is 'held' by these world
cities in these places. Sometimes excess capital is channelled out of 'emerging markets' and into 'developed markets', for instance through sovereign

wealth funds in the Gulf Region or China. This kind of temporal fix is less associated with world city formation since intermediation is not done by big global financial institutions, but rather conducted in-house by these funds (Behrendt, 2008; Clark et al., 2010). Alternatively to investing in 'developed' markets, excess capital can be absorbed in the local built form itself, leading to a spatial fix through various kinds of spectacular urbanization, a process which is more often mediated by foreign financial institutions. Constructivist critics, however, have asserted that world city formation can only be grasped when complementing an analysis of the dynamics of the world city network (as a proxy for how capitalism is spatially organized) with analyses of the 'local' production of the world city. A particularly important range of contributions have indeed disclosed the 'local' production of world cities by urban elites, ranging from examples of the construction of London or Singapore (Olds and Yeung, 2004; Massey, 2007). However, more than often the 'production' of world cities entails the interaction of global (economic) and local (political) elites across a range of scales, making it a 'glocal' rather than a local process (Swyngedouw, 1997). This is the story of Dubai I will discuss in more detail in the next section.

'world city' Dubai

The story of Dubai can perhaps best be told by the emblematic evolution of property prices in the emirate over the last five years (Figure 4.1). Foreign-owned property prices doubled between the start of the index in 2007 up to the outbreak of the global financial crisis in the third quarter of 2008.

Figure 4.1 Evolution of Dubai's foreign-owned property prices as percentage of 2007's first quarter
Source: Collier international, http://www.colliers-me.com/marketreports.aspx.

The final quarter of 2009 then saw a fast devaluation, bringing prices back slightly above the 2007 level at which they have more or less remained ever since. In many ways, this evolution invokes a typical boom-and-bust cycle, which characterizes contemporary finance-dominated capitalism (cf. the 2001–2 dot-com bubble). These cycles are marked by a period of strong investor confidence and speculation inflating prices (boom), to be followed by an endogenous/exogenous shock which undermines investor confidence. In this case the fall of Lehman Brothers and the fallout that hit Dubai's government-related investment agencies triggered a massive devaluation (bust), which gave way to the 2009 Dubai debt crisis (Bassens et al., 2010b). The 'strange' correlation between financial boom-and-bust cycles and property markets in general, and the construction of super-tall buildings in particular, has been famously captured by Lawrence's (1999) 'skyscraper index', which points to the peculiar coincidence of the (near-)completion of the highest building in the world and the outbreak of major financial crisis: in New York the Singer Building was completed in 1908 following the 1907 Panic and the Chrysler Building (1930) and Empire State Building (1931) following the Great Crash of 1929. In Dubai the 2008 property market collapse and following 2009 debt crisis presaged the completion of the 829m-high Burj Khalifa, currently the highest building in the world.[3]

In financial centres property markets in general and offices in particular are a store of value and represent a large chunk of the portfolios of financial institutions themselves (which are located in the city's business districts) (Lizieri, 2012). Financial institutions are hence not only the occupiers of office space but also its owner, which implies that property will feature as crucial assets since they serve as 'tangible' collateral in volatile financial markets. Financial markets ultimately affect urban property markets since financing often happens via the capital market. This implies that volatility in capital markets will lead to revaluations of property markets simultaneously across financial centres. Following a process of 'lockstep', as Lizieri (2012, 170) calls it, a downturn entails scarcer credit which depresses property values, but also a slow-down of work for financial institutions, which dampens demand for office space. As financial assets property is hence downgraded as collateral, which further depresses potential leverage and general activities of financial institutions – a process which is in fact the reverse of what happens during the upswing of markets.

Beyond this general effect there is also a direct relationship between the overall fate of the financial centre and the value embodied in the built form itself. Revaluations are, in other words, just as much geographically uneven. Property markets in well-established centres recovered rapidly to pre-crisis levels since they are considered safe havens for capital on the move, while riskier property markets in emerging financial centres such as Dubai experience longer-lasting devaluations. This connection, however, also works in the other way: financial institutions are crucially implicated in the constant struggle to keep the image of the financial center high as to counter potential devaluation of their portfolios. There is, then, more to be distilled from this story since there is a close relation between speculative investments in the built environment and the temporary 'fixing' of capitalism's crisis tendencies (Harvey, 1978).

Harvey reads the 'switching' of investments into the built form as a way for capitalism to manage a crisis of overaccumulation (which is of course apparent to an abundance of money supply and lower interest rates, see footnote 2), which is the result of the exhaustion of previous 'fixes'. As outlined in the previous sections, contemporary conditions of financial globalization make the effects and answers to overaccumulation inherently relational. This perspective then triggers the question where Dubai's capital is coming from, especially since productive industries are close to non-existent in the emirate. To start addressing this point, Table 4.1 details the stock of foreign direct investment (FDI) before and after the burst of the Dubai bubble, most of which occurred in finance and insurance sector (35.4 per cent) or in construction (34.5 per cent). What we see is that UK investments have always constituted the lion's share of Dubai's incoming FDI. Stocks held by investors from the Gulf Region are far more modest, with most of the capital flowing in from oil-rich Qatar and Kuwait in 2010. This suggests that the growth of Dubai has been mostly financed by UK investments or at least has been channelled through the United Kingdom, via a growing array of funds, asset management, banks and other financial

Table 4.1 Foreign direct investment stocks[4] in the Emirate of Dubai for 2006 and 2010

	2006			2010	
Country	FDI stock (million US$)	Share %	Country	FDI stock (million US$)	Share %
UK	4153	36	UK	7391	46
Japan	2494	22	Japan	2864	18
India	1126	10	Hong Kong	1530	9
USA	727	6	Switzerland	998	6
Netherlands	423	4	USA	981	6
North Korea	342	3	Kuwait	740	5
Iran	291	3	Qatar	565	4
Switzerland	246	2	India	446	3
Iceland	236	2	China	317	2
Turkey	226	2	South Korea	280	2
Others	1299	11	Others	467	3
Total	11560	100	Total	16113	100

Source: Dubai statistics centre, http://www.dsc.gov.ae/.

service firms in the City of London. Part of these investments may very well originate in the Gulf Region itself but have been recycled and re-imported in the region, a process mostly mediated by banks based in the City, which has a long business history in the Gulf.

Beyond these FDI statistics, we know that large UK banks such as the Royal Bank of Scotland, Barclays, HSBC and Standard Chartered have been heavily involved in establishing Dubai as a financial hub, through well-staffed regional headquarters (mostly in the Dubai International Financial Centre), but also as creditors of Dubai's 'world city project'. In 2009, when the Dubai debt crisis hit, they were 'exposed' to US$5 billion debt of Dubai World, one of Dubai's main government-related enterprises (*Financial Times*, 2 December 2009). In total UK banks were estimated to have lent up to US$50 billion to the United Arab Emirates, much of which has ended up in Dubai (*BBC*, 27 November 2009). Dubai's development as a 'world city' should thus be understood relationally: namely to a large extent as the result of the City looking for new solutions for overaccumulation, hence building 'The City-upon-the-Gulf'. This of course dovetails with the ambitions of the ruling elites in Dubai themselves and the supply-side urban development model – the Dubai-model which serves as a panacea for other cities in the Gulf Region and in itself is shaped on the Singapore city-state – they have been promoting for over four decades now.

This observation has important implications for how we read Dubai as a world/global city in light of the Friedmann–Sassen–Taylor framework. First, Dubai, as a debt-financed project in itself, is nowhere near to harbouring Friedmann's command-and-control or 'capital' functions. Dubai is very much at the receiving end as it serves as a site of opportunity, in fact a market in itself for (speculative) surplus generation for regional and global capital. This suggests that if Dubai is a world city, it is mainly so because it 'controls' access to its urban investment categories, which are mainly real estate markets and large infrastructure projects. In this light it can more readily be viewed as a 'gateway world city', not to the region as say Sao Paulo does for Brazil (Rossi and Taylor, 2006), but mainly to itself. On the other hand, large indebtedness can always trigger a situation when debtor owes the creditor so much that he in fact owns him. This may be the case for some UK-based financial institutions which have lent large sums to Dubai. Since Dubai now represents a substantial amount of (fixed) assets on the books of foreign financial institutions, a departure of a few influential investors may trigger a massive devaluation of large chunks of the Dubai portfolios. The need to maintain Dubai as an investment-grade category explains why UK investment appetite for Dubai remains high, especially now that more proximate 'developed' Eurozone markets are considered far from risk-free themselves. The relational construction of Dubai hence continues.

Second, most of the business of channelling capital into Dubai is performed by foreign financial institutions: the website of Dubai International

Financial Centre (http://www.difc.ae/) mentions that it hosts 16 of the world's top 20 banks, 8 of the world's top 20 asset managers, 4 of the world's 5 largest insurance companies and 6 of the top 10 global law firms. This seems to suggest that Dubai does serve as a site where specific 'knowledge' is available, although again this knowledge seems mostly related to what goes on in Dubai's markets itself, and is less relevant to reaping investment opportunities at the regional or global scale. This means that Dubai also falls short of being a global city in a Sassenian sense, as being a site from where centralized coordinating functions are performed in the expanding global economy. Dubai's (self)-categorization as a 'world city' is thus mainly falsified by referral to the growth of the APS complex in the city. There is indeed a large intermediation of these capital flows by Euro-American banks, and hence the growing entanglements with metropolitan centres in developed markets. However, the partial retreat of Euro-American banks in the wake of the 2008 crisis illustrates that this growth is best to be read as 'dependent' (*Financial Times*, 24 October 2011). Moreover, foreign intermediation seriously limits knowledge production by locals, which are notoriously underemployed in business and financial services even though government-sponsored programmes attempt to stimulate 'emiratization' of the workforce and seek international partnerships for local higher education, often as the offspring of US universities or UK business schools (see http://www.dubaifaqs.com/universities-dubai.php). It then seems that Dubai is temporarily enabling limited world city functions by 'borrowing' foreign knowledge.

Third, an extended definition of Taylor's monopoly formation through world cities is relevant for our analysis of Dubai as a 'relational world city'. Recently, there has been quite a lot of interest into Islamic 'interest-free' finance and the circuits of surplus creation it entails (Pollard and Samers, 2007). In contrast to conventional circuits, where Dubai still takes a secondary role (see the listings mentioned in the introduction), Dubai is allegedly emerging as a key hub in such 'decentred' circuits, many of which stretch out to Islamic markets in the Middle East, North Africa and South-east Asia (and Malaysia in particular). As a prime example of a niche where local cultural and religious knowledge is paramount and South–South connections are likely to be dominant, Dubai could very well be developing world/global city functions in this realm, contrary to conventional circuits, which are mostly dependent on knowledge in the leading world cities. However, recent work has shown that the geographies of Islamic finance in the Gulf Region are very much entangled with mainstay world cities (Bassens et al., 2010a) and for the larger part qualitatively similar to conventional modes of finance (Bassens et al., 2012a). In this light, Islamic finance in the Gulf Region constitutes one of the more recent niches in global finance, where innovations enabling religious and regulatory arbitrage allow for the accumulation of financial surplus. In this case a monopoly is produced through the construction of a global 'Islamic' market by conventional banks operating from the City of London and using Dubai as a fundamental cog to adapt and roll-out financial innovations conceived in overcrowded 'conventional' markets. In addition to monopoly through innovation, monopoly arises from tapping into knowledges at multiple locations. In investment banking and project finance, both of which are big business in Dubai, the translation, negotiation and introduction of financial products requires (i) the employment of a multisited APS complex to construct the financially successful product (e.g. an Islamic bond for a Dubai-based property developer listed in London, structured by a London-based bank and a Dubai-based global law firm); and (ii) the authorization of the product or deal by the so-called Shari'a scholars as a confirmation of its Sharia-compliance. These scholars, however, are more than often not Emirati but Malaysian expats or temporary residents, which indicates that the practice of borrowing knowledge extends to the field of Shari'a expertise (Bassens et al., 2012b). We should note that Islamic circuits that go South–South are emerging, in which conventional banks are less dominant and which mostly aim at channelling excess Gulf capital towards emerging 'Islamic' economies such as Malaysia.

To conclude, this chapter's point is that we have to be careful not to equate the spectacular and rapid urbanization *cum* APS growth in some cities in emerging markets with a 'natural' relocation of command-and-control functions to these places. Both aspects validate the idea of a broad-scale 'reorientation' of economic and financial geographies in the current age. Indeed, there is no reason to believe that this is not fundamentally reflected in massive urbanization and rapid growth of 'cutting-edge' urban economies. In this sense, cities like Dubai have indeed become 'world cities'. However, despite these 'images' of rapid world city formation, the presence of an APS complex can be misleading because it can signify dependent growth and mainly the profit of managing financial intermediation by foreign firms. For instance, instead of Dubai, it would be closer to reality to categorize Abu Dhabi or Doha as 'true' world cities with long-lasting command-and-control functions in a Friedmannian sense, since these cities are the basing points for capital linked to real oil power in SWFs and their global portfolios. Still, Dubai is a global city in a Sassenian sense since the globalization of finance requires new centralized functions and specific relevant knowledge in specific market niches. However, these functions may be of ephemeral nature since they are mostly linked to channelling regional/global excess capital in the speculative construction of Dubai. In this context, as developments in Islamic finance illustrate, Dubai's world cityness can best be understood by taking a relational reading of Taylor's ideas about monopoly formation in the realm of global finance.

This reading is framed in Sassen's project to study how the new *financial capitalist* empire functions. The realization of financial capital entails a complex set of processes which are inherently networked (realized via connecting multiple world cities) and relational (crucially dependent on mutual representation for capital formation to be legitimized, naturalized and eventually reproduced). Agreeing with Derudder et al. in this volume, the question of how crucial a particular city is for financial capital realization becomes a second-order one in such an economic reading of world cities. Having said this, the realization of financial capital is not just the outcome of a set of inanimate global processes. Rather, cities like Dubai have been 'produced' by an assemblage of entrepreneurial local ruling elites and 'global' (in this case mostly UK-based) financial elites. This implies that capital crucially depends on the agency of localized actors to realize itself. Strategic forms of urban entrepreneurialism via the built form, through 'cultural' strategies, or regulatory adaptations can hence be read as an effort to jump-start a city's role in global accumulation processes. However, it becomes clear that urban entrepreneurial policy does not end with attracting business to the city, but has the more fundamental challenge of embedding it and, far more importantly, redistributing the fruits of accumulation to its entire population. With these two dimensions being absent, future capital realization will eventually be frustrated, leaving the city empty-handed. As such it becomes clear that the growth of world city Dubai is one of the most emblematic examples of the constant struggle to find a spatial and temporal fix to the crisis tendencies of contemporary financial capitalism, and the challenges this creates for urban policy in its major nodes.

Notes

1. The views in this chapter arose from research funded by the Research Foundation – Flanders Grant No. 3E005811. The author thanks Ben Derudder and Michiel van Meeteren for their comments on an earlier version of this chapter.
2. Although 'world cities' and 'global cities' are often used interchangeably, it should be noted they actually refer to different notions about the relation between urbanization and evolutions in the global economy (see Derudder, 2006). A discussion of some of the main interpretations is provided in the second section. For reasons of terminological convenience, however, I prefer to use the term 'world city' as a catch-all term for these variegated definitions.
3. The intuitive validity of the index has given way to theorization, although mostly from economic perspectives. Thornton's (2005) discussion of the index, for instance, elaborates on the theoretical relationship between the construction of super-tall buildings and an interpretation of business cycles by the Austrian school whereby lower interest rates shift investments from short- to longer-term capital projects. In essence, the argument is that lower interest rates make it easier to purchase land, leading to increased demand for land, especially at top-location sites (e.g. central business districts). This in turn leads to increase in 'value' of land per unit, which drives parsimonious land-owners to build more capital-intensive (since interest-rates are low) high structures, limiting the total surface of land in use.
4. An investment that reflects definition of lasting interest made by an investor who is resident in one economy establishing a lasting interest in an enterprise (Direct

Foreign Enterprise) that is resident in an economy other than that of the investor. This means that the foreign direct investor owns 10 per cent or more of the voting power in that enterprise, which allows him to exercise an influence on decision-making, such process is called a Foreign Direct Investment (Dubai Statistics Centre, http://www.dsc.gov.ae/, accessed 24 September 2012).

5
The Historical Dimension

Peter Rimmer and Howard Dick

The history of urban settlement is as old as civilization, but reliable figures on size of population date back no further than the late nineteenth century. Even contemporary figures on urban size are bedevilled by inconsistencies in the definition of functional urban areas. Archaeology and literature give little better than orders of magnitude of the population of leading cities from their origins in the Tigris and Euphrates Valleys around 8000 BCE and in the Yellow and Yangtze Valleys from around 4000 BCE (Morris, 2010a,b). Comparative urban history is therefore a matter of looking for patterns and very long-term trends. This survey takes its starting point as the Roman and Chinese empires of around the beginning of the first millennium, thus a time period of about 2000 years.

Historical geography has to take as its frame of reference the known world. In the Roman and Chinese empires, the known world equated to the civilized world, beyond which lay the 'barbarians', albeit barbarians with whom it was possible to trade as well as to wage war and capture booty and slaves. While this known world was therefore fuzzy on the margins, it certainly did not equate to the modern perception of 'global', that is, the six populated continents as a single networked surface. The word international must also be eschewed as having no sensible meaning in eras before the rise of the nation-state. Nevertheless, the concept of 'world city' can be applied as signifying something more than 'great city' or 'metropolis'. As Lewis Mumford (1961, 639) suggested, the world city does not so much represent its own hinterland as bring together 'at least in token quantities all races and cultures'. As central to its (known) world, the world city is no different in kind from the global city, notwithstanding a multiplicity of nuances.

This chapter first sets out a simple model of urban evolution before applying the criteria to imperial cities, the new global order and a succinct case study of Shanghai. It then conceptualizes the impact of accelerating time-space compression on global networks over the past two millennia: the contemporary urban experience that is viewed through the roles of nation-states and multinational corporations, and the nature and vulnerability of global city space.

A world city model – evolution

The four most basic criteria for a world city are (demographic) size, (economic) role, (geographic) reach and (cultural) diversity. Size can be measured either by population or by area, but data are more readily accessible for the former, albeit usually no more accurate than half an order of magnitude. Function (or role) encompasses the mix of economic activities such as manufacturing, trade, finance and other services. Reach is about the articulation, intensity and extent of urban networks and the position of world cities as central nodes within those networks. Diversity is the cultural aspect of agglomeration, being the range and representation of non-local peoples with all their customs, everything that does not pertain to the immediate hinterland. Thus London is not England, Paris is not France, Jakarta is not Indonesia. These four criteria can be applied to give a snapshot of world cities at any juncture.

The next issue is what causes change over time. This simple model focuses upon technology and governance. Technology, the economic dimension, embraces production, distribution and consumption in urban space as manifest in such ways as the means of construction, transport, communications and, not least, public health (water and sewerage). Progress in most of these respects was very slow until the Industrial Revolution of the nineteenth century. The frontier of possibilities during the first two millennia therefore had a consistency that was broken little more than a century and a half ago.

Governance likewise has several levels and dimensions. At the very basic level it relates to the maintenance of public order, the rule of law and security of property within the city. Beyond this, it refers to the ability of some form of government bureaucracy to undertake public works and apply routines for their regular maintenance, failing which cities become unsustainable through crowding, congestion and disease. The third aspect of governance is the ability of overarching government, be it imperial or national, to manage a system of public finances as a pumping mechanism to provide enough resources to sustain a huge urban population that by its very nature does not produce more than a small fraction of its own subsistence, while also giving rise to an extraordinary demand for trade goods. In its most primitive form, the pumping mechanism may draw up resources by waging war, but ultimately cities require some accepted form of taxation and spending. The effectiveness of these forms of governance determines the extent to which a city can maximize its potential and sustain its population over centuries.

These functions of government translate into structures. Even if cities are not self-governing, they usually enjoy some measure of local autonomy, subject to the overarching sovereignty of the kingdom or, more recently, the nation-state. Kingdoms may be subject to the higher authority of empires or, as in China, be absorbed into them, and, in turn, as witnessed during the twentieth century, may be the product of their disintegration. The particular quality of modern nation-states is that their borders and jurisdictions are internationally recognized. This much at least has been an achievement of the United Nations.

Imperial cities

Rome of the first century CE has strong claim to being the first world city, notwithstanding the prior claims of Alexandria, Carthage and Babylon (Table 5.1). Estimates of Rome's population vary by several hundred thousand, but there is some support for the claim that by this time it was near enough to one million people and was the largest city in the world, west or east (Bairoch, 1988; Morris, 2010b). This massive population was sustained by a well-organized food supply from around the Mediterranean, including grain from North Africa, a well-engineered fresh water supply and sewerage system, and a tradition of and pride in urban government that was legitimized by impressive public works. The labour supply was ensured by slavery. So long as frontier wars captured enough slaves and other booty to cover the costs of garrisoning, the Roman economy was viable, indeed until the fourth century CE. The sack of Rome in 410 CE and again in 455 marked the end of its supremacy. The imperial centre moved east to more prosperous and secure Byzantium (Constantinople), though apparently the latter never grew larger than 500,000 people (Morris, 2010b).

China was forcibly melded into an empire during the third century BCE by the Qin (Ch'in), conquest of the Three Kingdoms, giving rise to the name by which the country is still known. Its raw military power soon gave way to the bureaucratic administration of the Han Empire, which for almost half a millennium coexisted at fingertips with that of Rome. The imperial capital of Chang'an was located in the fertile valley of the Yellow River on the site of the modern city of Xi'an, famous for the Qin dynasty tomb of the terracotta warriors. By the mid-eighth century CE at the height of the Tang Dynasty (618–907), its urban population within and beyond the spacious walled city is believed to have approached one million (Morris, 2010a,b; Modelski, 2003; Chandler, 1987), while the Eastern Capital of Luoyang (Loyang) may have reached 500,000 (Modelski, 2003), both surpassing Constantinople as the world's largest cities.

By the mid-seventh century the Eastern Roman Empire with its seat at Constantinople was shrinking in the face of first Persian and then Arab conquests. Following the death of Prophet Mohammed in 632 CE, Muslim armies occupied Egypt and North Africa as far as Spain, as also the area of modern-day Syria and Persia. In the mid-eighth century the Abbasid

Table 5.1 World cities

City	Era	Size Million	Empire	Other main cities
Rome	2nd BCE-5th CE	1.0 (1 BCE/CE)	Roman	Alexandria Carthage, Constantinople
Chang'an (Xi'an)	206 BCE-960	1.0 (700 & 800)	Chinese (Chin, Han, Sui & Tang Dynasties)	Luoyang
Baghdad	7th–16th	0.2 (1200)	Arab	Damascus, Cordoba, Cairo
Kaifeng	960–1127	1.0 (1000, 1100)	Chinese (Song Dynasty)	Guangzhou Fuzhou, Zhangzhou
Hangzhou	1127–1279	1.0 (1200)	Chinese (Southern Song)	
Jingling (Nanking)	1368–1644	0.5 (1400)	Chinese (Ming)	
Constantinople (Istanbul)	1299-early 20th	0.6 (1700)	Ottoman	Cairo
Lisbon	15th–20th	0.2 (1801) 0.6 (1930)	Portuguese	
Madrid	15th–20th	0.14 (1789) 0.4 (1868)	Spanish	Seville, Antwerp
Beijing	1279–1911	1.1 (1800)	Chinese (Yuan, Ming & Qing)	Canton Hangzhou Hankou
Amsterdam	17th–20th	0.22 (1700)	Dutch	Leiden, Rotterdam
Paris	17th–20th	1.1 (1851) 3.3 (1900)	French	Lyon
London	late 16th & early 17th-mid-20th	6.5 (1900)	British	Birmingham, Manchester, Glasgow
Vienna	1869–1918	1.8 (1900)	Austro-Hungarian	
Berlin	1871–1918	2.7 (1900)	German	
Tokyo	19th-mid-20th	1.8 (1900) 6.8 (1940)	Japanese	Osaka. Nagoya Kyoto
Moscow	1721–1917	1.8) (1915)	Russia	St Petersburg
New York	late 18th-mid-20th	10.2 (1936)	American	Chicago, Boston, Philadelphia

Source: de Vries, 1984; Maddison, 1998; Kotkin, 2005; Mitchell, 2007a,b; Morris, 2010a,b.

caliphate seized control of this empire and established its capital at Baghdad on a bend of the Tigris River. This strikingly beautiful new city was built in circular form on a Persian model, its walls being surrounded by a network of canals that both irrigated its hinterland and met the city's needs for food, water and sewerage. Estimates are that by the tenth century Baghdad had reached the threshold of one million people. However, just as the Roman Empire had bifurcated, so did the Muslim one. Displaced from Damascus by the Abbasids, the Umayyad dynasty founded Cordoba on the Iberian Peninsula as the capital of a Western caliphate to rival Baghdad in architecture, learning and commerce.

The great cities of the Mediterranean World from Carthage and Rome through to Constantinople had the great advantage of being part of a maritime world linking Europe, North Africa and what is now known as the Middle East. Whereas the Roman Empire spread eastwards, the Arab Empire spread westwards. Maritime supremacy was as important as military superiority. China, by contrast, was a more landlocked society. Nevertheless, a strategic aspect of the old imperial capitals of Chang'an, Luoyang and Kaifeng was their location at the end of the Silk Road, the caravan routes that reached across the deserts and high mountains of Asia into Central Asia and Persia to the shores of the Black Sea and the shipping routes through to the Mediterranean (Figure 5.1).

There was also a sea route linking the Red Sea and the Persian Gulf across the Arabian Sea to India and the Malay World. During the seventh and eighth centuries Arab seafarers traded via the Malay Archipelago as far as Canton (Guangzhou) in southern China. Arab trade routes thereby linked the world from the Iberian Peninsula around the world by both land and sea, as evidenced by coins, trade goods and monuments. Bounded though it may have been, it was in its slow, seasonal way a 'world system' (Wallenstein, 1974).

At the Chinese end of the world axis, a momentous change occurred with the southward shift in population and the locus of economic activity from the dry farming area of North China (millet and wheat) into the fertile rice-growing area of the middle and lower reaches of the Yangtze Valley. The decline of the old cities of the Yellow River was hastened by the conquest of northern China by the Jurchen (Manchu), who in 1127 seized the imperial capital of Kaifeng. Under the Southern Song (1127–1279), the empire consolidated in the Yangtze with a new capital at Hangzhou (Linan) with an estimated population of over one million. This was the city of Cathay whose splendours were later reported back to Europe by the Venetian merchant Marco Polo.

An era of around 500 years of flourishing urban civilization reached its apogee towards the end of the thirteenth century. The extent and the vulnerability of that world's interdependence would now be shown up by two terrible and prolonged catastrophes. First came the Mongol invasions.

68

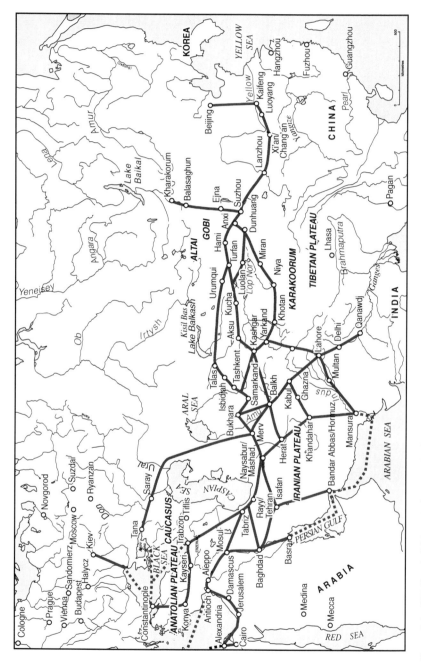

Figure 5.1 Silk Road: A historical network of East–West routes across Afro-Eurasia
Source: Routes generalized from Forêt, 2008.

Genghis Khan united the tribesman of the steppes into formidable mobile armies and by the time of his death in 1227 controlled an empire along the Silk Road from North China to the Caspian Sea. Subsequently Mongol armies reached as far as Egypt, Vienna, North India, Java and Japan. Although in 1279 the Mongols under Kublai Khan extended their control over the whole of the Chinese Empire and as the Yuan dynasty would rule for almost a century, their wider imperium soon fragmented into rival kingdoms.

Mongol rule may have facilitated the spread of the pandemic known as the Black Death, that is, the bubonic plague which in the mid-fourteenth century spread like wildfire from China along the Silk Road through Central Asia to the Crimea on the Black Sea, from where it was carried by Venetian and Genoese traders into Europe. Estimated urban death rates were a quarter to one-third of the total population with densely settled cities being especially vulnerable (Benedictow, 2004). Urban populations also declined because of the outflow of terrified people and the disruption of trade and commerce.

China proved to be more resilient than Europe, which took some centuries to recover. After defeat of the Mongol overlords, in 1368 the Ming Dynasty was proclaimed and ushered in almost three centuries of prosperity. The new Imperial Capital was at first established at Nanjing on the Lower Yangtze. By 1400 its population of around 500,000 made it the world's largest city, albeit just half the size of capitals before the Mongol conquest and the Black Death (Morris, 2010b).

The middle of the second millennium was marked by two great countervailing movements. Weakening of the Mongol kingdoms of Central Asia allowed the Ottoman Turks to seize control of the Black Sea, and the Levant. The capture of Constantinople in 1453 marked the end of the Roman-Byzantine Empire and a new era of Ottoman supremacy in the Eastern Mediterranean and as far west as the Balkans and Vienna. The sultanate controlled the Silk Road as far as China and from the capital of Istanbul (formerly Constantinople) at the mouth of the Bosphorus could regulate the flow of trade into the Mediterranean.

While a Muslim empire flourished in the East, in Spain the surrender of the Muslim kingdom of Granada in 1492 marked the rise of Christian Europe in the West. Seeking to circumvent Venetian-Ottoman control of the spice trade and Silk Road, the Portuguese king sent ships eastwards around the Cape of Good Hope to India and on to Malacca, the Spice Islands, China and Japan. Simultaneously the Spanish, with the aid of Italian capital and the navigators Christopher Columbus and Amerigo Vespucci, reached the Caribbean and the Americas as a bridge to the Spice Islands and China. These explorations and conquests not only opened up direct sea routes between Europe and Asia, but also, at great cost in disease and suffering, brought the two American continents into what was now truly a world economy.

These countervailing expansions collided in the Mediterranean. In the Battle of Lepanto (1571) the combined Spanish-Italian fleet destroyed the Turkish-Arab fleet near the entrance to the Adriatic, giving it command of the seas. Henceforth, the Ottoman Turks would control the North African shores of the Mediterranean, while the Christian powers, comprising Spain, including its territories of Naples, Sicily and Sardinia, the Republic of Venice, the Republic of Genoa, the Duchy of Savoy and the Knights of Malta, would control the northern shores (Braudel, 1973).

The opening of direct European trade routes to Asia and the Americas channelled enormous wealth back to Europe, not least massive amounts of silver. Yet these trading networks did not give rise to world cities in either Portugal or Spain, which were unable to transform those commodity and bullion flows into productive capital. Around 1600 Lisbon had a population of 150,000 but Madrid did not reach even that modest figure for another 50 years. Part of the reason was the drain of wealth to fund wars against the Protestant Kingdoms of northern Europe. The Spanish Armada (1588) and eventual Spanish defeat in the Low Countries ensured the eclipse of Antwerp as the northern trading hub and the emergence of first Amsterdam and then London as the new centres of maritime trade and international finance.

A significant factor in the economic stagnation of Spain was the expulsion of the Sephardic Jews in the momentous year 1492 (Gerber, 1992). A city cannot achieve world status without a class of people experienced and skilled in long-distance commerce and finance. The Muslim kingdom of Al Andalus (Granada), like that of the Abbasids and Ottomans, had been truly cosmopolitan, not merely tolerating, but allowing wealth and high office to talented Christians and Jews, who were merchants, bankers, lawyers and scholars. Their exclusion by Christian Spain brought about a great diaspora of this educated urban elite to other cities, not least to Antwerp, Amsterdam and London but also to the Ottoman Empire.

Asian trade was greatly disrupted by the intrusion of the Spanish and Portuguese followed in the seventeenth century by the Dutch and the British. Around the same time Chinese shipping was also being harassed by Japanese pirates (*wakō*) (Seyock, 2005; Schottenhammer, 2007). This gave rise to a momentous shift in Chinese attitudes towards the outside world. In the early decades of the fifteenth century, the eunuch Zheng He (1371–1433) led successive Chinese fleets as far as the Malay Archipelago, the Persian Gulf and East Africa. In 1421, however, after some years of preparation, the Ming Emperor relocated the imperial capital from Nanjing to Beijing (Northern Capital) near the Great Wall of China. The austere Forbidden City was laid out as the core of a grand city contained within massive high walls. Its logic was to defend the empire against invasion from the north relying on the Grand Canal from the Yangtze to Beijing to ensure the provisioning of the city. Though it was not deliberate policy at the time, this relocation of the capital to the distant north also marked a withdrawal of the Empire into relative seclusion, despite the maintenance of a carefully regulated tribute trade through the southern port of Canton (Guangzhou).

Reacting vigorously to Christian-Portuguese influence, the Tokugawa rulers of the recently unified Japan withdrew into even stricter isolation after 1633. Korea followed suit. Thus Northeast Asia, which had been so much a magnet for international trade and which continued to drain Europe of silver, all but withdrew from the world system.

In terms of city size, the outcomes of seclusion were counter-intuitive. Sustained by the remarkable efficiency of the imperial system of taxation and reallocation, Beijing became a prosperous capital of around one million people. Nor was it the only very large city in China, William Rowe (2009) estimates Hankou (Wuhan) also had that order of magnitude. Beijing's rival as the largest city in the world was the Japanese capital of Edo (Tokyo), which also grew to an estimated one million people. Yet neither of these huge cities had a world reach. Japan was all but closed to international trade and relations until the 1850s. The Chinese Empire maintained tributary relations and foreign trade through the port of Canton (Guangzhou). This was the reach of the Chinese Empire rather than the city of Beijing itself, Despite its being the Imperial capital and the controlling brain of the Empire.

In terms of relativities, Edo was the more extraordinary. By the eighteenth century the Chinese empire had a population of 200–300 million people, of which Beijing was therefore much less than 1 per cent. The population of the Tokugawa shogunate of the same period was smaller by an order of magnitude, perhaps about 30 million. The explanation for this anomaly is that Edo was the product of forced urbanization through the system of 'alternative attendance' whereby the shogun required each of the several hundred feudal lords (*daimyō*) to reside for part of the year in Edo with many of their samurai retainers and their families and attendants. The best evidence of the impact of this system is that when it was abolished in 1850s the population of Edo almost immediately fell by about half (Saitō, 1984).

The examples of Beijing and Edo influenced the thinking of Western philosophers and theorists, including Karl Marx and Max Weber, later also Karl Wittfogel (1957), to propose that these capitals were artificial cities for the display and consumption of oriental despotisms. In fact China and Japan were both functioning market economies (Skinner, 1964, 1965a,b; Sumiya and Taira, 1979). Arguably Beijing and Edo were as much centres of manufacturing and services as the later world cities (Curtis, 2009). Exotic as they may have appeared to nineteenth-century Westerners, they were harbingers of the modern mega-cities of Beijing and Tokyo.

By contrast, Europe's increasing prosperity did not give rise to large cities. In the mid-fourteenth century on the eve of the Black Death, the largest city in Europe was Paris with a population of around 200,000. Three centuries later that was the population of Amsterdam, which had succeeded Antwerp as the centre of northern European commerce and become in the hub of a truly global maritime trading empire. Its trading posts spread from New Amsterdam (New York) to the Caribbean and Brazil (Recife and Pernambuco) to Cape Town, the Red Sea and the Persian Gulf, Ceylon, the Malay Archipelago, Taiwan and Japan. The East Indian Company (VOC) managed a lively intra-Asian trade from Arabia to as far as China and Japan. Amsterdam possessed the full range of urban functions, its Seaborne Empire (Boxer, 1965) spanned the globe and its population was culturally diverse, notably as a haven for Jews and Protestants, but it was a city of only modest size by world standards of that age. The decentralized political and commercial structure of the Netherlands diffused the forces of agglomeration.

In the seventeenth century the most populous city in Europe was actually the Mediterranean city of Naples, whose population was twice that of Amsterdam (Astarita, 2005, 320). Naples was an ancient city, having had been founded in the fifth century BCE as the Greek city of Neápolis before being incorporated into the Roman Empire. Later the Norman/Vikings would rule, then France and Spain, but the city retained a measure of political autonomy. It benefited from its fine harbour and strategic location at the centre of the Mediterranean, adjacent to then fertile island of Sicily. Yet what is most remarkable about Naples is that, without being an imperial capital, it nevertheless flourished as a cultural centre – much more so than Catholic Rome – and also as a grand centre of consumption.

The first European city since Rome to achieve world scale in terms of population was London. Although an urban settlement since Roman times, around 1530 London still had only about 50,000 people, which increased to about 225,000 in 1603 following the influx of Huguenot refugees from France (Pevsner, 1957). By 1700, however, the population had soared to 600,000 (Morris, 2010b). Over the course of the eighteenth century the United Kingdom of Great Britain established naval supremacy over the Dutch and proceeded to establish a more sophisticated Empire. The main focus was the American and Caribbean colonies with the vast wealth of their slave plantations giving rise to a lively transatlantic trade. After the loss of the richest American colonies in the War of Independence, attention turned more to trade with India and China. The French Wars (1789–1815) led to the seizure of some of the richest Dutch and French colonies. By this time London's population had reached 1,400,000, dwarfing that of every other city in Europe (Landers, 1993).

A new world order

The end of the Napoleonic Wars in 1815 secured Britain's naval supremacy and global hegemony for a hundred years. This Pax Britannica was a time of peace in Europe, flourishing transatlantic trade, and accelerated colonial expansion on the periphery. In the mid-nineteenth century Britain's declaration of free trade together with the gold standard to calibrate national currencies laid the economic foundation for a new world order.

Nevertheless, what most distinguished the nineteenth century was the Industrial Revolution. The machine textile and metalworking industries of Great Britain destroyed the export staples of India and China and shifted economic power decisively to northern Europe and the transatlantic economy, the latter invigorated by the emerging powerhouse of the United States. Steamships and railways allowed intensive exploitation of global resources in the Americas, Africa, Asia and Australasia.

Railways also facilitated the emergence of new urban patterns. The booming manufacturing industries of textiles and metalworking were located not in London but in the Midlands, Lancashire, Yorkshire and adjacent to the Tyne and Clyde: the regional cities of Birmingham, Manchester, Liverpool, Leeds, Newcastle and Glasgow were linked by railways or fast coastal steamers. Railways also transformed the urban structure of London. Whereas the tightly packed, fire-prone City of London had long been the core, aboveground and underground railway systems together with tramways allowed London to spill out as a commuting city into the adjacent counties. At the beginning of the nineteenth century London was a city of one million people; by 1914, as imperial capital and service centre for most of the world, the population of Greater London was 7.5 million, dwarfing that of all other cities in the world (Ball and Sunderland, 2006). Even so, prosperity barely trickled down below the middle class. Just as in imperial Rome 2000 years earlier, millions were crowded into tenement slums and sickened on poor food, lack of light and foul air.

The First World War weakened Britain's global hegemony. Although Germany was defeated, putting and end to its imperial ambitions, the prime beneficiary was the United States, which in the 1920s enjoyed a period of unprecedented growth and prosperity. In the Pacific the main beneficiary was Britain's former ally, Japan. Unlike China, Japan had been able to maintain its territorial integrity. By 1894–95 early industrialization and modern armaments had made it strong enough to defeat first the Chinese Empire and, ten years later, Imperial Russia. These victories allowed Japan to lay the foundations of an Empire in East Asia. The First World War gave Japan opportunity to gain a foothold in Mainland China; in the 1930s its control was forcibly extended over all Manchuria, then north, central and the coast of southern China. By 1942 Japan's 'Co-Prosperity Sphere' also encompassed Southeast Asia as well as a large swathe of the western Pacific.

Japan's rapid imperial expansion was accompanied by the rapid growth of its capital, Tokyo. By 1900 Tokyo had become a city of around 1.8 million and, notwithstanding the devastation of the 1923 earthquake, by the mid-1930s had grown to almost six million, ranking ahead of Shanghai as the largest city in Asia (Morris, 2010b). Nevertheless, in terms of reach, it was a regional, not a world city. And, despite its impressive façade of modern buildings and infrastructure, Tokyo was still for the most part a low-rise city of wood and paper, a vulnerability that would be exposed by the bombing raids of 1944–45.

In the shadows was one other Asian empire. Despite its humiliating defeat by Japan in 1904–05 Russia or, after the revolution of 1917, the Soviet Union competed for territory in central and east Asia but, because of ongoing political turmoil and the constraints of a weak socialist economy, did not produce any very large cities. At its pre-war peak in 1939, the capital, Moscow, had a population of just over four million, Leningrad/St Petersburg three million.

In the early 1940s, amidst the bitter struggle of the Second World War, the world was therefore divided between four rival empires. The Anglo-American Empire, if it can be treated as a single entity, had been cut back to the British Isles, North America, Egypt, India and a large chunk of Africa, plus Australia and New Zealand – the 'red bits' – and hegemony over South America. By sudden, ruthless conquest, Nazi Germany controlled most of continental Europe, while the Soviet Union controlled all lands through Central Asia to the east. Finally, Japan controlled the territory from Burma in a wide arc as far to the northeast as southern Sakhalin (Karafuto) plus all of the western Pacific except for Australasia.

These four empires boasted four imperial capitals – London, Berlin, Moscow and Tokyo – but only two genuinely world cities, New York and London. The greater city was now New York, which as New York–Northeastern New Jersey Metropolitan District was recognized as the first city with a population over ten million, ranking ahead of Greater London with 8.1 million in 1931 (U.S. Department of Commerce, 1930; Craig, 1975). New York was the anomaly, not being a capital city, for that status was held by the much smaller Washington, DC, but nevertheless the gateway to what had become the world's biggest national economy. As symbolized by the world's tallest man-made structure, the Empire State Building (1931), it was also the frontier of modern technology. London was old, New York was new, also brash, vital and more cosmopolitan, invigorated by the most recent influx of refugees from Nazi Europe.

The new global order

Defeat of Germany and Japan and the collapse of those empires in 1945, also the fatal weakening of the British Empire and the residual French, Dutch and Portuguese empires, gave rise to a world of independent national states under the hegemony of the United States. Hitherto colonial cities had been kept small. In the 1930s even important ones like Singapore, Manila, Batavia (Jakarta) and Hong Kong were not more than about half a million people, though by 1931 Bombay and Calcutta stood out as having reached one million.

National independence triggered a new urban dynamic as central governments strived to establish national capitals with the outward symbols of the modern world according to the new international style of architecture. Independence also relaxed the colonial restrictions on rural–urban migration. Thus cities in India, Southeast Asia and even Africa such as Mumbai (Bombay), Kolkata (Calcutta), Delhi, Jakarta, Manila and Lagos suddenly exploded in size on their way to becoming mega-cities (Rimmer and Dick, 2009, 9). Yet such rapid urbanization was widely derided as 'pseudo-urbanization' or 'Third World urbanization', thereby perpetuating a view in the Western literature on cities that Asian, African and some Central and South American cities were not 'proper' cities according to Western norms (McGee, 1971, 2002). Nevertheless, few, if any, of these cities met the other criteria of being a world city: sophisticated urban functions and global reach were precluded by their neo-colonial status and the inward-looking, protectionist policies applied during the early decades of independence. India was a socialist, centrally planned economy and China even more isolated and autarchic.

Japan did not conform to this pattern. Upon the ruins of its cities and manufacturing industries, in the 1950s Japan began to lay the foundations for best practice, internationally competitive manufacturing industries, especially in steel and shipbuilding. From this base Japan embarked in the 1960s on the era of high-speed growth sustained at the hitherto unprecedented rate of 10 per cent per annum with electronics and automobiles becoming new leading sectors (Minami, 1994). In 1945 Tokyo had been a city in ruins. By the end of the 1960s it was a booming city of more than 20 million people, the largest in the world, though arguably still a national, not a world city, despite hosting the 1964 Olympics – and introducing the path-breaking 'Bullet Train' (Shinkansen).

During the 1960s, there began a sequence of technological changes that would transform the global division of labour and the urban pattern into contemporary form. The first of these changes was the introduction of jet aircraft to international passenger travel. By the end of the 1950s the introduction of the Boeing-707 and Douglas DC-8, followed in 1970 by the Boeing-747 Jumbo Jet, reduced travel times even between Europe or America and Asia to less than 24 hours, so that weeks-long voyages by international passenger liners were soon no longer commercially viable except for leisure cruising. Then in the 1970s the introduction to international shipping of containerized cargo handling reduced door-to-door transit times and together with savings in insurance and working capital dramatically reduced freight costs between continents. Although at first this new technology was simply a means of restoring the profitability of international liner shipping, it was not long before it triggered the unbundling of manufacturing into a New International Division of Labour (NIDL). American manufacturers were soon followed by Japanese and European firms in moving labour-intensive stages of production offshore to low-cost countries, especially in East and Southeast Asia. By the 1980s manufacturing in the United States, Japan and Europe was being hollowed out in industries ranging from textiles and clothing to electronics and automobiles using just-in-time (JIT) inventory systems and integrated door-to-door logistics.

The third wave of the technological revolution was in telecommunications and information technology (IT). As early as the 1870s telegraphic cables had reached around the world, reducing the transmission time for simple messages to around 24 hours (Dick and Rimmer, 2003, 37–72). By the 1880s the Bell telephone was being introduced to cities across North America, Europe and Asia, allowing instantaneous voice communications within cities. By the 1920s and 1930s telephonic voice communication was available at a price between continents, as also shortwave wireless. Wartime innovation led in the 1950s to the development of mainframe computers, which in the 1970s were scaled down to desktop personal computers that quickly replaced typewriters and allowed the storage and transmission of increasingly large bytes of data and information. By the end of the millennium, through the Internet, people around the world could be in almost instantaneous communication, as though working in an adjacent office. Intersecting with this technology was the development of smart phones as miniature computerized telephones able to log instantly into the global Internet.

These three technologies – fast air travel, cheaper and accelerated cargo movements, and instantaneous telecommunications – allowed corporations to become multinational manufacturers and retailers coordinating activities in dispersed locations through tightly controlled supply-chain logistics. The cumulative impact was most apparent in the rapid emergence of China since the 1990s as the prime global location of manufacturing industries. Although the Gang of Four were toppled in 1976, for the next decade or so China struggled with the internal reforms needed to re-establish a market economy. Until the mid-1990s South Korea, Taiwan and Southeast Asia were still the leading offshore production bases. Then in 1997–98 Thailand and Indonesia, also South Korea, were hard hit by the Asian Financial Crisis. China consolidated its standing as the preferred destination for foreign direct investment and since then has surpassed Japan's record of high-speed growth. Export production has concentrated along the seaboard in the Pearl River Delta around Guangzhou, the lower Yangtze Delta around Shanghai, and the Beijing–Tianjin–Hebei agglomeration on the Gulf of Bohai. One consequence has been accelerated urbanization.

Shanghai

By the end of the first millennium, the fertile delta of the Yangtze River had become the rice-bowl of the Chinese empire and the city of Nanjing (Jinling) was briefly the capital of the Southern Tang (937–76). In the thirteenth century Hangzhou became the capital of the southern Song (1127–1279), while Suzhou became famous as the centre of the silk industry. Shanghai was an urban latecomer, at first no more than a modest trading town in the coastal mudflats. Its commerce might have flourished more but for closure of coastal ports to foreign trade during the Ming Dynasty (1368–1644).

In 1841 Shanghai was seized by British naval forces and subsequently claimed as one of the first treaty ports under the unequal treaties imposed at the end of the First Opium War (1839–42). A small European settlement was established and began to flourish after 1861 when the Yangtze was opened to foreign steam shipping serving new treaty ports as far up the river as Hankou (now Wuhan). Two years later it only just withstood siege by the rebel Taiping armies, which had seized control of the delta and established their capital at Nanjing (Wood, 1998). Nevertheless, the International Settlement and the adjacent French Concession became not only the main centre of Western capital and enterprise on the China coast but also the crucible for modern Chinese enterprise (Figure 5.2). By the 1890s Shanghai

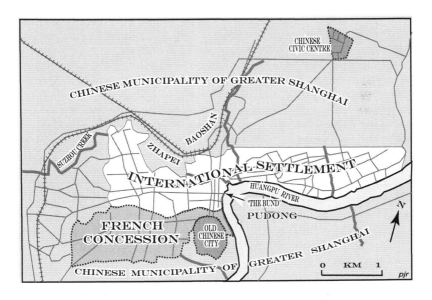

Figure 5.2 Shanghai in the 1930s
Source: Based on Dong, 2000.

Table 5.2   Shanghai's population at selected dates, 1860–2010

Date	Population Million	Date	Population Million
1860	0.15	1960	6.90
1890	0.42	1970	10.82
1900	0.65	1980	11.19
1920	1.00	1990	13.51
1930	3.12	2000	14.35
1940	3.49	2010	23.00
1950	5.41		

Note: 1870–1928 Chinese residents outside the Settlements constituted one-half to two-thirds of the population; after 1928 the Municipality of Greater Shanghai included a greater area of farmland than built-up area in its 829 sq.km (Murphey, 1953). After 1948 there were a number of boundary changes; the Municipality now covers 6,340.5 sq. km. *Source*: Mitchell, 2007a.

was also becoming China's main locus of modern industry, with the first machine textile mills being established along the Huangpu River together with flourmills, sawmills, shipyards and utilities.

In 1900 the population of Shanghai was estimated to have reached 651,000 (Table 5.2). Over the next four decades the remarkable thing about Shanghai was that it flourished despite all the turmoil in the rest of China. It transcended the collapse of the Empire in November 1911, the disintegration of the early Republican governments of Sun Yat-Sen and Yuan Shikai, the warlordism and Civil War of the 1920s, and the Japanese encroachment, even the vicious attacks on the Chinese City in 1932 and 1937. Being a party to the treaty port system, the Japanese mostly respected the integrity of the International Settlement and French Concession and wealthy Chinese capitalists and professionals also benefited from this protection. In turn, company registration under foreign jurisdictions gave some protection against the depredations of Chinese governments, be they warlords or the Kuomintang (Chinese Nationalist Party).

A peculiar feature of Shanghai society was the prominent role of the underworld crime bosses who operated under the benign protection of the French Concession. Most notorious of these figures was Du Yueh-sheng who not only became the public face of the crime syndicates but also even sat on the Concession's Municipal Council (Dong, 2000). This godfather controlled drug dens, gambling and prostitution, also the Chinese labour force on the docks, in coastal shipping, and in some factories. He worked closely with leading Chinese capitalists and in 1927 helped to broker the deal and organize the massacre of leftists that paved the way for Chiang Kai-Shek to establish his control over the city as the financial base to support his new Nanjing-based government and to finance the Northern Expedition to unify the country under the Kuomintang regime.

By the 1930s Shanghai undoubtedly qualified as a world city, ranking second only to Tokyo and slightly ahead of Osaka as the largest city in Asia. Boosted by a massive influx of refugees from the Sino-Japanese War, by 1940 its population had reached 3.5 million people, about half that of Tokyo (6.7 million). Overwhelmingly, it was a Chinese city. Within the treaty areas of the International Settlement and French Concession there was a cosmopolitan population of around 60,000, of whom Japanese, Russians, British, Germans and Austrians, Americans and French were the most prominent, but this veneer, though underpinning the city's image as the 'Paris of China', was less than 2 per cent of the total (Murphey, 1953). Second, Shanghai performed the full range of urban functions from the processing of primary produce through textiles to heavy industry, plus the key business services of banking, insurance and shipping. Its department stores along Nanjing Road were spectacular; its cinemas showed the latest Hollywood films; its dance halls and brothels were notorious. The only thing missing, and a notable contrast with Tokyo, was a large government bureaucracy, given that the capital was 300 kilometres upstream at Nanjing. Thirdly, the city's reach was very nearly global. Its Chinese business networks extended as far as Southeast Asia, Australia and California; its foreign networks of shipping, trade and banking linked it closely to Europe and to both coasts of the United States.

The 1940s, however, were a difficult time for Shanghai. After 1937 the Japanese invasion depressed commerce and in December 1941 Japan occupied the International Settlement, though not the much smaller French Concession. The surrender of Japan in August 1945 allowed a fairly rapid resumption of trade and industry but there were no reparations and reconstruction was cut short by accelerating inflation and eventual hyperinflation associated with the worsening Civil War with the Communists. By 1948, as Chiang Kai-Shek's Kuomintang/Nationalist Government began to transfer to the island of Taiwan, Shanghai capitalists began dismantling their factories and relocating, mainly to Taiwan or Hong Kong, though some would move as far away as South America. After the Communists occupied the city in May 1949, followed on 1 October 1949 by Mao Zedong's proclamation of the People's Republic of China, efforts were made to persuade capitalists, bankers, shipowners and factory owners to return to China and play a role in socialist reconstruction. By 1952, however, vicious anti-rightist campaigns along with the tensions arising from the Korean War (1950–53) had eliminated any possibility of a rapprochement between the Shanghai capitalists and the new regime. Their entrepreneurship and capital would drive the prosperity of Hong Kong as the 'New Shanghai'. Suppressed by China's Central Government, Shanghai itself stagnated for another three decades, to all outward appearances being trapped in a time warp.

Following upon the death of Mao Zedong and the fall of the Gang of Four in 1976, both leading to the rise of reformist leader Deng Xiaoping, declaration of Shanghai as an open city in 1984 stimulated its re-emergence onto the world scene. During the Maoist era Shanghai had remained an industrial city, but most of its sophisticated service functions had been allowed to atrophy as superfluous to a socialist system. As the door was opened for foreign investment, international banking, business and shipping services once again became essential. Between 1992 and the Global Financial Crisis of 2008, Shanghai experienced double-digit growth driven by exports from capital intensive, high-tech manufacturing and a property boom from redevelopment of leased government land.

What had begun as revival soon became a transformation even more remarkable than that seen in other leading Asian cities such as Seoul, Singapore and Kuala Lumpur. Demand for office space soon outstripped the modest, run-down facilities available in what pre-war had been the International Concession. A shiny, high-rise new CBD was opened up across the river in what had been the swamplands of Pudong. Nearby was constructed a new international airport joined to the rest of the city by expressways and high-speed rail; new container terminals were developed in Pudong and an even deeper port at Yangshan at the mouth of the Yangtze together with an International Logistics Park. By 2010 Shanghai had surpassed Hong Kong and Singapore as the world's largest container port. These huge infrastructure projects were complemented by public investment in expressways and the world's largest urban rail mass transit system. There was also investment in human capital, with Shanghai's older universities such as Jiao Tong and Fudan winning international prestige. All this attracted the regional headquarters of multinational corporations from Hong Kong, Singapore and Tokyo, together with skilled professionals such as software engineers and accountants. In the Maoist era the 'bourgeoisie' had been persecuted as counter-revolutionary, but now there re-emerged a prosperous Chinese middle class with a taste for a modern, westernized lifestyle. Not without social tensions, more and more of the city's crowded tenements were razed for luxury housing in gated communities, more and more cars came onto the roads, and big shopping malls displayed the familiar signs of globalization such as American fast foods and foreign brands. Shanghai's modern brashness and extremes of wealth and poverty are more than a little reminiscent of the pre-Communist era of corruption, prostitution, and crime.

Shanghai has enjoyed a degree of autonomy from the Central Government, thereby preserving the 'Shanghai way'. During the 1990s former

Shanghai mayors Jiang Zemin and Zhu Rongji rose to power in the Central Government, protecting Shanghai against too much interference and promoting its expansion into the Pudong New Area on the east side of the Huangpu (Lam, 1999). This so-called 'Shanghai Faction', out-manoeuvred the competing 'Beijing Clique' led by Chen Xitong (removed from office in 1995) and ensured a golden era as both the Municipal and Central Governments agreed on developing the Shanghai-Pudong area to become China's premier global city. The city's metropolitan footprint, manufacturing industries and property developers were allowed to spread into the adjacent provinces of Jiangsu and Zhejiang and the lower reaches of the Yangtze to form the greater Yangtze Delta metropolitan region with a population in 2010 of 105 million, of whom 80 million are considered to be urban (NBSC, 2011). The Delta's high-tech manufacturing centres of Suzhou and Wuxi are linked by fast trains and motorways to Shanghai (Fenby, 2012).

The spectacle of the 2010 Shanghai Expo showed that Shanghai is again a very cosmopolitan and global city, China's gateway to the world. Although Chongqing (29 million) in the highlands of Sichuan is officially the largest city in China according to the population of the total administrative area, this vast municipality, designed to counterbalance the emphasis on coastal regions, is only weakly integrated into the international economy and its true urban population is smaller than that of Shanghai (23 million) (NBSC, 2011). Almost as large is the national capital of Beijing (20 million), now incorporated, with its associated port city of Tianjin, into North China's premier development zone, but this sprawling agglomeration is also less globalized and dwindling water supplies threaten its long-term viability.

Thus Shanghai, like the megacities of New York and Mumbai, is an anomaly, a global city without any upper level of government (Lam, 2006). It has taken full advantage of a very strategic location and a populous and productive hinterland but, above all, its prosperity is attributable to a prevailing entrepreneurial spirit that can make something out of nothing. In that sense Shanghai is, by both Chinese and world standards, a born-new city. It has none of the ancient, imperialist heritage of Beijing or Nanjing: heritage in Shanghai means the façade of early twentieth-century Western office buildings along the Bund. This is not really a paradox. As Mumford recognized, the true global city, whether Rome, London, New York or Shanghai, least resembles the society in which it is embedded and, for better or worse, best epitomizes its aspirations for the future (Figure 5.3).

Time-space compression

Over two millennia there have been three turning points, all quite recent, that make the modern world and modern cities different in kind from

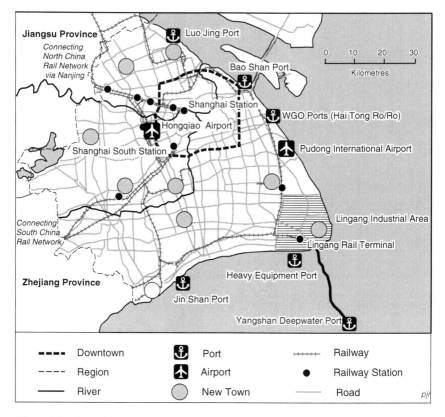

Figure 5.3   Shanghai in 2012
Source: Authors.

what had preceded them (Figure 5.1). First, was the Industrial Revolution of the nineteenth century with its more efficient technologies of
production, transport and communication, knitting the world together
in ways that hitherto had been unimaginable. Together with improved
health and sanitation, especially reticulated water and sewerage, they broke
long-standing constraints on urban size. Whereas for 2000 years the fea-
sible maximum population had been around one million people, by the
early twentieth century both London and New York were approaching ten
million.

The second turning point, following upon the end of the Second World
War in 1945, was the end of colonial empires and the emergence of a new
global order of nation states. The proliferation of nations together with
faster population growth and rural–urban migration led to the emergence

of many more mega-cities, albeit much less sophisticated in their infrastructure than London or New York, and in most cases without their global reach.

The third turning point, in the later decades of the twentieth century, was again technological, being the cluster of jet passenger travel, containerized freight and nearly instantaneous transfer of information that together have facilitated the shift of manufacturing away from the advanced economies of Europe, North America and Japan to low-cost countries, most notably China and India.

One notable aspect of this threefold transformation has been the rise of the multinational corporation (MNC) to coordinate production, distribution and finance activities that have been decentralized on an inter-continental and increasingly global scale. Headquarters and sophisticated control and research functions are located in relatively few cities in the northern hemisphere where there is a high degree of legal security, especially over intellectual property. At the same time, MNCs seek jurisdictions that are weakly governed, in other words, subject to laxity and loopholes that minimize scrutiny and tax liabilities. In that regard, the modus operandi of MNCs is not much different from that of criminal syndicates. It is no coincidence that MNCs, criminal syndicates and tax evaders are often found using the same offshore tax and financial havens. Ironically, Caribbean islands that used to be notorious for their slave plantations now thrive as tourist resorts and tax havens. Such financial off-shoring is no less important than the off-shoring of manufacturing.

A similar phenomenon is at work within large cities. There is a very long history of companies seeking to evade zoning restrictions and pollution controls by leapfrogging municipal boundaries. Likewise, workers and service employees tend to find lower cost housing on the urban periphery. Cities therefore tend to expand concentrically, often giving rise to doughnut effects and awkward lags in the adjustment of urban boundaries and responsibilities for infrastructure.

The history of 'global' networks for two millennia may be summarized most succinctly as the contraction of the main axis of east-west commerce. This has contracted from the ancient, diffuse and leisurely Silk Road to the twentieth-century High Street of leading port cities and is now collapsing into a frenetic Global City Mall where urban space so overlaps as to become almost simultaneous (Figure 5.4).

Until the fifteenth century the overland caravan routes of the Silk Road network linked the urban civilization of Han China to the urban civilizations of the Middle East and by extension to Europe. The corresponding sea route linked in the Malay Archipelago and India. By the seventeenth century there was also a Sugar and Tobacco Road extending across the Atlantic to the Americas. Passage across the Silk Road took about one year.

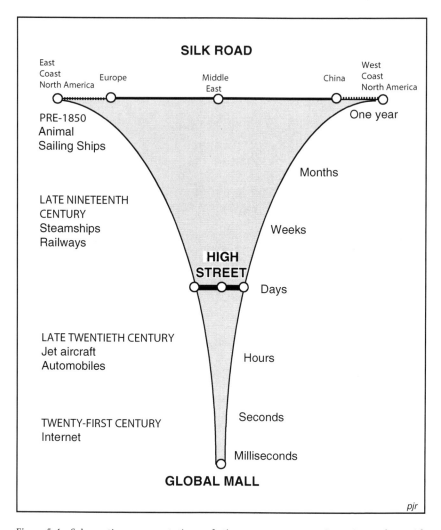

Figure 5.4 Schematic representation of time-space compression since the mid-nineteenth century
Source: Authors.

Over the course of the nineteenth century, steamships and railways allowed passage and movement to encircle the globe. Jules Verne (1872) captured the achievement in his book *Around the World in 80 Days*. Port-cities became waypoints on global routes along which travel was now to be measured in weeks. Cities still exotic to each other were thereby brought into much closer proximity, leading to obvious signs of convergence in infrastructure, amenities and lifestyle. This urban pattern might be described as High Street. Cities had their own addresses, but movement between them was now scheduled and predictable. This became even more apparent from the 1950s with the introduction of long-range aircraft and subsequently jet aeroplanes that reduced transit time to less than 24 hours, the same order of magnitude as a telegram.

Twenty-first century IT has brought cities into almost instantaneous proximity in terms of transmission of information, voice and even face-to-face contact. It is now quite practical to have meetings in real time between people in different cities, even though travel between them still takes some hours and days or weeks for the movement of goods. Discussion of this phenomenon has been in terms of new global cities. However, it makes sense also to consider the phenomenon as a global city-space that now almost transcends distance. In other words, rather than being discrete nodes in an urban network, cities have collapsed in and upon each other as a single global node, at least as far as elites and the burgeoning urban middle classes are concerned.

This new urban reality may be depicted as a high-rise building (Figure 5.5). The public space is the Global City Mall, a bright, well-structured space of food courts, department/anchor stores, stand-alone stores, entertainment zones and cinemas thronged with people with their smart phones, moving easily between floors by escalators that may be regarded as inter-city flights. Below in the basements and clustered around the outside of the building are stores and factories and crowded worker housing, beyond a wider hinterland from which resources are drawn. Above the mall are many levels of hotel rooms and residential apartments and in the upper stories the offices of parliaments and multinational corporations. In the penthouse suite adjacent to the casino are found the key decision-makers, not least bankers and financiers. Access to all levels is tightly controlled by access cards but information flows readily and instantaneously through the telecommunications core, beside which is the express elevator for movement between floors.

This depiction is, of course, a crude oversimplification, but it captures some essentials of the new urban experience. Whereas cities were once exotic to each other by their very natures, now the unique features of a city are often stylized and branded. Items of heritage are re-created as new wonders in foreign locations. Aside from such marketing, and the more persistent aspects of urban habitus, the external appearances of the built environment, the internal temperature-controlled spaces, furnishings, clothing, work habits and perhaps even food and language are more and more converging to a global norm.

What this model fails to address is governance. The whole building is managed according to a very awkward set of strata titles with no proper body corporate. Various nations and multinationals own floors and mall space

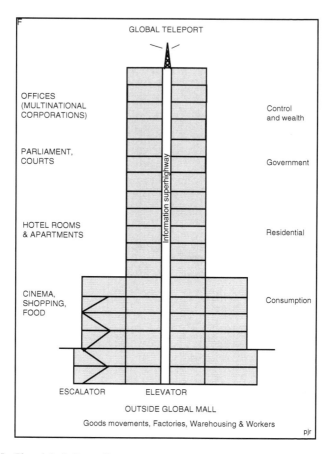

Figure 5.5   The global city mall
Source: Authors.

but seldom agree on how to manage their mutual interdependence. Individuals acquire access rights by virtue of their membership of a nation and these rights are to some extent reciprocal, but except for their own living space they have no other access rights to the upper floors and no say in what happens there. The whole building is therefore vulnerable to lack of agreement on overall management as well as a great deal of unevenness in the maintenance of nationally franchised space. Given the lack of awareness of and responsibility for anything that happens outside the building, there is also vulnerability to environmental catastrophe. If the power or water supply fails, or if epidemics break out, even a rampant computer virus, the prosperity and survival of this urban society is at risk. Global warming and rising sea levels pose a severe threat to many megacities situated in low-lying coastal zones. Rome has survived, though no longer as a megacity; some more recent megacities are likely to have much shorter histories. Urbanism is likely to endure but urban locations have been and will continue to be transient.

6
The Postcolonial Dimension

Vanessa Watson

Introduction

The postcolonial perspective has provided an important source of critique of global/world city scholarship. Jennifer Robinson's (2002) assault on this position accused global city theorists of leaving most cities in the world 'off the map' as they did not fit the particular and limited criteria which had been devised to classify global cities. Robinson called this a narrow vision of an imperialist approach to cities which are concentrated in only certain regions of the world and argued for a more cosmopolitan account of city-ness which draws on a greater diversity of experience available in 'ordinary' cities.

But there is a further reason why the 'global city' scholarship has been subject to critique. There are suggestions that it has had the (possibly unintended) consequences of encouraging all cities to aspire to 'global' status by mimicking the plans and projects of classified 'global' cities. For postcolonial theorists this is a good example of how unequal power relationships established under colonial rule persist into the postcolonial era, and come to both functional relationships and mind-sets. In the field of planning and architecture, many cities have adopted technocratic and modernist city plans (usually accompanied by vision statements declaring as aspiration to become 'world class cities') which exclude the poor, in the belief that this will somehow allow them to 'catch up with the West'.

More recently, Robinson's call to study a wider range of cities and activities within them has been picked up by a number of authors writing about cities in the global south – cities which do not fit the criteria of 'global cities' but which, they argue, are nonetheless as important and as instructive for urban scholars. A range of new terms has emerged to analyse and describe these cities: Ananya Roy (2011a) uses 'subaltern urbanism' to consider the 'slumdog' megacities of India; Solomon Benjamin (2008) refers to 'occupancy urbanism' and Gavin Shatkin (2011) to 'actually existing urbanisms'. All of these refer to alternative social dynamics in 'ordinary cities' where the energy and entrepreneurialism of the poor are as significant as the growth of finance capital in cities classified as 'global'.

The chapter considers firstly the various meanings of postcolonialism: as a temporal period, as a condition and as a source of critique and advocacy. It then moves to locate cities as a central element in postcolonial discourse and a key site where colonial and postcolonial relationships in their various forms have played themselves out. The third section of the chapter draws on the growing literature that argues for an alternative urban theory, particularly in the global South, which considers that all cities in the world (and not just global cities) are worthy of interest and study as they represent a full range of dynamics and lessons. This literature has also aimed to overcome problematic binaries of global and local, and to understand these wider relationships, and how they are expressed in cities, in a far more nuanced way.

The last section of the chapter turns to the case of Cape Town, South Africa, as an example of a postcolonial city which is quite definitely 'off the map' of the global/world city league tables, and yet has devoted extensive effort and public funds over the years to positioning itself as a world-class city. This ambition has in turn skewed public policy and investments as well as planning and architectural expression. Cape Town is also a good example of how the efforts of sectors of the elite, to achieve world-class status, are rarely uncontested: various Cape Town vision statements and policies demonstrate an interesting tension between the competing objectives of economic growth and redistribution. Moving beyond the global city scholarship can usefully adopt a postcolonial theoretical lens, which calls attention to the interface between central and peripheral nations and regions and questions of power which have shaped this relationship; the mutually constitutive role which this relationship has played; the issues which this relationship raises for understanding the geopolitics of knowledge; an interest in problems of difference, agency and resistance; and insistence on the maintenance of an ethico-political position in relation to planning and the future of cities in the global South.

Defining postcolonialism

'Postcolonialism' is a contested term. Following the useful extended definition of the term by McEwan (2009, 17–26) it can refer to a temporal period, a condition and a theoretical approach which can be both explanatory and critique. Temporally it refers to the period after colonialism (or after political independence) which ushered in, for many territories, a new era of postcolonialism with changed political, social, economic and spatial arrangements. Importantly, it does not suggest that colonizing powers had simply 'gone away': much of the current interest in postcolonial studies focuses on the ongoing relationships between colonized and colonizing territories, along with the persistent but changing nature of power relationships and inequalities which still shape the present.

Postcolonialism as a 'condition' refers to the political, cultural and economic (and urban) nature of societies living with the legacy of colonialism. Emphasis here has been on the highly diverse nature of the postcolonial condition arising from the differences in colonizing powers and in the territories which were colonized, as well as the temporal period during which it has occurred. Writings here have tried to avoid the false binary of colonial centres and postcolonial margins and noted that the effects were not simply in one direction, but also affected colonizing powers (and their cities) in profound ways. In this sense London, Paris and Madrid can also be described as postcolonial given the demographic, cultural and economic impacts which colonization and its ending have had on them.

Postcolonialism as theory and critique is concerned with explaining and criticizing the material and discursive legacies of colonialism which still shape present relationships. The interest here is in how postcolonial identities have been shaped, how colonial powers produced and used the knowledge of colonized peoples in their own interests and how this continues to structure inequitable relations between the two. These theories challenge knowledge and representation of the global South, particularly from sources based in the global North, and how the language of colonialism still shapes Western understandings of the world. Increasingly writers focus on overcoming the further binary of metropole/periphery in explanations of the changing postcolonial condition, and point to the complex nature of these interactions as well as the importance of agency in structuring engagements and outcomes. Critical analyses of the relationship between knowledge and power have been important in many of these ideas. In literary theory more specifically, there is an interest in how the colonized are represented in literature and how Western literature reflects assumptions of colonial superiority.

There is also a strong element of advocacy in postcolonial writings which challenges the inequalities and imbalances of the colonial legacy. Literary theorists argue the need to recover the experiences of the colonized, and to 'let the subaltern speak'. In other fields, writers point to the need to destabilize the dominant discourses of Western imperialism which are inherently Eurocentric and reflective of a dominant Western world view, and which attempt to erase the inequalities and differences which make up the postcolonial condition. Such authors call for the need to pluralize the production of knowledge, and demand more globally informed knowledge to 'unsettle' dominant Western-centric ideas and assumptions about the universality of Western thought and experience. These positions are often also concerned to surface local or indigenous sources of knowledge and thinking as a counter to a Western dominance of ideas.

Postcolonialism and cities

Cities have played a central role in processes of colonization and postcolonialism, yet writings on the two are frequently disconnected. Beall and Fox (2009) note that cities and their institutions were a major conduit for colonization, within both the colonizing and colonized territories. Where cities did not already exist they needed to be built, as outposts for colonial administration and control and as places to assemble, distribute and transport goods, services and people. Frequently this meant a coastal location linked to shipping routes, with further urban settlements and transport routes structured by the geography of primary products destined for the colonial market, and later by returning exports to the growing markets in these territories. Postcolonial governments thus usually found themselves with an urban and transport infrastructure oriented entirely to 'overseas' markets with poor integration internally.

At the level of the cities themselves, the impact of colonialism was profound. 'Colonial relations of domination were literally inscribed in the form of the built environment: in architecture, institutions and infrastructure of the city' (Beall and Fox, 2009, 50). This impact was obviously far greater in those regions where pre-colonial settlement was scattered and where new towns were laid out and built from scratch. This was the case in large parts of Latin America and Africa and in Australia. In many parts of the East, in contrast, the infrastructure of colonialism encountered long-established urban civilizations and here the encounter took very different forms again. But while highly diverse in implementation, the broad goals of colonizing powers tended to be similar: the dedication of particular urban areas to colonial settlers where efforts were made to recreate the urban forms and layouts from the colonizing territories; the separation of these areas from those to be inhabited by 'local' or indigenous urban dwellers; and often the separation again of those involved in colonial administration from 'the rest' – formal and informal labourers and the unemployed. Colonial towns were therefore usually highly segregated in terms of nationality, income and culture/race. Beall and Fox (2009) describe the overriding concern to protect colonial urban quarters from disease, nuisance and other pollutants, usually through the creation of a green belt or *cordon sanitaire* separating these from local residents.

Significantly, the vehicle for transferring and enforcing these visions of the ideal Western city in the colonies was urban planning legislation. As the concepts and tools of modern urban planning were refined and institutionalized in the UK, Europe and the USA in the first part of the twentieth century, so they were transferred to the urban centres in the colonies. Entire cities were laid out following the principles of European urban modernism, incorporating Garden City suburbs, boulevards and vistas, Le Corbusian towers, large public green spaces and efficient movement routes, a separation of urban uses, and control over densities and building materials. Hence planning came to be bound up with the 'modernizing and civilizing' mission of colonial authorities, but increasingly as well with the control of urbanization processes and of the rapidly urbanizing population.

As colonized countries gained independence and began to reshape political and institutional structures, colonial planning regulations and models remained largely unreformed. Many African countries still have planning legislation based on British or European planning laws from the 1930s or 1940s, and which has been revised only marginally. Postcolonial governments tended to reinforce and entrench colonial spatial plans and land management tools, sometimes in even more rigid form than colonial governments (Njoh, 2003). Important and capital cities in Africa were often the subject of grand master planning under colonial rule, sometimes involving prominent international planners or architects. Remarkably, in many cases, these plans remain relatively unchanged. The guiding 'vision' in these plans has been that of urban modernism, based on assumptions that it has always been simply a matter of time before African countries 'catch up' economically and culturally with the West, producing cities governed by strong, stable municipalities and occupied by households who are car-owning, formally employed, relatively well-off, and with urban lifestyles similar to those of European or American urbanites.

Planning in the subcontinent of India has had strong parallels with the African experience, given the common factor of British colonial rule. Limited health and safety measures at the start of the twentieth century gave way to master planning and zoning ordinances, introduced under British rule but persisting in postcolonial times. Ansari (2004) notes that some 2000 Indian cities now have master plans, all displaying the problems which caused countries such as the UK to shift away from this approach, and yet the main task of municipal planning departments is to produce more such plans. In Latin American cities as well, past colonial links played a role in transferring European planning ideas to this part of the world, but more general intellectual exchange reinforced this. Thus Buenos Aires developed strong links with French planners, architects and city administrators, and French experts were hired to prepare local plans. The 1925 master plan and zoning scheme were prepared by French architects, and the 1937 plan by French architect Le Corbusier (Novick, 2003). The Brazilian capital of Brasilia was planned by a local architect (1960) who was also a local pioneer of the modern architectural movement and strongly influenced by Le Corbusier.

Hence many expressions of postcolonialism, as defined above, are apparent in postcolonial cities with the planning system playing a central role in this. Urban visions and plans demonstrate a strong continuity from precolonial periods to the present, even when planning approaches have been revised in the previous colonizing territories. This 'colonization of the mind' is evident in the insistence by postcolonial politicians and the emerging middle classes for urban modernist plans which mimic Western cities with their glass box towers, Tuscan villas and gated villages. And in the previous colonizing territories of the global North, planning theories and models continue to emerge which assume global applicability, mentally erasing the great diversity of contexts across the world and assuming that if the rest of the global South has not yet caught up with the West, then it soon will.

However, this account of postcolonial cities can easily be accused of problematic binary thinking, which sees the colonial imprint on colonized cities as essentially imposed 'from elsewhere', and ignoring the fundamental role of 'agency' in shaping the form and functioning of postcolonial cities. This is important when it comes to considering how the postcolonial perspective on cities can provide a challenge to 'world cities' thinking. The next section examines some of the more recent literature which has explored how cities in the global South have been shaped by both global and 'external' forces as well as local and agency-driven forces.

Global and local: The shaping of postcolonial cities

Shatkin (2008) draws on the case of Metro Manila (in the previous Spanish colony of the Philippines) to ask if there is a growing convergence between recent urban interventions in the burgeoning mega-cities of the global South and large cities in countries such as the United States. Is there, therefore, a proliferating American urban model which will in future characterize global cities in all parts of the world? Shatkin (2008) questions what may be a simplistic interpretation of Philippines' new urban developments as purely a copying of an American model of urbanism and argues that instead influential local actors (in this case primarily property developers and their clients) have sought to selectively adapt international models of planning and design to the context of Southeast Asian urbanization. In a subsequent article Shatkin (2011, 79) further considers how global ideas of city-making are also countered by '... *actually existing urbanisms*, that are rooted in alternative social dynamics (informality, violence, alternative cultural, and social visions, vote-bank politics), and that resist worlding practice'.

In Metro Manila, a city of some ten million people, Shatkin (2008) shows how globalization has supported the emergence of a small but powerful elite made up of a professional and merchant class, along with foreign investors and ethnic Chinese business families. Interestingly, a significant part of the new demand for urban space comes from Philippine workers abroad who remit large sums annually to their home city. Urban space is also in demand from poorer workers and recent arrivals in the city from rural Philippines: occupying older buildings and informal settlements, they consistently challenge threats to the 'public city' from private developers and their government partners. The privatization of urban planning and development (as a new model of urban governance) has taken an extensive and all-encompassing form in Metro Manila that goes well beyond individual shopping mall and gated village developments. Here it is driven by private investment in cross-city transport schemes the purpose of which is to unlock the development potential of parcels of land serviced by the new movement infrastructure. In Metro Manila and other large cities of the East, these new developments are massive. Moreover they are scattered across the urban region and do not necessarily take on the 'edge city' form found in many US cities. These new systems of transport and residential/commercial development are overlaid onto the existing congested and decayed urban form but are detached from it, creating entirely separate pathways of circulation and land use. Shatkin (2008) refers to this as 'bypass-implant urbanism'. These schemes attract large government subsidies and this in turn drains public finance available for public space or to address the needs of poorer communities. The consequence is the steady decline of the existing older city, as well as the threatened and actual removal of communities who find themselves in the way of the new development projects and transit routes.

Private sector urban interventions as in Metro Manila, as well as intensifying competition for urban land in cities of the global South, has led to further research on forms of resistance to exclusionary urban land markets. Benjamin (2008) uses the term *'occupancy urbanism'* (which, he argues, avoids the binary of formal/informal) to refer to contested political and economic land-related processes in Indian cities. Here major infrastructure and urban mega-projects are subverted by alignments of shack-dwellers using their voting power, along with lower level bureaucrats and politicians, and small scale business interests. From a different starting point and using Henri Lefebvre as a theoretical frame, Roy (2011b, 8) explains urbanism in these contexts as four interrelated processes: as the production of space driven by forms of capitalism but also intertwined with local 'projects of space and power'; as a set of social struggles over urban space; as a production of the public apparatus, one element of which may be the planning system, which may be '... implicated in the efforts to constitute model citizens and institute civic norms'; and as a global process. This last process departs from the literature which focuses attention only on world or global cities, and adopts a position (the idea of worlding) which encompasses the full array of urban strategies from whatever source they may emanate.

This relatively recent work on the nature of 'urbanisms' in global South cities illustrates the ongoing ties between metropole and periphery, and the ways in which postcolonial relations and global economic relations have become intertwined. Most importantly, however, it also shows the crucial influence of local contextual factors in shaping cities, and how these social, cultural, political and economic diversities both capitalize on, and are subordinated to, broader global postcolonial and economic relationships.

Global/world cities and the need for postcolonial urban studies

The postcolonial literature on cities (discussed above) highlights both the temporal and geographical relationships which bind together cities across the globe, emphasizes the importance of 'agency' and the local in shaping these relationships, but also acknowledges the ongoing asymmetrical role of power and knowledge both between and within territories, which serves to support arguments that colonialism has not 'gone away', but has certainly changed its form.

In her groundbreaking article, Robinson (2002) challenged the 'global/world cities' thinking which had come to dominate the urban studies field. She argued that a structural analysis of a limited range of economic processes had been used to construct a categorization of cities which placed a small number of Western cities at the top of the hierarchy of cities (these were termed 'world' or 'global cities') and the rest as of secondary importance or even entirely irrelevant to the global economy, or 'off the map'. These world cities are classified as such because they serve as the organizing nodes of a global economic system and command dominant economic power. Robinson joins a host of other writers who have criticized the narrow economistic basis of this categorization, who have noted that this ignores the great diversity of economic circumstances of populations within these world cities, and who have pointed out the fallacy of regarding the rest of the world as economically irrelevant when the world cities and economies themselves could not survive without the resources and markets which they provide. Of more significance for this chapter, however, is Robinson's (2002) specifically postcolonial critique of the world cities literature. From this perspective she notes how the histories and experiences of these economically successful Western cities have come to shape urban theory more generally, thus inappropriately universalizing the experience of a limited part of the globe to the rest of the world. Moreover, the 'league table' approach to categorizing cities is pejorative: those cities which are consigned to the lower categories of the league table are therefore 'third world' cities, or 'not yet' cities, and still need to 'catch up' with those regarded as globally successful. Critical postcolonial theorists in a range of disciplinary fields, well beyond that of urban studies, have noted these tendencies to generalize from a Western experience to the rest of the world, as well as the ways in which power and knowledge interrelate to perpetuate a colonial perspective on which parts of the world are superior to others. Problematically, as Robinson (2002) points out, this modernist view of successful Western cities as models to be emulated by 'the rest', has unfortunate repercussions as poor city policies and budgets are skewed in favour of mimicking 'world-class city' attributes, and away from more pressing issues such as housing upgrade and urban services. League table theorizing in urban studies has also provided justification for poor-city politicians and officials to use outdated and inappropriate urban planning laws and visions from colonial times to demolish informal settlements, expel informal street-traders and invest in monumental buildings and car-oriented transport systems. Unreformed planning systems are frequently viewed as a reason for the marginalization of the poor in cities of the global South, yet it could be argued that the promotion of Western cities as an ideal to aspire to through the world-class cities position simply reinforces these older and modernist urban aspirations.

Robinson (2002) therefore argues that urban studies need to 'decolonise' its imagination about city-ness and rather to view all cities as 'ordinary cities'. This requires shifting the focus of urban theory to the diversity of urban experiences within the world as a basis for a more 'cosmopolitan' account of cities, and to the overlapping and multiple networks within and between cities which create generative potential and allow different city futures to be imagined. The kind of research generated by Shatkin and Benjamin (above) on 'actually existing urbanisms' and 'occupancy urbanisms' is directly in line with this thinking. An understanding of the actual complex and diverse processes taking place in cities in all parts of the world directly challenges the possibility of unsupported generalizations based on a limited number of Western cities. Robinson's argument is taken up in the planning field by Roy (2011b) who proposes the concept of 'worlding' as a counterpoint to the framework of global/world cities in urban theory. This concept '...seeks to recover and restore the vast array of global strategies that are being staged at the urban scale around the world' (Roy 2011c, 10). She notes that in some cases these are closely tied to elite aspirations and the making of world-class cities and in other cases may represent the kind of worlding from below that has been highlighted by Shatkin and Benjamin. Planning itself, she argues, is a worlding strategy (both in colonial times and in the present) as it acts as a vehicle for the transnational circulation of models, visions, best practice, technocratic expertise and modes of governing. Roy (2011c, 411) argues the need to set this against 'the counterpractices of critical transnationalism' working with different models-in-circulation which reflect the complex reality of urban life. The next section of the chapter aims to ground some of these ideas about world city theorizing and its postcolonial critique through reference to a case study: Cape Town.

The case of Cape Town

The territory which ultimately came to be called South Africa was settled for many thousands of years by ancestors of the nomadic Khoe-San people. In 1488 Portuguese navigators first rounded the Cape, opening up a sea route from Europe to the East, and in 1652 the Dutch East India Company established a permanent refreshment station at what is now the city of Cape Town. Dutch control of the territory came to an end in 1795 when Britain occupied the Cape in order to secure its trading route, although British rule only became permanent in 1814 when the Dutch formally ceded the Cape to Britain. In 1910 South Africa was granted the status of a self-governing colony, this lasting until 1961 when the country declared itself a republic and withdrew from the Commonwealth. As a result of these early Dutch and British influences, current South African common law still contains many elements of Roman Dutch law and English law, although the system of administrative law – and to a large extent the inherited planning system – is strongly British.

The concept of urban racial segregation, a defining characteristic of the pre-1994 apartheid government, in fact had its roots in nineteenth century British rule, as 'native locations' were established in and around the larger urban settlements. It was not until 1948, however, and the succession of the National Party in government, which the full apparatus of the apartheid project came into being. In the post-1948 period, apartheid (meaning 'apartness') involved the extension of various forms of segregation, which previously applied to Africans, to Indian and to coloured people as well. By the 1960s it involved racial discrimination in almost every area of life, with spatial separation in place at the local urban scale (in the form of planned segregated residential areas) and at the regional scale (in the form of demarcated African homelands). British and American urban planning models were adapted to meet the ideological requirements of apartheid: the Garden City and Neighbourhood Unit were widely used in Cape Town and elsewhere to plan new residential areas surrounded by green buffer strips and transport routes, for people of colour forcibly removed from previously mixed-race areas. The buffer strips and transport infrastructure segregated coloured, Indian and African races from each other and from white areas, and rendered them easy to 'seal off' in times of civic revolt. In essence apartheid was a policy that allowed white, and particularly Afrikaner, supremacy to survive in the face of growing African nationalism through the division and repression of people of colour. At no time, however, was apartheid unchallenged. By the end of the 1980s, increasingly organized resistance, largely orchestrated by the African National Congress (ANC), succeeded in bringing the apartheid government to the negotiating table and to the country's first democratic elections in 1994 (Harrison et al., 2008).

Throughout the 1900s South Africa's economy had followed a familiar colonial and postcolonial pattern of heavy reliance on the production and export of raw materials and natural resources (gold, diamonds and various metals) to the global North. However, local industrial protectionism post-War and the loss of certain overseas markets due to anti-apartheid campaigns had resulted in a relatively introverted and diversified economy. The reintegration of South Africa's economy into global markets following the elections of 1994 initiated a period of intensive economic restructuring. The lowering of protective tariff barriers in the face of aggressive competition from Asian producers induced a significant decline in sectors of Cape Town's manufacturing (in the previously dominant textiles, clothing and food processing sectors) which led to large-scale formal job losses. A depreciating local currency and the country's reintegration with world markets opened up export possibilities for certain agricultural products as well as the opportunity in Cape Town to expand the tourism sector (Jenkins and Wilkinson, 2002).

South Africa is currently classified as an 'upper-middle income' country by the World Bank and has an economy largely driven by the tertiary sector, although with high levels of poverty and inequality. Like most other postcolonial countries, it has continued to rely heavily on primary resource exports to the economically developed countries of the global North (although growing links with China and Japan have been emerging more recently). In the period after the ending of apartheid in 1994, a wide range of new policy initiatives were introduced at both national and local government level. While the need to address the racial inequities of the apartheid era through redistribution and improving public service delivery to previously neglected areas was an important element of government rhetoric, there was also a clear shift to more neoliberal and growth oriented policies.

By all accounts Cape Town is definitely 'off the map' of global and world cities: it does not appear at all in GaWC's (Beaverstock et al. 1999) map of alpha, beta or gamma world cities. It clearly does not meet the criteria for world cities, which, as Lemanski (2007) shows, are largely based on the need for urban economies to be integrated into Anglo-American (and not other) economic networks and capital flows. Yet 'being on the map' and becoming recognized as a global/world city has been at the forefront of the minds of city politicians whether the political party in power has been the supposedly more populist African National Congress or the more liberal political opposition. Jenkins and Wilkinson (2002) noted that post-1994 Cape Town's 'governing elite' moved to establish its priorities and objectives to align with the promotion of local economic growth, even if this occurred somewhat partially and selectively. The 1997 'vision' for Cape Town stated that 'In ten years the Cape Metropolitan Area will be one of the major tourist destinations of the world, especially noted for its natural environment and supported by a harmonious, tolerant and well-governed and educated people. The growing economy will be characterized by adequate housing and a low incidence of crime, making the Cape Metropolitan Area a global economic player' (quoted in Watson, 2002, 128). Fifteen years on, the hope remains: the current (2012) Integrated Development Plan for Cape Town has five strategic goals: achieving the 'opportunity city', the 'safe city', the 'caring city', the 'inclusive city' and the well-run city. Programmes for the first goal of becoming an 'opportunity city' include a partnership with the private sector and attracting globally important events, international tourists and investors.

Attempts by various local governments to rise up the global/world city league table have found expression in aggressive place-marketing, investment in tourism infrastructure to make Cape Town a global tourist destination, conference centre construction, the attraction of global sporting and other events (bidding for the Olympic Games in 2004; hosting the Soccer World Cup in 2010 at a cost for the stadium of US$ 600 million; and now achieving the designation as World Design City 2014), and a major waterfront development. Transport and other bulk infrastructure investments have supported these initiatives. Major new urban developments (e.g. the Waterfront and the large new retail and commercial node known as Century City) adhere to the vision of Western urban modernism and many new upmarket residential developments follow planning principles of 'gated villages' and 'new urbanism'. There has also been a proliferation of 'business improvement districts' (BIDs) and 'city improvement districts' (CIDs) established by private initiatives in more affluent areas and the central business area to improve security and public services, and in the latter case undertaking planning initiatives outside of the public authority. The central city CID has been particularly successful in maintaining property values in this area, hence continuing its attractiveness as an area to invest. Miraftab (2012) has argued that there is a close similarity between the old colonial practice of the segregated 'native location' in Cape Town and the present-day establishment of CIDs which segregate the city by class (and still largely by race) and exclude the poor from the wealthier parts of the city.

These various efforts to achieve global/world city status have skewed city budgets away from poorer areas and needs, although not entirely so. A central dilemma for Cape Town local government has been (and continues to be) between meeting the basic needs of the city's population and achieving global competitiveness (Lemanski, 2007) and the tension between competing demands of economic growth and redistribution has been reflected in almost every city 'vision statement'. As a number of authors above (Shatkin, Benjamin and Roy) have suggested, understanding contemporary postcolonial cities requires recognition of both continuing colonial ties and resistance to this 'from below'. As in other postcolonial cities, Cape Town's poorer communities have continued to voice demands (sometimes violently) for larger shares of the municipal budget and more spending on housing and basic services in their residential areas. Service delivery protests have become a frequent occurrence in Cape Town and in other South African cities. Non-payment of rates and public rentals (with 'bad debt' levels rising annually) is a further demonstration of non-compliance with City's expectations of 'good citizens'. Informal settlements (involving an estimated 174,000 households in 2009, or about 25 per cent of all households) have spread in Cape Town, both as new settlements on vacant land and as 'back-yard shacks' in formal low-income areas. The visibility of these shacks, particularly along the main access route from Cape Town's

International Airport to the city centre, has detracted from the desired vision of Cape Town as a world class, modern, Western city and it is not surprising that efforts have been made by the city to replace these with formal housing (e.g. the 'N2 Gateway' housing project). While huge disparities between rich and poor areas of Cape Town persist, it is also true that gains have been made by the poor: 'actually existing urbanisms' and 'occupancy urbanism' cannot be ignored in explaining the development of postcolonial Cape Town.

Conclusions

The City of Cape Town, along with many other postcolonial cities, therefore expresses, in its built environment and urban spatial pattern, its colonial and postcolonial histories on the one hand, and current tensions between 'world-class city' and 'inclusive city' aspirations on the other. It is possible to argue, certainly in relation to Cape Town, that global/world city aspirations express strong continuities with earlier relationships between South Africa and global North territories and are used to reinforce power and privilege in the city, even though some groups and individuals benefitting from this may be entirely local or indigenous. This is the case even though Cape Town remains 'off the map' in world city terms. Global/world city rhetoric (along with justification that the benefits of this will eventually 'trickle down' to the poor), even without success in the world city league table, is sufficient to bolster financial and political support for public actions which will attract international investors and tourists, with many of these actions taking place in and around the central business district, which also happens to be the site of the first colonial settlement.

Cape Town also illustrates the limitations of a purely 'structural' explanation of its postcolonial condition. The people of Cape Town, and particularly the poor, have resisted policies and programmes which do not directly benefit them, and through land and space occupation, through protest, and through financial non-compliance have carved out more or less precarious livelihoods in the city. Postcolonial critique also shows the danger of simple binary explanations here: urban Cape Town cannot be explained only in terms of a struggle between those with postcolonial ties and interests to the global North and the 'local poor'. Economic and social links between wealthy and poor, and between locally networked and internationally networked are complex and dynamic. Postcolonial studies and critique are therefore a valuable lens through which to expose global/world cities' thinking as partial and simplistic, and of little value to urban theory in understanding what are mostly 'ordinary cities'.

7
The Literary Dimension

Sheila Hones

Introduction

Despite a sustained interest in developing collaborations across the academic spectrum, the 'invisible college' (Acuto, 2011) of global city studies scholars still consists primarily of people working in the social sciences. As a result, one of the issues taken up by this collection of essays is the question of disciplinary diversity; the task of this particular chapter is to engage with the question of how work in the area of literary geography might contribute to global cities studies, and vice versa. The chapter includes three main sections: the first section introduces the proposition that academic argument and fictional narrative can both be understood as forms of textual interaction generating geographical knowledge, arguing that this provides the key link enabling collaboration between global cities studies and literary geography; the second section reviews the nature of literary geography, its relation to literary studies and to the social sciences, and the challenges it faces in engaging with scholarship on the global city; the third concludes the chapter with a brief unfolding of some of the points raised in the first two sections by reference to Colum McCann's novel *Let the Great World Spin* (2009).[1]

As Michele Acuto has noted, while the concept of the 'global city' in the academic social sciences has been the subject of persistent refinement and discussion, both in theoretical terms and as a research paradigm, in other academic fields and in non-specialist discourse the label 'global city' tends to carry a range of much vaguer connotations.[2] The very concept of the global city, as employed within this volume, rests on specific theoretical and metageographical foundations, and this throws up a major barrier to the integration of work in literary geography with specialized work on the global city. In the everyday geography of non-specialists, the global city is most likely to be imagined as a specific place with a self-evident, mappable, single location and a coherent history (New York, Tokyo, London), not as 'an inherently transitory phenomenon, a status of connectedness to the global' or 'an analytical construct' (Sassen, 2006; Acuto, 2011, 2954). Common-sense non-specialist geography is more likely to see the global city first as a place, and only much later as the representation of a spatial phenomenon, or as a transient nexus of connections that makes the global visible and tangible. What would it take to move literary geographers to engage with the detail and the specificity of theory and practice current within global city scholarship? And how, if they could be so moved, might the resulting work appeal to global cities scholars? Where, in other words, can we find the common ground for collaboration?

An academic article on the global city, analysing – for example – statistics generated by research into global financial interactions and the workforce geographies of transnational elites no doubt has a very different feel to an article performing the close reading of a novel. The first is working with facts, it would seem, the second with fiction; there is no obvious overlap here and no clear way in which the two might be understood to intersect. Nevertheless, these different articles can be connected in two potentially productive ways. On the one hand, a close reading performed in the context of current work in literary geography might well be making as much use of spatial theory as the paper using data analysis. Place, space, networks, scale, relational distance, metageography – all of these spatial themes and more are now quite routinely taken up in work in literary geography (Hsu, 2010; Preziuso, 2010; Hegglund, 2012). In that sense, literary geography has already shown a willingness to engage with theories and paradigms developed in the social sciences, so the challenge of motivating literary geographers to engage with global city theory may not in fact turn out to be an insoluble problem.

At the same time – and this is a more controversial argument – the apparently factual work of global city analysts cannot be separated from its textual articulation. The theoretical foundations of an article on global financial interactions, institutions and workers will have been developed, encountered and made familiar within its academic context in geography and urban studies, to a notable extent, through textually based practices. Typically, these practices will have included the collection and presentation of data, description, discussion, analysis and representation. In other words, knowledge about the global city even in the social sciences has largely been produced through the writing and reading of academic papers. This is an obvious point, of course, but its significance in the context of possible collaboration with literary scholars is that it demonstrates the important role that writer–text–reader interactions play in the emergence of the global city as a coherent subject.

In the social sciences, writer–text–reader interactions most often take place between academic colleagues; however, in the textual production of public knowledge about the global city, these interactions involving novelists, fictional texts and non-academic audiences are also significant.

So both academic and literary text-based interactions need readers: Colum McCann (2009, 360) is very clear on the point that a book 'is completed only when it is finished by a reader' and this can surely be applied to academic argument as well as fiction. One of the ways in which literary and reader response studies may be useful for global city studies is in drawing attention to the complexity of this collaboration, for example by showing how the ideal or implied reader usually indicated by the term 'the reader' is almost always in practice a not-ideal reader, one of many such not-ideal readers, many of whom will differ quite radically from the target reader the text implicitly addresses. Each one of these real readers will exercise their agency by engaging with the text slightly differently: in some cases inevitably misreading, in others, even consciously assuming the position of 'the resistant reader'.

Scholars working in the area of the global city engage with their readers in an attempt to affect, impact, reshape and rethink world geographies, to change the way space is envisioned, imagined, understood and practiced. Presumably, there is an implied social and political purpose here: to achieve a more accurate grasp of how the world works, and on the basis of that understanding to achieve progress, however progress might be defined. As Nigel Thrift (2003, 105) has argued, 'what we think of as "abstract" conceptions of space are a part of the fabric of our being, and transforming how we think those conceptions means transforming "ourselves." ' Academic articles, of course, speak most directly to an academic audience, and have the most direct impact on specialist geographical knowledge and practice, but the research energies of global cities scholars are surely not intended to make an impact only within academia. In the long run, their work is presumably also intended to have an effect on public, non-specialist geographies – which is to say, in J.K. Wright's terms, on geosophies: 'the geographical ideas, both true and false, of all manner of people – not only geographers, but farmers and fishermen, business executives and poets, novelists and painters' (1947, 1).

This means that in considering the spectrum of reader–writer text-based interactions which render the global city visible we are looking at a spectrum which includes both academic work in global studies and literary texts. One of the major practices involved in literary geography is the analysis of the ways in which literary texts not only reflect but also generate geographical knowledge. Novels and academic papers can both be understood as agents generating metageographical change; as a result, both can be read as active participants in the shaping and understanding of the global city concept. If, as Acuto (2011, 2970) suggests, the 'destination' for global city studies is 'a new way of looking at things', then the study of fiction, in addition to empirical research and theoretical debate, should be included within the repertoire of global city studies.[3] Fiction, like academic argument, not only represents and articulates geographical knowledge, but is also capable of changing it.[4]

It should probably be noted before moving further into this argument that – of course – such an emphasis on textual interaction is not intended to obscure the point that the global city always exists, in some sense, before theory, behind data, and beyond the pages of journals and novels: in other words, it clearly does have a physical and geographical reality. The point is simply that, as James Donald (2002, 47) notes, representations have real-world consequences, and whether those representations of the city are academic or fictional they can be understood to 'constitute mediated pedagogies of urban life'. Further, as Steve Pile (2002, 85) has pointed out, while the actual problems confronting modern cities are overpoweringly huge and alarmingly real, in the face of these problems storytelling is not simply a distraction: rather, Pile sees positive value in storytelling, envisioning a 'revolutionary practice' that relies on 'imagining and mobilizing better stories'.

The point here is simply that if we accept that the concept of the global city has become accessible and coherent within the social sciences largely through the sharing of texts, then we will have identified a point of entry into the college of global cities scholarship for literary geography. The emphasis made here on the importance of textual interaction to global studies scholarship is thus intended merely to draw attention to the way in which the recognition of that reality, the 'making visible of the global city' in particular terms, has developed out of a history of collaborative work based on empirical research and the refinement of theory, and that these two academic strands have both involved discussion, writing, publishing and reading – which is to say, expository and narrative practices. The gathering, presentation and analysis of data and the narration of theory are already standard practices within the 'invisible college'; literary geography can add to this the analysis and exploration of ways in which literary texts function in the generation and dissemination of new ways of understanding and experiencing the global city.

Literary geography and global city studies

A determined move towards increased interdisciplinarity is central to the project embodied by this collection of essays; the questions of what interdisciplinarity is, however, how it differs from transdisciplinarity (and other related concepts), and how it can best be conceived and practiced continue to be the subject of extensive academic discussion (Frodeman et al., 2010). The complexities of definition and practice involved in thinking through the practicalities of collaborations across academic disciplines are enormous, and clearly beyond the scope of this chapter; it is important to note right away, however, that the discussion in this chapter concentrates on literary geography, not literary studies. Literary geography cannot easily be named 'a discipline'; it is, rather, a collection of already interdisciplinary practices which overlap at various points. The relationship of literary geography to literary studies, on the one hand, and to geography, on the other, is unstable: for many literary critics, literary geography is practiced as a sub-field of literary criticism, while for many geographers, literary geography is practiced as a sub-field of cultural geography. A third variant (and there are more) emphasizes links between literary history, literary narratives and cartography. Sampling scholarly work from across the range of literary geography reveals a variety of very different framing assumptions about purpose and disciplinary context: but to oversimplify the distinction between two of the more prominent forms, literary geography with a strongly literary orientation tends to be much more invested in interpretation than literary geography as practiced within the context of cultural geography.[5] Nevertheless, no matter how the balance between the two primary informing disciplines is struck, it is clear that literary geography is already, in itself, an inter- or trans- or multi-disciplinary project. This means that when it engages with global city studies – another inherently interdisciplinary field – the resulting collaboration will be far more complex than it would be if it were two clearly defined disciplinary fields that were coming together.

Currently, the distinction between the more explicitly literary version of literary geography and the more explicitly geographical version is becoming less clear-cut, and several collaborative initiatives are currently underway to increase mutual recognition and communication.[6] In the context of collaboration with global cities studies, however, it seems likely that at present it is still the more geographical end of the spectrum of work in literary geography that holds the greater potential. This is mainly because of the difference in fundamental purpose indicated above: 'literary' literary geography is primarily interested in using spatial theory and geographical data to support the interpretation of text and the development of literary criticism and theory, while 'geographical' literary geography is more likely to be interested in analysing the ways in which literary texts articulate and produce geographical knowledge.[7] This is, inevitably, another oversimplification, and so a note of caution should be added: while Marc Brosseau did indeed draw attention to the ways in which 'the literary text may constitute a "geographer" in its own right as it generates norms, particular modes of readability, that produce a particular type of geography', in his influential 1994 paper for *Progress in Human Geography*, he also called for 'a much greater focus on the text itself', advocating an approach to literary text that was less 'instrumentalist', and a practice for 'geographical' literary geography that would follow literary criticism in taking time to respect the text as 'an intricate and complex signifying practice'.

While there are many potential avenues for productive collaborations bringing together work in global city studies and literary geography, more cooperative groundwork will have to be made to clarify the connotations and theoretical implications of apparently simple and apparently shared terminology. Doreen Massey (1992, 66) has noted how commonly authors talking about 'space' and the 'spatial' assume 'that their meaning is clear and uncontested', while in practice this apparently shared terminology works to conceal 'a debate which never surfaces because everyone assumes we already know what these terms mean'. This is not to say that everyone working in the collaborative area of literary geography/global city studies will need to agree on how key terms such as 'space' are being defined; it is simply to repeat the point that for communication to take place scholars need to be actively aware that the way they use apparently basic terms – the geographical vocabulary they take for granted – is specific, not obvious, and not necessarily shared. 'Place', 'space', 'networks' and 'the global' are prime examples of terms that will inevitably lead to miscommunication and inter-disciplinary confusion if they are not delineated carefully enough as they are brought into play. This is a continuing issue in interdisciplinary literary geography, within which different practices proceed along quite separate tracks laid down according to really different, fundamental assumptions not only about concepts such as 'setting' and 'place' but (as indicated earlier) also about what literary geography itself actually is and does: as the literary scholar Neal Alexander puts it, with literary geography 'we seem to be stuck with a term that is intrinsically polysemic'.[8]

In this context, it is critical that literary geographers themselves are explicit about what they are doing. Four examples should suffice to indicate the range of approaches and the resulting need for clarity. The research project currently working on a literary atlas of Europe, for example, makes its position and research parameters helpfully clear on its homepage: 'It all starts with the supposedly simple questions: Where is literature set and why there?'[9] Franco Moretti's influential (and controversial) explanation of literary geography in his *Atlas of the European Novel 1800–1900* is also unambiguous: 'this is what literary geography is all about: you select a textual feature... find the data, put them on paper – and then you look at the map' (Moretti, 1999, 13). Meanwhile the literary scholar Andrew Thacker has defined the practice of 'critical' literary geography as the 'process of reading and interpreting literary texts by reference to geographical concepts': his aim in the monograph *Moving Through Modernity* is the delineation of 'a vocabulary drawing upon concepts employed by theorists of space and geography for the interpretation of literary modernism' (Thacker, 2005, 2003). Hsuan Hsu and Martin Bruckner's *American Literary Geographies: Spatial Practice and Cultural Production 1500–1900* (2007), on the other hand, is an edited collection aimed at the analysis of 'concrete ways in which the spatial imaginary was produced, maintained, and transfigured over the course of four centuries'. The range of approaches currently running along parallel tracks in literary geography, broadly defined, suggests that to achieve coherence a future global cities literary geography would need to start not only with a catch-up review of theory and practice in studies of globalization, world cities and global cities, but also from a clear understanding of the research history and current range of literary geography.

To summarize, then, within the range of literary geographies described so far, the style which would be most likely to engage relatively smoothly with social science global city scholarship would probably be a variant of the geographically oriented form: one which was well informed about current spatial theory and research on the global city while also working from a thorough grounding in the theoretical and practical techniques of literary criticism. Thus while the purpose of this form of global city literary geography might be the elucidation of ways in which fiction, for example, mediated the public perception of global space, connections and distances, the methods by which that elucidation was achieved would be based on the close reading techniques typical of literary studies. The biggest challenge would remain the need for such a literary geography to be conversant with current theory and practice within research on the global city.

There is, however, one further angle of approach for a global cities literary geography that suggests itself. This is a quite different variant, one which instead of working from the close reading of texts focuses on the global spaces of literary production and reception. This suggestion arrives from two directions: on the one hand, there is an awareness within global cities studies that current research into global networks and infrastructures is focused too narrowly on topics such as the servicing of global capital. This means that the role of the global city in the circulation of cultural artifacts, knowledge and information is an area ready for development (Acuto, 2011, 2969). Fortunately, at the same time, the field of literary geography has already begun to develop a new line of work focusing on geographies of production and reception, which might fit quite neatly into this gap. In a 2010 review article for *Progress in Human Geography*, for example, Angharad Saunders (2010) identified the key ideas for textual geography as 'knowledge, practice, and poetics', including in her definition of literary practice not only 'genre, style and form' but also 'the material conditions of writing: the production, circulation and reception of the written word'.

These two aspects to literary geography – the literary and the material – have been neatly compressed in Jo Sharp's work on Salman Rushdie, in which she points out the ways in which 'Rushdie's global geo-graphing and the geo-graphing of Rushdie have come into conflict' (1996, 125). In her work on Rushdie and also in a later review article for *Area* Sharp makes the important point that authors have little control over how their work is read. So while 'Rushdie's work offers the geographer' – and no doubt many readers and critics – 'a world where the fluidities of hybridity and mobile spatial practices can play out', it is still necessary to analyse 'the contexts of writing and reception' in order 'to understand the novel's relationship with the world that it seeks to narrate' (Sharp, 1996, 126). Sharp (2000, 333) therefore argues for the need to approach literary texts not only as Brosseau's 'intricate and complex' constructions but also as entities with 'very material existences and detectable roles within society'.

In addition to her reminder that readers have their own agency, Sharp also usefully draws attention to the fact that this agency is exercised in very different ways by different readers. While it may seem that critics trained in the techniques of literary criticism have a more authoritative position as readers, or that their readings are more likely to access 'the real meaning' of a text, the recent move in literary geography to view the author–text–reader interaction as a spatial event undercuts that assumption by viewing specialist academic and non-specialist public readings 'not so much as essentially different practices but as the same kind of practice differently conditioned by context, conventions, and expectations' (Hones, 2008). The complex relational geographies of different readers will inevitably be woven into those contexts, habits and modes of reading. Literary critics in this configuration are just one genre of readers among many, and (outside the frame of academic literary studies) their readings are no more authentic or significant than others; one of the challenges for a global city literary geography would be to find a way to check the urge to interpret – to create an exhaustive or authoritative reading – with the acknowledgment that in a social science context the highly technical examination of a text may be of less value than an exploration of the full range of reader response as it can be understood in various spatial configurations. The reception of a literary work very likely has its own geography, and the spatial aspects of the ways in which a text has been 'received, interpreted and read by its various audiences' thus provides literary geography – and by implication any literary geography/global cities collaboration – with another important area for consideration.[10]

Where does the text happen? Like the global city, I would argue, it is an event with a highly complex geography, centered and diffuse at the same time (Hones, 2011). Reader response theory suggests that within literary studies there is broad consensus on three points fundamental to the question of reception: that 'the text is not a container of stable, objective meaning', that 'the reader is a producer of meaning' and that 'readings are necessarily various' (Schweickart and Flynn, 2004). Under these conditions, meaning can be understood as something which emerges in the interaction of various agents across space and time. If we take hold of the novel in this way, as a spatial event, an always emerging collaboration in space and time, then we have something which can only happen at the intersection of multiple participants, including author(s), editor(s), publishers, texts, teachers, critics and readers. The text, when it happens, comes into being in the interaction of differently contextualized processes, and these processes are each in themselves generated in the context of countless interactions across space and time. It seems that this concept of the text as event implies yet another way in which global city studies and literary geography might connect: if, as Smith and Doel (2011) assume, global cities should be understood 'as networks, rather than *in* networks', then a similarly subtle but significant metageographical shift might be applied to the conceptualization of texts. This is to say that the text, as it happens, can itself be understood as a network, and the implications of this potential comparison (between the global city and the global novel) might provide yet another productive area for future collaborations involving literary geographies and global city studies.

The author of this chapter's case-study text, Colum McCann, is of course a real person; he lives and works in New York City. Like New York City, he has a physical reality and a traceable historical geography. Born and brought up in Dublin, he holds dual Irish and US citizenship; like the city he now calls home, McCann possesses and exemplifies a 'connectedness to the global'. McCann's professional persona as well as that of his novels (the stories they tell, and the places they weave together) ranges far beyond the boundaries of New York City: McCann speaks at literary festivals around the world; he is celebrated with international prizes; and he is interviewed and reviewed in many formats – print and online – each with their own geographies of location and distribution, production and access. His books are globally available from real and online bookstores. Readers get hold of copies of the books, read them (perhaps translate them), write blog comments on them or discuss them in reading groups. In order for his novel even to begin to happen, McCann had to depend on inspiration from other artists and writers, local informants and experts, and the collaboration of editors and publishers; he has also benefited from a network of reviewers, blurb writers, promoters, awards and judging panels, book festivals – and, of course, from his audience.

As studies in the global city and literary geography begin to work more closely together, an interest in the global geography of reception could well be expanded to a wider interest in the relationships between new forms of global space, modern literary production (including authoring, publishing, printing, selling and promoting) and modern literary reception (including reviewing, blogging, face-to-face and online reading group activities). So while the concluding section of this chapter concentrates primarily on examples of geographically oriented close-reading, looking at the ways in which McCann's novel *Let the Great World Spin* facilitates for the reader (or even demands of the reader) a particular understanding of space as networked and global in scale, there remain a range of other possibilities, as suggested here, for the analysis of the novel's global geographies of literary production and reception.

Let The Great World Spin

The historical default definition of literary geography as the study of 'literature and place', with 'place' in this configuration being understood most commonly in relation to narrative setting or to cartographies of author biography, throws up a serious issue for a global cities literary geography.[11]

The increased willingness of literary geographers to engage with spatial theory and to think through the geosophical foundations of their work offers some hope here, although the conventional approach to literary geography, emphasizing as it does the concept of setting, clearly derives from and depends upon a mosaic metageography. This 'container space' approach is grounded quite conventionally in the assumption that at any naturalized scale (global, national, regional, local, etc) global space is made up of separable parts such as neighbourhoods, cities, regions, areas, nations or continents which, within the spatial logic of an assumed scale, fit together neatly with minimal overlapping. Colum McCann's novel *Let the Great World Spin* can be read within this metageography; it cannot, however, be identified in any straightforward way as a novel 'set in New York', nor even as a novel with scenes taking place in a set of discrete locations – New York, Dublin, Cleveland, Palo Alto, Little Rock and New Orleans. The metageography of container space is challenged in the event of *The Great World* by the way in which its narrative style performs and draws out from its readers an alternative metageography, resisting a static view of world space in order to emphasize instead a global space of interconnectedness and networks, a space in which events happen simultaneously in multiple locations and in which locations embody multiple historical and social dimensions.

Let the Great World Spin is, then, a novel 'set' in New York, but a New York that is as unset as a global city can be. Just as the structure of the novel depends on multiple intersections of different plot lines, different historical geographies and different social groupings, the New York that it narrates is itself a network, a nexus, a transient collection of collisions. Michele Acuto has suggested that in the context of global city studies this aspect of McCann's fictional New York usefully 'speaks to the inevitable instability of the "city"', in the sense that the networks which define the global city are subject to constant change; it is a useful reminder that 'the master category "city"' can so easily be taken for granted 'while the city itself is in continuous flux'.[12] Indeed, as McCann describes it, *The Great World* is the story of 'a collision, really, a web in this big sprawling complex web that we call New York'. It performs and momentarily stabilizes this web in its presentation of 'a story of lives entwined in the early 1970's ... [most of which] takes place on one day in New York in August 1974', following 'the intricate lives of a number of different people who ... accidentally dovetail in and out of each other's lives on this one day ...'[13]

In order to portray this web, dramatized by collisions between lives, histories and geographies, McCann organizes the narration of *The Great World* into 13 chapters (and one photograph). The opening chapter is presented in the voice of a third person narrator: 'Those who saw him hushed. On Church Street. Liberty. Cortlandt. West Street. Fulton. Vesey.' The remaining 12 are each narrated from the perspective of one of 11 major characters: some in the first person ('I stood looking around for Corrigan'), others in a third person voice that is limited, mainly, to a single point of view ('Most days, he had to admit, were dire'). The single day which functions as the narrative axis around which the novel's multiple stories revolve is a fictional version of Wednesday, 7 August 1974, the day on which the French wirewalker Philippe Petit performed his famous tightrope crossing between the two towers of the World Trade Center. In the novel, an unnamed wirewalk artist not only provides the narrative centre of consciousness for two chapters, but in addition his performance of the highwire walk across the space between the newly completed towers provides one of the key narrative hubs through which the various individual stories connect. Some characters see the performance; others hear about it; another sees a photograph of it; yet another is the judge in front of whom the wirewalker appears after his arrest; two more are also under arrest and appearing in the same court at the same time. The first 12 chapters take place at the time of the 1974 wirewalk performance; the 13th and final chapter is set 12 years later in 2006, and is narrated by a character who has briefly appeared earlier, as a small child.

Readers have variously taken *The Great World* as a 9/11 novel, even though the events of 9/11 are never directly mentioned, and as a novel about the 1970s; within the American literary tradition, it has been read both as 'a New York novel' and as a work of 'immigrant fiction'; beyond that, it has been read within the tradition of Irish literature, and it has also been read as an example of the emerging genre of 'world fiction'. Taken together, the various literary, historical and contextual aspects of *The Great World* suggest that it would work well as the subject of an extended case study in literary geography and the global city. On the one hand, its literary themes and intertextual references provide excellent material for close readings of the ways in which the text event articulates the global city, made in the tradition of text-analysis and also reader-response approaches to literary geography; on the other hand and in terms of the social processes of its creation, production, dissemination and reception, it provides equally promising material for a literary geography approach focused on the ways in which literary production and consumption rely upon, emerge out of and also produce global city networks.

I would like to end this very brief exploration of a few of the many possible literary responses to the challenge of global city studies by focusing on one of the ways in which the novel's narrative style works to articulate New York as a global city, not least by enabling readers to experience a non-mosaic global space, a strongly connected space – to use Doreen Massey's phrase – of simultaneous heterogeneity (Massey, 2005, 105). In what follows I will simply try to sketch out, using four paragraphs from the text, an indication of how the narrative of *The Great World* articulates a complex, globally folded setting, anchored by reference to New York. The first quotation is taken from a scene in which the wirewalker prepares for his New York performance in a distant rural setting: I take this as an example of the narrative articulation of New York as a global stage, a place for performance, a place which draws global attention. In this scene, the wirewalker is rehearsing in isolation – in a meadow near a log cabin – the walk he will perform for the world in New York; as a result, he has to be in two places simultaneously:

> There were times when he was so at ease that he could watch the elk, or trace the wisps of smoke from the forest fires, or watch the red-tail perning above the nest, but at his best his mind remained free of sight. What he had to do was reimagine things, make an impression in his head, a tower at the far end of his vision, a cityline below him. He sometimes resented it, bringing the city to the meadow, but he had to melt the landscapes together in his imagination, the grass, the city, the sky.
>
> (McCann, 2009, 161)

In the meadow, he is also in the city; he melds the two places together in his mind, and in his embodied practice. As he leaves for the city he is still in two places – en route, and yet remaining in the meadow, behind himself: 'He'd look over his shoulder and see that figure, neck-deep in snow, waving good-bye to himself'.

The second example comes from a chapter focalized through a computer programmer in Palo Alto: I take this as an example of New York as a place always globally co-present and accessible in the technologically mediated space of connections. Here, computer programmers in California who have learned of the wirewalk through the ARPANET are hacking their computers through to public phone booths located near the towers. If their calls are answered, the programmers ask for eyewitness descriptions.

> – I'm telling you, José, we're in California.
> – You're trying to tell me I'm talking to a computer?
> – Sort of.
> – You're in California...? People! Hey, people!

> He says it real loud, holding the receiver out, and we can hear voices chattering the wind... some sirens going in the background, big high whoops, and a woman laughing, and a few muffled shouts, a car horn, a vendor roaring about peanuts, some guy saying he's got the wrong lens, he needs a better angle, and some other guy shouting: Don't fall!.
>
> (McCann, 2009, 180)

The participants in this scene are distant but co-present: on the east coast, the spectators are at ground level; on the west coast, the programmers are in a basement laboratory. Both parties are intensely focused on the wirewalker, high above street level, and all of the action is connected in real time. As one of the programmers explains, 'It's about being connected, access, gateways.....' (McCann, 2009, 197).

The Palo Alto chapter not only describes this kind of technologically medi-ated connectedness but actually enables a reader to experience and in a sense participate in the heterogeneous simultaneity of time-space as the narrative cuts back and forth in (fictional) real time between the programmers in their basement and events in Manhattan. In the passage above, which is located by the focalization primarily in the Palo Alto basement, the Manhattan sounds are mediated through the telephone receiver, but because anyone who has read the novel's opening chapter ('Those who saw him hushed') will have already experienced these sounds and the related action from a Manhattan street-level perspective, the back-and-forth in this chapter effec-tively locates the reader in two places at the same time, which is to say that it effectively disconnects the Palo Alto action from a frame setting, and through that dislocation pushes a reader into an experience of the kind of interactive space which enables the global city.

My third example comes from a chapter narrated by a Colombian nurse, living and working in New York. This paragraph articulates the dislocated location of New York in a slightly different way, generating a palimpsest of the city as destination, of here-and-now memories, made up of multiple arrivals and departures. Adelita's narrative articulates this folding of space and time: in a moment of intense happiness, she feels as motionless and yet as able to slip from one time and place to another as the wirewalker in his moment of concentration:

> I know already that I will return to this day whenever I want to. I can bid it alive. Preserve it. There is a still point where the present, the now, winds around itself, and nothing is tangled. The river is not where it begins or ends, but right in the middle point, anchored by what has happened and what is to arrive. You can close our eyes and there will be a light snow falling in New York, and seconds later you are sunning upon a rock in Zacapa.
>
> (McCann, 2009, 279)

Where the Palo Alto chapter narrates non-mosaic space in its creation of multiple settings interacting simultaneously in a literal sense, Adelita's men-tal merging of New York and Zacapa narrates the conflation of different places at different times into a single present moment 'in the middle' poised between distant locations and between past and future.

The fourth quotation comes from the novel's final chapter. Here the cen-tral character, living in 2006, is looking at a photograph taken in 1974 of the wirewalk in progress. The photograph includes not only the towers and the artist, but also an airplane apparently – an optical illusion – about to crash into one of the towers. Readers of the novel will be already familiar with this photograph, which is inserted between chapters eight and nine as a half-page greyscale reproduction. The photograph has been shot upward, from ground level, between the two towers, and shows clearly the stretched wire and two cavalleti (stabilizing wires), the tiny figure of the wirewalker, and his eight meter balancing pole. At the extreme top left of the shot there is an airplane, its nose apparently only meters away from the left-hand tower, its left wing and part of the tail cropped by the upper edge of the photograph. This is, in fact, a documentary photograph given a fictional attribution in the text. The original (historical) photograph was taken by Vic DeLuca for Rex Images on 7 August 1974, and shows the real Philippe Petit walking. In the novel, however, the photograph is attributed to the amateur photographer Fernando, who is the central character in the sixth chapter, with the implication that this is the photograph he takes just after the end of his chapter, as he comes up out of the subway to witness the wirewalk in progress. With the caption 'photo: © fernando yunqué marcano' this pictorial quotation from the historical archive thus becomes part of the fictional world of the novel, thereby folding narrative space in yet one more way by linking the narrative-internal (diagetic) space and the external (extra-diegetic) space of the author, publisher, text and readers.

Given the way in which the photograph suggests that the airplane may be about to hit the left-hand tower, it also functions as another conflation of spatial dimensions, of time and location: in this case, 7 August 1974 and 11 September 2001. This is one of the points that so fascinates Jaslyn about this photograph: the way in which it collapses time in the repeated space of an iconic New York location. I take this as an example of the global city as a nexus; as something which endures; something which holds together.

> A man high in the air while a plane disappears, it seems, into the edge of the building. One small scrap of history meeting a larger one. As if the walking man were somehow anticipating what would come later. The intrusion of time and history. The collision point of stories. We wait for the explosion but it never occurs. The plane passes, the tightrope walker gets to the end of the wire. Things don't fall apart.
>
> (McCann, 2009, 326)

Here, at the start of the final chapter – which completes the weaving across space and time of the novel's many threads – Jaslyn's narrative explicitly draws attention to the idea that places and people are connected by stories, images, histories, memories: and not just connected, but also constituted out of those connections. At the same time, the photograph is itself both part of the fictional, imagined New York of *The Great World* but also and at the same time part of the documentary archive of the historical New York. As a result the photograph functions to connect multiple New Yorks – the city at different times, in different textual and actual dimensions, and across the entire range of the text event of *The Great World*.

Two of the key locations in the novel are New York and Dublin, and as the narrative threads back and forth between these two places, it connects them and, at the same time, suggests how Dublin is part of New York, and New York part of Dublin. 'Ireland is an everywhere now', McCann remarks in conversation with novelist Nathan Englander; Englander follows this up by noting that while New York contains 'many worlds' and can feel like 'a sort of elsewhere sometimes', it is still a 'wonderful, singular, unified city'.[14] As Doreen Massey (1994) has explained, it is possible to understand place in precisely these terms: 'what gives a place its specificity is not some long internalized history but the fact that it is constructed out of a particular constellation of social relations, meeting and weaving together at a particular locus'. And much the same could be said, in fact, of the novel: just as for McCann the city of New York is 'the collision point of stories', *The Great World* itself can only happen in a collision. In this sense the reader, engaging with the text, not only reads about the interconnectedness of New York and of global city space but actively shares it.[15] The text event of *The Great World* becomes part of the event of New York as a global city; the novel, its author and its readers not only collaborate in the articulation of global city space but also participate in its production.

Notes

1. Starting from the point that the world city narrative is already 'one of the most interdisciplinary among the social sciences', Acuto (2011, 2953) calls for 'an eclectic understanding' of the global city 'that can speak beyond the [invisible] college' of world city researchers.
2. On the problems inherent in interdisciplinary collaboration, even within geography, and the miscommunication easily generated by terminology which appears to be shared but is in fact not, see Bracken and Oughton (2006). Bracken and Oughton argue that 'interdisciplinary projects must allocate time to the development of shared vocabularies and understandings'.
3. Quoting Henry Miller.
4. In their introduction to the *Blackwell City Reader*, Bridge and Watson (2002, 7) highlight the importance of geographical imaginaries 'to illustrate the power of ideas, the imagination, representations, and visions in influencing the way cities are formed and lived'.
5. For more on this point, see Hones (2008) and compare with Thacker (2005), written from the perspective of literary studies.
6. See for example the online bibliography http://literarygeographies.wordpress.com/ (started in 2012) and associated cross-disciplinary literary-geographical projects currently under development.
7. The literary scholar Neal Alexander, for example, sees his work as 'developing modes of close reading that are attentive to the kinds of geographical imaginations that are manifest in literary texts', personal correspondence with the author, 20 March 2012, (Alexander and Cooper, 2013; Alexander, 2011).
8. Personal correspondence to the author, 20 March 2012.

9. http://www.literaturatlas.eu/?lang=en.

10. On geographies of reception, see for example (Keighren, 2006; Livingstone, 2005; Machor, 1993; Secord, 2000).

11. Literary geography is still popularly associated with the study of 'landscape in literature', as exemplified by literary gazetteers and atlases, for example Bradbury (1998). As evidence of the continuing public interest in this approach, see the 2012 British Library exhibition 'Writing Britain', examining 'how the landscapes of Britain permeate great literary works'.

12. Acuto, personal correspondence with the author, 11 December 2012.

13. http://www.colummccann.com/interviews/LTGWSinterview.htm.

14. McCann, C and N. Englander. 'A conversation with Colum McCann and Nathan Englander', in *Let the Great World Spin* [appendix: A Reader's Guide] 371, 369.

15. Richard Carter-White, personal correspondence with the author, 14 January 2013.

8
The Virtual Dimension

Mark Graham

> The most profound technologies are those that disappear.
>
> (Weiser, 1991, 94)

The cartographic attributes of the invisible[1]

Cities are comprised of bricks and mortar, concrete and glass, roads, rails, pipes and cables, people, plants and animals. The layers of cities also include the many histories, memories, legends and stories that people ascribe to place (Crang 1996; Graham 2010). Yet cities have been going through two important transitions that have brought into being new dimensions that profoundly matter for the ways that we interact with our urban environments. Cities are no longer just confined to their material presences: they have become both digital and digitized.

Within the global city literature, much has been written about the ways that both social/business and material/infrastructural networks crucially matter to the development of cities (e.g. Acuto, 2011). But this chapter focuses on another component of our urban environments: the many, often invisible and ephemeral, digital layers of cities. The virtual elements of cities are immensely significant. Cities ooze data; they are structured by code and software; they cast innumerable digital shadows.

The goal of this chapter is to interrogate these virtual layers of the city. By asking what they are, where they are and why they matter, we can then explore their significance for global cities. Specifically, with a case study of user-generated content about the city of Jerusalem, we can ask whether contemporary Information and Communication Technologies (ICTs) are reinforcing dual urbanisms and splintering cities or if their potentially open nature allows for a bypassing of concentrations of power that have always been found between and within global cities (Sassen, 2007). The rest of this section now reviews some of the key ways in which the virtual dimensions of cities influence the social, economic and political characteristics, experiences and interpretations of cities. Four concepts are particularly useful in describing the intersections between the digital and the material: palimpsests, augmented reality, code/space and digiplace.

Palimpsests

The notion of a palimpsest was first employed to refer to medieval writing blocks that could be reused while still retaining traces of earlier inscriptions. Because those earlier inscriptions could never fully be erased, every writing block was a composite containing traces of all inscriptions (Crang, 1998). The notion of a palimpsest thus becomes useful for describing the urban environment. Cities are incessantly made and remade, and layered with historical, contemporary, tangible, intangible, visible, invisible, material and virtual elements. Digital urban layers can take myriad forms. The most visible of which are probably the digital maps that many people use to navigate through cities. Google, Yahoo!, Apple, OpenStreetMap, Baidu and many other companies and organizations all host publicly accessible platforms that reflect cities. However, these services also become the platform for an almost unimaginable amount of additional content that both reflects the materiality of cities and augments it with additional content. This additional content is comprised of photographs, blogs, tweets, social media checkins, webcams, videos and Wikipedia articles. These layers of digital representations are then further reproduced and repurposed in the ways that they annotate the urban environment (see Figure 8.1 for an example of the layering of digital content onto the materiality of the city).

Figure 8.1   The material/digital palimpsests of Manhattan
Source: Google Streetview.

The virtual content layered in and over cities is also not just of-the-moment, but also of-the-past: allowing for an 'unavoidable continuity' of the city's geography (Beauregard and Haila, 2000). Some of these layers are relics of earlier events, places and experiences (for instance, old user reviews that hover over particular places). Other layers are much more current (for instance, the incessant posts in microblogging services that react to live events).

This peculiarity of the city as a material/virtual palimpsest means that the city itself can be experienced in entirely new ways. Not only do we no longer experience and interact with the city solely from our grounded offline positionalities, but we also experience many traces and data shadows of the city from earlier points in time. In other words, the enrolling of innumerable digital layers into the palimpsests of our cities has fundamentally changed what the urban environment is and what it means to many of its inhabitants. Importantly, this leads us to wonder whether the material/virtual palimpsests of cities are able to encourage more generalized and less geographically unique digital layers, or if the selective reflections and representations of the city reinforced fragmented and splintered urbanisms. Furthermore, does this mean that the cities with the most visible digital presences are better able to project themselves and reinforce their global city statuses? These questions will be picked up again later in the chapter.

Augmented realities

We therefore need to ask how to conceptualize the ways in which the hybrid material/virtual layers of cities are experienced. It is here that the idea of 'augmented reality' is particularly useful. The term originated as a way to describe head-mounted digital displays that were used by Boeing workers on assembly lines. However, since then, the term has been more broadly applied as a way of describing experiences of place that are supplemented with digital information.

Graham, Zook and Bouton (2012) note that the trend towards digital augmentation can be traced via three successive moments in the development of Internet practices and technologies: the growth of authorship, the emergence of a geospatial web (or Geoweb) and the rise of the mobile web. The rapidly increasing number of content contributors coupled with the ability to easily annotate places in the Geoweb has resulted in dense layers of virtual information augmenting some parts of the world. Furthermore, as ever more people use connected mobile devices (i.e. smartphones and tablets), layers of information over cities are no longer just accessible non-proximately. In other words, we are able to bring in all of this information into our portable, mobile devices. It can all augment the ways in which we bring place into being whilst we are in place, enacting place. We quite literally have access to all of the information augmenting our cities in the palms of our hands.

We know that representations of places are more than just lines and shapes on maps. Geographers have argued that spatial representations are not neutral, but entail power-laden stabilizations of understanding (Pickles 2004). Augmented information shapes what is known and what can be known about cities. This discoverable knowledge, in turn, influences the myriad ways in which urban spaces are (and can be) experienced. We should therefore be increasingly concerned with the ways in which augmented inclusions and exclusions, visibilities and invisibilities will shape digital representations. As we experience not just the city, but the augmented city, digital geographic representations don't just influence how we think about places, but also, in a very real sense, influence how we move through, interact with and enact place.

Code/space

Before discussing the issues of power and voice in layers of the augmented city, it is important to point out that digital representations are not the only way that immaterial information mediates our urban experiences. Equally important is the role of software or code (i.e. formalized rules for information into other outputs and representations). As Amin and Thrift (2002, 125) note, 'The modern city exists as a haze of software instructions.' Nearly every urban practice is becoming mediated by code.

Dodge and Kitchin (2004, 2005) construct a useful typology of the ways in which code influences everyday life. They distinguish between 'code/space', 'coded space' and 'background coded space'. Code/spaces are parts of our cities in which code or software in essential to the production or enaction of that space. A failure of code in such spaces inevitably results in a serious disruption of those spaces (ticket machines at a train station would be an example of this). Coded spaces also rely on code to function, but a failure of code would not render the space unusable (a busy traffic intersection would be an example). Background coded spaces are dormant until accessed (for instance, with a mobile phone) and transformed into code/spaces or boded spaces.

It is also important to point out that many code/spaces and coded spaces don't just alter the ways that cities are enacted and brought into being for their inhabitants, but also emit data shadows and information trails. These emitted shadows of 'big data' can take a variety of forms, but most are manifestations or by-products of human/machine interactions in code/spaces and coded spaces. We now see hundreds of millions of connected people, billions of sensors and trillions of communications, information transfers and transactions producing unfathomably large data shadows. Examples include geolocated mobile phone data showing spatial patterns of conversations, real-time electricity usage and records of all underground journeys taken with smartcards (such as London's Oyster, Hong Kong's Octopus and New York's MetroCard).

These data streams and shadows are increasingly being used to govern, plan and regulate cities. *The Economist* (2012), for instance, asks:

> ... how will data change cities? To get an idea, look at how racing cars have changed. Mechanics used to do all the fine-tuning on their vehicle before a race. Now they sit in front of big screens, monitoring the data that comes in from the hundreds of sensors attached to the car – and make adjustments in real-time. One day city hall may be as packed with screens as a Formula 1 pit.

When using data about the city, policy makers and researchers no longer just take snapshots in time or samples from particular people and places. In other words, policy processes that shape global cities are likely to be ever more data-driven. Although many local governments and private sector entities do not fully know how best to utilize such a panoply of data, we are seeing an increasing number of examples of ways that urban data shadows can be fed back into algorithms and urban layers, and services; and ultimately have significant effects on how people move through the city.

The layering of the city with socially powerful code is perhaps best expressed by Crang and Graham (2007, 789):

> The distributed processing in the world around us is often claimed to be a pervasive or ubiquitous computing environment: a world of ambient intelligence, happening around us on the periphery of our awareness, where our environment is not a passive backdrop but an active agent in organizing daily lives. The spaces around us are now being continually forged and reforged in informational and communicative processes. It is a world where we not only think of cities but cities think of us, where the environment reflexively monitors our behaviour.

Digiplace

Because urban data shadows are now so unfathomably large, complex algorithms are needed to sort, rank and order the virtual layers of cities. It is these algorithms that form an important part of our final concept that is useful for elucidating links between the virtual and the material: 'digiplace'. Digiplace is a heuristic for the subjective mixing of code, data and material places (Zook and Graham, 2007a, b and c). It 'encompasses the situatedness of individuals balanced between the visible and the invisible, the fixed and the fluid, the space of places and the space of flows, and the blurring of the lines between material place and digital representations of place' (Zook and Graham, 2007b, 1327). Or following Julie Cohen's description of the Internet, it could be said to be 'an experienced spatiality mediated by embodied human cognition [...that] is relative, mutable, and constituted via the interactions among practice, conceptualization, and representation'

(Cohen, 2007). In other words, digiplace becomes useful as a way of bringing together the material and digital layers of the city, understandings of how the virtual can augment the material through technological mediations and analyses of the power that code has to shape the ways that place[2] is brought into being.

Importantly, digiplace is also a way of imagining the highly subjective and individualized experiences of the melding of cities and information. Cities (or places) have never been statically and objectively knowable. The London that I know is very different from the London that anyone else knows. This is not because of any particular insights into the workings of the city that I personally possess, but rather is because we know, experience and enact fundamentally different cities. But, because of the complex and targeted algorithms used to mediate our interactions with and use of urban augmentations, digiplaces can potentially become further reified, segmented and individualized. There is nothing inherently problematic about the fact that fundamentally different cities can be presented to us, but when combined with other issues of power, voice and information inequalities, the opaque and selective digital mediations of our cities can start to become cause for concern. It is to these worries that the rest of this chapter now turns.

Virtual challenges: Big data and the ephemeral, augmented city

This section highlights four main concerns related to the virtual geographies of global cities. First, the issue of information absences is addressed. Here, the worries surround the variable amounts of information about places, as well as issues of voice in the specific ways that places are being represented. Second is the issue of informational presences. The unprecedented explosion in urban data shadows has serious implications for privacy and how cities are perceived. Third and fourth are the interlinked issues of ghettoization and the ephemerality of local information. The targeted nature of urban information, code and data shadows means that we all experience fundamentally different cities: a concern that has far-reaching implications for how we should think about cities.

Virtual absences

As discussed earlier in the chapter, the ways that cities are represented have important repercussions on how we perceive, interact with, augment, move through and enact our urban environments. As such, the informational shadows of cities truly matter. Mapping content indexed in Google Maps is a useful way to explore these layers of information about material places (because it is the world's most used website, and aggregates a huge variety of data sources). In Google (a service with a stated aim to 'organise the world's information and make it universally accessible and useful'), we see that some cities are covered with highly dense virtual layers of content and information, many others have only very sparse virtual presences (e.g. Graham and Zook, 2013). The Tokyo metropolitan region (with a population of about 35 million people), for instance, is layered with more content that the entire continent of Africa (with a population of over one billion people). Examinations of other platforms for digital layers and representations of cities (e.g. Flickr, Wikipedia) display similar patterns of absences and presences. In other words, most data currently do seem to indicate that the density of information is highest in the usual suspects in the global cities literature, while other cities are simply left off the map.

Not only are representations of urban environments characterized by highly uneven geographies, but the production of those layers are equally concentrated. Despite the fact that there are now over two billion Internet users, a very small minority tend to produce the bulk of digital information. Nowhere is this more apparent than in Wikipedia (a free encyclopaedia with a mission to 'contain the sum of all human knowledge'). Wikipedia in theory allows anyone with an Internet connection to make changes and contribute content. In practice, however, we see stark geographic and gendered inequalities (Graham, 2011; Lam et. al. 2011).

For instance, we know that there are more edits that originate in Hong Kong than the entire continent of Africa combined (Graham, 2012). Or if we look more closely at the Middle East and North Africa (see Figure 8.2: which is a map of contributions to all language versions of Wikipedia[3]), we can see similar measures of the uneven amount of participation from

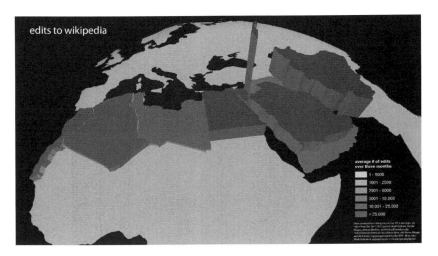

Figure 8.2 Edits to Wikipedia in the Middle East and North Africa
Source: Author.

different places. The map gives us a sense of how many Wikipedia edits come from Israel compared to other countries in the region. In other words, Israelis are far more active in creating/reproducing knowledge in one of the world's most used websites than their counterparts in the rest of the Middle East and North Africa. There are actually almost as many Wikipedia edits that come from Israel (215, 333) as from the rest of the entire region combined (254, 089).

Some of these informational absences undoubtedly come from disconnectivity and poor communications capabilities. Other absences also arise from informational fragmentation (e.g. in China and a handful of other countries, viable competing services exist to challenge global standards [Sina Weibo instead of Twitter, Baidu Baike instead of Wikipedia, etc.]) and censorship at either micro- (e.g. workplaces) or macro- (i.e. countries) levels.

But why should we care if London is covered by a denser cloud of information than Lagos? Why does it matter if some places are digitally mirrored by content that omits the voices of women, minorities, the oppressed, the invisible? Why do these augmentations really matter? The first part of this chapter attempted to expand on how these digital layers of cities both shape and are shaped by the material urban environment and the ways that we enact it. However, a brief anecdote from an interview that I conducted in 2012 might also help to ground the importance of informational absences and presences in a concrete example. As part of a research project that I run that looks into how altered communications capabilities are changing East Africa, I interviewed a travel agent in Nairobi, Kenya.

The travel agent was telling me how the faster internet that he now has allows him to offer more regional tours to nearby countries like Rwanda and Uganda. I then asked for more details about what this specifically meant. What is it that he is doing now that he couldn't do before? The answer was 'Googling many more things – faster – more efficiently'. But I pressed the issue, what did this mean? What information was Google giving him that allowed him to learn more about new places and offer them as destinations to his clients? Well, the answer was actually Wikipedia. Google would lead him to relevant Wikipedia articles, and he would read about national parks, adventure activities and a range of other sights and then relay that information to his customers. This may seem like a relatively trivial story. However, it succinctly illustrates how geographic representations don't just influence how we think about places, but also, in a very real sense, influence how we move through, interact with and enact place. In other words, there are real, material consequences for cities and places absent from digital representations.

Virtual presences

The lack of information about, or contributions from, many cities in the world is only one way that certain people and places can find themselves at relative disadvantages. The massive data shadows (i.e. geocoded information or digital representations of place) over many parts of the world can cause a few important problems of their own. As virtual layers of cities become ever more influential, there will be increasing needs and pressures to study, map and understand them; and because these virtual layers almost entirely exist in digital form, the data lend themselves more easily to certain types of analysis. In particular, this means that we are increasingly in an age of 'big data' in which samples, inferences, speculations and hypotheses are no longer necessary (Graham, 2012). The data shadows that we emit about so many social and economic activities can be harvested across entire countries and populations in a relatively easy manner. As such, services like Google's Flu Trends[4] and Mood of the Nation[5] are increasingly being set up to use 'big data' as a social/economic/political mirror. There is similarly a growing emphasis by global and globalizing cities on big data and data-based strategies for 'global' growth (a trend that means that people and organizations with data analysis and mapping capabilities will hold increasing sway over many allocations of resources).

However, as we increasingly come to rely on 'big data' shadows, there is a lot that can be lost. Having more data about any particular process or practice does not necessarily equate to having more insights. Large-scale analyses of large-scale datasets necessarily cause us to ask only certain types of questions and derive only certain sorts of answers. Geodemographics have, for instance, been used by financial institutions from the urban to the national scale for loan-scoring and credit-worthiness checks (e.g. Goss, 1995). In an era of 'big data', a lack of codified data can therefore mean lack of access to necessary financial resources. In other words, financial risk (among many other things) is intimately tied to codified and standardized information. Places with thin data shadows can therefore suffer from exclusion and barriers simply because of an absence of data rather than actual higher risk. The increasing reliance on 'big data' shadows can also start to self-reinforce the importance of those very shadows, with the viability of less automated methods of scoring and analysis (e.g. meetings, conversations) ever more undermined.

Irrespective of these absences, the simple presence of data itself can potentially also begin to have unanticipated consequences for cities. Not only are there ever-larger data shadows to urban environments, but much of that information is in the form of open and accessible data. Open data are undoubtedly a useful tool for accountability and civic responsibility, but they don't come without risks. If data are open and there are relatively transparent feedback mechanisms between those data and the allocation of resources, then we might expect citizens to begin to actively attempt to shape and manipulate those data (in other words, people will start to 'game the system'). This was observed on an online crime-reporting tool in Portsmouth, England, where citizens reported 136 crimes in order to demand stronger police presence (despite there being only two crimes on the street).

A very different example of the feedback mechanisms between digital geographic data and the city has been reported by Gibbons.[6] He noted that only a year after the unveiling of online street-level crime maps in the UK, 11 per cent of people had not reported a crime because of worries that recording crime would serve to lower house prices. What we are then seeing are changing relationships of signification. As our everyday urban experiences become increasing infused with and augmented by digital spatial information links between signifiers and their original signified concepts can quickly become lost and repurposed.[7] Another especially relevant concern in many of the world's most wired cities is the issue of privacy and a decreasing ability for networked urban citizens to expect anonymity. It has long been possible for state security agencies to piece together detailed pictures about all but the most reclusive of citizens by triangulating sources of information like mobile phone calls, credit card purchases and travel card journeys. However, private firms are now beginning to develop an equal amount of sophistication in the methods that they use to make inferences about urban inhabitants.

For instance, in mid-2011, a panicked user of the social news website Reddit posted the following message to fellow users[8]:

> So I've been planning on getting engaged and have been researching diamonds and rings online, before going out to buy the perfect ring. Only problem is Google has been watching and is now displaying adverts and commercials for diamond engagement rings on all the websites I visit!! I must have visited over a hundred diamond websites in the past 2 weeks while she has been away, so Google now thinks I just fucking love diamonds and can't get enough of that shit.

The replies to the user's post luckily allowed him to quickly change his privacy settings and dispel the incriminating advertisements. But this story points to a much more interesting (and potentially frightening) trend. Because of the significant data trails that many of us leave as we live in and move through urban environments, businesses can have an ever more powerful role in shaping and controlling global cities. Private firms are able to (fairly accurately) predict where we will be at any given moment, and what we will be doing, buying and looking at. This, in turn, allows much deeper and more intrusive targeting and the elimination of any semblance of anonymity. Apart from privacy issues, more accurate targeting and customization raise concerns that are addressed in the following section.

Ghettoization

Cities have never been stable, homogenous experiences. My experience of Manchester is unique, as is the urban experience of the other two million people who live there: we all inhabit the same geographic area, but ultimately encounter and enact very different cities. It might be assumed that the virtual dimension to cities allows people move away from the grounded and material nature of urban splintering (e.g. Graham and Marvin, 2001) to have more homogenous urban experiences due to the fact that we all access the same virtual representations. However, in many ways, accessing augmented digital information allows us to reify and reinforce the existing ways that we enact and understand cities. The rest of section discusses two important ways in which digital ghettoization can happen before turning to a case study that illustrates some of these processes in augmented reflections of Jerusalem.

Language is an obvious but crucially important way that different annotations and augmentations of the same place can be constructed. Representations and digital elements of cities can sometimes exist in hundreds of languages,[9] all of which highlight, describe, critique and order place in unique ways. A simple example from Bangkok can illustrate these very different linguistic shadows of place. In the maps below, Google Maps[10] was queried for content about Bangkok containing the words 'temple' or 'วัด' (temple in Thai). The size of the circles in each map indicate the amount of content that Google indexes about that particular part of the city (Figure 8.3).[11]

We can note that mapping references to 'temple' in English, unsurprisingly highlights high-profile tourist destinations. In contrast, Thai content highlights entirely different parts of the city. We see a focus on the Temple of Dawn and the many other temples on the eastern bank of the river. There are also clusters of content around the Golden Mount, Chinatown and the temples in Sathon (e.g. Wat Yan Nawa). Again these are locations in the city that are more likely to be known and frequented by Thais than foreigners. This case of temples, indexed by Google in Bangkok, doesn't tell us much about temples or Bangkok; but it does illustrate how fundamentally different virtual layers of the same city exist for English and Thai speakers.

Another important way that digitally augmented information can lead to a ghettoization of urban experiences is through what Eli Pariser (2011) has termed 'filter bubbles'. An example of this is a conspiracy theorist searching for information on the Internet and then only receiving content that supports rather than challenges his or her views. Graham and Zook (2013) have then built on Pariser's ideas and applied them to a spatial context. They argue that 'a combination of the rhetoric of coded objectivity of algorithmically ranked maps, alongside active targeting, and customization of search brings into being a representation of the world which reinforces much of what is already believed, serving to reinforce Pariser's filter bubbles. Geocoded content is thus increasingly fragmented into individualized representations that ultimately enable the construction of self-reinforcing information cocoons' (Graham and Zook, 2013, 41).

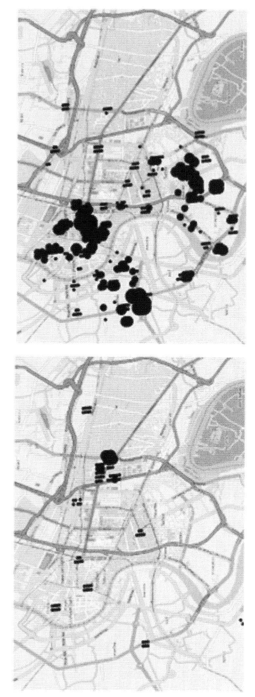

Figure 8.3 References to 'temple' in English (left) and Thai (right) in Bangkok
Source: Author.

In early 2012, Microsoft made headlines with a patent that proposed offer tailored and selective representations of cities available to users of one of its apps. The app, which later was dubbed the 'avoid ghetto' app, was tailored to allow pedestrians to avoid certain 'undesirable' parts of cities. The proposal attracted much criticism, but illustrates just one of the ways that as personal data shadows become more encompassing and code becomes more sophisticated, the virtual dimensions of cities can become increasingly tailored and personalized.

Does it matter that different representations of a city are being produced and reproduced for different people? Urban inhabitants are accessing not just bubbles of filtered information, but also information on fundamentally different cities. Balkanized bubbles of augmented urban information have the potential to reinforce real, material, balkanized spaces. As a result, we need to ensure that urban research maintains a focus on mapping and theorizing how the fluid and sometimes fleeting representations that exist on the internet might reinforce balkanized hermetically sealed imagined spaces.

Ephemeral cities

Not only do the virtual layers of cities help us to enact fundamentally different places, but they also underscore the ephemerality of places. Doreen Massey (2005) argued that places (or bundles of space-time trajectories) are necessarily ephemeral temporary constellations. In other words, cities never were and never will be fixed and static entities. However, because of the increasingly hybrid material/digital nature of urban environments we now see a much more rapid reconfiguring of the raw materials of cities than ever before. Almost every platform and repository of digital geospatial information is characterized by some degree of informational flux, but it is in information search that we can observe the unfixity of information at its most powerful. We see the increasing relevance of local search through the battles that are played out in order to be listed on the first page of results for search terms, the multi-billion-dollar industries of search advertising and search engine optimization, the fact that the utility of large directories of information has long since faded, and the fact that many urban inhabitants now access and find local services through searches on mobile phones and local mapping services. Search engines and practices of local digital search thus play a central role in the ways in which much of the world accesses, enacts and brings into being specific types of information.

This local information, as mediated through search engines (a simple example of this would be a local search for a bicycle mechanic or public swimming pool), has become unfixed and destabilized. First, every search relies on a vast 'ecosystem' of networked information that is both created and ordered by a crowd of contributors. The incessant online activity of millions of people means that not only is content itself constantly changing, but so are the preferences that feed into rankings that separate the visible from the invisible. A related implication is that large global cities covered by 'thick' layers of content will likely also be the places that are also characterized by the most significant amount of informational ephemerality. Second, the sorting algorithms that mediate the enormous amount of crowd-sourced content have become spatially, socially and temporally unfixed. Information accessed through search engines is thus de-centred and destabilized. In other words, answers that search engines provide to our questions vary substantially based on our social, spatial and temporal positionalities. Furthermore, each time that we are presented with (and influenced by) temporally, socially and geographically targeted content, created and filtered by a crowd of millions, we reinforce the power of that content. The ephemerality of urban information ultimately means that it becomes increasingly difficult for different people discover authorial intent and to share bundles of space-time trajectories. Customization, targeting, rapidly switching networks and the temporal unfixity of information all increase the difficulty of talking about what is 'at' any particular place. Yet, it remains important to do just that, and understand how particular places are represented and brought into being.

The digital layers of Jerusalem

Before concluding this chapter, it will be useful to ground some of these discussions about the coming together of code, content and the city with a case study of one particularly contested place: the city of Jerusalem. Jerusalem is a city that is home to about 800,000 people. It is a holy city to Christians, Jews and Muslims and is therefore ascribed with particular importance by adherents of all of those religions. Western neighbourhoods of Jerusalem are primarily populated by Jews and have been under Israeli rule since the 1948 Arab-Israeli War. East Jerusalem, by contrast, has been administered under Israeli rule since 1967. It is home to 98 per cent of the Muslim population of Jerusalem and is home to 261,000 Muslims and 196,000 Jews (Chosen and Korach, 2010). Importantly, despite formal control over East Jerusalem by Israel, the city is the desired location for any future Palestinian state.

As mentioned earlier in this chapter, the city also exists in 162 languages in Wikipedia. These layers of the city form part of the palimpsests, augmented realities, code/spaces and digiplaces of the city. Each of the 162 descriptions is also created by a different set of editors (although there are undoubtedly overlapping contributions from some multilingual authors) with a different audience in mind (i.e. the authors of the Jerusalem article in the Estonian Wikipedia would likely expect most readers to be Estonian). The net result of this activity is 162 articles, each substantially differing from the other. None are direct translations from another version, and all significantly or slightly choose to represent the city of Jerusalem in different ways.

It is instructive to examine three of the most relevant versions to the populations of the city: the Arabic and Hebrew versions because of the significant Arab and Jewish populations of Jerusalem, and the English version because of the visibility and widespread repurposing of content in English on the Internet (as well as the fact that many Palestinian Arabs and Israeli Jews are fluent in English and can therefore participate in the editing of the English version of the article in Wikipedia). Translations[12] of the introductions to the three language versions (from the versions that were publicly available on 17 July 2012) are given below. It is worth noting that all three editions of Wikipedia share the same commitment to a 'neutral point of view' as a core principle upon which all articles must be based.[13]

Arabic version

Al-Quds (in Hebrew: Yerushalim) is the biggest city in Historical Palestine in terms of area and number of residents, and the most important one religiously and economically. In the Arabic language it is known in other names, such as Beit al-Maqdis, Noble Al-Quds and the First Qibla. Israel names it officially Urshalim al-Quds (in Hebrew: Yerushalayim al-Quds).

The Arabs and the Palestinians consider it the capital of the future State of Palestinian as given in the Palestinian Declaration of Independence that took place in Algiers on 15 November 1988 (for their historical ancestors, the Jebusites, were the first who built the city and resided in it until the 5th millennium BC), whereas Israel considers it its united capital, following its annexation of the city's eastern part in 1980, which it occupied after the 1967 War (the Jews consider it their religious and national capital for more than 3000 years). The UN and the international community do not recognize Al-Quds as the capital of Israel and consider East Al-Quds part of the Palestinian Territories, and do not recognize its annexation to the Hebrew State with some exceptions. Al-Quds is situated within the range of the Hebron Mountains, in the center of the region that lies between the Mediterranean and the western edge of the Dead Sea. This city grew and expanded its boundaries greatly compared with previous eras.

Al-Quds is considered holy to the followers of the three Monotheistic faiths: Judaism, Christianity and Islam. For the Jews, it became the holiest site after Prophet and King David conquered it and turned it into the capital of the United Israelite Kingdom around 1000 BC. Then, his son Solomon went on to build the First Temple in it, according to the Biblical text. For Christians, the city has become a sacred site following the crucifixion of Jesus Christ on one of its hills, called Golgotha, around 30 AD, and after Saint Helena found the cross on which He had been hanged inside the city after about 300 years, according to the New Testament. As for the Muslims, Al-Quds is the third holiest city after Mecca and

Al-Medina, and it is the first qibla, for the Muslims turned their faces to it during their prayer, after receiving this commandment around 610 AD. It also represents the place from which the prophet of Islam, Muhammad Ibn Abdullah ascended to heaven, according to the Islamic doctrine. As a result of this high religious importance, the Old City is home to many religious sites of great importance, such as, the Church of Resurrection, Al-Buraq Wall and Al-Aqsa Mosque. This is despite its area of 0.9 square kilometers (0.35 square miles).

Here, the first paragraph clearly places Jerusalem within Palestine (rather than Israel). The rest of the introduction makes it clear that the city and its governance are highly contested both by many of the city's inhabitants and by the international community. The remainder of the section then stresses the unique nature and the enormous religious significance of the city itself.

Hebrew version

Yerushalayim is the capital city of the State of Israel and the biggest city of Israel. The governmental institutes of Israel are situated in Yerushalayim: the Knesset, the Supreme Court, the presidential residence and the premier's residence.

The city's name in English, French and German is Jerusalem. In Arabic it is Al-Quds or Urshalim. In Modern Greek Ιεροσόλυμα. In Spanish Jerusalén. In Italian Gerusalemme. In Russian Иерусалим. Yerushalayim is situated on the Judean Mountains on the water divide of the Western Land of Israel, between the Mediterranean and the Dead Sea at a height of 570 to 857 meters above sea level.

The city is sacred to Judaism, Christianity and Islam, the monotheistic faiths, and it was the center of the Jewish People's life in ancient times and its object of yearning while it was in exile. Being a center in the world of the believers, the city was a focus of wars and conflicts that continue to this very day. Since the end of the 19th century, the New City's neighborhoods developed around the Old City, and they constitute today the overwhelming majority of the city. At the center of the complete city stands the Temple Mount which separates West Yerushalayim from East Yerushalayim.

In 1981, the Old City of Yerushalayim was declared a World Heritage Site by the UN-affiliated UNESCO, and it is in the list of endangered sites.

The Hebrew version of the article interestingly presents a very different representation of Jerusalem. The city is clearly defined as being the capital of the State of Israel. It is again unambiguously presented as being within Israel with text that states that it is Israel's largest city. In fact, the heavily contested nature of the city is barely mentioned in the introduction (nor is the fact that the city is the desired capital of a future Palestinian state). It is also worth noting that while the Hebrew article uses an article template dedicated to Israeli localities, the Arabic article uses a general city template, in which the country is listed as 'Historical Palestine', and two mayors are mentioned – the Palestinian-appointed mayor and the Israeli-appointed (and de facto) mayor.

English version

Jerusalem . . . is the capital of Israel, though not internationally recognized as such, and one of the oldest cities in the world. It is located in the Judean Mountains, between the Mediterranean Sea and the northern edge of the Dead Sea. If the area and population of East Jerusalem is included, it is Israel's largest city in both population and area, with a population of 801,000 residents over an area of 125.1 km2 (48.3 sq mi). Jerusalem is also a holy city to the three major Abrahamic religions – Judaism, Christianity and Islam.

During its long history, Jerusalem has been destroyed twice, besieged 23 times, attacked 52 times, and captured and recaptured 44 times. The oldest part of the city was settled in the 4th millennium BCE. In 1538, walls were built around Jerusalem under Suleiman the Magnificent. Today those walls define the Old City, which has been traditionally divided into four quarters – known since the early 19th century as the Armenian, Christian, Jewish, and Muslim Quarters. The Old City became a World Heritage site in 1981, and is on the List of World Heritage in Danger. Modern Jerusalem has grown far beyond its boundaries.

The English version offers yet another interpretation of place. This time, Jerusalem is presented as the capital of Israel, but its disputed nature is clearly highlighted. Many Palestinians might, however, take issue with the fact that mentions of Palestine are absent from the introduction. It is the English version that is also the site of a particularly heated disagreement about how best to cartographically represent the city. The first map that I could find in the history of the Jerusalem article[14] appeared in July 2008 and is displayed below in Figure 8.4. The map's use of colour distinguishes between Israel and the West Bank and Gaza Strip (Israel being a lighter shade and the Palestinian territories being a darker shade that is identical to the colour used for the foreign territories of Jordan and Egypt). In July 2009, this map had been replaced by the image in Figure 8.5.

This simplified inset map conforms to the standard of inset maps in many other Wikipedia articles about cities. It is worth noting that the Palestinian territories are no longer depicted in the same colour used for

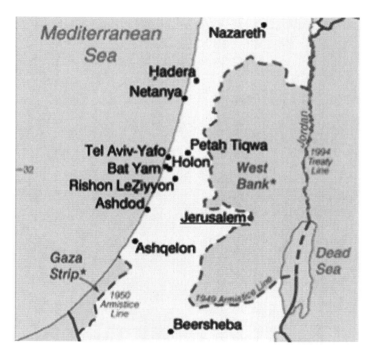

Figure 8.4 Inset map in the Jerusalem Wikipedia article in July 2008
Source: http://en.wikipedia.org/wiki/File:Jerusalem_Israel_Map.png.

foreign countries. However, it remains that the visual effect of the map still serves to place Jerusalem within Israel rather than the Palestinian territories due to the yellow tone used for the shape of Israel.

The image was briefly replaced with a close-up of the city as a way to resolve the dilemma, but in September 2011 was reverted to Figure 8.5 with the following comment[15]: 'changed location map to Israel instead of Jerusalem, to make it more clear where Jerusalem is (because adding a location map of Jerusalem itself to demonstrate Jerusalem's location is not useful)'.

Further revisions then appeared in 2011, which reversed the way that the Palestinian Territories had been de-emphasized on previous map. Figure 8.6, for instance, draws the Palestinian Territories as a more highlighted part of the map. Jerusalem, however, still appears to fall entirely within the Israeli part of the map. This issue is then resolved in the current (at the time of writing) map in Figure 8.7. Here, the urban form of the city is unambiguously spread across two political boundaries.

The disagreements about how best to represent the geographic location of Jerusalem can be seen most vividly on the article's 'talk pages'

Figure 8.5 Inset map in the Jerusalem Wikipedia article in July 2009
Source: http://en.wikipedia.org/wiki/File:Israel_location_map.svg_

(en.wikipedia.org/wiki/Talk:Jerusalem). On those pages, some users passion-ately argued for the use of maps that clearly depict Jerusalem as being an Israeli city. Others assert the need for cartographic depictions that either highlight the fundamentally contested nature of the city,[16] or the fact that it is also considered to be a Palestinian city. While consensus is preferred in disagreements on Wikipedia, conflicts also tend to have winners and losers.

The case of Jerusalem highlighted not just the ways that the same city can have very different digital shadows for different communities of people, but also the complex processes of negotiation that define our urban environments. Although the disagreements about maps in Jerusalem seem to have settled on a particular spatial representation that is potentially

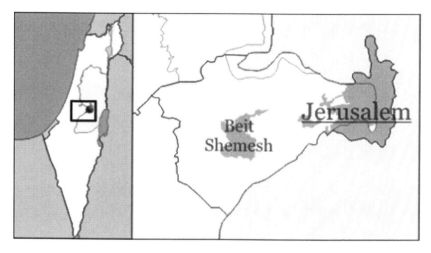

Figure 8.6   Inset map in the Jerusalem Wikipedia article in 2011
Source: http://en.wikipedia.org/wiki/File:Jerusalem1map.png.

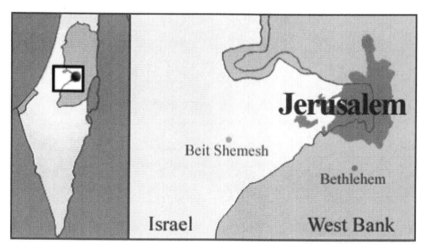

Figure 8.7   Inset map in the Jerusalem Wikipedia article in 2012
Source: http://en.wikipedia.org/wiki/File:Jerusalem_WBIL.jpg.

acceptable to a significant number of Wikipedia editors, there are countless other places and processes less subject to such an intense public gaze.
Potential disagreements derive not from objectively false information about
a place needing to be replaced by objectively true information, but rather
because of multiple, conflicting truths. In other words, the digital layers and

augmentations of cities are inherently socially constructed and subject to the uneven geographies of power and voice that characterize contemporary societies.

Conclusions

The complex ways in which digital content is fixed, ordered, stabilized and contested fundamentally change how we augment, enact and bring our cities into being. Cities are now layered with digital information and lines of code that are both unevenly distributed and power-laden. Our urban experiences, interactions and understandings are increasingly mediated through the ways in which digital content and code are brought together, fixed, ordered, stabilized and contested, and the virtual palimpsests that now form an integral part of our cities are likewise influenced by older, offline patterns and processes of voice, representation and power.

Visibility and voice in the urban environment thus have both material and virtual components. In many ways this can provide space for resistance to entrenched and uneven power relationships. The possibilities afforded by digital tools and technologies allow for transparency and accountability and even new types of protest, repurposing and occupying. But, ultimately, we need to ask who gets to represent people and places and who doesn't, which parts of the world are over- and under-represented, what types of content and information are more and less likely to be visible in digital representations, how does the blending of code and content shape our everyday life, what are some of the hidden dimensions/power relations in how we use digital tools and information, how do personal and social positionalities play into issues of voice and representation online, what does it mean to 'volunteer' information/labour, what is the role of the state in regulating digital information and representations, what are the potentials for social justice in the digital realm and what domains of contemporary life have been left relatively untouched by digital code and content? The answer to many of these questions, unfortunately, seems to be that the digital layers of cities can also simply reinforce the fragmented and splintered urbanisms that characterize global cities and further exclude and marginalize those that are already disempowered. In other words, the virtual layers of urban environments do not seem to allow for a wholesale bypassing of concentrations of power that exist between and within cities, and are by no means a panacea to any of the most significant problems faced by cities around the world.

Does this mean that we will see a path-dependence of the powerful enacted and re-enacted? Does this mean that digital democracy (or the tyranny of the majority) will quite literally crowd out certain opinions, voices and content? More concerning is the fact that in a destabilized and de-centred cloud of information, there are few ways to gaze through the opacity built into the system. How do we then map and measure, study and critique these increasingly ephemeral tools that so many of us rely on for our informational needs? Perhaps most importantly, who stands to benefit and who stands to lose, which voices will be loudest and which will be silenced in an informational ecosystem of ephemeral content? The answers to these questions are, in many cases, still unclear, but we can attempt to answer them with algorithmic archaeology, sustained critical inquiry into the geography of information, and by keeping a focus on the complex and often opaque virtual informational layers of cities.

Notes

1. This phrase was coined by William Gibson in his 2008 novel *Spook Country*.
2. The notion of 'place' in this chapter is not an allusion to Agnew's (1987) fixed and territorialized vision of 'locale'. Recognition of the blended and layered ways in which the digital and the material layers of cities are experienced and enacted is rather an extension of work in geography that recognizes the fundamentally relational natures of place (e.g. de Souza e Silva, 2006; Nicholls, 2009). Pierce et al. (2011, 54), for instance, remind us that place-making is an 'inherently networked process, constituted by the socio-spatial relationships that link individuals together through a common place-frame'.
3. In order to make the map, quarterly data about the total number of edits to emerge from any territory (i.e. the amount of content that people are producing in each country) were taken and averaged over a two-year period (2010–1).
4. This service is able to harvest Google searches on flu related topics (e.g. 'fever', 'sneezing') and predict the geographic spread of flu faster (by two weeks) than the best Centres for Disease Control and Prevention estimates.
5. Mood of the Nation (http://geopatterns.enm.bris.ac.uk/mood) is a tool that uses geolocated tweets and sentiment analysis to compare different regions of the UK on four types of emotion (anger, fear, joy and sadness).
6. See Steve Gibbons' blog 'Crime Nudge' (2011) available at http://spatial-economics.blogspot.co.uk/2011/07/crime-nudge.html.
7. The Internet is littered with examples of very rapid repurposing of ideas and signs in ways that lose the original signifier–signified links. One famous example of this comes from the coming together of the 2010 Vancouver Winter Olympics and the 'pedobear' Internet meme ('pedobear' is a meme popularized by the 4chan image-board. The 'pedobear' image represents a pedophilic bear used for humorous purposes and often employed to mock (human) pedophiles. In 2010, a Canadian artist decided to edit the image of 'pedobear' into a photograph of Vancouver Olympic mascots (many of which look surprisingly similar to 'pedobear') and upload the image to his blog. The image was then indexed by Google and subsequently found by journalists around the world seeking a quick image for a Vancouver 2010 story in their papers. A handful of newspapers and magazines around the world then used the altered version of the Winter Olympics mascots in their stories instead of the original.
8. The conversation is available at: http://www.reddit.com/r/AskReddit/comments/j7lw6/google_is_about_to_ruin_my_engagement_surprise/.
9. The Wikipedia article about Jerusalem, for instance, exists in 162 languages.

10. It is important to point out that many groups of people also simply use different platforms from one another (e.g. Europeans are more likely to use Twitter and Chinese are more likely to use Sina Weibo for short messages). However, the purpose of focusing on just one platform (i.e. Google) here is to point out that even within the shared sources that we use, very different augmentations of place can happen for different people.

11. See Graham and Zook (2013) for a more detailed discussion of the methods employed to generate these results.

12. These translations were all kindly carried out by Dror Kamir. Many of the insights in this section of the chapter also come from email conversations and a content on Kamir's blog: http://anduraru.wordpress.com/2010/09/13/exploring-basic-bias-on-wikipedia/.

13. The 'neutral point of view' policy furthermore stipulates that 'the principles upon which this policy is based cannot be superseded by other policies or guidelines, or by editors' consensus' http://en.wikipedia.org/wiki/Wikipedia:Neutral_point_of_view.

14. The following discussion of inset maps refers entirely to the English version of the article rather than the Arabic or Hebrew versions.

15. http://en.wikipedia.org/w/index.php?title=Jerusalem&limit=5000&action=history.

16. Interestingly, the city boundaries in Figures 8.6 and 8.7 are the post-war boundaries set by Israel in June 1967 and encompass some Palestinian towns that were not previously considered to be part of the city of Jerusalem.

9
The Cultural Dimension

Oli Mould

Introduction

As Raymond Williams argued, 'culture is one of the two or three most complicated words in the English language' (Williams, 1985, 87), and I would argue that perhaps 'city' is one of the other words. Therefore, to attempt to describe the relationship between culture and the city is to open a Pandora's box of experiences, emotions, practices, places, memories and moments. From the theatre districts of Broadway in New York and the West End in London, via the mosques of Istanbul to the subcultural activities of graffiti artists or underground raves in Shanghai, culture has a very intangible, tacit and complex affiliation with urbanity. From Saskia Sassen's original articulation of global cities, academic literature has focused almost exclusively on the political economic functions of these cities, and how they exert hegemonic power *globally*. The work of the Globalization and World Cities (GaWC) group based at Loughborough University in the UK, under the directorship of Peter Taylor (see Taylor, 2004b), has also done much to forward the rhetoric of global cities as existing within, and the creators of, a worldwide network of advanced producer service (APS) firms, which are often used as a means to quantify how 'global' a global city is. In counterbalance to this, critiques of the global (and world) city concept have focused on how there is a Global North bias to those cities which are considered 'Global', with other cities being framed in the 'development' debate (Robinson, 2002; Watson, this collection). Ancien (2011) also finds there to be a lack of political engagement in the current global city concept that can devalue its analytical functionality. While these are valid critiques, this chapter will focus on another concept that is also lacking from current thinking within global city literature, namely that which deals with the amorphous and complex issue of culture.

There has been a notable shift in the 'variables' used in global city measurement to include cultural factors, which have splintered into a number of different themes. For example, there is now the use of cultural industries as a means of assessing cities in a global hierarchy. The works of Krätke (2003) and Watson and Hoyler (2010) have expanded the weaponry of global city measurement (beyond APS firms) to include media, creative and cultural industry indicators. Culture in an urban context can also refer to major (or 'mega') events, such as the Rio Carnival or the Olympic Games, as well as smaller film or literary festivals. Also, often the heritage of a city is celebrated. Culture has also been used as a 'source-ground' around issues of social justice and economic growth (Miles and Paddison, 2005, 833). However, it is perhaps the work of Richard Florida (2002, 2005) that has done the most to alert urban policy makers to the importance of culture to a city's *economic* prosperity. The drive to attract the so-called 'creative class' has had many cities around the world initiating large cultural projects to boost their city's provisioning of the arts and culture, which are viewed as what the creative class looks for when decided where to live. However, there are many critiques of such policies, suggesting that they are the latest iteration of neoliberal urban renewal strategies, and as such continue to proliferate the social inequalities associated with them (for the most vehement of such critiques see Peck, 2005, 2011). As such, culture while utilized in part to contribute to the global city paradigm (in that it is used to ameliorate city competitiveness internationally) is still an inherently political economic tool, as it is often used by many cities as a means to an economic developmental end.

To describe this process, the chapter will be in three main parts. The first will detail how 'culture' has infiltrated the global city concept, but has been, in a sense, 'hijacked' by urban entrepreneurial strategies that seek to utilize the rhetoric of culture for the purposes of infrastructural development and economic growth. It will do so through the 'top down' examples of such developments, namely cultural quarters and media cities, which are two urban initiatives that involve developing large areas of city for cultural and creative industry infrastructure. The second part of the chapter will then go on to describe other forms of cultural activity that are not 'sown up' in the global city concept, at least not in a formal sense. Subcultural activities and urban subversions are proliferating in cities all over the world (Daskalaki and Mould, 2013), and can embody distinct cultural empowerment of particular citizens, but can also be used as a further 'bottom up' tool of global city development and capitalist appropriation. The third part of this chapter will outline how these issues of the schisms between the concepts of culture and the global city play out in Copenhagen, Denmark.

Culture 'from above'

Ever since Saskia Sassen wrote the book *Global City* in 1991 (revised in 2001), the term has infiltrated much of social science and humanities literature, and has become a buzzword in urban policy realms. It is difficult to avoid in the mainstream media and advertising material for cities around the world. Leafing through glossy promotional magazines on an international flight, or thumbing through a city hotel's in-house local events pamphlet, the term 'global city' is often used in reference to the multitude of cultural provisions on offer, from Asian fusion cuisine to African film nights. However, despite the term being used to showcase the cultural diversity of a city, Sassen's original meaning of a global city was one of financial and economic might (see Parnreiter, this collection for a comprehensive historiography of the term); global cities are those which command and control the global economy. She argued that:

> ...these cities now function in four new ways: first, as highly concentrated command points in the organisation of the world economy; second, as key locations for finance and for specialised service firms...; third, as sites of production...; and fourth, as markets for the products and innovations produced.
>
> (Sassen, 2001, 3)

Through the agglomeration of APS firms, certain cities (she identified London, New York and Tokyo as the triumvirate of contemporary global cities) have influence on the flow of finance, goods and labour through the world. Headquarters of major banks, insurance firms, management consultancies, accountancy and advertising firms (collectivized as APS firms) all have high-level offices residing in these global cities. As such, the key decisions about the location of global capital (financial and human) are made in these locales (Derudder et al., this collection). The work of GaWC built upon this idea and through intense research on the world's largest APS firms, devising a ranking of cities based on their 'networked-ness' within the world economy. The delineation of particular cities into 'alpha', 'beta' and 'gamma' cities (the classification chosen to mirror that used for celestial stars, as it was a 'universe of cities') was a groundbreaking methodological moment. It soon infiltrated public urban policy and gradually city governments all over the world became fixated on where they were placed in the rankings, and what they needed to do in order to climb them (Giffinger et al., 2011). The systematic reproduction of these rankings over the last two decades, and the countless other bodies concocting ranking of their own, ossified the urban government disposition to enact policies to aid the ascension of these rankings. Being at the top brought with it a sense of gravitas that your particular city was a global city, and hence part of the elite group of cities that, according to the theories, 'commanded' the world economy.

Given the recent financial crisis, is it perhaps questionable to argue that the global economy is, or has ever been 'controlled and commanded', yet the concept of the global city as a concentration of financial strength persists. And in an attempt to become a global city, urban governments jostle with each other to attract the headquarters and regional offices of major APS firms. Since the turn of the century, however, there has been a shift in gaze of city officials from attracting firms headquarters to attracting people, more specifically, the creative class. Richard Florida's hugely popular book *The Rise of the Creative Class* published in 2002 outlined that in fact, rather than people following jobs, it was the jobs that were following people. In other words, global firms will be attracted to cities that had a creative and talented workforce. This controversial narrative is not without its critics, yet the governance structures in many (mainly Western) cities saw this as a way of stimulating their economies, the majority of which had been in recession due to global financial crisis. Florida's book, and his numerous accompanying speaking engagements, encouraged cities to focus on attracting the creative class, and to do so a city needed a provision of culture, tolerance and diversity. The nature of Florida's methodologies and the numerous indexes he creates in order to rank a city's ability to attract creative people are highly debated. The critiques are multifaceted, but the important critique for this chapter is the one that focuses on how cities are taking the essence of Florida's theories and using it to justify vast amounts of investment in urban renewal projects. Such projects are predicated on seemingly 'fuzzy' concepts of liveability, creativity and innovation (Markusen, 2006), without any consideration of the broader cultural issues of social inclusivity (Miles and Padisson, 2005). Peck (2011, 482, emphasis added), when referring to Amsterdam's uptake of creativity policies, argued that

> At the same time that creativity constitutes a soft hegemonic veneer, an overarching metanarrative, that in Amsterdam holds together a disparate assemblage of economic, *cultural* and housing initiatives, it is also a uniquely slippery and interstitial formulation, one that exists in the cracks between extant policy fields, connecting them in new ways, opening up new spaces of synergy in the (under-resourced but over-mandated) sphere of urban governance.

As such, the development of culture in cities is ideologically yoked to the attraction of human capital (and the financial rewards this theoretically reaps). So culture within urban policy necessarily entails a narrow focus on the provision of cultural assets, rather than focusing on culture as a much broader community and social good (Castells, 1983). New art galleries, museums, theatres, even sports stadiums have been built with the mindset of improving a city's cultural provisioning and thereby being a more attractive place for the creative class to live (Evans, 2009). Through the prism of 'attracting creativity', major infrastructural developments are being undertaken, often under public–private partnership initiatives. Some cities have been successful (the so-called 'Barcelona model' (e.g. Degan and

García, 2012) has been heralded as a success as it involved issues of social cohesion as well as economic growth), while others have been critiqued for using culture as a guise for standard infrastructural and economic development, or 'soft' marketing and public relations purposes (Hansen et al., 2001; Peck, 2011).

Along with Barcelona, the development of the Guggenheim museum in Bilbao in 1997 is often depicted as an iconic example of how a specific arts and culture development (rather than a city-wide policy change) has been used for regenerative purposes: the so-called 'Guggenheim effect' (Scott, 2006; Plaza et al., 2009). Other cultural-led regeneration activities around Europe developed in parallel with Bilbao, perhaps spurred on by the recorded success in boosting tourism and economic vitality to the area. In the UK, for example, the late 1980s and early 1990s saw the development of what later became known as 'cultural quarters' (CQs). The premise of a CQ is now firmly entrenched into urban policy in the Global North (particularly in the UK and Western Europe) and involves an area of a city given over to 'arts and culture', in the broadest definition possible. Often in collaboration with real estate contractors and urban consultant specialists, urban governments identify an area of the city that is in need of development and engage upon a systematic 'rebranding' process around the premise of culture. This may often involve building a large anchor institution such as a modern art gallery (as in Bilbao), a theatre, museum, cinema or other cultural premises. Often designed by an iconic architect in a unique and striking style, these anchor institutions are seen as a catalyst for nearby development, in the hope it will stimulate cultural production and consumption activity to proliferate (Evans, 2005). Other CQs will be smaller in scale, offering boutique production spaces for cultural industry companies, such as exhibition spaces, rehearsal and recording studios, art-house cinema combined with consumption facilities (Brown et al., 2000).

Many cities throughout Europe (in the UK alone there are over 35 designated CQs) are developing CQs based on this specific formula. The economic success of Bilbao and the proliferation of CQs around the world have created a 'best fit' model (Montgomery, 2007) that spreads from city to city and across national borders. This prescription for a successful CQ is reminiscent of what McCarthy (2005, 297) calls the 'serial replication' of CQ across the UK and Europe, in which different local city governments implement policy models they have seen to be successful in other cities. And now, as different cities compete for human capital under the rubric of the 'creative class' these CQs become important areas in the perceived attractiveness of a city. As such, they have become inherently sown into the global city discourse. The international success of cultural regeneration mediators and global urban consultants (Evans, 2005) has catalysed the proliferation of these CQs and contributed to the 'creative policy fix' that is creating an 'isomorphic network of creative urbanism' (Peck, 2011, 21).

If CQs represent a physical and infrastructural appropriation of the 'network of creative urbanism', then so too do 'media cities'; although with perhaps a more 'traditional' political economy. Recently, some local urban governments have been providing a focused and pragmatic cultural policy that centres on the cultural and creative industries, manifesting in a purpose built cluster of cultural and creative industry activity. Media Cities then, as they have become known, are being constructed around the world. So far, notable media cities can be found in Dubai, Salford in Greater Manchester, Brooklyn in New York, Abu Dhabi, Seoul and Copenhagen (more of which will be discussed later in the chapter). City councils, often led by private real estate and investment interests, are offering large swaths of their city as potential sites of massive redevelopment. Many cities already had recognizable clusters of cultural and creative industry activity mainly due to incumbent businesses recognizing the value of agglomeration and assimilating a cluster over time (Scott, 2006). However, these media cities are often large-scale, meta-planned, hi-tech media industry provisions designed to attract international companies. Goldsmith and O'Regan (2003, 33) note that the media city has been 'recast as a form of commercial property/industrial park development' which has a primary goal of attracting international business. As such media cities are perhaps the latest iteration of the 'high-tech fantasies' that proliferated in the 1980s and 1990s (Massey et al., 1992). They are often privately owned, and therefore tightly securitized, have on-site luxury residential accommodation and have auxiliary cultural amenities. The role of media cities for the urban governments that build them is to attract large, global media and creative industry firms, and the economic benefits that they offer. As such, while they are providing assets that are designed to attract the creative class, their primary goal is to attract the firms in the first instance (thereby running counter to a core Floridian ideal).

So while pushed through urban policy processes under the rubric of cultural development and attracting the creative class, CQs and media cities have underlying gentrifying characteristics that adhere to the global city paradigm in that they prioritize those developments that will bring about economic prosperity. This is not to defenestrate the role of culture in these developments completely; however, to take a broader view of culture that includes social justice (akin to the Barcelona model) then it could be argued that for CQs and media cities, at best, there is a distinct lack of cultural and social engagement, and at worse, they actually increase social inequalities in the locales (Christophers, 2008).

Culture 'from below'

The global city's use of culture, as has been detailed so far, is as a means to an economic end. This is perhaps unsurprising, given that the paradigm of the global city itself was theoretically tailored to a political economic discourse in the first instance. But the debates within the literature hence and its diffusion into public policy, particularly surrounding the integration of cultural issues into the global city, have progressed at a funereal pace when it comes to those cultural activities that lie 'outside' the narrow capitalist-inflected definition. In other words, culture within the global city paradigm has so far been limited to what it can achieve for economic and political development. This lack of academic attention to other thematic dimensions of global city status is not limited to culture, however broadly defined. As other chapters in this edition point out, there is a myriad of other ideologies that remain conspicuous by their absence in mainstream urban policy studies. However, the rubric of culture has been so widely co-opted by economic forces that culture in the global city paradigm often gets lost to a consumption/production nexus (Scott, 1997, 2006; Pratt, 2008). A reading of culture that lies beyond such an ethos is often couched in community, subcultural, activist and/or social justice issues. Culture when not an immediate commodity to be packaged and consumed is often posited against, or at least at odds with a global city paradigm and the economic development, gentrification and social inequalities that that can entail (Jacobs, 1969; Castells, 1983; Harvey, 2003a; Marcuse, 2009). Without delving into the complexities and nuances of the 'Right to the City' debate (which extend far beyond the remit of this chapter), in these instances, activist and/or 'grassroots' movements of urban action that are seen as having a strictly urban culture (such as the recent Occupy movements in a number of global cities across the world) are vehemently opposed to the processes of the global city (financialization, gentrification, commercialization of cultural goods, etc.). So in this respect, these cultural activities are somehow 'outside' (perhaps a more suitable spatial metaphor in this case is 'below') the global city.

Urban subcultural studies too can often imply anti-hegemonic city rhetoric (Pinder, 2005), with one discourse involving the practice of urban subcultures that re-appropriate the urban environment for their own creative and cultural desires (Daskalaki and Mould, 2013). Culture in these instances is manifest (or articulated) by a shared system of experiences, emotions and beliefs within a group of people practicing a similar 'art'. Stemming from and drawing upon the philosophies of the work of The Situationists (and the writings of their main protagonist Guy Debord) in the 19050s and 1960s, many urban subcultural activities are concerned with creative and often playful interjection with the urban environment. Pinder (2005, 150) noted how

> Through playful practices, he [Debord] and his colleagues intended to extend the nonmediocre part of life, to reduce the empty moments of life as much as possible and to enhance the freedoms of cities .... In this way a ludic spirit ran through ... early situationist engagements with

urban space. The groups' practices also had an agonistic dimension, through their critical and oppositional approach to existing norms and socio-spatial relations.

The work of the Situationists has heavily influenced the study of urban subcultures. And given how the re-appropriation of urban space is conducted playfully and creatively, these processes are very much part of the cultural articulations of contemporary urban subcultures. Take parkour for example, which has become an immensely popular subcultural pastime in cities throughout the world. While the definition of parkour has been debated in terms of its meanings, from a purely practical perspective, it involves people (usually able-bodied, male and in very good physical condition) who run, jump, roll, somersault, climb and generally interact corporeally with urban (and peri-urban) environments (Mould, 2009). Numerous parkour studies have commented on the shared belief system by traceurs (people who practice parkour) and how the act is extremely creative and immersive in the urban environment (Saville, 2008; Mould, 2009; Sharpe, 2012). It has a clear commercial appeal to filmmakers and advertisers due to its spectacular corporeality, but despite the global proliferation of parkour (catalysed by online viral videos), it has maintained its community and subcultural characteristics. Although financial reward is a clear motivation for some (and in these cases, they clearly add to the Floiridan style of urban cultural development), the majority of traceurs continue to participate in this culture for more social and emotional reasons (Gilchrist and Wheaton, 2011).

The presence of a parkour community is not a prerequisite of being a global city; there will be very few city governments who *prioritize* parkour activity over the more 'traditional' characteristics of global city activity, despite welcoming it as a pastime. Parkour communities will perpetuate *as an intergrated process of*, not in spite of, global city production. The multicultural demographic characteristics of global cities will catalyse (although perhaps not instigate) the coming together of like-minded people (i.e. traceurs) to perform their art. In other words, while the global city paradigm itself does not include parkour as part of its *raison d'être* (unless it is a packaged and commercially viable format such as its use in advertising), the by-products of the nuances of global city characteristics will facilitate it. Factors such as the restriction of public recreational space in global cities force traceurs to congregate in parks and other suitable places that are perhaps on the margins of global city functionality (derelict buildings, infrequently used office buildings, etc.). Moreover, the attempts at control and restriction of such activities by urban officials (as they do not add any commercial value to the global city) can have a rallying effect and increase the sense of community and increase the 'strength' of the subculture.

This process is mirrored in countless other subcultural activities such as skateboarding, graffiti (Kramer, 2010), yarn-bombing (Moore and

Prain, 2009) and many others. Despite their marginalization from the global city paradigm to date, they form a cultural milieu which has been given credence and validation in recent years as they are represented as 'cool' and 'bohemian'. Subcultural practice of global cities have been present for decades, if not longer, yet it is only comparatively recently (perhaps fuelled by the uptake of the Floridian paradigm) that they have been seen as contributing to a sense of collective urbanity that can be capitalized upon. Zukin (1992) argued, in relation to New York City, that the cultural diversity that characterizes the city is now (through political manipulation or economic developmentalism) representative of the 'authenticity' of the city. Through the various processes and manifestations of gentrification in New York City, it is this process which Zukin sees as the artificial creation of a type of authenticity. 'Authentic' places are not those infused with cultural history, but those with a desire from the people to maintain a stylistic quality that is conducive to their own life style, and therefore one which catalyses a gentrification narrative.

As such, subcultural practices 'from below', while often starting out as on the periphery of global city debates, can find their way 'in' by means of commercialization, adding further cultural dimensions and iterations of the global city. Skateboarding, graffiti, parkour, yarn-bombing, urban exploration are all examples of subcultural activities that have become 'part' of the global city (at one point or another) in that they have been used to propagate urban capitalist development. However, this is not to deny the continual 'activist' or 'subversive' nature of these activities as they will continue to be the fundamental ethos of these subcultures. But such subcultural activity represents how the global city's cultural dimension can be appropriated 'from below'. Culture, as we have seen then, can take many 'forms' when talked about in relation to the global city, and the chapter so far has represented these through top-down and bottom-up characteristics. While this duality can obfuscate the complexities of cultural interaction in global cities, for illustrative purposes, the following section will highlight how these two different 'types' of global city cultural appropriation play out and get intertwined in Copenhagen, Denmark.

Culture in Copenhagen

The city of Copenhagen, according to GaWC is a Beta+ world city (Taylor et al., 2010). Along with other cities such as Prague, Vancouver, Bangalore, Tel Aviv and Berlin, Copenhagen is a second tier city in terms of its importance in the world economy. The ranking of cities in this way (and the associated limitations) have been discussed earlier in this chapter. But it is worth reiterating that given Copenhagen's 'status' as a Beta+ city, it is no surprise that the city government has been enacting policies of urban renewal and development in an attempt to attract investment, jobs and prestige on a global stage (Hansen et al., 2001; Bayliss, 2007). In many respects then, Copenhagen is much like many other cities around the world. However, when looking specifically at cultural policies for urban renewal, Copenhagen becomes one of a smaller number of cities that adopted a 'creative city' strategy relatively early on. It can be traced back to the latter years of the twentieth century, making Copenhagen one of the very first cities in Europe, possibly the world, to holistically engender the prevailing urban development ideas of the time, namely those around creativity and cultural boosterism and the 'creative city' idea more generally.

However, resonating with Peck's (2005) subsequent critiques of such policies, (Hansen et al., 2001, 866) argued that

> the rhetoric of the creative city, at least in the Copenhagen context, is remarkably void of policy recommendations, substantial alternatives to property-led development, or any clear notion of how the creation of the creative city is to differ in any way from business-as-usual urban redevelopment. It therefore remains a disguise for these very activities it pretends to replace.

The importance placed on cultural assets as a way of attracting footloose creative labour was bound up in a wider governmental strategy of implementing a creative city. Heavy investment in cultural infrastructure was green lit on the premise that it will boost the city's attractiveness to footloose capital and the creative class. Within Copenhagen, there were a number of these investments, as noted by Bayliss (2007, 896):

> The areas of culture and creativity have ... witnessed considerable developments. Firstly, the city has benefited from major additions to its cultural and recreational infrastructure. Whilst the Opera House is foremost among the new attractions, other developments include Arken museum for modern art and an enlarged Statens Museum for Kunst (national art museum). Amager Strandpark, an artificial beach built out from the coast to create a lagoon, opened in 2005. A new theatre on the waterfront, floating harbour stage, as well as concert hall and golf course in Ørestad are on the way. Fixtures on the cultural events calendar include the International Film Festival and the Jazz Festival.

So the development of cultural infrastructure has been immense. Since the developments noted above, the construction of Ørestad has continued (albeit tempered heavily by the global financial climate). This development was part of a wider 're-structuring' of the municipality's urban development programme towards a progressive neoliberal agenda that prioritized real estate and infrastructural development over social justice (Majoor, 2008). Included in the development is DR Byen, a site of multiple media companies

Figure 9.1   DR Byen, Ørestad, Copenhagen
Source: Photo by Julian Birkinshaw.

(including new offices, studios and locations for the whole of DR, Denmark's national broadcaster), a large concert hall, a university and housing. The concert hall (on the left) and the new DR studios (on the right) can be seen in Figure 9.1 above.

This media city is a flagship development for Copenhagen and is located at the north end of the Ørestad development. The transit-led mega-development of Ørestad was gargantuan, with huge infrastructures (a new metro line, hundreds of office, educational and residential buildings as well as DR Byen) constructed in an attempt to attract international capital (Knowles, 2012). DR Byen, Copenhagen's media city, represents the largest single development in Ørestad, and signifies the use of cultural production and creativity as a means (or justification) for large-scale development. The importance of attracting creative class workers and creative industry firms to the Copenhagen government is a clear strategy of urban renewal, and the immense development of DR Byen indicates how cultural assets have become central to this strategy. Couple this with the other large-scale developments noted by Bayliss (2007), the 'culture from above' in Copenhagen, is very evident.

However, due to the ongoing financial 'issues' engulfing Europe and the rest of the world, many of the developments in Copenhagen have been shelved (or scrapped altogether), particularly in the Ørestad development (Grabar, 2012). Still under construction (the long-term plan includes

30 years of development (Knowles, 2012)), there are now many areas of Ørestad that are vacant lots or halted building sites. Many of these sites are situated adjacent to and therefore isolating larger residential buildings. Rather than let these sites lie dormant, community groups (local residents, city-wide sports groups and the factions of the city municipality) have commandeered these buildings sites and erected temporary sports areas within them. One such site has been labelled 'plug and play' and consist of temporary basketball, netball and football courts, a roller-skating circuits, water sports area and even a parkour park (see Figure 9.2).

Containers are used to store the sports equipment, and the surfaces, courts and areas themselves have been built using the concrete foundations that were already in place. The re-use of these buildings' sites as areas of (sub)cultural interaction and play, and the initiatives by local residents, is a clear example of how a 'culture from below' is being manifest in world or global city functionality. In other words, these 'plug and play' areas are culturally orientated offerings that are not as 'tied up' into the global cities paradigm as DR Byen might be, but still exemplify how 'culture from below' is (or perhaps should be) a further part of the cultural dimension of global cities. The presence of a parkour park for example is a clear indication of how the subculture has been assimilated into the cultural provisioning of

Figure 9.2   Parkour plug and play 'park', Ørestad, Copenhagen

Copenhagen as a global city, despite it being a marginalized subculture in other parts of the city. Other parts of Ørestad have also used parkour to engender it cultural urbanity. The film *My Playground* (2009) showed traceurs performing parkour in and around one of the residential buildings in Ørestad. The building (called 'Mountain Dwellings') is an iconic development, and the architects and developers worked with the filmmakers to encourage the use of the building for parkour. The film shows a parkour group (Team Jiyo) throughout Copenhagen, but with a focus on how they interact with the architecture of Mountain Dwellings. The unrestricted use of parkour in this area is again another instance of how a subculture, which has previously been marginalized and criminalized (and in some cities, still is), has been embroiled within a cultural inflection of the global city paradigm. While not part of a formal identification of the 'creative industries' or a subset of the 'creative class', these traceurs and the filmmakers exemplify how this cultural activity (willingly or not) is becoming part of the over-arching paradigm of Copenhagen as a global city (see Daskalaki and Mould, 2013).

There are other, more contested areas of Copenhagen's cultural urbanity. The area of Christiania in the Christianshavn area of Copenhagen is a 34-hectare site of former army barracks. In 1971, squatters entered the area, and now, there are 888 permanent inhabitants. In 1976, a court ruling ordered the eviction, but the rule was never enforced as a special law was passed to allow the area to exist as a 'social experiment' (Moeller, 2009). The open sale and consumption of cannabis has been a source of tension within the local community, but

> ... the cannabis market in Christiania has functioned as an accepted and integral part. During police interventions, it has even been physically defended by locals and sympathisers. Since the market has been operating for such a long time, a set of explicit 'conduct norms' have evolved.
> (Moeller, 2009, 338)

The 'conduct norms' of the prohibition of other drugs, not selling to minors, no photography and no running, have meant that it is now Copenhagen's second biggest tourist destination and with profitable businesses thriving. The implicit subcultural activity within Christiana is clearly at odds with the city's official policies (and it is sometimes the site of violence, arrests and general unrest); yet its international appeal to tourists means that it has obvious positive economic externalities. The anti-hegemonic tendencies inherent in Christiana and its supporters have clear commensurability with the recent Occupy and other social justice movements and the wider debates around the Right to the City, and as such are at odds with much of the rhetoric of the global city. So to infer that it could ever represent a cultural dimension of the global city is a difficult line of argumentation, but it represents the complexities, schisms and general messiness when considering cultural aspects of the global city paradigm.

Conclusion

Any attempts to debate the cultural aspects of the global city will inevitably unravel the intense complexities, fierce contestations and ubiquitous contentions that are bound up in our limited descriptions of culture of the global city. The paradigmatic history of the global city has been slow to acknowledge the role of cultural assets, with the traditional focus on the political economy of their command and control functions (Sassen, 2001; Taylor, 2004b). While culturally orientated characteristics have been considered, they have tended to continue the economic or commercial rhetoric, namely by considering the cultural or creative industries instead of APS firms, or the role of large-scale cultural planning projects on the global competitiveness of the city. In other words, when global city debates focus on culture, they have moulded it to fit its current methodological agendas (see Krätke, 2003; Watson and Hoyler, 2010). As such, subordinate or more peripheral readings of cultural urbanity or culture as a means to social justice have rarely been discussed as a viable characteristic of global cities.

Through a theoretical and metaphorical demarcation of culture form above and culture from below, this chapter has highlighted the different ways culture has been assimilated (or least attempted to be assimilated) into the global city paradigm. This dualistic narrative is of course merely diagrammatic; to suggest that these processes are in and of themselves dichotomous would be naïve. For the purposes of descriptive clarity, they have been isolated using this vernacular. The caveat is that a deeper analysis would highlight how these 'two processes' are often bound up together, to such an extent that a binary becomes unhelpful. However, where such a dichotomous model does help is in isolating those cultural practices that contribute to a city's neoliberal economic development, and those where its contribution is not immediately clear. The construction of cultural institutions is a common urban development process, but when it is done under the political rubric of 'creativity' or increasing a city's attractiveness to the creative class, it becomes something qualitatively different from a social development strategy. It gets tied up into the global city narrative as increasing a city's international competitiveness. Likewise, the presence and growth of urban subcultures is part of the everyday urbanity, but when they become appropriated by more official or commercial institutions, or used as a means of place marketing, then they become part of the story of the global city development and capitalist accumulation.

In Copenhagen, culture as a concept has been utilized prominently for well over a decade as a political means to justify large-scale investments. It exemplifies how urban management in the twenty-first century has taken a different view of culture, one that is intricately linked to economic development (a link made all the more viable by the popularity of the concepts of the creative city (Landry, 2000) and the creative class (Florida, 2002, 2005)). But concurrently, Copenhagen can also highlight instances of subcultural, marginal or informal activity that has in some cases been 'brought in' to the global city paradigm through commercialization of activities, but in other cases, how it has reacted against urban officialdom and is rooted in social justice. However, mirroring the conceptual caveat flagged above, a deeper study of these phenomena in Copenhagen would reveal how these processes are not as dichotomous as has been suggested, but in fact there are many people, policies, processes and places that enmesh these seemingly different cultural characteristics into a complex, interconnected network of cultural appropriation.

The marriage of the concepts of culture and the global city is an uneasy one, with tumultuous relations at times. This is brought about by the tacit and intangible nature of culture, and the pragmatic, evidence-based nature of mainstream global city debates; as such they make for uneasy bedfellows. Despite this, cultural characteristics (those which go further than an economically restricted description) of global cities do persist, and so to include these themes into a more holistic narrative of global cities is a progressive measure, and one that would enlighten the complexities of global city development.

10
The Architectural Dimension

Kerwin Datu

Introduction

When we think about the architecture of the global city, often we have in our mind's eye a certain kind of rather spectacular imagery, which may entail crystalline skyscrapers, luxurious residential complexes, rich cultural buildings or works of breathtaking avant-garde design. The discourses surrounding these kinds of architecture can be equally spectacular, studded with vocabulary like 'starchitects', 'the Bilbao effect' and the 'icon'.

But these images and concepts constitute a highly selective and vastly incomplete vision of the architecture of the global city, and can be misleading for those who commission and produce this architecture as much as for the researchers who study it. This raises two particular challenges, which this chapter seeks to address.

The first challenge is to overcome the self-selectiveness of what we think the architecture of the global city to be. To address this, this chapter proposes that researchers need to fix their analysis of this architecture within a framework that identifies the operational connections between architecture, cities and globalization, as well as sufficiently identifying the diversity of architectural landscapes subject to these connections. The framework proposed here is an extension of Sassen's (2001) method of analysing global cities, namely that the production of architecture is bound up within the social production and reproduction of the global city itself which she describes. By tracing this cyclical process – from the production of the global city to the production of architecture and through to the impact of architecture and its production on the production of the global city – the full extent of what we mean by *global city architecture* can be identified and its social import determined.

Other useful frameworks are briefly mentioned here as well. The Schumpeterian concept of creative destruction (Schumpeter, 1942; Harvey, 1981) explains how globalization processes assist in the displacement and replacement of architectural landscapes within cities. The logic of competition between cities, especially the activities of city marketing

(Ashworth and Voogd, 1990) and place promotion (Gold and Ward, 1994), explains how city leaders demand specific kinds of architecture in order to promote their city with specific kinds of images. The second challenge is how to treat the spectacular imagery that dominates and even obscures our understanding of global city architecture. This chapter proposes that the prevalence of this imagery be given its proper place within the frameworks outlined above. There are scholars and critics who attempt to discount the visual, representational, 'spectacular' or 'iconic' dimensions of architecture, implying that they distract us from the arguably more important social functions and impacts that architecture must attend to (Lees, 2001; Sudjic, 2005). However, this stance merely precludes the important scholarly task of understanding why the architecture of the global city should abound with such spectacular imagery in the first place, and of understanding why the neglect of its social impacts happens so often.

Rather than see the image of architecture as a distraction, we need to identify its place within the framework of the production of the global city, and thus be able to weigh its impacts against those of other aspects of architectural works and their production.

The proposal put forward here is that the image(s) that a work of architecture or indeed an entire architectural landscape projects is something deliberately constructed by those who commission and design that architecture, and is intended to communicate specific messages to a remote target audience by the transmission of those images through various media. When it comes to global cities, the key ingredient in understanding this is the concept of scale. While the image that works of architecture project in the media may have various intentions (secure more work for the architect, attract visitors to the institutions, etc.), in the context of globalization and cities these images and the messages they convey are intended to be communicated at the global scale, to audiences far removed from the geographic, social, economic and political contexts of the physical work itself. As a result, the gulf between the construction of the image of a work of architecture and the construction of the physical building anchored in and responding to the needs, values and expectations of its local setting is at its widest in global cities. It is a great challenge for researchers to analyse the intentions and the impacts operating at both of these scales simultaneously, often because they are seemingly incommensurable, but it is important to find ways to combine these analyses rather than to discount the import of one or the other.

Global city architecture: More than the 'spectacular'

The practice of architecture provides our collective imagination of the global city with its most potent visual image: the city skyline. Some of the most iconic images of cities are the most famous skylines in the world, for example

Manhattan in New York or Hong Kong set against its hills. Alternatively, the image of a global city that architecture provides may be encapsulated in a single 'iconic building' (Jencks, 2005) – an individual work of architecture that captures the world's imagination and fuses with the identity of the city within the global consciousness. Some of the most effective architectural icons of recent decades are the Sydney Opera House by Jørn Utzon, the Pyramide du Louvre by I. M. Pei and Partners, the Bilbao Guggenheim Museum by Gehry Partners, 30 St Mary Axe (nicknamed 'the Gherkin') in London by Foster and Partners, and the Burj Khalifa in Dubai by Skidmore Owings and Merrill. Another yet a no less spectacular and selective image of global cities is to see them as homes to the world's most innovative architects and other designers dictating global fashions and trends from their bases in districts like Clerkenwell in London or Chelsea in Manhattan, or through publications like *Wallpaper, Domus*, or *Architectural Review*.

When a global city wishes to illustrate its supremacy as an economic capital, these are naturally among the images it invokes. Likewise when a city aspires to become a global city, it is these images it turns to for inspiration. There is a tendency for leaders to take a very superficial reading of global cities (especially of very new cities such as Dubai and Singapore), to seek to replicate their image by assembling what they believe to be the necessary parts – skyscrapers, shopping malls, railways, etc. – and to eliminate from view all that seems at odds with such an image – history, temporality, dilapidation, informality, spontaneity.

There are two misconceptions involved in these kinds of efforts. The first is the belief that global cities do not also contain these elements of decay within their environments, and the second is that it is necessary to actively eradicate them to become a global city. Neither of these is true of course; it is simply that global cities rarely advertise the fact. But to the people who inhabit global cities, there are always areas large and small known and even cherished for their decay, their decadence, their street life, their chaos, their resistance to planning and control, or just their simple ordinariness. The concept of the 'ordinary city' (Robinson, 2006) is a useful reminder that despite whatever classifications are applied to a city, such as 'global' or 'world' city, there are many more mundane facets to that city than those indicated by such an appellation. Likewise the architecture of any city we might call 'global' extends far beyond that which we associate with the city's 'global' face into a landscape of ordinary buildings and spaces that comprise the rest of the city.

In this light there is no categorical distinction between a 'global city' such as Singapore and a city that aspires to become one such as, say, Surat. Both may desire to have 'global' architecture, and both will necessarily contain ordinary buildings, and neither city's makers may rightfully focus on one to the neglect of the other. When we talk about 'the architecture of the global city' then, we are compelled to talk about all of its architectures, whether they fit our image of what a global city should look like or not. However this is not to say that when discussing 'the architecture of the global city' we should dilute our focus to any architecture in any urban area. Rather it is to change the way we narrow our focus. We do not focus on architecture within specific 'global cities', but on architecture produced by processes of globalization, whichever cities they are found within. At the same time it is to broaden our discussion beyond the stereotypical images we often envisage.

Identifying global city architecture: The production of the global city

What then can be meant by the architecture of the global city? How can we identify it? This must be done in tandem with the task of delineating the global city itself. Here however we have a reasonably sound methodological footing. In her own iconic work, *The Global City* (2001), Saskia Sassen as a typical sociologist takes an interest in how this social condition reproduces itself – how is it that global cities continue to dominate the global economy throughout time? Her thesis was that a global city is one that comprises a core community of advanced business functions – corporate headquarters, financial institutions, accountants, lawyers, management consultants, media, design and communications – whose collective decisions determine the flow of vast sums of capital and other resources around much of the globe, including into their own city, thus reinforcing the city's position within the global city network year after year.

We can use this as the starting point for our understanding of global city architecture, moving from the production of work to the production of space and architecture. The complexity of the advanced business functions in the global city core produces work for several thousands of highly educated professionals who must congregate not only within the same city but within the same neighbourhoods within that city to collaborate effectively, such as New York's Lower Manhattan, Paris' La Défense or London's Canary Wharf. But the professional and personal needs of these businesses and individuals in turn produce work for several thousand more workers to be employed in sectors such as retail and local services, hospitality, waste and sanitation, construction and maintenance.

All of these activities produce spatial needs in the form of operational, residential and recreational spaces. For the professionals these include premium office spaces, residential developments, leisure and sporting facilities; for other workers it implies the retail and hospitality spaces they may operate within as well as the usually lesser quality residential accommodation they may find or have provided to them within the city. These spatial needs generate demand for certain kinds of architecture, whose qualities typically depend on the economic status of their users. The hierarchical nature of a global city's labour force gives rise to large economic and social inequalities, and these are expressed in its architecture as much as in any other material dimension of a city.

At the top of this hierarchy of architectural quality are the skyscrapers and other forms of premium developments designed to compete in an extremely heated commercial tenancy market to attract the greatest immediate demand from global business, what Sklair (2005) calls the 'corporate fraction' of the 'transnational capitalist class'. The result of this competition is that almost all developments at this level are pushed towards architectural qualities that denote values prized by commercial tenants, in particular reliability, security, flexibility, prestige and low running costs. The architectural qualities that result may be described as dematerialized and minimalist, where the messiness, physicality and the natural aging of traditional building materials are suppressed, concealed or engineered away, as is much complexity of detailing, so that the building demonstrates and signifies those prized values, or in other words projects an image that corresponds with them. This leads to an overwhelming uniformity of architectural expression in global cities throughout the world which can be observed at a glance. Even at the scale of the individual building many design motifs can be seen to repeat themselves *ad nauseam* across several global cities. This leads many to complain that globalization encourages a homogenization of the world's cities, causing one to be indistinguishable from any other.

For the building types that seek to attract the global city professionals themselves, such as residential developments and retail facilities, the set of values that architects must respond to changes somewhat, allowing for a freer universe of architectural expression. Prestige and luxury remain important, as do lifestyle amenity and a sense of exclusiveness. But to answer to the greater individualism of users' tastes, the architecture of these types becomes stylistically more diverse, while often more explicit in its stylistic borrowings from other centres or architectural cultures. For example, architects may borrow consciously from Italian hilltop cities, royal Japanese gardens, Moroccan bazaars, Manhattan art deco, Parisian art nouveau or London townhouses, notwithstanding the fact that the climatic, topographic or social contexts that generated those architectures may have nothing to do with the settings they are applied to. But these adaptations can occur so readily only because such tropes are easily recognized by the well-educated and well-travelled professionals they seek to attract, and may be associated in their minds with the values mentioned above. Adding to the criticisms levelled at skyscrapers, the indiscriminate blending of styles at this level of architectural production may lead to critiques that global cities become too *diverse* in their architectural expression, as the local vernacular and traditional urban form become supplanted by a pastiche of artificial and alien styles, yet at the same time may still result in homogenization of the world's cities by reducing them to the same eclectic blur of styles.

Alternatively, many clients may have more sophisticated tastes and use their developments to participate in the architectural avant-garde, commissioning buildings with a specific intent to push the forefront of contemporary design or exploit it as a market advantage. This hints at another dimension of global city architecture, which is that for many architects the most vibrant global cities are those that play host to the most innovative communities of architecture studios and schools, where the most forward-thinking ideas and technologies are developed and put into practice, and where their output finds its most receptive audiences, for example Los Angeles, Rotterdam and Barcelona.

While there is usually little overlap between the small creative firms that populate these cities and the large commercial architecture offices employed in the most premium global city developments, the commercial and the creative sides of the industry converge in the production of the architectural icon – a building which seeks to be both a landmark within the urban landscape as well as within the global consciousness. The use of a creative designer in a highly visible premium development is almost always a conscious commercial decision intended to gain a market advantage, and yet the instinctive conservatism of commercial developers expresses itself here as well, again through the tendency to hire the most well-established and prominent of avant-garde designers rather than take a chance on smaller firms. Thus the creation of a 'star system' of architects in which the most visible projects are awarded only to the most well-known, and thus least risky, creative designers such as Zaha Hadid, Frank Gehry, Renzo Piano and Norman Foster.

So far this is the 'global' face of architecture, Sklair's 'transnational capitalist class' (Sklair, 2005; Adam, 2012), but what happens beyond these landscapes? Lower down the architectural hierarchy are the spaces produced for the workers who support the core global city professionals rather than for those professionals themselves, and for which economy of means is usually the overriding factor. This may mean living in poorly maintained housing projects built by the government, by one's employers or by the wider private sector, or overcrowding in older generations of housing stock maladapted for multiple tenancy. The lack of disposable income available to such workers to spend on their living environments means that housing developers do not see them as a profitable demographic to cater to, and expend little consideration on their architectural quality. Likewise, because they are not considered a lucrative source of economic growth, city leaders focused on growth spend little energy trying to create an architectural environment that will attract them.

On the other hand, because there is little expectation that such projects will be profitable, there is less concern to hire the most commercially reliable architects to design them. Social and low-cost projects become a space where smaller, cheaper architectural practices may be given the opportunity to build, or where more risky architectural ideas can be experimented with, especially in European cities with long traditions of social housing. More enlightened industrialists may also seek such architectural experimentation in their working environments as a means to improve morale and productivity, reduce operating costs or gain other efficiencies. The experiments enabled by less visible projects such as these become opportunities for a more sustainable spectrum of technologies and values to enter into the production of architecture elsewhere in the global city. The same goes for many other building types that are indirectly generated by the population growth associated with globalization, among them schools, universities and hospitals.

Global city architecture and displacement

These are all architectures installed by the processes of globalization; one may also talk of architectures within global cities that are displaced by the very same processes, or that have been condemned to neglect in anticipation of them. These may include many areas with heritage value, such as the *hutong* (alleyway) districts of Beijing or the courtyard houses of Dubai, which cannot be rapidly adapted to the density and use requirements of a globalizing city. These architectures are not necessarily dichotomous; later generations of globalization may cannibalize architecture installed by earlier generations, for example. Another line of social theory helps us to understand how the architecture of the global city is produced in this sense. Joseph Schumpeter's (1942) conception of 'creative destruction' argues that capitalism proceeds by seeking to *create* new opportunities for profit-making, and when these opportunities can only be exploited by coming into conflict with existing assets, the ensuing competition or crisis causes some of these assets to be *destroyed*. This is especially true in times of general economic crisis, where the same profit streams have been growing for a generation or more, all existing avenues for further growth have been exhausted and society as a whole must reorganize itself for new opportunities to emerge, usually with great social and political pain.

David Harvey (1981) brings a geographic dimension to this process with the concept of the 'spatial fix', part of which is the notion that new opportunities can be found by forcing open new geographical spaces for globally mobile capital to operate within. These may be new countries, as when corporations decide to move into 'emerging markets', new cities or new neighbourhoods within cities, such as when city leaders earmark and redevelop special zones within their territories to attract global business. These 'new' areas are naturally inhabited by existing 'assets' – existing living and working spaces, businesses, residents and communities. Many institutions and regulations must be pushed to evolve in coordination in order to make it economically and politically palatable to destroy these assets. For example development plans may be revised to allow increased densities on different sites, causing sites to be worth more if the existing low-density buildings upon them were to be demolished and larger buildings erected than if they were simply allowed to earn rental income as they are.

These theories imply that the displacement and destruction of the existing architectural landscapes of global cities are essential features of global capitalism. They take various forms including eviction (the displacement of individual residents and other tenants by force of law or violence), gentrification (the displacement of whole communities or socioeconomic strata from a neighbourhood through market forces) and demolition. In all three of these forms of displacement, political ideologies and allegiances may be invoked beyond pure economic arguments. A political discourse may arise to demonize residents or communities that an economic elite wishes to evict, for example by accusing them of antisocial or criminal behaviour such as drug dealing, extortion or land grabbing. The political significance of an architecture may be employed against it, such as in the case of the Ottoman-era Ajyad Fortress in Mecca, a beautiful citadel whose demolition to make way for the rather more crass and infinitely more commercial Mecca Royal Hotel Clock Tower could occur only in a political context that denigrated Ottoman heritage and influence within Saudi Arabia.

In other cases the destruction may be more aesthetic than physical. In many cities the heritage value arises through the homogeny of architecture within historic neighbourhoods, and is destroyed not by their demolition, but by the juxtaposition of incongruous styles and forms. London's skyline is preserved through the use of 'protected vistas' which prevent new construction from intervening within sightlines from prominent hills to specific architectural landmarks within the city, especially St Paul's Cathedral and the Palace of Westminster. Tall buildings between or beyond these landmarks would destroy these cultural assets without any physical demolition being required. And even when it avoids these sightlines, a tall building may still interfere with the cultural value of other architectural heritage. It has been argued, not least by UNESCO, that the erection of the Shard at London Bridge by Renzo Piano Building Workshop at a height of 309.6 metres overshadows the World Heritage–listed medieval Tower of London to such a degree that the Tower can no longer be appreciated as before, and perhaps ought to lose its listed status.

The purpose of enumerating all of these landscapes, whether produced or displaced by the processes of globalization, is to demonstrate the breadth of the phenomenon that we may call global city architecture, and to show how our image of the subject may need to expand if we are to begin to manage and analyse it all effectively without the selective filter of prejudice or our yearning for the spectacular.

The producers of global city architecture and the logic of competition(s)

Within these processes, however, what causes the agents who produce these architectures to do so? What values and ambitions motivate them? While the theories of social production and creative destruction explain the structural drivers of global city architecture, other literatures explain the actions of individual stakeholders. For city leaders, their actions are most commonly inscribed within a logic of competition – competition with other cities to attract businesses, investment and highly-skilled workers. Winning this competition is often captured by the stated objective to become a 'world class city', a city whose business amenities and physical environment meet the standard of any of the world's most prominent business capitals.

Within this logic, city leaders embark on several coordinated strategies, including infrastructure investment to meet the perceived needs of these businesses, marketing campaigns, trade relations and other image-making exercises. Some of these activities generate architectural needs directly, such as airports, road and rail infrastructure, hotels, convention centres and business parks. For others, the architecture is generated indirectly through policies and political decisions that favour specific kinds of architecture.

At the level of individual developments, the mechanics of commissioning, designing and constructing a building helps to explain the architectural character that emerges. In many global cities, policies and institutions have been developed ostensibly to ensure the architectural design quality of buildings. Competitions may be organized voluntarily by clients or mandated by government policy for projects of sufficient size or social significance, and may consist of written expressions of interest or drawn design proposals. While at first glance the competition of ideas that these processes generate appear to be in the public interest, a closer understanding of how architectural ideas are produced under the pressure of competitions gives cause for scepticism. As the critic Witold Rybczynski surmises, 'the charged atmosphere promotes flamboyance rather than careful thought, and favours the glib and obvious over the subtle and nuanced' (Rybczynski, 2002). The competition brief may explicitly call for an 'icon' or a 'landmark' building, goading architects to produce spectacle rather than a considered response to local needs.

The architectural historian Charles Jencks suggests that the purpose of an icon is to play the role of the 'enigmatic signifier', to hint at many meanings while explicitly targeting none of them, allowing observers to attach to it whichever meaning is most significant to themselves, increasing its potency as a cultural object (Jencks, 2005). Yet this hardly seems like the real intention behind the demand for an icon. If icons are 'signifiers', then I would argue that they are not intended to be 'enigmatic', but rather to come to signify quite explicitly the prestige of the cities they are placed in. Any enigma observed in the form of such buildings is not the result of a desire to evoke multiple meanings in a postmodern sense so much as it is to avoid explicit analogies or references to other works that might distract the observer from the intended response, which is to see the project and the city in a more positive light. From the designer's perspective as well, the enigmatic quality is often due to a desire to differentiate the design from its precedents, to arrive at an original form that demonstrates the architect's talent as a creative professional, rather than necessarily a wish to pursue formal abstraction. The creation of an icon is used as a project's 'unique selling point', a most conventional commercial imperative.

When city leaders request an architectural icon, they may be seeking to replicate what is known as the 'Bilbao effect' – the supposed effect that the popularity of the Bilbao Guggenheim had in turning around the economic fortunes of the city after its opening in 1997. Whether or not the Bilbao effect exists is itself highly contested. It is true that the opening of the museum preceded a significant short-term boost in tourism to the city, but less certain that this generated any significant economic development in other sectors in turn (Gomez and Gonzalez, 2001; Jones, 2004). And city leaders often place too much emphasis on the quality of the architecture itself, forgetting that the museum was anchored in a long-term urban redevelopment plan (Adam, 2012) and backed by a formidable and proactive marketing machine which may in fact have made the difference between Bilbao and any number of other global city pretenders. In the wake of the Bilbao Guggenheim many other Spanish cities of similar scale rushed to produce similar institutions, such as Valencia's City of the Arts and Science and the Auditorio de Tenerife both by Santiago Calatrava, and Santiago de Compostela's City of Culture by Eisenman Architects, none of which have had the same impact while placing enormous financial strain on their governments.

A related phenomenon is the stated demand for a supertall building, usually for the tallest building in the world in one category or another. While for clients of such buildings – as in Dubai, Kuala Lumpur, Shanghai and Taipei – supertall buildings demonstrate their arrival in the peerage of global cities, for many critics they reveal nothing other than the insecurities of those clients (Dovey, 1996; King, 2004). The critic Jonathan Glancey notes that supertall buildings are 'increasingly symptoms of "second-city syndrome"' (Glancey, 1998).

These experiences reinforce the lesson that for all its seductiveness, architecture cannot simply be entrusted with the task of consolidating a city's position on the world stage; at the very least it must be accompanied by other economic strategies to ensure that any short-term gains translate into development in other sectors of the city. But for researchers it also shows that fundamental to the analysis of global city architecture is identifying the intentions and the values of those that create it, and the mismatch between these intentions and values and the real impacts of the completed work.

Scale and image

We have identified that globalization produces several kinds of architecture, some of which are highly visible, some often neglected both by city makers and by researchers. We have identified that these architectures are not produced for their own sake but for specific economic functions, intimately tied to profitability and the logic of competition between places, though not always assured of success. But more than other forms of architectural production, the architecture of the global city forces researchers to consider the question of geographic scale.

Peculiar to the processes of globalization is its use of architecture in the image-making of the city at the global scale. It is wrong to discount the practice of image-making in the analysis of this architecture but it is also wrong, as Lees (2001) argues, to restrict one's analysis to the representational dimension of architecture. The image-making and the materiality of architecture must both be evaluated; the special lesson of globalization is that these aspects have a tendency to operate at different geographic scales, and cannot be weighed easily against each other.

While in most other contexts city makers are usually preoccupied with providing sufficient space for various local activities or satisfying a specific market demand, in global cities their sights are much more firmly fixed on using architecture as a medium of communication, and to a much wider geographical audience. Thus different types of architecture are generated at different scales even within the one project, responding to different (and sometimes contradictory) socioeconomic intentions and impacts at each scale. For global cities a common example is architecture intended to attract certain business interests operating at a global scale, while physically suppressing street-level and other local business interests to do so.

Singapore

As stated above, one may observe in many city leaders a desire to reproduce a certain image of the global city within their territories. What is this image? For one government-appointed master planner in Dar es Salaam, 'Singapore is his role model, and he favours big projects to clear slums and build bridges, roads and out-of-town settlements' (Boyle, 2012). Elsewhere 'Singapore, that paragon of order and control that is the antithesis of India's messy urbanism, is widely admired by India's bureaucratic elite' (Chattaraj, 2012). Or this: 'the idea of a world-class city [...] is a slogan, as if devised by a marketing agency, to sell the latest fashions in cosmetic urbanism [...] now Dubai, now Singapore, sometimes with a hint of the Manhattan skyline' (Echanove and Srivastava, 2011). Time and again, city leaders in the developing world cite Singapore as an image they want to replicate. And it is an arresting image, with recent projects like the Marina Bay Sands by Safdie Architects, the United Overseas Bank Plaza by Kenzo Tange Associates and the Sail at

Marina Bay by NBBJ transforming the skyline. But as with all global cities, it is an incomplete image, and in fact the most important architectural lessons to be taken from Singapore lie elsewhere in the city.

Nevertheless, if this is the lesson that other city leaders take away, the city leaders of Singapore themselves are partly to blame. The Singapore government's Urban Redevelopment Authority (URA) actively promotes its urban development expertise through external consulting activities and technical assistance conducted by the URA Consulting Group. By promoting themselves and their urban planning achievements through such an agency, Singapore is in a position to project the image it chooses and to shape the image that its foreign partners receive, and sadly it has proven more interested in promulgating its spectacular modernity than its extraordinary achievements in public housing. Part of the difficulty is the cognitive gap between the experts in Singapore and their audience in other cities. In Singapore, the dominant planning discourse is now one of 'sustainability', a natural concern for a mature city whose economy is driven by advanced consumption. But the meaning of the discourse can easily be misunderstood by leaders of cities in the early phases of rapid urbanization, who have yet to shift their mindset from one of resistance to urbanization to acceptance and accommodation of it. For a leader in a context such as Lagos or Kinshasa, the bewildering expansion of the urban agglomeration seems unsustainable itself. Faced with this, Singapore's discourse of 'sustainability' may be misinterpreted as reinforcing its belief that this rapid expansion is something to be resisted, limited, controlled, whereas it ought to be interpreted as a call to reorganize one's local institutions and technologies to meet future resource demands. There is, therefore, a translation task to be undertaken to ensure that the lessons a city like Singapore has to offer are not distorted by the prejudices of city leaders in other contexts.

Because while the benchmark that global cities such as Singapore set is a product of the spectacular imagery already discussed, the image that Singapore projects is in many ways a by-product of its 'global city' efforts in housing and other fields, not its explicit objective as it is for the cities that strive to match it. For example, the history of Singapore's housing shows that architecture was a means to an end, and that ultimately it strove for global city status more through the character of its people than through the character of its architecture per se. While visitors from the developing world come to Singapore today and see a landscape free of the shacks, tenements and overcrowding which pervade their own city, this was not true for most of the twentieth century, when immigration caused Singapore's population to balloon. Housing surveys in the 1950s reported population densities of up to 50,200 persons per square kilometre in the city centre; in one part of Chinatown 'over half of the residents lived in cubicles with an average size of about 9 sq m.; a high proportion of these cubicles had no windows; sanitary conditions were intolerable and the buildings completely dilapidated.'

Outside the centre, 'squatter settlements mushroomed' (Eng and Savage, 1985, 56).

The diagnosis was a general shortage of housing, not just for the urban poor but for families of all levels of income. The colonial government response was to embark on a public housing programme overseen by the Singapore Improvement Trust (SIT), though its first satellite town, Tiong Bahru, was aimed at the open market rather than the urban poor. Like contemporaneous housing schemes in Western Europe, the design of Tiong Bahru reflected the modernist themes of the architectural avant-garde, with streamlined curves, flowing internal spaces, facades articulated with long balconies and ample windows for light and ventilation. In the independence era this effort was scaled up dramatically under SIT's successor the Housing and Development Board (HDB), which ranks as one of the world's most successful public housing programmes of the late twentieth century. Whereas many developing-world cities emphasize the 'eradication' of slums and pay less attention to the obligation to rehouse their residents, Singapore's focus was on restructuring the centralized economy to provide housing at such a rate that slums need no longer persist. Between 1960 and 1990 the HDB constructed 669,247 dwelling units (Teo and Huang, 1996, 314) by the end of which it housed '87% of the country's population' (Teo and Huang, 1996, 307) of three million people, an extraordinary result. A lot of the design quality of Tiong Bahru was lost as rate of production increased and concrete tower blocks became the dominant form; nevertheless a concern for the liveability of both the buildings and their interiors remained a hallmark of Singapore's government-built housing.

For example, 'housing estates were planned along the lines of the "neighbourhood concept" of the European postwar new towns, with some modifications to suit [...] the Asian communal way of living' (Eng and Savage, 1985, 58). With regards to the units themselves, 'the Design and Research Unit was established by the HDB specifically to study and advise on ways to improve the standard of flats', which led to 'flats with larger rooms and improved ventilation and fixtures' (Cairns and Jacobs, 2008, 1979). And in the 1990s it took to 'using highly visible designs to add variety to the skyline of the estates and to the facades of blocks', and expanded its tradition of 'courtyards, walkways and pavilions [...] meant as areas for interaction' (Teo and Huang, 1996, 307). A famous feature of Singapore's public housing is what is known locally as the 'void deck', in which the ground floor is left open, avoiding the inherent insecurity of ground floor apartments and providing a large covered open space for various communal uses (Ooi and Tan, 1992; Goh, 2003).

One of the reasons the new nation generated such a successful housing programme was the need to establish social cohesion after the ethnic tensions that produced it, and a sharp trajectory of economic expansion and housing construction were both seen as essential to this objective (Sim et al., 2003). Architecturally, this means that the values of social cohesion and interaction came to be expressed throughout the public spaces and common areas of its housing. Even 'the move from a "modern" to "post-modern" architectural style' in the 1990s was done to make public housing more responsive to 'public input and expression' (Goh, 2001, 1589), an important democratizing initiative.

This was not simply an internal objective but part of a drive to 'mark Singapore's arrival as a global city' (Goh, 2001, 1589). As Goh notes, 'in his 1999 National Day Rally speech entitled "First-world Economy, World-class Home", Prime Minister Goh Chok Tong explicitly links Singapore's economic competitiveness with changes in the housing landscape', and indeed 'HDB's concept plans for the public housing estates of the 21st century, with their greater degree of client feedback, greater diversity of styles and emphasis on lifestyle and amenities, are clearly part of a larger national project of creating an attractive living environment by global standards' (Goh, 2001, 1598–99). The important lesson here is how Singapore stakes its reputation as a global city not so much on the visual appearance of its housing architecture as on the values integrated within its production and use. This is very different to the reading made by aspiring global city leaders on their visits, who often see little more than a landscape of spectacle and 'order and control' that they have failed to impose on their own populations. It is also important to note that Singapore's efforts are applied just as much to its public sector projects, whereas in many aspiring global cities most of the emphasis is on speculative real estate developments with little social dimension. This is not to say that Singapore is necessarily a picture of architectural virtue, but shows that while city leaders around the world might aspire to replicate what they perceive to be the image of Singapore, the architecture of this global city is far more complex and instructive than even what Singapore itself perceives it to be. It is also worth noting that Singapore constructed its model of a global city in positive terms – social cohesion, a global standard of living, a knowledge economy – rather than the negative terms expressed by other leaders – cities without 'slums', without 'mess', without 'disorder'.

Conclusion

This very brief case study of Singapore shows not only how the image of one global city's architecture may be misleading and obscure more instructive analyses of its architectural production, but also how the image itself and its communication at the global scale becomes a factor in the production of architecture in other (would-be) global cities and therefore must be analysed at the same time. These are the challenges then that future scholars of the architecture of the global city must confront: how to anchor their analyses within an understanding of the breadth of interactions between the processes of architecture, urbanism and globalization; how to appreciate the dialectic between the visual, representational, spectacular and media dimensions of architecture and its physical, functional and social dimensions; how to appreciate the dialectic between the global, local and human scales of these dimensions; and ultimately, how to unravel and thus be able to challenge the assumptions, values and intentions informing the production of architecture.

11
The Geopolitical Dimension

Michele Acuto

Introduction

Thinking of cities and world politics might, to many, appear like a futile exercise. When trying to pair the 'global city' phenomenon with those methods and considerations typical of the political sciences, one might be prompted to ask a question that American political scientist John Mollenkopf (1992, 24) posed almost two decades ago at the outset of his research into New York City: 'Is urban politics worth studying at all, or is the urban political realm so subordinate to, dependent on, and constrained by its economic and social context that factors from this domain have little independent explanatory power?' Why should we bother with the nuances and intricacies of politics within cities if at the end of the day these are but a subject of broader forces and institutions? Is the modern metropolis a worthy object of political inquiry in itself or should it be subsumed under bigger trends and wider complexities?

Global cities, as highly interconnected places on the world map, are at the fulcrum of this dilemma. They present us with ever-changing assemblages of urban and global dynamics and entanglements of macro processes such as global trade, micro realities such as those of housing and metropolitan transport, while 'meso' contexts such as those of the nation state are conjunctly in a state of flux. This chapter aims at disentangling this complexity by highlighting, first, that global city urbanists have already encountered these political challenges, second, how political views into the globalizing metropolises are especially crucial in the contemporary scenario.

The politics of the global city

Global cities and politics have long been entangled but their relation has generally been uneasy. Indeed, Patrick Geddes' 1915 venture into the evolution of cities, which many locate at the outset of global city research, originally set out to 'escape' the abstraction of politics to move into the concreteness of the city, which however was by Geddes' own admission the cradle that originally prompted the rise of politics as organized *polis* (Geddes, 1915; Hall, 1998). By many accounts, cities and politics have since their very birth been in a mutually constitutive relationship. Yet, the contemporary global city scholarship has largely struggled to highlight this. For instance, in Saskia Sassen's analysis of the late-1980s (and 1990s in the second edition of her *The Global City*) the realm of urban politics occupied a secondary positioning beyond social structures, economic processes and labor relations – a role that did not warrant politics' explicit attention in her work until recently (Sassen, 2001, 2007). Politics was also marginalized in John Friedmann's research program of the 'world city hypothesis' (1986), which once again focused on migration, capital and hierarchical tendencies among key global hubs with only passing mentions to the government of these cities.

This is of course not to say that government has been absent altogether in the evolution of the global city tradition. Politics have certainly been embedded in several of these founding studies. Nonetheless, little explicit and purposefully framed analysis of the political texture of the globalizing metropolis is presently available. This is perhaps because global city politics occupy a grey zone between urban studies and political science. Attention to the political dynamics of the global city has for the most been confined to local government studies and case-specific literatures on major metropolises. Contexts such as London and New York have in this sense a well-established lineage of work available on their urban politics but these studies have for the most part struggled for broader significance (Trounstine, 2009). At the same time, a risk that many urbanists have run in the past few decades is that of veering away from other political spheres to privilege the 'urban' – thus risking a dangerous reification of what the political confines of the city are. The main challenge for the contemporary global city researcher, then, is how to step beyond mere localization and reconcile the complexity of urban politics with broader political literatures such as those of international relations theory (IR) or global governance. To tackle this agenda, however, we need to be wary of what (political) grounds global city scholars have already covered, starting with the localized reality of the globalizing metropolis.

The local politics of the global city

For long, politics proper have remained somewhat 'black-boxed' behind core concerns of the global city literature such as transnational connectivity, socio-economic re-structuration or structural violence. As Mark Purcell (2002, 27) has argued, much of the limited literature that specifically addresses this theme still 'argues that there is a need for an expanded set of theoretical tools to understand the new politics in global cities'. This of course does not mean that urban studies more in general have lacked an appreciation of the political construction of the city – whether global or not. From this angle the city has been represented not just as result of sporadic encounters in the social spaces of humanity. What urban historians such as Mumford, Weber or Tilly have long taught us is that the nature of the city as settlement (*urbs*) is necessarily coupled with that as an association of individuals, as *civitas* (Isin, 2003). Yet civitas is not a purely self-organizing aggregation of people: the city is a centre of concentration of the practice of social arrangement and power relations, and thus a *polis* in the sense that it is constituted not just by people, but by socially organized people (the *civitas*) that rely on political settings to orchestrate their 'coming together' and producing the actor dimension of the global city. The city is, as David Harvey (2003b) put it, a 'body politic', a collective organization that supports human life like a porous ecosystem of interdependent parts whose nature was inherently political ever since its beginnings. As a political milieu, the urban is the context of cooperation and contrast, crystallized in more or less juridically formalized institutions that regulate city life, and criss-crossed by power structures stretching not solely across its texture but beyond. How the global city is governed, which authorities have a say in these practices, who composes its political community (or *civitas*) and what mechanisms of integration define the confines of the metropolis as a political system (or *polis*), matters fundamentally in that it allows us to understand the premise of the city's geopolitical agency, as well as its direct impact on other spheres of global governance. The analytical challenge here is that, when we move 'into' the global city, we might easily get lost in its complexity and stunned, as French urbanist Patrick Le Galès (2002, 183) reminds us, by an 'émerveillment du tout collectif'. Overwhelmed by multiplicity and diversity of actors, dynamics and technologies present in these strategic centres of globalization, we could easily abandon ourself to meta-theoretical speculation, particularistic exploration and eulogistic praise of global cities, going astray into their worldwide connectivity. The task of a renewed global city scholarship, then, is to reconcile the appreciation of the political texture of these metropolises with wider international processes while not reifying the city and its limits.

Now, as I have argued elsewhere (Acuto, 2013a), what remains predominantly overlooked by global city scholars in political terms is the dynamic of *becoming* 'global' city. While increasingly popular, there remains in the literature some substantial limitation in defining the process that *leads* to the emergence of global cities and in the *politics* that have a key stake in this. Olds and Yeung (2004) have in various occasions called for renewed attention by global city analysts to the role of process and governance in the making of global cities. Once we look at the dynamics that lead to the emergence of a metropolis as 'global' city, and take into account the 'glocal' (Swyngedouw, 1997) specificity that encounters both exogenous pulls (like that of the global economy) and localized contexts (such as those of urban government) that sustain these, the present geography of world affairs presents us with a much more complex political picture than most global city literature gives away. To highlight how there is no single model of the 'global city' but rather a plethora of 'differential pathways' for global emergence, Olds and Yeung demonstrated how contemporary global city models leave many unanswered questions about how global cities come into being. Crucially, they prompt us to ask, what political and governance processes are involved in the globalization of the modern metropolis?

A further analytical evolution, as suggested by Purcell (2002), is not to forget the rising importance in global city politics of new social movements among marginalized populations, which have been playing an increasingly influential role in the definition of the political texture of these cities. While the literature on these micro and non-governmental actors is still relatively underdeveloped, the discussions on global cities of the past few decades have gone to some important length in terms of defining the central questions for these political claims beyond govern*ment*. As Sassen and several other global city scholars interested in social movements have noted, the global city is a prime gateway for bottom-up claims and for challenging the established nature of urban, national and international politics. The global city offers a unique 'space of engagement' (Cox, 1998; Sassen, 2007) where the traditional boundaries of dependence, domination and control can become object of contestation and even potential evolution. If Purcell focused his analysis on the struggles over charter reforms in Los Angeles, this has equally been the case with most of the now popular Occupy movements, and a similar argument can also be developed for the uprisings of the Arab Spring, which all point to the growing potential of major urban contexts to serve as springboard for global and transnational processes (Köhler and Wissen, 2003; Al Sayyad and Massoumi, 2012).[1]

However, as Purcell noted in his study of Los Angeles, these dynamics do not undermine the importance of studying the government of global cities. Rather, the claims of new social movements and the challenges of the 'dual' and 'right to the city' literatures suggest that 'both formal political structures and electoral politics remain significant features of global city politics' and that 'if the new social movements are to have a lasting and transforming impact on global city politics, part of their project will have to engage such formal politics' (Purcell, 2002, 25).

Here a few recent contributions from planning and geography have sought to formalize a view of the local construction of the global city. As Peter Newman and Andy Thornley (2011) described in *Planning World Cities*, a growing number of metropolises have formulated a 'response to globalization' and to the fragmentation highlighted above by developing what is generally know as 'strategic urban planning' (SUP). SUP indicates a citywide policy with specific spatial implication for geographical areas within such conurbation, and targeted at the establishment of policy priorities. SUP has, in fact, become not just a policy orientation but also a political strategy sought after by subnational governments in order to develop productive engagements with a global audience (UCLG, 2010). This focus is based on the assumption that 'global city-making' is not only a process of urban management. Rather, it offers a politically driven conjugation of a complex twofold dynamic of centralization and spatial dispersion through which metropolises seek to assert their role in the networked texture of the present world system. As Newman and Thornley suggest, SUP provides a vantage point to scrutinize the assemblage of city-specific governance structures into networks capable of providing a 'localized' (but by no means not just 'local') response to the disaggregating dynamics underpinning world affairs. A focus on strategic planning then might be an analytical middle ground to unpack the conscious (i.e. 'political') globalization of the global city. SUP is not just branding, nor it is exclusively in the hands of local governments, as a plethora of other actors intersect with such networking dynamics to formulate strategic planning responses. Likewise SUP does not deny the residual centrality of government but rather allows for a multiplicity of actors to be taken into consideration. In turn, when considering more explicitly these political dimensions whether as a space for engagement of strategic construction of the global city, scholars are prompted to open the 'black box' of urban politics in highly internationalized cities In turn, this brings about a gamut of epistemological challenges for urban as much as political theorists, touching in particular upon issues of political community and leadership. Before stepping on to these challenges, it is equally important to understand how similar problems arise from a political scholarship, that of *international* politics, which has until recently received almost no consideration from the global city literature.

The international politics of the global city

How can we then systematize the global city's international relevance to depict this as a context of localized politics with more-than-local significance that intersects, but is not merely subjected to, the dominant 'meso' level of state politics? On the one hand, Purcell's focus on new social movements offers a bottom-up take on the 'production' of politics with global resonance in the globalized metropolis. On the other hand, Newman and Thornley's emphasis on strategic planning promotes a top-down understanding of the continued relevance of city government without disembodying this from both international and urban frames. Yet, both approaches might still be too confined to the purview of the 'city' as central scale for analysis of these processes. Could we then go further into the 'global' political relevance of these cities?

An alternative solution to considering these 'urban politics' as politics *in* the global city, as localized assemblage of governance structures, might be one of looking at the politics *of* the global city as an actor in the wider geography of world politics. It is then equally important to step further to take into account the active political engagements emerging *from* these cities and casting their influence on international relations. Almost in parallel to the urbanist literature, cities have also been presented by some international theorists as potential diplomatic agents (Melissen and van der Pluijm, 2007). One line of inquiry that has progressively crept in literatures beyond urban studies and geography is therefore that of the city as an international actor.

However, contrary to urban studies and local government analyses, international studies have to date offered a very limited theorization of the 'global' influence of the global city. For long this discipline has been limiting the consideration of cities to a subjected position met with assumptions of 'separateness, discontinuity and exclusivity' (Hocking, 1999, 17; Acuto, 2010, 426) that have for long placed cities as passive subsets of the national. Only until very recently, IR has been characterized by a general lack of studies capable of demonstrating that cities 'are not passive spaces suffering the indiscriminate exercise of top-down logics' (Le Galès, 2002, 262). Progressively, a niche interest in urban issues in international relations and a revival of an often overlooked lineage of research concerned with the diplomacy of sub-national actors (Hocking, 1993; Hobbs, 1994) have made their way into key international theory conferences and journals. This is for instance the case of Sofie Bouteligier's *Cities, Networks and Global Environmental Governance* (2012). Through analysis of two transnational municipal networks, Metropolis and the C40 Cities Climate Leadership Group, Bouteligier has illustrated how cities fulfill the role of strategic sites of global environmental governance, concentrating knowledge, infrastructure and institutions vital to the function of transnational actors. On a similar analytical pathway, the edited collection *Cities and Global Governance* (Amen et al., 2011) has called for innovation in international relations theory by providing examples of the different intersections between the local and the global and how these alter the conditions resulting from globalization processes.

In this sense, global environmental politics is where the theorization of cities as actors in international affairs has perhaps been most productive. Several studies of cities and climate change point us in this direction. Over more than a decade of research on the topic, scholars like Bulkeley and Betsill (2003) have provided an extensive array of analyses of how cities have been pursuing transnational networks and decentralizing local government initiatives to tackle environmental challenges beyond the realms of national and international politics. Importantly, these authors have often argued that urban governance on climate protection issues is fundamentally tied to the relations between the municipalities and other levels of decision-making within the state and the international system, which are developed by networking different spheres of authority. While these works have excavated deep into the geopolitical role of cities in responding to climate change, much of this literature has generally remained relegated to environmental politics, with relatively low attention on behalf if international relations and diplomacy scholars not directly concerned by these themes. IR has in turn rarely been addressed by these approaches. As Simon Curtis (2011) pointed out, a greater attention to the role of cities poses fundamental questions for IR theorists and can illuminate the changing nature of the international system by highlights how cities are essential to processes of globalization, providing a material and infrastructural backbone for global flows, and a set of physical sites that facilitate command and control functions for a decentralized global economy.

Overall, this embryonic scholarship calls upon global city theorists to move beyond localism or globalization to incorporate agency in the political presence of these metropolises into international discourses. Yet there remains a conspicuous gap in providing theoretical bridges between the extensive scholarship developed in urban studies and the vast debate on the transformations of the present world order in international studies. The limits of this discussion, however, are twofold. On the one hand, there remains a struggle for relevance vis-a-vis urban studies beyond global city theory. On the other hand, accounts of 'city diplomacy' (Melissen and van der Pluijm, 2007) run the risk of reifying the 'city' into a hardened category and simplified unit within broader pictures of international affairs with little appreciation for the inner political complexity of these metropolises. Conjunctly, these shortcomings are met on the ground by mounting political challenges that analyses such as those of Purcell's new social movements or Newman and Thornley's strategic planning have only begun to unpack.

Political challenges[2]

Transnational constituencies?

Thinking of politics *in* and *of* the global city means, in practical terms, considering the role of publics, constituencies and representatives on the urban landscape of highly globalized metropolises where the relationship between government and governance is being questioned. This is not just a function of the growing business influence that is progressively the central agenda of local governments. Ade Kearns and Ronan Paddison (2000), for instance, have aptly pointed out that these transformations set three interrelated challenges for city government: first, 'interurban competition has become fiercer' due to the heightened interconnectedness and pervasive territoriality of the global market; second, 'homogenising' global pulls are 'accompanied by simultaneous attempts to develop a city's local distinctive culture to attract business investment'; third, 'cities have viewed national governments as less able to help them and less relevant to their fortunes'. This brings us to a further complication. In the global city the 'local' is not just the French in Paris and the British in London: foreigners become 'localized' through their interplay with a particularly 'open' urban, while local cultures and affiliations are themselves hybridized by the globalizing influence of the city, which questions many of the traditional boundaries of group affiliation such as kinship, family and ethnicity. Global cities put in direct confrontation logics of group affiliation with those political notions of membership ('sovereignty' and 'citizenship' *in primis*) which are more or less formally remodelled, stretched, pierced and 'glocalized' through that open geography with global tendencies represented by these post-industrial metropolis. At the individual level, by producing endless cosmopolitan encounters, the global city resets the parameters of individuality as they relate to those traditional cultural, religious and political affiliations that embedded people into the state-centric system of the past centuries. This provokes a social tension whereby, as Ken Booth put it, 'identity patterns are becoming more complex, as people assert local loyalties but want to share in global values and lifestyles' (in Lipschutz, 1992, 396). The mobility-inspired and heterogeneous nature of global cities provides a fertile ground for social confrontation, thus inspiring socio-political changes in the parameters of social membership. By putting the 'local' in direct contact with the 'alien' and opening breaches through the encasements of the national that can offer global gateways to the multitudes, the post-industrial metropolis becomes a strategic terrain for conflict, socio-cultural hybridization and, ultimately, political challenges. As 'incomplete societies' (Le Galès, 2002) in constant change, global cities are characterized by a multiplicity of confrontation among indigenous and foreigners, rich and poor, legal residents and illegal migrants, all of which claim stakes as members of the various 'communities' hinged on the global city. Urban governance, defying much of the conventional statecraft logic and admitting countless 'external' influences as well as 'internal' exclusions, becomes a battleground where multiple and often competing visions of what the global city should be converge. Rights, duties and benefits of participation to this policymaking dynamic are thus twisted as the globalization of urban planning and the 'glocalization' of urban politics redesign the logic of urban governance. The idea of political membership, in the global city, assumes novel characteristics and becomes tied to alternative sources of liberties and political involvement. Providers of entitlements and facilitators of political action now range beyond the institutions of the nation state, with governance spheres above and below it both functioning as guarantors of rights and claimants of duties, and the global city seems to be acting as a core re-articulator of this process.

Central to this discussion, however, is a question that has a well-developed lineage within the global city literature. As articulated by a number of research programmes, not everyone can equally take part in, and benefit from, the globalized dynamics of the global city: politics in these urban contexts are a prime instrument for scholars to unveil the unequal construction of the metropolis and the possible, or denied, avenues for change. If we look into these dynamics, as Massey (2007, 215) noted in relation to the socio-spatial structuring of London, 'it becomes necessary to ask, when speaking of global cities, *whose city* is at issue here?' This is not just a matter of unveiling elites, as the urban politics scholarship suggested above has discussed at length. Rather the 'whose city' question is, then, crucial today more than ever because of its incomplete character. While it might be simplistic to paint stylized images of global cities in the hands of a fixed elite or purely left at the mercy of global markets, asking 'whose city' becomes less of a question and more of research programme. Considering the challenge of who participates in the government and governance of these metropolises has a crucial positioning as both an analytical orientation for urban researchers as much as a critical sensibility for the broader global city scholarship.

The rise of mayors?

The 'whose city?' question confronts us not only with political community challenges but also with the issue of authority. Who is 'in charge' in these globalizing metropolises? Surprisingly, even though the question might appear rhetorical to many, the attention that the literature has thus far paid to city leadership is minimal at best. As David Satterthwaite (2009, 4) recently argued in an editorial for *Environment & Urbanization*, mayors are often mentioned in a substantial percentage of the urbanist literature 'but rarely are their roles discussed in any detail'.[3] Even those well-established repositories of local government analysis, or the expanding genus of studies concerned with city networks that span far beyond metropolitan boundaries, have to date fallen short of providing academic and general publics with a comprehensive overview of 'glocal' political role of mayors. Quite practically, city leaders are frequently a component, but almost never the object, of large portion of studies, reports, columns and collections concerned with illustrating the changing nature of urban governance and the complex shifts underpinning city management.

Despite the scholarly oversight, the influence of global city mayors in global governance has steadily expanded over the past decade. This growing transnational agency has mostly rested on a self-appointment by cities to the central stage of global policymaking. Metropolitan leaders have been particularly prolific in catalysing international attention to cities. They have increasingly become the object of interest by international bodies such as the UN, as well as regional and transnational organizations such as the World Bank and the European Union.

Where these mayoral efforts might have been most significant is in the realm of global environmental governance. Local issues have long been part of the broader agenda of international environmental politics since its early days: one of the outcomes of the 1972 Stockholm UN Conference on the

Human Environment was the initiative to convene a 'Habitat' conference specifically focused on local environmental issues in 1976 in Vancouver. This trend continued also after Rio and through the Agenda 21 push, with a second conference (Habitat II) held in Istanbul in 1996. In this sense, the UN remained all throughout the end of the last century a core driver of this 'urbanization' of environmental issues. For instance, through the United Nations Environment Programme and in collaboration with the International Union of Local Authorities (IULA), the UN has prompted the International Council for Local Environmental Initiatives (ICLEI), which has to date become a well-established representative forum for local governmental action on sustainability issues. City leaders have thus progressively moved from ceremonial and advocacy roles to facilitating and policymaking functions. Many mayors hold today a stable position in the negotiations surrounding the UN Framework Convention on Climate Change, and their presence tends to mirror a general respect for their managerial expertise and planning 'know-how'. Crucially, this presence then injects urban features in wider international processes. For instance the United Towns Organization, IULA and ICLEI were instrumental in pushing for the inclusion of a local agenda as part of the broader Agenda 21 commitments of the Rio de Janeiro Earth Summit in 1992 (Gordon, 2007). ICLEI cemented this effort in 1993 launching the Cities for Climate Protection (CCP) Campaign with the aim of gathering a coalition of local governments sufficient to account for at least 10 per cent of the global GHGs emissions (Bulkeley and Betsill, 2003). CCP is nowadays often cited in the environmental scholarship. Of course, ICLEI and its CCP are by no means the only urban-based networks now present on the global environmental scene. If from the 1970s through the mid-1990s most of the focus on cities was being developed through the UN and in international fora, since then two trends have revolutionized the participation of cities in global governance. First, city networks have grown exponentially in numbers and membership. Second, cities have progressively carved a more extensive role in environmental governance.

We are then confronted with a (re)emerging internationalization of city leaders into global political spheres. If throughout the latter part of the twentieth century cities had developed some international structures for city-to-city cooperation, an evolution of the traditional 'city twinning' practice that has long-lived historical roots, we are now witnessing the sprawl of complex transnational networks with pervasive policymaking capacity. Different from what we could call a 'first wave' of city networks, cases like the Climate Leadership Group (C40) are today centred upon not only mayoral relations with overseas peers, but also by the cross-national integration of a myriad of local government departments and, even more importantly, by the hybridization of these links with a mounting variety of non-governmental actors from major multinational corporations like Honeywell to key technology developers like Siemens and powerful international bodies like the OECD.

London: Politics *in* and *of* a global city

The sprawl of city networks and contemporaneous emergence of 'new' internationalized cities onto the center stage of world affairs presents us with a disorienting variety of trends, cases and inner complexities for a mounting number of global cities. It might then be useful to consider here a well-know case of global city, that of London, in relation to an emblematic area of politics, environmental governance, to illustrate the complex multi-scalar ramifications of politics *in* this metropolis as much as of politics *of* London in the international arena. The British capital has certainly been a well-established cornerstone of the development of the global city literature. The importance of the politics question for global cities was indeed mirrored in Peter Hall's original 1966 work on the 'world cities' with explicit reference to London. As Hall put it, both third and first world metropolises share a common governance problem: 'that of devising an effective and economical system of local government which can organize those services that must be handled metropolis-wide; which can ensure effective delivery of those other services that must be provided locally [...] and that can secure the necessary public finance to do these things in an efficient and equitable way' (Hall, 1966, 22). Undoubtedly then, London is one of the foremost examples of metropolises that have sought to establish themselves as 'global'. In this sense, there is a long-lived experience of global city politics in the British capital, which for many centuries has had to reconnect localized development with worldwide connections. While it might be nearly impossible to trace this lineage in the little space available here, the contemporary development of London in the third millennium, characterized by a marked internationalization and by the development of London-wide governance structures such as the Greater London Authority (GLA) and its Mayor of London, could offer a productive case study.

Global city politics in London

In spite of its long-lived centrality in international affairs, London's primacy in the world system has been challenged by both wider and more localized political-economic dynamics. Since at least the 1970s the city has encountered those new geopolitical processes described above by Kearns and Paddison (2000), which have tested its catalytic interconnectedness. The city has had to face the problem of distinguishing its centrality as diverse from many of the 'newer' global cities sprawling, for instance, in East Asia. At the same time, London has been confronted by a series of governmental drawbacks spurred by the decline of the United Kingdom as a key global player after World War II and by the retreat of the state on the local front through the 1980s and 1990s (Hebbert, 1998). Central in its continuing globalization and vivid testimony of the global city challenges summarized above is the role of the GLA in the present internationalization of London. While there is today a wide and well-established literature on the politics of London that cannot unfortunately be summarized here (Travers, 2004), the more recent experience of the GLA with planning and with defining the identity of the capital as a particular global city among its many competitors is telling for our discussion.

From the very start of the GLA experience with Mayor Ken Livingstone, London was never to be 'just' a global city. The mayor had a vision of an 'exemplary' metropolis not solely 'prosperous' but also 'green' and connected.[4] In the early 2000s, an extensive series of initiatives signalled the GLA's attempt to mobilize London's politics in a 'green' direction. In order to do so, and in the wake of the central government's limitations, Livingstone had to rely on an extensive participation of the private sector in the delivery of both basic environmental research and planning, as well as in the promotion of 'green' innovations for metropolitan politics. This was echoed globally when London secured the Olympics in 2005 – a case that, as I have discussed more at length elsewhere (Acuto, 2013c), is emblematic of the political-economic construction of the capital as 'global' city. The Olympics can serve as a platform for more than athletic competition: they are contexts of political repositioning and international posturing. This, in London, became a matter of displaying environmental leadership to the masses that converged, virtually and physically, on the British capital. In bidding for the 2012 Olympics, London had promised to provide 'the greenest Games ever' to the global audiences of the games.

The profile of the London 2012 games fast emerged as more than just cosmopolitan, with the London Organising Committee of the Olympic and Paralympic Games (LOCOG) and the GLA group planning on delivering environment-friendly events and activities and then-Prime Minister Tony Blair pledging to make London 2012 'cutting edge example of sustainability'.[5] Since the bid, London has put much emphasis and mobilized considerable paradiplomatic structures to bring about this green vision. Johnson and the GLA have been interpreting the Olympics as an unparalleled chance to reaffirm London's centrality in the global urban efforts against climate change. Besides, authorities in London also feared the possibility of a weak Olympic theme as the summer games might be seen as standing as 'an island between Beijing and Rio'.[6] If Beijing 2008 was about China's opening to the world to demonstrate the maturity of the East Asian giant, and Rio 2016 should be a similar reaffirmation for Brazil as the unique host of the first South American Olympics, and London seemed to many as having 'to rely on less-transcendent material as it hosts the summer spectacular for the third time'.[7] To back up with concrete initiatives on the ground that welcoming and cosmopolitan theme that, obviously, has been an underlying reality of most Olympics to date, London rolled out a substantial green strategy to turn the 2012 games into an unprecedented policy effort for urban sustainability. The Olympics, in this sense, offered to the GLA a unique chance to promote London's green urbanism. London's 'green Olympics' strategy was centred around a number of environmental actions originally developed in partnership with BioRegional and WWF in the 'Towards One Planet 2012' statement following the bid. Core among the variety of green initiatives announced in this formulation of the 'green Olympics' were projects that concerned the sustainability of the Olympic complex, the carbon footprint of the games, the centrality of public transport, a food vision for the event and a zero waste commitment for the duration of the Olympics. London was in this sense determined to make of the games not only a temporary window into its sustainable urbanism, but also a lasting imprint on the city's development.

The role of the mayor remained a crucial one throughout. Identified as the representative for London, Mayor Livingstone cemented his role as spokesperson for the metropolis and 'planner in charge' for the Games' operationalization. In this sense, the mayor sought the candidacy both to reinforce London's 'global' image as well as to access a large-scale urban restructuring that would have probably been impossible otherwise. Obviously, the redevelopment of East London and the redevelopment of venues for the 2012 Games were among the most pervasive actions taken by the city to shape the Olympics. Venues have not only been designed with a strong emphasis on ensuring a green the Olympic legacy, but also with the aim of showcasing leadership in sustainable innovation. This included the retrofitting of existing complexes (Wimbledon, Excel, Lords and Earls Court), as well as new venues like the Olympic Stadium and the Aquatics Centre, which have been built in areas determined to be in 'need of a sustainable legacy' as opposed to those zones where there is no 'need' for a green legacy, which host temporary venues in iconic places such as Hyde Park. While all of these initiatives account for substantial influences on the Olympic context and on the future of London's 'sustainable' development, much of the planning for the Olympics has also focused on transportation as an often-overlooked element with a substantial imprint on London. Transportation has been a major target of Olympic redevelopments and upgrades. London invested over £11 million in walking and cycling routes leading to Games venues, and promoted an Active Travel Programme managed and delivered by Transport for London (a body part of the GLA) and aimed at enhancing sustainable alternatives to public services such as cycling. Tested during the Games, these planning modifications have become part of the everyday texture of the metropolis.

This brief excursion into the recent definition of London's Olympic profile illustrates many of the theoretical and challenging markers sketched in the previous section of this chapter. Certainly, it tells us a story that has at its heart the importance of the internationalization of London as a component of a more-than-local geography of socio-economic relations. Likewise, it testifies that global cities can display a capacity to control this global development and points once more at the importance of local government and in particular mayors as key hinges in stirring the direction of a global city's globalization. Yet, it also sustains many of the critiques sketched in the previous chapters and in the introductory reviews of the global city literature. The internationalization of these metropolises is deeply embedded into the ambiguous, if not deleterious, effects of neoliberalization and of the 'business privilege' (Newman and Thornley, 2011, 144) that dominates the governance landscape of these metropolises. Yet, how do these considerations relate to the *international* scholarship on global city politics?

Global city politics of London

The production of a 'global city' through the Olympics testifies to the explicit attempt by London authorities to present the city to the world as a leader in sustainable urbanism. However, if we also admit some diplomatic (or 'paradiplomatic') capacity for these metropolises as the international theory literature has been suggesting, then we need to step beyond planning and urbanism and look at whether London might also be a player in the dynamics of world politics.

This is perhaps best represented by London's experience with the C40, a network of major metropolises committed to curb climate change and currently headed by New York mayor Michael Bloomberg. Not surprisingly, the C40, which has increasingly catalysed media and policy attention worldwide, was kick-started by Livingstone in 2005. C40 has since been developing regular summits, strategic implementation workshops and, perhaps most significantly, sowing close ties with key international players such as the Clinton Foundation, the World Bank or the OECD. Yet, since the 2006 partnership with the Foundation's Climate Initiative (CCI), C40 has also witnessed a mounting influence of American cities, New York above all, at the expenses of the British capital. Since Toronto mayor David Miller replaced Livingstone as chair of the Group in 2008, London has progressively lost a central positioning in steering the direction of the C40. Under Bloomberg, the World Bank has eventually become a key partner. An MoU was signed at the 2011 C40 Sao Paulo summit, while the group has merged with the CCI and steadily expanded its global reach. Albeit still a founding member of the C40 steering committee and a well-respected actor in the proceedings of the Group, London has arguably lost its primacy in the C40 network and Boris Johnson, Livingstone's successor, has generally occupied a secondary role behind the direction of Bloomberg, Clinton and several growing voices from Asia and South America.

London's role in the C40 has mostly been based on the assumption that city-to-city cooperation allows greater international influence than individual municipal action. At the heart of Livingstone's original diplomatic efforts that set up the C40 network in 2005 was the assumption that pooling the potential international leverage of global cities would have led to substantial improvement on their separate capacity to tackle issues such as climate change. This has recently confirmed throughout the eight years of the C40's experience by the network's success in catalysing key transnational actors like the World Bank, and has been further sanctioned by the C40 chairs that succeeded Livingstone, and in particular by Bloomberg. The C40, then, testifies to the development of a diplomatic track in parallel, and even partial contrast, with state politics. The case of London's diplomacy for the Olympics, instead, points at a different approach to cooperation: since the competition for the games puts in direct competition cities, London has relied here on joint efforts with its central government and on direct negotiation with an international organization like the IOC. So, while London was not the sole initiator of this diplomatic effort, the city has generally been invested with a catalytic role and carried out city diplomacy with the consent of the state, rather than in parallel with the state, but in potential contrast with other cities.

In the pooling process of the C40 London has demonstrated an outgoing entrepreneurial approach based on summitry, *ad hoc* technical consultancies and policy coordination efforts, and more traditional city-to-city relations. This type of city diplomacy has been pinpointed on the rhetoric that international processes have been lagging behind in terms of action on the ground and have become dissociated from the everyday (urban) determinants of climate change. Oriented in this critical way, the city diplomacy of the C40 has also very often resulted in a relatively adversarial positioning against states, which are perceived by cities as slow and ineffective bureaucratic machines that are entangled in the possibly unsolvable deadlocks of the multilateral process. This orientation has progressively flourished on the initial accusations moved by Livingstone, and reached a point where mayors now generally blame the international system for its diplomatic shortcomings. In the case of the Olympics, instead, London has relied on an 'inward' entrepreneurial approach where city diplomacy has functioned as a pivot for wider processes and initiatives. In this instance the city has largely avoided clashes against the state, which has on the contrary been a core partner of the GLA throughout the bidding, planning and delivery processes.

Key theme of the diplomatic case of the C40 is, of course, that of climate change. Sustainable urbanism is in this sense presented as a core solution to the challenges of global warming but metropolises are also engaged in the city diplomacy of the C40 for developmental reasons. Sustainable policy and green retrofitting are seen in this case as core assets for the success of truly 'global' cities in the contemporary global market. As confirmed by the several studies now available on city diplomacy for climate purposes (Bouteligier, 2012; Acuto, 2013a), local governments have been pushing on a green agenda not just because of a cosmopolitan rationale but also, if not chiefly, due to the competitive advantages that green urban redevelopment and international leadership on liveability and sustainability can offer at present. 'Quality of life' has in fact become a recurrent mantra of these diplomatic efforts as much as liberal statements on cooperation and relative gains more common to the international process. Much of the same can be argued in terms of theme of the Olympics. Sustainability has in this sense been merged with the cosmopolitanism rhetoric typical of the games, and has been promoted down to the most mundane practices such as food or waste management thanks to the comprehensive planning capacity allowed by such large sporting event. Green, in the Olympic case, has not only been associated to planning more in general, as in the C40, but even more markedly with a change in the way the city and its 'citizens' (whether local or temporary) operate. The GLA's emphasis on sporting activities has been a core bridge between big picture thinking of urban planning and the 'small'-scale societal developments of, for instance, cycling and recycling.

In terms of delivery of these approaches, mayors and city leaders are central in initiatives like the C40 and the Olympics, which have progressively taken on their prerogatives the duty of partaking in global debates and providing 'local' solutions to 'global' challenges. Likewise, non-governmental brokers like the Clinton Foundation have also been invested with increasingly central roles in global city politics due to their essential bridging role with global market tools and forces. Partnerships with NGOs and public–private negotiations have therefore become the norm in city diplomacy as cities have sought alternative pathways to international cooperation. Once again, the Olympics case confirms this logic. To implement the green strategy the city and its governmental partners have relied heavily on the advantages and language of public–private partnership and have been shying off large corporate giants like McDonald's or BP. Key in developing this bridge have, just like in the C40, been the mayor and his executive team, as well as the planners that have provided technical backing to the initiatives of the city's leadership.

Overall, both the Olympics as much as city networks like the C40 present a crucial testimony as to the multi-scalar reach of global cities like London. These transnational processes allow for substantial globalization initiatives but also present many chances to transform diplomacy into practical action. London's engagement with a crucial international theme such as sustainability is a vivid demonstration that global cities matter for IR because they participate in world politics by recasting several boundaries of the 'international' and often challenging the pecking order of the dominant state-centric hierarchies of global governance. At the same time, however, cities can also function as catalysts for political alignments that not only conjugate state, international and transnational processes, but also reach deep into everyday lives – a bridging function that could after all prompt an even more multi-scalar appreciation of the geopolitical dimension of the global city.

For a *global* politics of the global city

Liberating us from stereotypical images of states and cities as limited containers, the global city scholarship has had an important stake in creating a more fluid image of our contemporary society and could have a crucial say in developing a holistic understanding of what politics is in a time of visceral challenges. As illustrated above, some advancements in the study of the political dimension of global cities have already pushed us in this direction. Yet, scholars in both urban studies and IR should not limit themselves to the investigation of, respectively, the politics *in* and *of* global cities. Rather, I suggested, we might now be able to join in these analytical advancement and step beyond scholarly divides to develop perspective on the global city that reconnects inner governmental challenges to international dynamics as much as to mundane realities. The ultimate possibility of a geopolitical look into the global city, then, is that this fluid view can further what Massey called a progressive 'geographical imagination' capable of looking 'both within and beyond the city and hold the two things in tension' (1999, 161). The politics of the global city, in fact, force us to continuously link the 'urban' both with the international and the local, to maintain a 'glocal' viewpoint and repeatedly refer to situated as much as globalized practices. Yet, to step to this global sense of politics a greater attention is needed for a realm of urban and international affairs that has, not just in the global city literature but in urban and international studies more in general, received very little attention: the every day. As David Ley (2004, 151) pointed out, the scholarship on global cities has a marked tendency towards a dangerous 'underdevelopment of human agency and everyday life' and, crucially for politics, the 'disappearance of the citizen' from the landscape of the globalizing metropolis. Overwhelmed by the transnational flows and networks that define the 'global' nature of these cities, the mundane experience of the individual subject in the global city is often sidelined in much of the literature and in the almost totality of the press. This is a theoretical evolution, then, that begs not just for a multi-disciplinary bridge between international and urban analysis, but also for a concerted effort aimed at reconciling all sites of politics in, of and through the global city – a task no single theorist or theoretical perspective might be able to achieve individually.

Scrutinizing global city politics, then, demands as much for an inherent interdisciplinary collaboration as for an attention for the development of these metropolises 'on the ground' of everyday affairs. This is not a call for middle grounds, nor one for simplifications. It would be easy to advocate a political internationalization of the global city scholarship, but this would jeopardize the refined urbanist sense of the city as a complex socio-technical reality whose limits are precarious and whose politics are inherently contingent. What investigations of new social movements such as those of Purcell and Sassen or refinements of the study of urban governance like those of Newman and Thornley all point at is that the global city scholarship has the capacity to step beyond its disciplinary confines and begin fruitful conversations on the diverse political relevance of these metropolises. Likewise, it might be equally misleading to lead a charge for the localization of international theory into the minute detail of urban politics as this analytical step might betray the effective 'big picture' outlook so characteristic of IR. Rather, global city politics demand for holistic programmes of research that attend to both the contingency of urban studies and the abstraction of IR, and to do so support the growth of collaborative research and cross-disciplinary bridges – possibly the only pathway to a truly 'global' account of the politics of the global city.

Notes

1. Of particular relevance here is the recently launched initiative Theatrum Mundi led by Saskia Sassen and Richard Sennet that, among other themes, focuses on the streets of major global cities as platforms for new socio-political assemblages. For a summary in relation to the Arab Spring and new social movements see Saskia Sassen, 'The Global Street' *Huffington Post Blog*, 10 March 2011, available at http://www.huffingtonpost.com/saskia-sassen/the-global-street_b_989880.html.
2. This section builds on work resulting from a Fellowship at the University of Southern California's Center on Public Diplomacy, published in Acuto (2013a, 2013b and in particular 2013c). I owe some particular thanks to Jessica Castillo and Emily Schatzle at the University of Southern California for the research support during these inquiries.
3. The only conspicuous exception might be that of the journal *Local Government Studies* that, with a mostly UK- and Europe-centric focus, has gathered some interesting analysis of the election, leadership process and governing coalitions sustaining mayors. Yet, this has to date not stepped beyond the confines of this more traditional political science analysis, and has born very little consideration as to what 'international' role these elected officials might play.
4. See for instance the foreword to the 2008 consolidated version of the Plan. Mayor of London, The London Plan: Consolidated with Alterations since 2004 (London: Greater London Authority, February 2008), p.xi.
5. 'London 2012 to be the greenest ever', *BBC News Online*, 23 January 2007, available at http://news.bbc.co.uk/1/hi/uk/6289357.stm.
6. Christopher Clarey, 'London's Games, an Island Between Beijing and Rio', *The New York Times*, 7 May 2012.
7. Ibid.

12
The Security Dimension

David Murakami-Wood

Introduction

This chapter considers the urban dimensions of security and insecurity, specifically in relation to the contemporary urban condition represented by the term 'global' or 'world city network' (Taylor, 2004b). It takes a Foucauldian biopolitical approach to security/life adjusted by Mbembé's necropolitical considerations of insecurity/death, and focuses on the way in which global circuits of security knowledge (McCann, 2011) are deployed to govern populations insecure and marginalized in the global city, the new urban outcasts (Wacquant, 2008) or the 'precariat' (Standing, 2011). These global circuits of security knowledge are illustrated with the case of Rio de Janeiro. Drawing on interviews conducted with a range of senior police officers, government officials and community representatives, the discussion identifies six examples of circulating global security knowledge which have been brought to bear on the recent management of the favelas of Rio de Janeiro: military intervention in Haiti; the transformation of Bogota in Columbia; the Zero Tolerance model of Giuliani in New York in the 1990s; Israeli community policing; sports mega-events; and technocratic surveillance. It concludes that the Rio case indicates that global cities are rarely simply receivers of security knowledge but, whether successful or not, become sources of new security knowledge that continues to circulate in the global city network.

Global urban (in)security

For urban studies and geography, the city is both referent and at the same time the terrain of study, and thus, some analyses or urban (in)security draw more on top-down assumptions that consider the (in)security *of* the city and others from the bottom-up that consider (in)security *in* the city. However, it is also the case that the referents have been shifting: on the one hand, as Jon Coaffee and I argued in 2006, 'security is coming home' – there has been a long term towards the (military) securitization of the urban and domestic, accelerated by 9/11 and the subsequent War on Terror; and on the other hand, critical approaches to international relations, security studies and geopolitics have meant that the formally top-down approaches have become increasingly aware of social, cultural and psychological concerns. This has meant that the referent object of security in most contexts is almost always multiple and contested.

As Sigmund Freud argued, existential or psychic insecurity is a fundamental feature of the human condition (Wolstein, 1987), and certainly such existential insecurity can be seen to underlie many contemporary developments, in particular efforts to defend personal and territorial space against the threatening Other. But security and insecurity are also material and measurable: matters of life and death and the distance between. In the initial lectures that make up *Security, Territory, Population*[1] Michel Foucault (2007) argued that security was the primary object of government. This he referred to as biopolitics, the management of life itself and as Dillon and Lobo-Guerrero (2008) have pointed out, '[t]here is no biopolitics of this, or a biopolitics of that. When one says biopolitics one says security; albeit in a certain way.' 'Biopower', which consists of biopolitics plus the kinds of specific disciplinary mechanisms Foucault outlined in his earlier work like *Discipline and Punish* (1977), is applied to constantly mobile and changing populations. The concept, therefore, is also mobile and dependent on the conception of 'life'. Equally, neither insecurity and security are simply material states of existence, but also processes, either movements towards greater security and the 'capacity for taking action to secure a better future' (Ericson, 2007, 4) or the risk of an increasingly insecure existence (c.f. Beck, 2002).

Risk management is for Dillon and Lobo-Guerrero (2008) already embedded within the calculations around life that constitute Foucault's notion of biopolitics. However the opposite of security, insecurity, needs to be thought of as more than just 'the opposite of life' or one outcome of biopower. Insecurity is a condition approaching death, or its nearest equivalent living state, what Giorgio Agamben (1998, 2005) called 'bare life', wherein survival can be the only objective. In living with risk, the insecure live with varied probabilities of approaching bare life or death. Drawing on Agamben, postcolonial theorist Achille Mbembé (2003) argued that in the age of terror and counter-terror, the management of death or those in the bare-life subjectivity of the 'living dead', bodies marked for death, has become a significant variation on the Foucauldian notion of biopower, or what Mbembé called 'necropower'.

As Foucault emphasized, biopower (and therefore also necropower) operates through territory as well as on population and neither security-life nor insecurity-death are equally shared across societies or distributed evenly across space, but are continuous produced and reproduced outcomes of processes of sociospatial construction, whether resulting indirectly from spatial fixes to crises of capitalism (Harvey, 2001) or directly from actions with security as their specific objective.

Foucault was writing primarily with reference to two spatial scales: firstly, the body in the institution and secondly, the nation state: cities do not figure very strongly in his analysis. However, it is clear from a historical analysis of urban formation that the city is a biopolitical mechanism, and not for the popularly understood defensive function of city walls – in fact a much more complex and variable feature than earlier writers knew – but for the fact that cities concentrate populations in space, and allow first sovereign power but then to be effected over people in a way that could not be carried out so easily over a more dispersed population, indeed in many ways a city is as much the designation of a kind of population as it is a space. The specific forms of power included violence, human surveillance through agents and spatial control through internal and external walls and gates (Coaffee et al., 2008). This is what Mumford (1961) observed, some time before Foucault even considered the biopolitical, when describing cities as a function of the pathology of rulership. Although, as Janet Abu-Lughod (1989) demonstrated, urban networks have a long history, economic and sociospatial transformations made the global urban network of the twentieth century very different from the far less intensely connected cities of previous centuries. By the early 1900s, the networks of economic relationships linking cities in the mediaeval and early modern period had moved from geographically limited mercantilist world economies (Braudel, 1984) into a single more integrated world system of liberal capitalism (Wallenstein, 1989). Thus cities in the modern industrial nation state were not the same as cities in the pre-modern period, and cities in an era of post-industrialism and globalization are different again; however, the seductions of creating a purely linear pattern should be avoided. First of all, as Foucault observed, although the governmentality (the art of government) has evolved and new ideas have emerged over time it is not that one form of governmentality entirely replaces another, but that all continue to be available and can be deployed on different territories and populations in a variety of configurations. This is partly because there is never a singular 'population'. The first lesson from Abu-Lughod, Mbembé and other writers of (post)colonial theory and history is that we should throw out the imperial universalism that would have a western/northern development pathway as what constitutes 'human' history, and relatedly, understand that in practice colonial nations and hegemonic classes produced (and continue to produce) such discourses at least partly with the aim of constructing certain kinds of bodies and territories. In this context we can see the emergence of an urban necropolitics, where some are marked for inclusion and life, and some for exclusion and death (or bare life).

Since the end of the Cold War, there has been a confluence of related understandings with the spatial: from Barry Buzan (1999) in international relations/security studies describing zones of peace, through Scott Lash and

John Urry (1994) in sociology who separated the world into 'tame and wild zones', to urban studies and geography, in which King (1990), Mollenkopf and Castells (1991) and Saskia Sassen (2001) among many others have talked of the 'dual city'. None of these theories are simple core/periphery or inside/outside models; all to some extent acknowledge what Buzan calls 'interleaved zones of living' (Buzan, 1999, 10), that is that the new territories and populations produced in contemporary governmentality are at once differentiated – not part of a general civilizational 'progress' – yet temporally and geographically proximate.

In the contemporary period, we have seen a more clearly emerging division between kinds of (in)security that affect different cities and also different groups and social classes within cities, as a rapidly neoliberalizing capitalism took hold in the second half of the twentieth century (see e.g. Peck, 2010). The end of Fordism and the advent of neoliberal globalization have led to the partial reconstruction of class divisions on a global scale, generated huge inequalities within cities and in particular led to the vast expansion of global south cities (Montgomery et al., 2004).[2] Combined with the continued legacy of the colonial city (King, 1990) this had led to internal divisions, with a privileged overseer class living alongside but separate from a vast pool of insecure migrant labour. This can be macro-exclusionary, as in the new city-state models of governmentality which entirely exclude both city builders and/or the mass of the regular urban working class from the city, either being kept in external camps, as with the builders of Dubai, or having to cross national border controls to work and return home each day, as in the case of Singapore (Davis and Monk, 2007). This can also happen against design intentions. Brasilia, the 'utopian' modernist capital of Brazil, created by avowed socialist architects Lucio Costa and Oscar Niemeyer, has become exclusionary in its evolution. Only the middle class of government workers are able to afford to live in the clean modernist housing surrounding the government core, and the working class of cleaners, shop workers and labourers are bussed in, in the morning, from less salubrious satellite cities via the underground bus station and bussed out again, in the evening.

However, for most global cities, these macro-exclusionary modes are only part of the story. As Davis and Monk (2007) show, biopower in the urban context is not exercised in strict territorial divisions by sovereign power. A complex geography of micro-exclusion has emerged, produced by a shifting assemblage of state and private power: thus terms like 'splintered' (Graham and Marvin, 2001) and 'fractured' (Koonings and Kruijt, 2007) have come to describe the new physical and economic landscapes of global cities. In Brazil, this has been well described by Teresa Caldeira (2001) as a 'city of walls', in which it is not the state's sovereign power alone that produces territorial division but the retreat of the state – or the fact that it was never quite as extensive as was imagined in the first place – and its supplementing or replacement by overlapping private security companies and economically differentiated self-protection.

Within this fractured urban network, Garland argued that societies are now characterized by 'a generalized insecurity deriving from the precariousness of social and economic relations' (Garland, 2001, 133). Loic Wacquant (2008) has defined this as a situation of 'advanced marginality' which although its particular sociospatiality differs from place to place, has common features, and more recently Standing (2011) has characterized those in this situation of permanent insecurity as not a new proletariat but a 'precariat' whose conditions of life and existence are constantly in question.

Importantly, this is not because they are entirely outside of global circuits of urban knowledge (McCann, 2011) but because they are the immediate 'Other', a new 'dangerous class' (Standing, 2011), and in particular the security knowledge generated and applied in the global urban network is directed at solving 'them' and the existential security problem that they represent to the wealthier classes, in other words at securitizing their existence for the benefit of the mainstream society. This can take the form of either biopolitical projects for inclusion, or necropolitical projects to exclude or remove them from the existential sphere of consideration of the wealthy, either through mass imprisonment – whether that be through a prison-industrial complex as in the USA or the transformation of whole cities into open-air prisons, as in the Gaza Strip in Palestine – or through continued repression or mass movement elsewhere.

Yet, the global urban circuits through which such knowledge flows are not so direct, and also have other sources and connections, and in practice this ideal-typical division is more complex. Partly this is because, despite its waning in a neoliberal era (Brown, 2010), the nation state has not gone away and remains a significant force, partly because neoliberalism demands constant intervention to function (Peck, 2010) but in some cases it also remains a social democratic force. In addition, the complex nature of government in practice means that 'the state' can be at once national, regional or local depending on the particular city in question and each level of the state can have potentially contradictory orientations. Finally, state organizations, at whatever level, have their own institutional trajectories and may also be very different from each other: there can be multiple bodies concerned with police and security, for example, each with their own priorities, histories and cultures. Finally, one of the major characteristics of the current form of 'neoliberalizing government' (Brenner et al., 2010) is a constant churning of transnational 'policy innovation'. Such policy learning takes place not just between states or urban authorities or between elite politicians and policy-makers, but often between mid-level bureaucrats of various specific organizations, state or private, united by their technical expertise and specialisms – a group Larner and Laurie (2010) in their work on the simultaneous globalization and privatization of water policy, term 'travelling technocrats'. I will now turn to a particular example of this complex and differentiated reproduction of (in)security in the global city network, in Rio de Janeiro, and its particular 'precariat': the residents of the informal settlements (favelas). I will consider what flows of security knowledge circulate, binding the global city network together while generating multiple forms of macro and micro-exclusion around and within global cities.

(In)security in Rio de Janeiro

Rio de Janeiro has a complex governmental and security landscape. The city has its own government under the *Prefeito* (Mayor),[3] responsible for some aspects of security, particularly emergency services, disaster preparedness and low-level crime through the *Guarda Municipal* (City Police) (GM).[4] The city sits within the *Estado* (state) of Rio de Janeiro, under the *Governador* (Governor),[5] responsible for the *Polícia Militar* (Military Police, PM),[6] the enforcers and *Polícia Civil* (Civil Police, PC),[7] the detectives. The situation is complicated by the existence of the notorious Batalhão de Operações Policiais Especiais (Police Special Operation Battalion, BOPE),[8] a semi-independent force within the PM. The Federal Government of Brazil is responsible for most social policy and also has its own *Polícia Federal* (Federal Police, PF), responsible for anti-corruption and cross-border crime. This multilevel, multi-agency structure results in constantly changing and potentially contradictory government directions. In the mid-1980s while the country was still ruled by the military (until 1985), socialist Lionel Brizola was Governor of Rio. When César Maia, a moderate social democrat, was Mayor from 2001 to 2008, the country switched from a centre-right government to the first ever leftist presidency, under Luiz Inácio Lula da Silva ('Lula') from 2003 to 2011. The national government remains with Lula's Workers' Party, but the state elected a more right-wing governor, Sergio Cabral, in 2007, and the city followed in 2008, electing Eduardo Paes.

Despite nominally universal citizenship, the most marginal have remained often outside official recognition (Holston, 2008). Historically, such invisibility meant no protection against arbitrary detention, torture and death, as was the case during military rule. Militias (*Autodefesas Comunitárias* – Community Self-Defence organizations, ADCs) remain at large in Rio de Janeiro, and as a report to the state legislature in 2009 revealed, involve members of the army, police forces and local politicians (ALERJ, 2009). To counter this at national level, Lula introduced programs, which endured beyond his tenure, including *Fome Zero* (Zero Hunger)[9] and *Programa Bolsa Família* (PBF) (family support program)[10] as well as the national biometric Identity Card.[11] These are all biopolitical measures, aimed at creating a material and psychic sense of inclusion and are extraordinarily popular, even the ID card scheme (Murakami Wood and Firmino, 2009), unlike such measures in some global north nation states (Bennett and Lyon, 2008).

For those who are the generally willing subjects of such measures, particularly the most marginal, those living in informal settlements known as the *favelas or morros*[12] of Rio there has also been long-term policy oscillation between deliberate state ignorance and problematization (Perlman, 2009). However, with their continued growth, and immediate proximity to some of the wealthiest communities in the city, ignoring them has become impossible. Instead, the question is the nature of the problem they present: whether one of crime and security or one of social policy.

The former problematization sees the morros as a source of threat: the morros are controlled by armed drug gangs, and no-go areas for non-*moradores* (residents). And many morros are indeed controlled by gangs associated with the cocaine trade, affiliated either to the Commando Vermelho (Red Command, CV) or it offshoots, particularly the Amigos de Amigos (Friend of Friends, AdA) (Arias, 2006). The answer in this case has been necropolitical: either obliteration, expulsion and/or rebuilding along official lines, or police invasion and retreat. The latter perspective in contrast works in a more conventional biopolitical manner by incorporating morros into wider society through the provision of infrastructure, education and social services.

The biopolitical problematization predominated in two particular periods: firstly, under Governor Lionel Brizola, who concentrated on the building of schools in morros, as well as the upgrading of some services, and more recently under Mayor César Maia, whose *Favela-Bairro* (Favela to Neighbourhood) program was endorsed by major international institutions and donors from the UNDP to the World Bank (see e.g. Moreno-Dodson, 2005). However, more recently the pendulum has swung back towards the necropolitical problematization; however, instead of a purely hardline approach, there is a two-handed strategy. Both the city and state are united in an approach to the morros characterized by Mayor Eduardo Paes as 'choque de ordem' ('shock of order'). Favela-Bairro has been abandoned in favour of a new policy of 'pacification', in which special Military Police *Unidades de Policía Pacificadores* (Police Pacification Units, UPPs)[13] occupy selected morros, driving out gangs and instilling state control. After the restoration of state authority, social programs are introduced, very much in the way that 'hearts and minds' programs are introduced in the aftermath of military invasions. When I visited in 2009, the program had just started with three communities, Santa Marta, Cidade de Deus (the 'City of God' of movie fame) and Jardím Batan. By December 2012, it covered 28 morros (see Table 12.1), including the biggest and most complex of all, Complexo do Alemão and Rocinha, and involved around 8,000 officers. According to the state security administration, by 2014 there would be more than 40 UPPs involving 12, 500 police officers.[14]

It is clear from talking to those involved in the development of the UPP strategy that the long-term ambitions remain broadly biopolitical and inclusive.[15] According to a former PM colonel-turned-state security

Table 12.1   UPPs in Rio de Janeiro, December 2012

Year	No. of New UPPs	Running Total of UPPs	Communities Occupied by UPPs (Date Occupied)
2008	1	1	Santa Marta (19/12)
2009	4	5	Cidade de Deus (16/2), Jardim Batan (18/2), Babilônia e Chapéu Mangueira (10/6), Pavão-Pavãozinho e Cantagalo (23/12)
2010	8	13	Ladeira dos Tabajaras/Cabritos (14/1), Providência (26/4), Borel (7/6), Formiga (1/7), Andaraí (28/7), Salgueiro (17/9),Turano (30/10), Macacos (30/11)
2011	5	18	São João, Quieto e Matriz (31/1), Coroa, Fallet e Fogueteiro (25/2), Escondidinho e Prazeres (25/2), Complexo de São Carlos (17/5), Mangueira/Tuiuti (3/11)
2012	10	28	Vidigal (18/01), Fazendinha (18/04), Nova Brasília (18/04), Adeus/Baiana (11/05), Alemão (30/05), Chatuba (27/06), Fé/Sereno (27/06), Parque Proletário (28/08), Vila Cruzeiro (28/08), Rocinha (20/09)

Source: Secretaria de Estado de Segurança do Rio de Janeiro (SESEG), 2012.

administrator, this is all about demographic transformation – it is a question of population management, 'favelas in Rio de Janeiro these days have 150,000–200,000 residents, they're cities and they need support from visible policing integrated within the community'.

The result of this biopolitical understanding is that the forms of control that are envisaged as necessary cannot be the traditional military solution:

It's pointless to place half a dozen police in the Complexo do Alemão where there are fifty or sixty rifles on the street in the hands of traffickers throughout the day. It's ineffective. If I need to bring the presence of the state to these people I have to give social infrastructure and policing, but not of the invasive kind – as if it was enemy territory, going in and killing a dozen people and then retreating.

Where does this combined approach come from? From the interviews, six recurrent sources of global urban security knowledge were identified[16]: Brazil's own history and politics; regional examples of postcolonial military intervention, particularly Haiti; regional urban innovation, particularly in Colombia; New York and 'Zero Tolerance'; Israeli community policing; the influence of sports mega-events; and finally, technocratic models of surveillance.

The first source was in PM references to Haiti, which has seen highly militarized security aid becoming the normal response to disasters that have afflicted the country and the city of Port-au-Prince in particular (see Mullings et al., 2010; Zanotti, 2010). This discourse recognized Rio de Janeiro as a 'dual city' and those who mentioned Haiti or Port-au-Prince generally also mentioned New York, as if Rio was at once both New York and Port-au-Prince which, in terms of its inequalities, is a fair description. However, the references to Haiti were not about poverty but about pacification. As one former senior officer in the BOPE argued:

> The armed forces prepare peacekeeping units and could prepare units to operate as they do so in Haiti. As peacekeepers and not as a force to intervene in a war against an enemy from another country, what we have here is not a conventional war, however the weapons are for war – mines, grenade launchers – the casualties, deaths and victims are from war.

There can be no better example of security 'coming home'. In this discourse, the moradores are an internal urban colonial Other – unruly and violent subjects who need to be subdued in the only manner to which they are accustomed, war. Furthermore, this is justified because of international knowledge and the signifiers of war, the presence of international aid bodies: '[t]he Red Cross are active in our territory, the UN also. If they see this as a war type situation why does Brazil not see this?'

The second circuit was also regional, but related not to the 'bad example' of Haiti, but the 'good example' of cities in Colombia, as one senior military police officer said:

> We are doing something other countries have also done – Colombia had its' 'choque de ordem' based on studies by academics from the humanities. Antanas Mockus, the ex-mayor of Bogota together with Fajado in Medellin undertook urban re-organization in their cities, street planning, buildings, street traffic. This isn't simply an idea that was born in Rio de Janeiro.

Several exemplary global cities and 'heroic figures' were invoked by interviewees. But both Mockus and Fajado are from the political centre-left, opposed to the rightist national government of Colombia and have deployed a variety of sociocultural, educational and other initiatives as well as programs for the democratic accountability of police (Moncada, 2009); both have more in common with César Maia than with the current regime in Rio. Such examples were appealed to as free-floating signifiers, matters of purely operational policy that could be shared and adapted without any consideration of context.

The third source of security knowledge was another exemplary global city and 'heroic figure': New York and ex-Mayor Rudolph ('Rudy') Giuliani. Giuliani's 'zero tolerance' approach to policing based on 'compstat' crime mapping technologies is presented as a unique success story, despite evidence that different policies elsewhere produced similar results (Greene, 1999) and that deeper underlying trends might have been the cause (Bowling, 1999). But Giuliani has based a career in urban security consultancy[17] on this perception of success and is a frequent speaker in urban management and policing events worldwide, part of the 'elite networking' in crime control policy (Jones and Newburn, 2002). Giuliani was mentioned by name by both police and community representatives, the former approvingly, the latter mockingly, and shortly after the interviews in 2009, was briefly mooted as a special security advisor to Rio for the forthcoming mega-events (Globo.com, 2009).

The fourth source is Israeli community policing. Several officers involved in UPPs have been sent on training courses in Israel. One such fast-rising junior female officer described it this way:

> There is a lot of excellent voluntary work in Israel, because the history of the country, years of attacks, has led to this.... The city council there is doing good work for citizenship and I was there to visit these projects to see if they could be useful here.

Rio de Janeiro was not the only Latin American city sending officers and officials on these training courses, 'the course was with other Latin American people also connected with this type of work. They were from Chile, Argentina, Peru, Panamá, Guatemala...' However, she was also aware of the ambivalent reactions that this course generated in Rio:

> People thought, 'Ah she went to Israel to do a course on guerrilla warfare' which is not true at all... on the one hand it's good because the traffickers think, 'Wow she's going to Israel'. But for the community this was a bit worrying, but I asked for calm and explained that the course was on community work and not associated with crime. Nevertheless they still asked, 'But if it's community work why Israel? Why not France?'

Why not indeed? Once again, the answer seems to lie in the way in which policing is seen increasingly as a value-free form of street level security bureaucracy whose lessons are transferable irrespective of policy and political context. Official analyses of community policing models in Israel from the mid-'90s stress the transferability and generalizability of the lessons learned (see e.g. Weisburd et al., 2002). However, unlike the 'elite networking' of both Mockus and Giuliani, this is the policy learning of Larner and Laurie's (2010) 'travelling technocrats'.

The fifth source of security knowledge is the travelling circus of the global city network: sports mega-events. Rio de Janeiro is hosting the 2016 Olympic Games and part of the 2014 FIFA World Cup. Sports mega-events are a significant element in economic competition between global cities and security is now part of the management of reputational risk that enables global cities to attract further investment (Coaffee and Rogers, 2008). It is clear from the interviews, other academic research (Gaffney, 2010) and recent media reports (Glenny, 2012) that the securing of the games entails the increasing insecurity of the marginalized residents of morros that are either perceived as significant threats to order – in that they harbour active and armed gangs – or who are occupying space required for event venues or are simply alongside major routes into the city where they might detract from visitors' aesthetic experience and generate psychic insecurity.

Finally, tying many of other sources together is what I have previously termed 'globalizing technocratic surveillance' (Murakami Wood, 2011b). However, in that work I concluded that this was not yet a significant influence in Rio, despite the use of video surveillance (closed circuit television, CCTV) for traffic control and in some wealthier districts like Copacabana (see Cardoso, 2012) the unexpected introduction of CCTV into UPP-occupied Santa Marta in late 2009 (see Murakami Wood, 2011a, b). All PM officers interviewed were sceptical about the value of CCTV, with the exception of the director of the then relatively small and antiquated central PM CCTV control room. One senior figure in BOPE was openly contemptuous, and another PM commander certainly did not see CCTV as a panacea: 'a policy of security cannot in my view be based on surveillance cameras. Surveillance complements visible policing on the streets, along with a show of force.' Senior officers in other police forces had greater enthusiasm, particularly in the then relatively weak GM, which had an old emergency control centre that they wanted to transform into a more modern operation. However, by 2012, Rio had not one but two integrated control rooms under construction or in operation, and a vastly expanding network of cameras. The first is ostensibly not a police control room, but exactly what the GM officer had hoped for: the hub of a so-called 'Smart City' initiative, the Centro de Operações Rio da Prefeitura (Rio Prefectural Operations Centre)[18] largely funded by IBM, to harness 'big data' to solve multiple problems of urban government.[19] This mayoral initiative links weather forecasting, traffic control and emergency services in a single large control room, with real time monitoring and response. Its focus is on anticipating, preempting or responding to emergencies, including in particular landslides caused by flooding, and traffic accidents. This is important for the security of residents of the morros, who tend to live on land that is very steep and/or vulnerable to flooding. In 2010, a landslide in one of the communities that I visited in the previous year, Morro dos Prazeres, killed 34 people. However, the mayor's response was to sign a decree ordering the evacuation of Prazeres and 157 other 'high risk' areas (*Guardian*, 2010). That the mayor was motivated more by necropolitical security considerations than humanitarian motives became clear within a year as a topographical study indicated that only a relatively small area of Prazeres was actually at serious risk (*MundoReal*, 2011).

Future directions

The integration of Rio de Janeiro into global circuits of urban security knowledge looks set to accelerate and intensify. The Smart City control room is being joined by a new police control centre bringing together all the forces under the Security Secretary of the State of Rio's mandate. This promises much but has been continuously behind schedule. Part of this project will involve acting as a command and control centre for the FIFA World Cup in 2014. Although sports mega-events have often been seen as a driver of security innovation in cities (see Bennett and Haggerty, 2011), it seems that in Rio, the Cup and the Olympic Games are additional drivers to an already-expanding neoliberal security agenda.

Rio is not simply a passive receiver of sources of information circulating in global urban knowledge networks. Just as Favela-Bairro circulated as a social exemplar, so Rio's contemporary biopolitics is a discursive resource for other global cities, for example, what Rio Smart City might mean in India (*Economic Times*, 2012). This is no accident: the city has relentlessly promoted the initiative through social media and slick online video marketing which describes the centre of operations as the 'heart and soul of Rio',[20] and Eduardo Paes himself has been presenting himself at 'progressive' public, like the TED talks, as a forward-thinking techno-savvy mayor who can manage his city in real time from anywhere in the globe.[21] At the same time, other Latin American cities, in particular Buenos Aires in Argentina, have been eyeing the UPP model (Galdo, 2011). And more generally, Brazil's example is also being eagerly promoted by the American state as the democratically acceptable face of urban securitization. Thus the humanitarian aspects of the UPP program are emphasized and personalized: for example in 2012, Major Pricilla de Oliveira Azevedo, former commander of the first UPP in Santa Marta, was named by the State Department as one of its 'International Women of Courage'.

But Rio's security agenda is not going unchallenged, from three main sources. Firstly, the occupations of the morros have not ended gang violence: in 2012 it was reported that the UPP in the Morro de São Carlos had to be reinforced by a significant BOPE operation (G1, 2012), and also in that year, a female PM officer was killed in Nova Brasília (de Menezes, 2012), the first UPP death and a blow for a program that has tried to freshen the violent macho image of the PM by pushing female officers to the forefront.

Secondly, pushing out drug gangs from the morros of Rio has resulted in a large upsurge of crime in places to which they have been displaced, in particular the neighbouring city, Niterói (Roller, 2012). This has generated calls for the extension of an already very expensive program – estimates for just the initial occupation of Complexo do Alemão alone are more than 160M Reais or about $80M US) – to other cities in the state. And finally, there is the emergence of an anti-occupation and anti-surveillance politics (Murakami Wood, 2011a; see also Glenny, 2012). This is to be found in some UPP-occupied communities but has allies among middle-class human rights advocates and left-wing politicians. The long-term fate of the current security initiatives in Rio could depend both on future state and city elections, and on what happens during the World Cup and Olympics. However, even if the initiatives are seen as unsuccessful, it does not mean that they will not continue to circulate within global urban networks of security knowledge. As Clive Norris (2012) has argued with respect to CCTV, despite its manifest failure, it not only continues to spread but the discursive influence of such globally circulating security objects can often be redoubled because, as Brenner et al. (2008) observe, in an era of neoliberalizing government, failure merely generates a perceived need for further biopolitical innovation.

Notes

1. Before security is largely abandoned as a theme in favour of governmentality in the later lectures.
2. Or, to use Wallenstein's (2000) term, a 'transition' to an as yet uncertain new form of global economic organization.
3. http://www.rio.rj.gov.br/.
4. http://www.rio.rj.gov.br/web/gmrio/principal.
5. www.rj.gov.br.
6. http://www.policiamilitar.rj.gov.br/.
7. http://www.policiacivil.rj.gov.br/.
8. http://www.pmerj.rj.gov.br/bope/.
9. http://www.fomezero.gov.br/.
10. www.mds.gov.br/bolsafamilia.
11. http://www.brasil.gov.br/para/servicos/documentacao/conheca-o-novo-registro-de-identidade-civil-ric.
12. Although most in Brazil use the terms *favela* and *favelados* (favela dwellers), those living in these areas prefer the term, *morro* (hill) and *moradores* (hill-dweller) as less pejorative.
13. http://www.rj.gov.br/web/seseg/exibeconteudo?article-id=1349728.
14. See Note 12 supra. It should be noted that there are somewhere around 200 morros in the city of Rio de Janeiro.
15. All interviews were conducted in March and April 2009. For the purposes of this chapter, I have not identified individuals except by an approximate description of their official role.
16. There were also other local and national sources, but these are outside the scope of this chapter.
17. http://www.giulianipartners.com/default.aspx.

18. Centro de Operações Rio da Prefeitura website http://www.rio.rj.gov.br/web/ corio.
19. IBM Smarter Cities Challenge http://smartercitieschallenge.org/.
20. Centro de Operações Rio da Prefeitura 'Centro de Operações Rio, o cérebro da cidade' https://www.youtube.com/watch?v=Li28GiLGS7k.
21. See the TED Talk 'The Four Commandments of Cities'. ted.com http://www.ted.com/talks/eduardo_paes_the_4_commandments_of_cities.html.

13
Global City Challenges: A View from the Field

Glen Searle

This chapter addresses the challenge of identifying and (re)assembling the different dimensions of, and perspectives on, globalization in an emergent global city, Sydney. Its main purpose is to show how the challenges that face Sydney as a global city can be understood in a more nuanced way that both enlarges our perspectives on the processes of globalization and illustrates the interconnectedness of the challenges that these processes generate.

The chapter first traces the emergence of Sydney as a global city. It then considers how symbolic elements have been used to underpin the idea of global Sydney, and the related issue of built form distinctiveness. This is followed by consideration of the city's socio-economic polarization and related multicultural challenges that have intensified under the influence of steadily expanding globalization. Urban development planning challenges arising from Sydney's rise to global status are then explored. The individual globalization themes developed in the preceding chapters of this book are woven into the narrative in this chapter on global Sydney and its challenges and summarized at the end.

The rise of global Sydney

Sydney was Australia's first European settlement, founded in 1788. It has kept its position as the nation's prime commercial centre and largest city over most of the period since then, except when Melbourne had commercial leadership from the late nineteenth century to the mid-twentieth century, and when it was the biggest city from the late 1850s to around 1900. Sydney's national commercial leadership up to the period of contemporary globalization emerged in at least two phases. The first, in the colonial era up to the1850s, was based on Sydney's large and rich hinterland, centred on exports of wool through Sydney. Melbourne's hinterland was settled later, and over the next century produced less than half the wool – Australia's main export up to the 1960s – that was grown in Sydney's catchment (Davidson, 1987, 82–83). However, with the discovery of gold in central Victoria in 1851, Melbourne's population increased rapidly as it provided supplies and services for the goldfields, and wealth flowed back to it. It soon passed Sydney as Australia's biggest city, a position that was reinforced by burgeoning manufacturing production under a protectionist colonial government (Kitchen, 1934, 51). With a bigger population, and control and management of the nation's main mines, Melbourne also became the financial capital of Australia (Shann, 1933). The severe depression of the 1890s ended the first wave of Melbourne's growth: more than 100 public companies defaulted within nine months from July 1891, and in two years Melbourne lost nearly 50,000 of its population (Cannon, 1986, 18, 24–26, 48).

Sydney's population surpassed Melbourne's in the first decade of the twentieth century, but Melbourne retained its financial leadership. This leadership was reinforced by Melbourne's status as the national capital and location of the federal Treasury from 1901 to 1927, when Canberra became the capital. But Melbourne's financial ascendancy slowly waned. In recognition of Sydney's greater population and the concentration of federal government departmental head offices in Melbourne, the headquarters of the government's new Commonwealth Bank had been located in Sydney since 1912. The production of wool in Sydney's New South Wales hinterland continued into the twentieth century to be more than double that of Melbourne's hinterland of Victoria (Davidson, 1987, 82–83). This made Sydney the nation's biggest wool export port, and generated lending business for Sydney's banks, particularly the Bank of New South Wales, Australia's largest, which was traditionally the biggest lender to Australia's wool industry (Holder, 1970, 267, 281). Australia's first air service to the UK was started in 1934 by Qantas from Brisbane (where Qantas then had its headquarters), but by the late 1930s the service had been switched to Sydney's Mascot aerodrome. Melbourne did not have a designated international airport until 1950 and, unlike Sydney, could not take Boeing 707 aircraft until its new airport opened in 1971, placing it at a disadvantage for international tourist and business travel. The difference was critical as contemporary globalization from the 1960s onwards relied upon air linkages to the US and Japan, which favoured a Sydney gateway.

Melbourne still had the headquarters of 50 of the top 100 Australian companies in 1953 to Sydney's 37. But by 1973 the positions were reversed, with Sydney having 50 head offices of the top 100 compared to Melbourne's 39 (Taylor and Thrift, 1981, 100). This was paralleled by changes in financial flows: by around 1970 the turnover on the Sydney Stock Exchange surpassed Melbourne's for the first time (Bain, 2007, 56). A futures exchange was established in Sydney in 1960 with the support of the state government (Bain, 2007, 236), and by the late 1970s had expanded into trading financial contracts. This placed the exchange, the only one in Australia, in a strong position to control Australian trading in financial derivatives which became central to the expansion of the global financial system from the 1980s (Harvey, 2005, 33). Sydney's national commercial leadership was also strengthened from around the 1960s as state-based economies became more integrated into the national economy, with state-based businesses being taken over by national companies in processed food production and department store business, for example (see also Gibson and Horvath, 1983).

In 1983 the new Australian government adopted measures to deregulate the financial system, involving floating the Australian dollar, reduced monitoring of international capital flows, reduced controls over the operations of non-traditional and foreign financial institutions and over the range of tradable financial products (O'Neill and Fagan, 2006, 209), and allowing a number of foreign banks to obtain full banking licenses to operate in Australia. This effectively enabled Australia to fully participate in the global financial system that had rapidly expanded with the financial deregulation which followed the end of the Bretton Woods system in 1971.

A second feature of evolving globalization also had significant implications for Australia. By the 1980s a third global economic bloc was emerging in the Asia Pacific area to challenge the American and European blocs as the shift of goods and services production from developed countries accelerated. This increased the imperative for multinational companies to establish regional headquarters (RHQs) to service and control their operations in Asia Pacific countries. Australia's common time zone, its large Asian language immigrant population and its base of advanced professional services and associated skills were advantageous for attracting such RHQs. Perhaps more importantly, the economic rise of the Asia Pacific bloc produced a growing middle class cohort that generated demands for international tourism and English language higher education. Australia's unique tourist attractions and its respected tertiary education institutions that taught in English meant it was well placed to meet these demands.

A third globalization dimension was also significant. The General Agreement on Trade and Tariffs led to a gradual worldwide diminution of trade barriers, which was accelerated by multilateral treaties and by standardization of trade agreements when the World Trade Organization agreements took effect in 1995 (Harvey, 2005, 92). In Australia, the high import tariffs that had, since federation in 1901, underpinned a large manufacturing sector relying on local markets started to be reduced from the early 1970s. In the mid-1980s there were unilateral long-term reductions in import protection in the automobile and the clothing, textiles and footwear manufacturing sectors, compensated by government-funded industry restructuring plans. By 2001, Australia was considered to have the lowest overall barriers to trade and investment among all OECD nations (OECD, 2001, 118). Resulting import competition had a major impact on Australia's largest manufacturing sectors, particularly in Melbourne.

When these various changes caused Australia's economy to become much more integrated with the global economy from the mid-1980s, Sydney was positioned to be the city through which Australia's principal global linkages were made. The city's national commercial leadership had led to financial leadership, and its futures exchange gave it a head start in participation in trading of derivatives and foreign currency that underpinned the rapid expansion of the global financial system. Commercial leadership also gave Sydney the strongest advanced producer services base especially in law and information technology, which interacted synergistically with the finance sector in activities such as new share offerings and mergers and acquisitions. This base has also enabled Sydney to provide a major share of high level services to mining firm head offices in Perth and Brisbane that control the massively increased exports of coal and iron ore to Asia (Spiller Gibbons Swan Pty Ltd and National Institute for Economic and Industry Research, 2000). Sydney was the country's main international and communications gateway with the most direct flights to foreign destinations (Searle, 1996, 14), which was a key advantage for attracting international business travel and associated investment as well as tourists from overseas. The city's natural attractions of its harbour, beaches and climate and its global icon, the Opera House, were also a major advantage in attracting overseas investment and tourism. (The author recalls bureaucrats in the Department of Decentralisation and Development in the late 1960s saying that they only had to show overseas businessmen the view of the harbour from the department's 12th floor windows to clinch a decision to locate in Sydney.) By the 1980s, Sydney's commercial expansion and its amenity were attracting the biggest share of immigration, with more than a third of Australia's new migrants choosing to live in Sydney. With a much-increased share of migrants coming from Asia, it meant that Sydney now had a large number of residents who spoke an Asian language. This was to prove a significant attraction for multinational companies establishing technical support services in Australia for their Asian customers and their Asian branch operations. Sydney's universities, which included two of the top eight in Australia, then provided the foundation for the next phase of the city's globalization. Large numbers of Asian students started tertiary studies in Australia from the late 1980s as Asia Pacific young adult numbers and aspirations increased (Hugo, 2006) and an 'education export' industry developed to eventually challenge gold as the nation's third most valuable export. By 2011 there were around 560,000 international students enrolled in Australia, including over 200,000 in higher education (Australian Education International, 2012).

Thus Sydney's historical and geographical circumstances have seen it emerge as Australia's global city. The national commercial preeminence was a firm foundation for global connections. These dimensions ensured Sydney would become Australia's global city after 1960.

Current signifiers of global Sydney

The outcome of the changes overviewed above is expressed in a range of indicators of Sydney's current global character. In 1983 the city was already the preferred location of Australia's foreign banks, with 73 having offices in Sydney compared with 6 in Melbourne (Bain, 2007, 13). This preference continued following deregulation of the financial sector, when the majority of new foreign-owned banks and investment banks setting up in Australia chose Sydney for their head offices (Bain, 2007, 12). In 2010, the volume of futures and options derivatives traded on the Australian Stock Exchange (with such activity being centred in Sydney) ranked the exchange number 21 in the world (Futures Industry Association, 2011). The Australian foreign exchange market, also focused on Sydney, in recent years has had the seventh highest turnover in the world (Department of Industry, Tourism and Resources, 2006). By 2005, more than 60 per cent of Asia Pacific's regional headquarters established in Australia by multinational companies had been located in Sydney (New South Wales Government, 2005). Major Sydney firms have, in turn, become significant players in foreign markets, with Westfield being the world's largest operator of shopping centres; QBE Insurance derives most of its revenue from overseas and is the world's 18th largest general insurer (2012); while Qantas is the world's 13th largest airline in passenger numbers (2012). By 2012, international education was worth $6 billion a year to New South Wales, with 171,000 international students – nearly all of them in Sydney – enrolled, including 110,000 from Asia (Patty, 2012). Sydney is also Australia's major destination for international tourists. In 2011, Sydney accounted for 42 per cent of all passenger seats on flights to or from Australia (Bureau of Infrastructure, Transport and Regional Economics, 2012), and over 30 per cent of international visitors (Tourism Research Australia, 2012).

The globalization of Sydney's economy and society took a specific character that emerged from the city's history and geography. In turn, this has generated a set of challenges that refract general globalization imperatives through a distinctive local lens. The following sections draw on key themes in the chapters of this book to discuss these distinctive challenges, but it is worth first summarizing the basic dimensions that frame Sydney's globalization issues. The first concerns problems of providing infrastructure, services and housing for Sydney's growth in general, and globally driven growth in particular. For example, what are the fiscal and environmental limitations to producing sustainable development? Is problematic housing affordability a necessary corollary of a global city? A second dimension involves the interrelated challenges of ameliorating the socio-economic polarization that is characteristic of global cities, and of enabling the cultural diversity of Sydney's immigrants to enhance the city's life and character. Another framing dimension relates to Sydney's built form distinctiveness: does the steady global homogenization of new developments matter in the context of the city's existing global icons? The following sections provide a contribution to discussion of these issues.

Globalization, image, built environment

Sydney's rise to global status has inevitably generated a new layer of development over the city. This has been basically led by the requirements of global activity, and is reflected in commercial investment in office buildings, transport and logistics facilities, educational use and residential space at high densities.

At a broader level the state has attempted to use major developments to actively promote Sydney's global image – notably the year 2000 Olympic Games. This has contrasted with the accidental role that Sydney's truly global icons – the Opera House, the Harbour Bridge and the Harbour itself, all of which predate Sydney's global phase – have played in attracting global activities. However, the fundamental question arising from the new built environment of global Sydney concerns its impact on Sydney's sense of its distinctive physical identity, and what might be getting lost.

This question has arisen most strongly in regard to the state-led redevelopment of Darling Harbour, adjacent to the CBD. This project, conceived in the early 1980s, was intended to capture an increased share of already expanding tourism numbers coming to Australia. It incorporated major exhibition and convention buildings, a harbourside market and a hotel along the foreshore, a maritime museum and Sydney's first casino. The scheme was controlled by a special development corporation with planning powers to authorize and fast track developments so that the project could be the centrepiece of the city's bicentennial celebrations in 1988. The inspiration for the scheme was Baltimore's Harborplace development, led by developer James Rouse, who was employed by the state government to be a consultant for Darling Harbour. Not surprisingly, the outcomes at Darling Harbour embodied several of Baltimore's elements, notably the harbourside market. Darling Harbour's development has been criticized as having a 'grim familiarity' and being 'monotonous and inevitable' (Sudjic, 1993, 300). In the process, the possibility of using the historic wool stores, the old power station and other remnants of the precinct's history as the leitmotif of redevelopment was spurned. Instead, an overseas model was transposed because it had proven successful, albeit in a different historical and geographical context.

Two development outcomes at Darling Harbour demonstrated the consequences of disregarding local context. The first was the construction of a monorail instead of a tram line to provide necessary public transport from Darling Harbour to the Sydney CBD (Daly and Malone, 1996; Searle, 2008, 215). The monorail was opposed by the City Council because of its negative impacts on city streetscapes. The elevated line ran in front of historic building facades, off-horizontal on sloping streets, scything the integrity of the streetscape. The government was forced to exempt the monorail from state planning legislation to circumvent city council rejection of the line. The other Darling Harbour development that imposed a decontextualized outcome was the Sydney Casino, which would pay a licence fee that defrayed much of the Darling Harbour redevelopment costs (Searle and Bounds, 1999). The casino was built on the site of a former power station that could have potentially been redeveloped as a gaming venue, retaining its built heritage. However, this could have constrained the government's license fee. The winning US-Australian partnership instead opted for a US-style casino complex of three towers of up to 19 levels (to provide harbour views for hotel guests) in 'ziggurat' form. There was significant local community opposition to the casino. But one prominent residential activist accepted the reality of the casino and successfully worked with the developers to incorporate sandstone cladding to make the casino look a little more like a traditional Sydney building (Hillier and Searle, 1995).

Sydney's most striking development response to the possibilities of globalization has been the stadiums and other projects constructed to host the year 2000 Olympic Games. The Olympics were sought by the government in large part to make Sydney more conspicuous on the global map of investors and tourists. The focus of construction for the Games was at Homebush Bay on surplus government land where the two main stadia, several smaller venues and the Olympic Village were built. These developments, particularly the Olympic Village, provided an opportunity to demonstrate, albeit with a state subsidy, how more sustainable urban development in Australian conditions could be achieved through passive and active solar energy features and water recycling (Searle, 2012). The master plan adopted for Olympic Park was devised by a US landscape architect, George Hargreaves. While the plan skillfully integrated the disparate venues that had been developed in a locationally ad hoc fashion, the plan's main axis, Olympic Boulevarde with its vast width of 170 meters, reinforces the constructed emptiness of the precinct outside major events. The post-Olympics master plan is attempting to insert greater vitality into Olympic Park with new high-rise residential and commercial development.

By contrast Fox Studios, another new global entertainment venue developed on state land, has successfully adapted the built heritage of its old inner city Sydney Showground site. All significant heritage structures have been preserved. Former show pavilions have been converted into movie production sound stages and exhibition and concert venues. The showground ring is being reused as a village green for temporary entertainment such as circuses and a twice-weekly farmers' market.

Such fusing of global activities into the older building fabric not only allows the character of the city's built environment to organically evolve à la

Jane Jacobs (Jacobs, 1961). It also avoids the risks of constructing specialized facilities for global activities, especially global entertainment, that can later lie underused when the original activities move on. The venues built for the Olympic Games are a classic illustration of these risks (Searle, 2002, 2012). The main indoor and outdoor stadia, both privately developed, each failed to attract a regular flow of events in the years after 2000. As a consequence the main outdoor stadium was eventually sold at a price much below the original construction cost, with a total loss of investment equity. A number of the other specialized venues constructed for the Olympics such as equestrian, rowing and shooting facilities have required state subsidies to keep operating.

An earlier venue constructed with state funding to host global entertainment told the same tale. In 1989 the government announced it would help to fund construction of a motor raceway on state land at Eastern Creek in outer western Sydney to host the Australian round of the motor cycle grand prix, and to bid for a Formula 1 grand prix race (Searle and Bounds, 1999). Hosting the motor cycle race would provide an opportunity to strengthen Sydney's global awareness, with up to 300 million viewers around the world expected to watch the event. The raceway was awarded the motor cycle round for six years from 1991. But crowds were less than a quarter of those forecast, and financial inducements by the Victorian government allowed it to recapture the race in 1997. Since then the raceway has not held an international event, though it hosts an annual round of the local V8 Supercar series. Whether this justifies the original raceway costs to the government of $140 million is doubtful.

The most recent attempt to proactively generate major globally oriented development in Sydney is at Barangaroo, a 22 hectare state dockside site on the western side of the CBD at north Darling Harbour. The project is intended to provide 508,000 square meters of floor space, mainly in three office towers, to 'secure Sydney's role as a global financial services hub in the Asia Pacific region' (Barangaroo Delivery Authority, 2010). Whether the provision of office space alone will attract global functions is uncertain at this time. Notwithstanding this concern, the project has caused central issues relating to the impact of globalization on Sydney's built form to be revisited. In this case, the proposed development is seen by professionals as failing to properly connect and align with the historic city grid (City of Sydney, 2010). Moreover, the project is seen to lack fine-grained urbanism and to have restricted potential for spontaneity and change, features exacerbated by having only one developer (see articles in the May/June 2010 issue of *Architecture Australia*).

Contestation over the project has also shown how the global icon of Sydney Harbour is fiercely safeguarded by the community. Three separate community groups were formed over concerns about the excessive height and bulk of the scheme, but in particular about the perceived threat from a proposal for a red-tinted high-rise hotel jutting into the harbour. The hotel had been proposed by the project's lead architect, Lord Richard Rogers of the UK, as an iconic 'statement'. For the community groups, this was seen as the thin edge of the wedge, a precursor to allowing widespread incursions into the harbour. Their protests, and an 11,000 signature petition to state parliament, caused the incoming state government in 2011 to delete the proposed pier and its hotel as well as make other project modifications.

This in turn raises questions about the impact of global 'starchitects' such as Rogers on a global city like Sydney. Does the supposed excellence of their architecture outweigh its homogenizing and de-localizing effects? There is a debate in Australian circles about whether a truly 'local' commercial architecture is possible in the context of large scale national, let alone international, architectural practices. As Bryant (2012) has noted: 'The botched [Barangaroo] tendering process... revealed how international architects, in this case Richard Rogers, can still lord it over the locals. The original competition winner, Hill Thalis, had the project taken away from him.' In the early years of Australian modernist architecture it had been possible to discern distinctive local styles, notably the curving forms of several of Harry Seidler's buildings in Sydney. But Sydney's globalization has been accompanied by increasing use of world starchitects, employed so that projects can be noticed. Conversely, a major developer believes that leading international architects want to have Sydney, with its world city status, on their projects' lists (Dennis, 2012). One example is Renzo Piano. His Aurora Place (2000) development in fact responds to local context with a curved and twisted main façade that is intended to correspond spatially with the Opera House down the street, and extensive use of terracotta cladding to reflect Sydney's traditional residential roofing material. Recently Frank Gehry, of Guggenheim Museum Bilbao fame, has designed a central Sydney university building with a 'crumpled' façade that is, inevitably, unlike any existing building in Sydney (although it uses Sydney's traditional sandstone as a material) but which could itself eventually become an icon for the city.

So perhaps the infusion of new designs from the starchitects will bring a richer, if potentially less locally grounded, architectural palette to Sydney. The blandness of much of the central city development in Sydney's boom years of the 1980s certainly supports this notion, as demonstrated by the international hotels constructed to accommodate the influx of tourists from overseas. These were built to an international template designed to maximize yields, featuring unarticulated façades with serried rows of windows that ignored contextual fenestration. This is illustrated by the Intercontinental Hotel, constructed around the 1896 sandstone state Treasury building which provides restaurants and bars: the plain 1984 hotel tower above with its grid of small rectangular windows does not attempt to reference the elaborate Treasury façade with its Greek-style portico. Perversely, the very blandness of most of central Sydney's modern architecture has allowed the city to provide an indeterminate global city backdrop for shooting Hollywood studio movies, as in *The Matrix* (1999).

The building of global Sydney is still a work in progress. Even so, the government's desire to attract more and more global activity has seen it and the city council turn to more ephemeral strategies to attract international attention. In this, the city has returned to its world icons and deployed them as transient artifices. In 1996 the city council started its New Year's Eve fireworks display, which incorporates fireworks on the Harbour Bridge and on barges in the harbour itself. The first show featured an 'Olympic Torch' on Sydney Tower to symbolize the countdown to the year 2000 Olympic Games. The global dimension of the fireworks has remained significant, as they are shown on television around the world as the first celebration across the globe of the New Year. In 2009 the government put on the first annual Vivid Sydney festival, to attract tourists in the off-peak early winter period. The festival is badged as an 'ideas' festival with a series of music and other creative events, designed to 'showcase Sydney as the creative hub of the Asia Pacific' (Destination NSW, 2012). The visual backdrop to the festival is large-scale 3D moving mapping projections on the Opera House and two prominent public buildings on the harbour nearby, in addition to illuminated skyscrapers. Thus both the Harbour Bridge and the Opera House have been commodified and made hyper-real for the tourist/global gaze.

Globalization, social diversity, polarization

Sydney's globalization from the 1980s has brought not only increasing ethnic and cultural diversity, but also greater socio-economic polarization. Together, they have produced a more spatially divided city. Such an outcome has been the norm across most capitalist cities over the last 30 years as neoliberal urban governance has accentuated the basic tendencies of capitalism to produce spatially uneven landscapes. However, globalization has given Sydney's inherent spatial division an extra intensity and variety.

The most evident contribution to economic polarization from Sydney's globalization has come from the wave of analysts, dealers and traders who have been at the heart of the expanded and diversified financial sector. As in other global financial centres, these occupations have been paid very high salaries and bonuses over the last two or three decades (Baum et al., 2006, 1572). Producer services occupations supporting the finance sector, such as lawyers, accountants and specialized consultants, have also increased significantly in number and received very high incomes. All these jobs are very centralized in and around the CBD, due in large part to the importance of face-to-face meetings for information exchange, negotiation and the generation of trust, and to the speed with which needed services can be supplied. Much of the wealth of these workers has been spent on very expensive housing in the highest amenity areas, notably those around the harbour near the central city. The most obvious physical manifestation of this has been the development of luxury high-rise apartment blocks in and near the city centre, usually with harbour views, and often converted from office blocks which had a lower premium on views.

The result has been significant extra pressure on Sydney's housing costs. While average housing costs rise as city population increases as existing land supply becomes more sought after (Abelson, 1993), Sydney's high paid global activity employees have accentuated this effect. As Sydney's globalization gathered pace between 1986 and 1996, the city's average household incomes rose, whereas Melbourne's fell, helping to explain Sydney's higher housing prices (Yates, 2001). By early 2012, established houses in Sydney were being sold for a $605,000 median price compared to $468,000 in Melbourne (ABS, 2012a). Sydney's ratio of median house price to median household income of 9.2 was 'severely unaffordable' and the third worst of cities in global Anglophone countries, according to the 2012 Demographia housing affordability survey (Demographia and Performance Urban Planning, 2012). These high housing costs have forced more households into private rental accommodation, and required them to pay higher rents. In 2009–10, 21.1 per cent of all Sydney households had housing costs of 30 per cent or more of gross income (the usual benchmark indicating housing stress), compared to 15.5 per cent in Melbourne. Households renting privately in Sydney paid 23 per cent of gross household income on average in housing costs versus 19 per cent in Melbourne (ABS, 2011).

The lower income households that have been most affected by Sydney's high housing costs have included a significant number generated by global activities, countering the high income beneficiaries of globalization. They include jobs such as cleaners and security staff for the global sector offices. They also include those servicing the international tourism industry such as kitchen hands, waiters, cleaners, taxi drivers and hotel janitors, many of them taken by immigrants. This industry has, like finance and producer services, become concentrated in central Sydney, this time because of the global icons there and the historic Rocks district. The result has been new international hotels and the growth of restaurants, cafes and retail outlets relying heavily on tourist trade. Tourism development has also been stimulated by the growth of the overseas backpacker market, leading to a demand for accommodation and eating and drinking facilities in the bohemian Kings Cross district and other inner suburbs. In central and inner Sydney, the focus of global jobs, a total of 4,300 hospitality workers (64 per cent of all such jobs in central/inner Sydney) and 1,900 cleaners (71 per cent) commuted in each day in 2001 from other parts of Sydney where housing costs were lower (Yates, Randolph and Holloway, 2006). Those who did live in central Sydney most often had their housing costs supported by other incomes in the household (61 per cent of hospitality workers living and working in central/inner Sydney were neither the main household earner nor their spouse/partner, and 45 per cent lived in shared households (Yates et al., 2006)). At the same time, manufacturing competition from Asian countries, exacerbated by the lowering of import tariffs, has caused blue collar jobs in middle and outer suburbs to disappear and unemployment there to rise. Since 1983, Sydney has lost its last car assembly plant, its remaining television set production and its last major white goods factory, inter alia. Thus Sydney has become spatially polarized into an eastern half that has more globally oriented jobs with generally higher incomes and housing prices especially around the harbour, and associated glitz such as expensive bars, restaurants and nightclubs in its inner areas, and a western half with lower paid jobs, lower cost housing and an increasing share of the poor.

Many of the low paid jobs generated by global activities, particularly in restaurants, are occupied by overseas students. The government's 20 hour a week overseas student work restriction means they have to take low paid casual work (Nyland et al., 2007). Sydney's high housing costs force many to look for work beyond 20 hours, making them vulnerable to exploitation and underpayment. The *Sydney Morning Herald* (Whyte and Lucas, 2013) reported in 2013 that 43 Sydney restaurants were known to pay below the minimum wage, with the worst conditions at Chinese and Japanese restaurants. Inadequate incomes force overseas students into living in overcrowded rental accommodation, illegal boarding houses and significant distances from educational campuses, according to a government task force (Kembrey, 2012).

Until Sydney's contemporary globalization phase started in the 1980s, low cost housing was available in the inner city as well as the outer suburbs and many middle suburbs. By that time, however, the gentrification of inner suburbs was well under way, a process that was reinforced by the influx of high paid global jobs. As the globalization of Sydney's economy intensified during the 1990s, the housing price premium of the inner city increased, a trend that is continuing. In 1994, average housing prices 5 km from the CBD were around 50 per cent higher than they were 45 km from the CBD; by 2002, the premium had increased to around 100 per cent (New South Wales Government, 2005). The significant amenity differences between Sydney's inner suburbs and outer suburbs away from the coast have accentuated this premium. The inner suburbs have harbour views, sea breezes in summer and access to beaches, with the result that 25–44-year-old households, for example, are prepared to pay a stronger locational premium for inner suburban housing compared with similar households in Melbourne (Yates, 2001). But even so, western Sydney housing prices have remained relatively high by national standards. Consequently, since the 1980s there has been significant out-migration from Sydney, especially to South East Queensland to take advantage of the latter's lower housing costs and perceived attractive lifestyle.

This migration out of Sydney has corresponded with a rise in overseas immigration into Sydney, coinciding with the expansion of global activities since the 1980s. An increased emphasis on skills as a permanent entry requirement has seen a large increase in Asian immigrants, in particular, with many such immigrants coming from overseas students who have completed their qualifications in Sydney educational institutions. Forty per cent of Sydney's population in 2011 had been born overseas (ABS, 2012b), and those born in Asia comprised an increasingly important share. Those born in China comprised 3.4 per cent of the population, for example, and 6.5 per cent claimed Chinese ancestry. While many Asian immigrants have been able to establish themselves in prosperous suburbs such as Chatswood on the North Shore, the majority have found this difficult, and have concentrated in cheaper housing areas in the middle and outer west and south-west. Asian students have been a major market for new high rise housing around the Chinatown/southern CBD area.

Sydney's heightened multicultural persona has brought its own contributions to Sydney's globalization. One of the darker dimensions of globalization across the world has been the growth of international drug trafficking. Some of Sydney's Asia Pacific population has challenged more established local gangs and become involved in trafficking of drugs, as the movie *Little Fish* (2005) so harrowingly depicted in its 'Little Saigon' locale in western Sydney. Nevertheless, populist perceptions that concentrations of Asian immigrants generate higher levels of gang wars and other criminal activity have not been borne out by statistics. A study in 1998 found that rates of crime in 'Little Saigon' – Cabramatta – were unexceptional (Birmingham, 1999, 423). By contrast, some Chinese Hong Kong migrants qualifying via the business start-up category have been able to send their families to live in Sydney, but remain in Hong Kong to continue their business there as 'astronaut immigrants' (Pe-Pua, 1996). Most emigrants from China/Hong Kong have chosen to live in apartment blocks, avoiding the alienating quality of desolate outer suburban living experienced by the Hong Kong family shown in the movie *Floating Life* (1996). In general the new Asian population of Sydney has brought enhanced vibrancy to older multicultural centres such as Chinatown and Cabramatta, the Vietnamese focus in western Sydney, and generated new multicultural foci across the west and south-west suburbs.

The oldest cultural group in Sydney, the Aboriginal population, faces its own challenges from the city's globalization. The main Aboriginal concentration has been in inner south Redfern, centred on the Block, where 102 old terrace houses had been bought for the existing Aboriginal community with federal government funding in the 1970s. These were eventually demolished to rid the precinct of drug-based crime, and there are plans for the Aboriginal Housing Company to replace them with apartments. Nevertheless social problems have remained. A long history of hostile relations between police and the Aboriginal community culminated in a riot outside Redfern station in February 2004. This flash point was a principal trigger for the formation of the state government Redfern-Waterloo Authority in 2004. The Authority was set up with special powers to address social problems in Redfern and adjacent Waterloo by creating jobs and constructing new housing. But a sub-text was the potential for redevelopment around Redfern station which would allow the area to link into the 'knowledge economy' because of its location in Sydney's 'global arc' stretching from the airport to the south through Redfern and the CBD to the Macquarie Park hi-tech area to the north-west (Jopson and Ryle, 2004). There has been little evidence of such development thus far, and it remains to be seen whether the desire to 'fill in' Sydney's global spaces will eventually threaten the Redfern Aboriginal community.

Another cultural community that is being intersected by globalization is Sydney's gay and lesbian population. This has always been part of Sydney society, though mostly covert until homosexuality was decriminalized in 1984 (Falconer, 2010, 187). In 1978 a march through city streets by gay rights protestors demanding repeal of anti-gay laws grew to 2,000 participants and was attacked by police in the process of making many arrests (Falconer, 2010, 187–188). This was the genesis of the annual Gay and Lesbian Mardi Gras parade through the inner east, featuring gaudy and provocative choreography, floats and costumes. It has become a global tourist event, with many of the crowd of several hundred thousand who watch the parade each year flying in from overseas to attend.

Globalization, infrastructure and planning

Sydney's global status is not something that the city can take for granted. However, its present global activities present a range of planning and governance challenges centred on infrastructure and housing that are being addressed in an often less-than-adequate fashion. There has also been a tendency to be somewhat complacent about its continuing ranking as a global city.

The main infrastructure deficiency emerging since Sydney's current globalization phase began concerns transport. In particular, there has been too little public transport infrastructure built in response to the growing population and employment. For example, although job numbers in the CBD increased from 145,000 in 1991 to 227,000 in 2006 (Xu and Milthorpe, 2010), the only new public transport infrastructure capacity added in central Sydney since the 1970s has been a light rail line (1997) which takes less than 5,000 commuters each day. As a result, overcrowding on trains and buses serving the CBD has become worse. Current transport planning for the global office precinct at Barangaroo fails to heed this lesson, with 13,000 new rail commuters expected to be working there by 2021 to be funnelled into Wynyard station, where there are no plans to expand capacity despite it being forecast to be at capacity by 2017 even without the Barangaroo development (Saulwick, 2011). A major independent inquiry found that without a second rail link across the harbour, the city's rail system will face 'paralysis' by 2022 (West, 2010). The state government's new transport plan released in 2012 (NSW Government, 2012) includes a second harbour rail crossing, as well as four new motorways, as the centrepieces for Sydney's expanded transport system, but sees them as long term initiatives with no starting dates or proposed funding. The parallel transport proposals of the government's Infrastructure NSW agency released around the same time exclude the new harbour crossing but include similar motorway proposals (Infrastructure NSW, 2012).

At the heart of the state government's incapacity to properly commit to an adequately expanded public transport system is a desire to keep its AAA credit rating, as a positive signal to investors. This sets a limit on the extent to which the government can borrow to fund transport and other new infrastructure. Motorways remain an attractive option because of their potential to levy tolls to pay for construction costs and thereby allow borrowing for construction to be shifted to the private sector. This philosophy has allowed the government to largely complete the *Roads 2000* motorway plan it published in 1987. However, this strategy has resulted in the new motorways quickly filling to capacity in peak hours, with extra lanes already being added to the M2 and proposed for the M4 East. The wider issue is that the AAA rating might mean little for those investing and working in Sydney's global arc if public transport there continues to worsen: inadequate transport provision is already lowering Sydney's rating in global indexes.

Nevertheless at the heart of global Sydney, Sydney City Council has shown how an imaginatively creative vision could produce a central city that lives up to its global city status. Its strategic plan (City of Sydney, 2008) contains ten key project ideas as part of an integrated strategy for a 'green, global and connected' city, including transformation of the main George Street thoroughfare into a car- and bus-free boulevard served by light rail connecting Central Station to the harbour. This would free the street from the existing logjam of buses bringing commuters and shoppers into the city, with the 6,000 bus daily trips in the CBD being a major contributor to central city congestion. To legitimize and strengthen the case for state government financial support for a light rail service and its approval of the necessary street closures, as well as business support, Lord Mayor Clover Moore has tapped into global policy arenas and paid for a leading expert on car-free city policies, Jan Gehl, to help produce detailed plans.

Planning for Sydney's most important single item of global infrastructure, the airport, is also troubled. A joint 2012 study by the Australian and NSW governments (Steering Committee, 2012) reported that if a decision to build a second airport was not made quickly to alleviate capacity constraints at the existing airport, the economic costs to Sydney would be considerable. Between 2012 and 2060, an average of 12,700 jobs would be foregone annually in the state, and by 2060 the foregone gross state product would be $17.5 billion. While airport expansion is a difficult planning issue for global cities in general, it has been bedevilled by a notable lack of political will in Sydney. A site for a second airport at Badgerys Creek in outer western Sydney was bought by the Australian government over 20 years ago, and was reaffirmed as the best site for a new airport by the joint government study in 2012. However, successive state governments have ruled out the site because of local opposition and the possible loss of parliamentary seats, despite planning controls that have restricted new residential development under the proposed flight paths. The present state premier has stated his preference for Canberra airport to be expanded to meet Sydney's needs, connected to Sydney by high speed train. This seems a quixotic stance: over a distance of 290 km, the costs of a fast rail line by itself are very likely to approach that of a second airport in the Sydney basin, and there is no international example of a global city relying on an airport at such a distance.

The affordability of Sydney's housing is another major planning issue arising from globalization, due to flow-on impact of the high incomes of many global sector workers on house prices. This situation has been exacerbated by significant state and local government taxes and charges amounting to 23 per cent of the cost of a greenfield dwelling in 2009, and 16 per cent of the cost of an infill dwelling (National Housing Supply Council, 2010). Since 2007, state government charges for greenfield developments have included a levy, originally set at $355,000 per residential hectare (about $24,000 per dwelling), to help fund regional roads and land for state infrastructure such as schools and health care. Such costs formerly came out of general state budget expenditure, and the levy reflects the government's reluctance to commission new infrastructure, however essential, without some form of non-public financing in order for the state to remain creditworthy. The major government policy response to high housing costs over the last three decades has been to enforce a higher share of denser residential development through planning controls (Searle and Filion, 2011). This urban consolidation policy was intended to lower dwelling costs by making better use of existing infrastructure in conjunction with the smaller land area needed per dwelling (as well as produce other planning benefits such as reduced car use). But such potential savings from higher density development have been offset by greater development and construction costs, with the result that the total cost of an infill dwelling in Sydney is virtually the same as a greenfield dwelling (National Housing Supply Council, 2010).

More direct state responses to the problem of housing affordability have been limited. Federal assistance for state public housing programs has been replaced from 1996 by rental assistance payments for low income earners and state stamp duty concessions and bonus payments to first time home buyers. Without commensurate increases in housing supply, such measures tend to drive up the general price of housing. The state's urban development agency, Landcom, has a target of 7.5 per cent of its housing to be affordable by moderate-income households, though this effectively excludes the bottom one-third of households. Local council requirements from developers for affordable housing as part of developer contributions or inclusionary zoning are not common. The state government has been reluctant to mandate such requirements as it probably sees these as driving up general housing costs.

A final challenge in planning for global Sydney relates to the need for economic development policies, in addition to infrastructure and housing measures, that ensure Sydney remains an attractive destination for global activities. Sydney's success in hosting the Olympic Games has reinforced a sense of complacency at state government level about its appeal for such activities. The state's expenditure on tourism promotion, for example, has been less than Melbourne's state of Victoria. The cost of accommodation for international students is very high by world standards, but the government has failed to respond with funding to ameliorate this. The government has put much less funding into advanced research infrastructure to promote the global ranking and international attractiveness of its universities to students compared with the Victorian or Queensland governments. The fortunes of the international finance sector depend more on national, not state, policies and laws, but growing competition from Singapore and Hong Kong for global financial services is not being factored into planning. There are signs, though, that the state government is becoming more proactive in attracting global activity, such as the intended expansion of the Darling Harbour convention centre so it can host very large international conferences.

Sydney and dimensions of the global city

Sydney's contemporary manifestation as a new global city is refracted through the various dimensions explored in previous chapters of this book. One layer of understanding is yielded by viewing its history, picking up on the demonstration by Rimmer and Dick in Chapter 5 of how the steady convergence of time-space over history has produced a new kind of world city. It is no accident that Sydney, seen as being globally remote for most of its history, became a global city when time-space convergence allowed it to tap into the possibilities generated by the economic rise of the Asia Pacific zone. Similarly, Sydney's emergence as a global city illustrates the way in which the production of specific global network connections – global relationalities – is fundamental to global city emergence, as demonstrated in Chapter 3. In Sydney's case, this was tied to the new links and connections with the Asia Pacific zone. Chapter 3 has shown that Sydney is significant in the global connections of Hong Kong and Taipei, for example.

Such connections have arisen as older links with the UK and Europe faded, illustrating Castell's (1996) thesis that globalization strengthens some international connections while weakening others.

Viewing Sydney's history in postcolonial terms, following Watson's perspective in Chapter 6, further enriches an understanding of the city's global ascent. Sydney's colonial era set in place many of the necessary conditions required for its later emergence on the world stage. These included the colonial elimination of most of the indigenous population in the city's hinterland and the consequent freeing-up of land for wool, wheat and mineral exports that underpinned Sydney's national commercial ascendancy. The subordination of the Aboriginal population also provided carte blanche for the introduction by the British government of its governance institutions, education system and infrastructure networks that underpinned the emergence of an advanced national economy from which Sydney was able to launch its global status. Australia's primacy in wool production led to the world's first traded wool futures, which in turn was the precursor to Sydney's futures exchange, a cornerstone of its global finance sector.

While a focus on the economic and financial dimensions of the global city (Chapter 4) can cause other dimensions such as those discussed in this book to be overlooked, this chapter has shown that Sydney cannot be understood as a global city without first understanding its economic and financial roles. Chapters 2 and 4 have emphasized the role of advanced producer services beyond servicing just the global command and control activities in their own global city. In Sydney's case, the most important advanced producer services are financial services, but their global role has differed from cities such as Dubai (Chapter 4): this role has been mainly one of being a conduit providing foreign capital for local property development and housing loans, equity investments, and infrastructure and other capital expenditure items.

The contribution of culture to global city complexity, brought out by Mould in Chapter 9, has been significant in Sydney. The year 2000 Olympic Games were the most significant event in Sydney's short global city history, a fitting symbol of the importance of sports in the city's cultural landscape, and one which has increasing links into global sporting networks such as rugby and football. The Olympics required security services to be provided on an unprecedented scale. The expertise thus developed led to the export of security planning expertise by an Australian firm for later Olympic Games and other global major events, echoing the case of Rio de Janeiro discussed by Datu in Chapter 10 on the security dimension of global cities. The city's most important examples paralleling the alternative, community-based cultural activities described by Mould can be found in its minority cultures. The Mardi Gras parade of the gay and lesbian community; the annual Chinese New Year festivities in central Sydney; and several festivals held by Sydney's Indian community all reflect Sydney's multicultural complexity. In turn, this emphasizes the role of high immigration, increasingly from Asia, in producing Sydney's global status, a dimension discussed by Parnreiter in Chapter 2. In this, immigration has refracted and reinforced the socio-spatial polarization that characterizes global cities (Chapter 2). Here, the swathes of sprawling low income housing and humble flats in western Sydney with inadequate access to jobs are at odds with the virtual Sydney picture (the virtual city being a corollary of the global city, as discussed in Chapter 8) of harbour, vibrant centres and beaches. Instead, the Harbour Bridge and Opera House are transformed by fireworks and surface images that produce a hyper-reality beyond the virtual. At the same time, movies and TV shows centred on immigrant themes have perhaps been the most distinctive contribution of fiction to the production of global Sydney. The importance of literature in the production of the global city, as elaborated by Hones in the case of New York in Chapter 7, is not particularly evident in Sydney.

The architecture of Sydney reflects to a degree the propositions about global city architecture put by Datu in Chapter 10. There is an increasing intervention by global 'starchitects' into the city's built fabric, although the extent to which this is diminishing built form heritage does not yet seem as significant as that posited by Datu for Singapore. And, of course, Sydney's most famous icon, the Opera House, was designed by a Dane and is now on the UNESCO World Heritage List. The flow has also gone the other way, with local architects drawing on the experience of designing Sydney's Olympics venues being selected to design six major venues for the Beijing Olympic Games.

The geopolitical dimension, canvassed by Acuto in Chapter 11, has a distinctive contribution in Sydney. Unlike his case study of London, the political structure underpinning Sydney's global status is not multi-scalar but essentially uni-scalar, with the state government using constitutional powers to control and run the global city agenda (Searle and Bunker, 2010). Nevertheless, the Sydney City Lord Mayor has drawn on global city planning policy networks and used these to obtain state government support for a new light rail system as part of the city's global planning actions.

Conclusion

Sydney's emergence as a global city came about in the first place because of its commercial leadership within Australia at the beginning of the current globalization era in the 1970s. This was reinforced by the accidental possession of features that were, by then, world icons – the harbour, the Sydney Harbour Bridge and the Sydney Opera House. The global activities it has attracted have inevitably placed strains on the city's built environment and infrastructure, and on its social fabric. The spatial polarization of the city has been accentuated, sharpening an existing urban divide in which geography has given eastern Sydney a blessed amenity stemming from its harbour, bays and inlets, beaches, rolling topography and a warm temperate climate moderated by summer sea breezes. This geography, the associated lifestyle and the world icons will continue to give Sydney an advantage on global attractiveness tables. But this heritage is in danger of being countered by failure to adequately respond to the challenges of globally based growth. To Sydney's advantage here, however, is the existence of a vigorous public discourse about the need to protect the city's assets and overcome its transport and other deficiencies, which is difficult for the government to ignore. And in the longer term there is the prospect that the infusion of great cultural variety that has come with high immigration into Sydney over the last 30 years will, à la Peter Hall (1998), produce a city with enhanced creativity and dynamism.

Conclusions

Michele Acuto and Wendy Steele

Displacing the global city

In the so-called 'urban age' the twenty first century global city looms large as an increasingly omnipotent construct. As we have seen throughout the collection, this 'triumphant' concept has conquered most urban practice (Glaeser, 2010). There are no limits, it seems, to the prospects and possibilities of global cities as super structures of the super species in the age of the anthropocene. Responding to these totalizing views and the careless rhetorical application that characterizes much of the public discourse on the 'global city', several have called for grounded research wary of the complexity of the emergence of globally networked places. The fetishization of the idea of the global city has for instance been called into question by Neil Brenner and Christian Schmid (2012) who have argued that this is but one moment among many in the geography of our urbanizing planetary conditions. Their plea is for a greater focus on the processes of what they describe as 'planetary urbanization' which involves both the material conditions of 'concentrated urbanization' (i.e. the global city, big infrastructure) amidst the reorganization and transformation of the urban fabric through 'extended urbanization processes' (i.e. mass rural population displacement, worldwide shipping lanes, deforestation in the Amazon, the internet, climate change). After decades of urbanist scholarship on this theme, then, it has become necessary not to abstract the global city from the very conditions that allowed for its rise, as much as from the broader historical context it is necessarily embedded into. As Jennifer Robinson (2006), Olds and Yeung (2004) or Brenda Yeoh (1999) before them, to cite but a few, Brenner and Schmid exhort us to step beyond the confined analytical box of the traditional global city view, embracing wider geographies, more complex multiscalar processes, changing socio-political dynamics and ultimately new urbanist methodologies.

These critiques have, as we noted in the introduction, progressively raised critical questions about the limits of the global city. Far from being hermeneutically sealed, the contemporary global city is porous in both theoretical nature and impact. The contested identity of the 'global city' and its conceptual (non-identical) twin, the 'world city', have thus manifested as both an idea and a material condition of local/global processes that stretch the interdisciplinary boundaries of the global city research agenda. What makes a city 'global' for example has often become a signifier for the power and limitations of modernist dualisms that include (but by no means limited to): abstract/material; local/global; centre/periphery; production/consumption; fragmentation/heterogeneity; economy/culture; affluence/decay; control/chaos; formal/informal; fixity/mobility; and the spectacular city/the 'ordinary' city.

Seeking to offer a range of possible alternatives to the dualist and rhetorical limits of the global city scholarship, we have ventured on the largely unexplored path of multi-disciplinarity. This was not, however, a search for a 'new' theory of the global city, but rather a proposition for a gathering of alternative approaches to what has, after all, been an extremely productive line of urbanist inquiry for the past few decades. Calling for a critical re-reading of the idea of the global city from standpoints as different as literature, politics or history, we have not only sought to expand the horizons global city thinking. Equally, we have attempted at a collection of grounded experiences from many different metropolises. We searched as much as for novel theoretical inspiration as for a mix of vignettes of practical relevance for those ordinary urban practitioners that, to paraphrase De Certeau's lines (1984, 128) that opened our inquiry, often stand below the threshold at which the visibility of the global city begins, following a globalizing 'urban text' that they write without often being able to read it. To offer alternative readings of this text, and to mirror the growing expansion of the global city literature beyond the well-trodden paths of urban studies and economics, we have taken unusual grounds and some theoretical risks. Our ultimate goal was not of rejecting the lessons that works such as those of Sassen, Brenner or Friedmann have offered us. Instead, we attempted to complement here these views with new and sometimes unexpected analytical ventures. *Dis*-placing, rather than *re*-placing, the global city has been the main aim of this collection. So what, if anything, have we learnt from this experiment with wandering in the global city through a variety of disciplinary eyes?

Charting cross-disciplinary paths

It might be easy, at this point in the collection, to offer some totalizing manifesto for a 'new' global city research, perhaps echoing Friedmann's 1982 hypotheses, or even Hall's 1966 planning review of the 'world cities'. For attractive that such a solution might be, we would like to limit our editorial judgment to distilling some of the major themes that emerged in the collection. We do this not by the means of some groundbreaking pronouncement, but rather by relying on what might perhaps be powerful and yet easily dismissed evidence from the pages of this book: global city scholars *are* engaged in a much wider analytical effort than critics often assume and global city research, even if broadly understood or occasionally solicited, is rich in innovation and inter-disciplinary bridges. If we have started here from the challenges moved by global city 'discontents' (Sassen, 2007) to the dominant paradigm, we now move on to two key issues that, in our opinion, emerge from the research efforts of this book. First, we highlight the importance of not forgetting the 'city' in the 'global city' construct. Second, we underline the cross-cutting calls for a reflexive discussion on the expanding variety of global city standpoints and, conversely, methodologies deployed to understand global cities.

The 'city' after the global

The global city unbound, in terms of traditional disciplinary moorings as well as in its conceptual and spatial scope, has been a key cross-cutting theme of most chapters in this book. The increasing interest in the 'global city' as both a cross-disciplinary idea and set of practices is characterized by divergent translations and tolerance-testing eclecticism. Friedmann (1995) described this divergence as part of the nature of the global city paradigm, as not only a polarized social entity, but also a 'dual city' in a scholarly sense, where theory soars into the abstract thereby neglecting its other face, its rootedness in the everyday practices that constitute the production of history, institutions, culture and politics. Sociologists such as Anthony Giddens pointed at this as a process of 'distanciation' (connection through presence and absence) and 'disembedding' (lifting social relations out of local conditions and restructuring across time and space). The significance of transcending boundaries captured in terms such as 'glocalization' (Swyngedouw, 2000) and 'deterritorialization' are then central to understandings of contemporary global city challenges and practices. There is, after all, still a city of concrete, cables and people in the midst of all of that 'global' that crowds academic papers and urbanist practices. The challenge that confronts us when facing the global city is then twofold: on the one hand, developing an appreciation that displaces the dominant economic-centric model of the city, and on the other hand allowing for the city's influence not to dissolve in so much globalization, whether theoretical and practical.

So, to begin with we need to investigate alternative stories of the rise, evolution and revolution of these metropolises that go as many remarked in the book, beyond what Bourdieu (1985, 723) called 'economicism' or the predominance of economic determinism that is here reflected in the primacy of global economic processes in global city research. This, as much as the rhetorical abstraction of the 'global city' construct of many PR campaigns, renders other practices and processes nearly invisible. However, at the same time we also need not to disregard the importance of economics and finance in charting the present geographies of the global city in a predominantly neoliberal scenario. This is a challenge that has for instance emerged in Oli Mould's account of the cultural geographies of the global city. As he pointed out, and as Kerwin Datu echoes in his sketch of the architecture of Singapore, much of what we could tag as a 'cultural turn' in global city planning has been fronted by many critiques, which have been suggesting that this 'creative class' appeal is but the latest iteration of neoliberal urban renewal. Beyond a cultural veil, the problematic proliferation of social inequalities continues to splinter the global city. As Mould underscores in his conclusions, culture can be utilized in part to contribute to the global city paradigm both in a practical sense (as a policy priority) and in a scholarly vein (as a cross-disciplinary extension), but it also still stands as 'an inherently political economic tool' that is 'often used by many cities as a means to an economic developmental end'. This, then, is not just an analytical whim: the effects of rhetorical abstraction are very real. Take Vanessa Watson's discussion of Cape Town in her postcolonial geographies chapter. As she pointed out, this instrumentalization is the case even though Cape Town remains a city partly located 'off the map' in most world city terms. Watson reminds us that, even without apparent success in 'league' tables, the global/world city rhetoric is 'sufficient to bolster financial and political support for public actions which will attract international investors and tourists', ultimately shaping part of the African metropolis. So how can we balance an appreciation of the economic (and financial) bases of the global city while not surrendering the whole construct to an economicist viewpoint?

A partial solution arises from Christof Parnreiter's introduction. As he suggests, it might be necessary to 'return to the beginnings' in order to revitalize global city research, thinking more seriously about the call that opened Sassen's *The Global City* by asking for an attention to agency and the practice of global control. If in Sassen's terms this meant only a partial displacement of the corporate concentration of power, many of the chapters in this book have offered snippets of the more complex agency of the city in the global. For example, David Bassens remarked that it is imperative to remain careful 'not to equate the spectacular and rapid urbanization *cum* APS-growth in some cities in emerging markets' with a what might appear at first sight as 'natural' relocation of command-and-control functions to these places. Capital, culture, political connections and even literary accounts do not simply travel undisturbed across urban 'hubs'. Those very hubs are in fact loci of planning, financial practices or cultural hybridization that transform and shape the ebbs and flows of globalization, and that can actively respond to the regional, international and global contexts around them. The city as a complex of people, but also as a localized governance structure, acts and re-acts. In Michele Acuto's chapter, this meant understanding the global city as a possible participant to international processes. Similar active roles can also be traced in, for instance, David Murakami-Wood's story of Rio de

Janeiro changing responses to urban insecurity, or in Glen Searle's account of Sydney's multiple authorities seeking to develop favourable conditions to attract global activities, and having to respond to their necessary local consequences. This is equally testified in Peter Rimmer and Howard Dick's historical narrative that, despite the far-reaching description of millennia of urban history, still calls for a greater emphasis by global city scholars on governance as a key dimension to relate to those many challenges that have tested globalizing metropolises through the ages and that are faced with problems of near-unprecedented reach like climate change or pandemics – themes that a contemporary scholarship of the city, whether 'global' or not, can no longer afford to ignore.

Paying closer attention to the agency of the city in the complex of globalization dynamics can in fact also allow for a global city scholarship that is truer to its urbanist origins and that is capable of offering 'in depth' accounts of production of new urban spaces. For example, Datu has pointed out how an important lesson we can derive from the case of Singapore is of how the city-state has been staking its reputation as a global city not just on visual appearance, housing architectures and iconic developments, but also as on the values integrated within the production and use of these material developments. As he notes, there remains a limiting abstraction of the 'global city' strategy deployed by Singaporean authorities, who are often seen as promoting little more than a landscape of spectacle and 'order and control'. In this case, then, a superficial and rhetorical abstraction of the 'global' features of the metropolis fail to address the fundamental fact that, thanks to the particular governance conditions and commercial success of the city-state, the production of the global city extends here to efforts applied just as much to its public sector projects, whereas, as Datu remarks, in many aspiring global cities 'most of the emphasis is on speculative real estate developments with little social dimension'. Attention to the agency of the global city becomes, then, as much a normative imperative for research as a crucial methodological anchor for its database, taking us to the question of global city empirics and to the challenges of eclecticism.

Global city methods, medleys and responsibilities

Once the 'city' has surfaced again in our analytical horizons as a responsive element in the global city narrative, we are, however, tasked with not replicating the limits of the dominant discourse criticized in the introductions to this volume. As Watson underscores, the global city scholarship has often been subject to critique because 'it has had the (possibly unintended) consequences of encouraging all cities to aspire to "global" status by mimicking the plans and projects of classified "global" cities' and therefore reiterating unequal and structural power relationships. These shortcomings, however, are not just limited to the reiteration of global city logics. Rather, as several contributors reminded us in this volume, they have also arisen from poorly reflexive, where not uncritical, deployment of global city 'methods'. Friedmann's original call is in this sense partly betrayed: if the 'world city hypothesis' was meant as a research programme, in many cases global city analytics have had a dangerous tendency to totalizing accounts and simple testing of the 'hypothesis' rather than following the author's caveat that this approach was 'neither a theory nor a universal generalization about cities' (Friedmann and Wolff, 1982, 70). As Ben Derudder, Michael Hoyler and Peter Taylor pointed out in their network rejoinder to the global city scholarship, attempts at solid analytical development of this programme, as with the Globalization and World Cities project and its interlocking model, went to great length to devise complex depictions of the changing geography of city-to-city connectivity. Yet the wider public quickly got seduced by a search for rankings and hierarchies that represent only the surface of the iceberg of global city theory. This cookie-cutter application of globalist discourses and competitive views of the 'global' city as a 'better' or more 'highly ranked' city than many other 'ordinary cities' (Robinson, 2006) has animated much of our decision to search for alternative disciplinary accounts. Symptomatically, as Derudder, Hoyler and Taylor noted for instance in their summary of GaWC's founding mission, neither Friedmann nor Sassen had 'devoted much attention to a methodical analysis of how and why cities could qualify'. Quite simply, since the early 1990s, 'global city' has been a theory in search of more reliable methods.

As with agency, this demand for theoretical solidity has been voiced by Parnreiter in reviewing how the global city scholarship has been confronted by the need to empirically corroborate the global city concept and to offer substance beyond the globalized abstraction of its core discussions. As he remarks, lack of information on global city features and processes, as well as several critiques of the globalist ethos of this academia have often to do with *empirical* rather than a conceptual problems. This does not, however, mean dispensing of the long-lived global city literature altogether. Rather this research programme should, Parnreiter reminded us, be wary of its solid scholarly foundations and 'where global city researchers have endeavoured to investigate mechanism of economic command and control, they have found it'. Can this be replicated beyond the economy into the complex medley of global city 'dimensions' gathered here? While this collection might only account for a very preliminary step into cross-disciplinary global city discussions, our editorial judgement tells us that Parnreiter's cautious optimism might be after all exportable to the wider audience of those that have engaged with the global city beyond urban studies.

Predictably, our assignment to the authors gathered in this book, based as we wrote in the introduction on a collection of 'disciplinary standpoints', has produced a variation of methodological approaches even within the limiting constraints of the chapters' literature review/case study formulation. For instance, Rimmer and Dick felt the need to devise their own historiographical model to trace the *long durée* (Braudel, 1983) of the world city phenomenon. Similarly, Murakami-Wood deployed a variation on a Foucauldian biopolitical framework and Acuto called for an integration of urban governance with the internationalized viewpoints of diplomacy and world politics. On their part, instead, Derudder, Hoyler and Taylor went at great length to illustrate how GaWC responded to Friedmann's and Sassen's methodological shortcomings to continuously refine a quantitative network analysis of globalization and cities, while David Bassens demonstrated in his account of Dubai how this framework can also be coupled with a qualitative discussion of a city's evolution. Many other chapters took us on even less common grounds for the global city literature. For example, Mould hinted at ethnographic engagements with the cultural texture of the global city, while Sheila Hones took us through a close reading of a fictional account of New York. When taken collectively, all of these ways of appreciating the global city speak to the vast and growing multiplicity in viewpoints that can be taken to recast our scholarly engagement with these metropolises. This is not to say that the realm of global city 'dimensions' is presently limited. The practice and public discourse over global cities has certainly been proactive in expanding the problem field of the 'global' and the analysis of the determinants of globality in cities. Mould has for instance evidenced a noticeable shift in the 'variables' (far accurate than they might be) that are being used in global city measurement to branch out to cultural factors, including for instance cultural industries as a means of assessing cities in various global hierarchies. Nonetheless, this practice-driven expansion requires, as many chapters noted, some more solid scholarly reflexivity to prevent the hijacking and profit oriented co-optation of innovative methods. For example, Mark Graham has underlined how the increasing reliance on 'big data' shadows in new accounts of the city's virtual geography (or 'palimpsest' as he puts it) can also start to 'self-reinforce the importance of those very shadows', with 'the viability of less automated methods of scoring and analysis (e.g. meetings, conversations) ever more undermined'.

One suggestion came in this book from GaWC's illustration (also echoed by Bassens, Acuto, Murakami-Wood and Watson) of the importance of acknowledging the more refined grain of global city studies, and the inherent relationality of the global city idea. So, for instance, Derudder, Hoyler and Taylor pointed out how the 'ultimate objective' of GaWC's IWCNM model 'is not to produce a global ranking of cities' but rather the real analytical interest lays 'in revealing the functional and spatial outline of the transnational urban networks in which cities are enmeshed'. As they point out, rankings can certainly be produced via these methods and can in some cases serve as 'a useful introduction to an analysis of connectivity' in the world city network, but these instruments are 'neither a goal in itself nor the privileged way of conveying results'. These methods offer instead both a representation of how substantially more refined global city methods might be vis-á-vis their rhetorical reflections, as much as an important snapshot of the two-way connection between cities and globalization. For instance, as Bassens' narrative on the developments of Dubai's networked positioning in Islamic finance illustrates, the idea of 'global city-ness' or 'world city-ness' can be 'best understood by taking a relational reading of Taylor's ideas about monopoly formation in the realm of global finance'. The story of the successes of places like London, Shanghai or New York cannot be told if not relation to other cities, broader flows, and mutually constitutive relationships of the 'city' and the 'global' (Taylor et al., 2013). Yet, this progressive understanding of the city as equally structured subject of, and structuring agent in, broader processes presents the present scholarship with a test for our scholarly tolerance of eclecticism. The multidimensional global city that emerges from such account, as Murakami-Wood reminds us in his discussion of urban (in)security, is both 'referent and at the same time the terrain of study'. This, however, is further complicated by the fact that such referents have also been shifting: as he for instance suggested reviewing the state of the scholarship on this dimension, formally top-down approaches have also become increasingly aware of the micro-social, cultural and psychological concerns that for long characterized bottom-up discussions, ultimately underlining how this referent object is in most cases 'almost always multiple and contested'.

Even when the global city is paired with extremely abstracted reasonings such as those of international relations (IR) theory, as in Acuto's case, scrutinizing urban politics necessarily demands as much for an inherent interdisciplinary collaboration as for an attention for the development of these metropolises 'on the ground' of everyday affairs. This means that the global city scholarship does not need brand new models, but rather careful cross-disciplinary integration of analytical frames. In Acuto's chapter, for example, we are reminded that it might be highly misleading to lead a charge for the localization of IR into the minute detail of urban politics as this analytical step might betray the effective 'big picture' outlook so characteristic of IR. Rather, investigating global city politics demands for holistic programmes of research that attend to both the contingency of urban studies and the abstraction of IR, and thus support the growth of collaborative research. In this sense, cross-disciplinary linkages also forge connections between diverse registers and appreciations of the global city. For example, as Mould noted in his contribution, 'the marriage of the concepts of culture and the global city is an uneasy one, with tumultuous relations at times'. Mould argued that this is principally brought about by the 'tacit and intangible nature of culture' clashing with 'the pragmatic, evidence-based nature of mainstream global city debates' therefore making for two 'uneasy bedfellows'. Similar arguments have also been hinted at on postcolonialism by Watson or on literature by Hones: for as apparently easy as we might have suggested them, multidimensional engagements on the ground of the global

city remain challenging thought experiments. However, despite this difficulty, the practice of global city urbanism reminds us that such ventures are
not impossible. As Moulds underlines, cultural characteristics that go further than an economically restricted description of global cities do persist
in the everyday reality of urban planning and city life and so, as he puts
it, 'to include these themes into a more holistic narrative of global cities is
a progressive measure' which would equally 'enlighten the complexities of
global city development' as well as better match the multiplex and blurred
realities of urbanist practice out there. Global city studies should, then, be
required to make amend of their inherent need to acknowledge and engage
with other methodologies, perspectives and assertions about the nature and
the most appropriate ways to appreciate the role of these cities. For example, Derudder, Hoyler and Taylor noted how, if GaWC's approach provides
'one specific method to approximate these networks' and if its analyses 'can
be tailored to specific research interests', one should not infer that IWCNM-
inspired research is to be seen as opposing qualitative research. Rather, the
authors reminded us, eclecticism is a necessary step for this approach to
thrive. GaWC's quantitive network analysis, then, was presented here 'as
part of a much wider, critical-realist methodology where extensive research
may provide formative input to intensive research that takes the [global
city] research agenda further'. Likewise, Datu has remarked how an investigation of the built form of the global city needs to start from overcoming
the 'self-selectiveness' of what we think the architecture of the global city
to be. When we choose to provide a view of the global city from a specific disciplinary (or indeed methodological) standpoint, we should be held
accountable for the limitations that such a specific approach implies.

Sheila Hones reminded us of this caveat in her account of the fictional
New York of *Let the Great World Spin*. As she points out, just as for McCann
the city of New York is 'the collision point of stories', the book itself 'can
only happen in a collision'. The reader that is engaging with the text, Hones
reminds us, not only reads about the interconnectedness of New York 'but
actively shares it' so that in this sense 'the novel, its author, and its readers not only collaborate in the articulation of a global city space but also
participate in its production'. This is then what we, as editors, would consider perhaps the most important lesson 'learned' from the cross-disciplinary
venture gathered this book. If much can be said and criticized, as we are certainly guilty of, about the misinterpretation of the global city scholarship
by the general public and by some academics, we should make amend here
of the important role that global city authors also have in shaping people's
imaginaries *of* these metropolises and, ultimately, people's practices *in* these
metropolises. Challenging is then the position of the analyst vis-à-vis his
or her 'field', as represented in this volume by many different disciplines as
much many different cities, and the consequences of his or her particular
way to narrate it. This is of course no novelty in social science, and it is not

surprising that such a suggestion has emerged from a discussion of the global city entrenched in literary theory. Edward Said's famous essay on the relation between 'the world, the text and the critic' has for instance pointed this out by reminding us how textual accounts have ways of existing that 'are always enmeshed in circumstance, time, place, and society' (Said, 1975), and that the texts we produce have necessarily a way of existing beyond our pens and keyboards, which in turn have a core stake in producing a particular snapshot of a moment in time. In this sense, as global city scholars we need to remember that we are ourselves responsible for the formation of a 'global city culture' that now pervades everyday talk and very real urbanist practices, and we need to own such culture with a spirit of openness and critical inquiry. The true global city challenge, then, is not just that of not losing the 'city' in the 'global city' but also that of remaining liable for the ways global cities are read, interpreted and practiced, and be ready to answer rhetorical abstraction and problematic social practices with the consciousness of having, at least partly, been involved in the production of such dominant discourse. The global city scholarship should then come with a sense of 'intellectual responsibility' (Chomsky, 1967) towards its publics and its object of study for as authors of worldviews we should also be wary of the impact these have on the very worlds we describe, and of the alternative ways one could tell 'our' story – a challenge that makes us only hopeful for more eclectic and innovative global city research.

Global City Challenges:
A Sympathetic Postscript

Roger Keil

Reflecting on what might be left to say at the end of this important and necessary book might start with a determination of its positioning in a larger debate. Probably to the astonishment of its originators – among them John Friedmann, Goetz Wolff, Peter Hall, Peter Taylor, Saskia Sassen – the concept of global and world cities has proven to be one of the most enduring ideas in the field of urban studies. An idea allegedly first sketched on the back of an envelope by Friedmann after perusing an in-flight magazine with its maps of carrier connections, has grown to be the centerpiece of a growing body of work in the social sciences on the role of major, internationalized cities, in the original formulation command centers of the global economy or basing points of global capital, riven with economic polarization, social fragmentation and political strife. The history of the 'paradigm' is aptly sketched out in Parnreiter's opening chapter to this volume. It has been subject to quite a few summary treatments in the past (e.g. Brenner and Keil 2006; Brenner and Keil 2011). More recently, the range of publications has been dramatically widened by encyclopedic collections that have cast light on all manner of aspects related to world city formation and global city relations (e.g. Derudder et al., 2011; Taylor et al., 2013). I am making no difference here between global and world which I consider a tactical, not a strategic differentiation.

This current collection can duly claim its rightful place in this growing range of publications. Well edited, with many cross-references among the chapters, it is both true to tradition and breaks new ground in areas often under-researched in the literature. It is a theoretically and conceptually sophisticated book, yet its aim is also to connect global city theory to political practice. This is significant as one could argue that the book thus takes the project of thinking about globalizing cities back to its roots in the political necessity to deal with rather new and challenging conditions of the political at the outset of the period of globalization. While inspired by theoretical breakthroughs in World Systems Theory and the realization that the world had entered a New International Division of Labor by the 1970s, the original impetus for thinking through the socio-spatiality of the world city in its networked character came from the point of view of the practitioners in those newly globalized urban areas. Friedmann and Wolff noted that in this context 'the central issue is the control of urban life' and that '[p]lanners are directly engaged on this contested terrain. They are called upon to clarify the issues and to help in searching for solutions. Obviously, they will have to gain a solid, comprehensive understanding of the forces at work. And they will have to rethink their basic practices, since what is happening in world cities is in large measure brought about by forces that lie beyond the normal range of political – and policy – control. How can planners and, indeed, how can the people themselves, living in world cities, gain ascendancy over these forces? That is the basic question' (cited in Brenner and Keil, 2006, 58). *Global City Challenges,* with the Editors' claim to be 'a collaboration geared towards providing a practice-oriented review of this scholarship that is critical and case-based' (Acuto and Steele, in this volume), fits well into this framework.

While such a claim is made, it must be avoided, of course, and the authors in this book mostly do, to cater to the strategists of 'world class city' programmatics in various cities around the world to assemble the constituent parts that make up a global city in their view. The task must remain to critically confront the real project of world city formation and not to cave in to the demands of global city makers for a scholarship that provides roadmaps for success which naturally are laced with contradiction.[1] In this sense, even the practical strategic direction devised by Friedmann and Wolff – to be better world city planners and political actors – ultimately leads back to studying world and global cities predominantly as a theoretical object, and not as an object of the desire of those who benefit from its existence.

Now that project has come a long way since about three dozen global city researchers met in Virginia in the spring of 1993 to discuss the papers that were ultimately edited under the title *World Cities in a World-System* (Knox and Taylor 1995). At the time, the project was still marginal to the field of urban studies, faced with considerable legitimation issues, nascent in its methodological and conceptual approaches and selective (if not to say exclusive to a degree) in its global reach. The situation is different now, and this book is testament to the wide range of thematic reach, methodological pluralism and geographical extent present in the work done under the heading of global and world city research. This is heartening in many ways but has also led to considerable openings for criticism launched at the entire enterprise of studying cities in global networks and hierarchies as we will see below.

This book gives us a good snapshot of what is currently debated in the literature. The world city literature has now become a palimpsest, a layered set of parchments inscribed, erased, re-inscribed by multiple generations of global city researchers. The term itself entered the popular English language discourse at the time of the release of the film version of Umberto Eco's *The Name of the Rose* in the 1980s, billed as a palimpsest of the novel, and had a powerful if short career in the requisite postmodern treatises of the decade which also gave birth to the concept of the world and global city. Both David Harvey and Edward Soja refer to it in their work. Mark Graham, in his contribution to this book, takes up palimpsest again and makes specific and productive use of it in the context of his discussion of the virtual dimension of world-cityness. There is a certain parallelism and congruence here between the palimpsest nature of the global city and the equivalent character of the sedimentation of our collective knowledge on the subject. Despite the remarkably multidisciplinary and multi-layered project of world city research it must be asked, though, how it has seemingly come to be dominated by mostly geographic thought? Born from the disciplines of history, economics, planning and sociology for the most part, the debate on global cities today is mostly internal to Anglo-American Geography.

A few themes present themselves as urgent throughout the book, which also have significance beyond these pages. The 'dimensions' discussed in the volume are both clearly delineated in their own right, with a set of intellectual approaches, methodologies and concepts attached but also overlapping to provide an interlocking and dialogic framework. From the perspectives of those dimensions, the various chapters explore the rapidly changing notions of global/world, city/urban and crisis/stability that have characterized the dynamic global urban system in the past generation. A complex landscape of continuity and change persists. David Bassens, for instance, in his contribution to this book describes the emergence and subsequent slide of Dubai as a function of global capital switching in the context of overaccumulation when he argues 'that the growth of Dubai and some other financial world cities in emerging markets can only be explained as a temporary fix for overaccumulation. This happens through the production of world cities as emerging markets in themselves – a process which is crucially mediated by institutions operating from the 'capitals of capital' in the world.' Not much would need to be changed to demonstrate the similarities of 1980s Los Angeles to present day Dubai. Back then, in the early days of global city formation during this current period, there was the expectation that the Southern California metropolis might become 'the capital of the Pacific Rim' or 'the capital of the 21st century'. In hindsight, that period of world city formation may be chalked up mostly to giant, temporary influx of Japanese capital during the time of the bubble economy in that country's land market. Los Angeles did not achieve the kind of overarching global status it was expected to gain at the time. A boom and bust regime is still inscribed deeply into the architecture of the global city network (Keil 1998). Maybe Dubai is currently experiencing its Los Angeles moment.

What characterizes this book, like the global city literature overall, is a certain Eurocentrism. There is very little sustained interest outside of the West (and outside of the emerging economies such as Singapore, Korea, Brazil to name a few) in the specific theory of global cities as it is on display in this book. There is also a dearth of work overall, yet also in this book, that is produced on issues of diversity and alterity, most notably class, gender and race. Still, the chapters of this book demonstrate convincingly that the intellectual apparatus of world city theory is sharp enough to make such topics central to future investigation. In that context, the rudimentary ideas about class that existed at the outset of the era of globalizing cities will have to be differentiated as notions of diversity have pushed to the fore of the sociological view on today's globalized metropolis.

That the world has ostensibly become more complex and multi-dimensional since the Cold War origins of world city theory is hard to deny. The idealized virtuous cycle of the globalization of capital, culture and labor that characterized the perception of much early globalization literatures has also now been recast as a potentially vicious cycle of potential network failure and catastrophic connectivity (Keil 2011). More important still than complexification of the world itself have perhaps been the ways of knowing that world. The challenges faced by global city thinking now are posed by new voices that have changed the 'geographies of theory' to use a term often associated with Ananya Roy (2009) and shifted our view back from the western hegemony of the dominant global city to the 'ordinary city' anywhere (Robinson 2006). It has been argued accordingly that we have now moved the overall project from looking at global cities as a distinct group of large powerful internationalized centers to 'globalized urbanization' more broadly (Brenner and Keil 2011). More recently, even, a passionate case has been made to speak about 'planetary urbanization' instead of global cities, to move our perspective from the methodological 'cityism' of global city theory to the Lefebvrian notion of 'urban society' (Brenner and Schmid 2012).

This refers us finally back to the political questions with which we opened this short discussion. Friedmann and Wolff in their original formulation paint a picture of political disengagement, a global city divided into citadel and ghetto, with the poor sequestered like a virus as the ruling elites remake the city in their image. While they considered the world city 'in any event immune to revolutionary action' (2006, 63), lacking a political center, they also admit that in those hubs of the global economy 'localized conflicts may suddenly erupt into a worldwide crisis' (2006, 65). The early presence (or prescience) of the centrality of political action and the persistence of the political theme in global city research outside its current geographical core belies the repeated observation in this book that there is a 'political deficit'.[2] Just as the political imperative was present in Friedmann and Wolff's seminal text, so it is today. The most pressing issues of global city theory are political. Perhaps it is too easy to confuse the alleged 'political deficit' with the felt deficit of the state, as if global cities were sculpted at the hands of global capital alone. Yet, the state's role in global city formation has often been noted.[3] What has been missing, perhaps, and where there has been a real deficit, is to examine the role of non-statist politics in the emergence of the global city. A 'politics of urbanism' that is based on 'seeing like a city' (Magnusson 2011) may be the better way to go about this than referring back and forth between the hegemony of (transnational) capital and the hegemony of the (transnational) state in the formation of the world city. If that direction is taken (and there are many examples for that in this book), we stand a chance to retain global city research as a constitutive part of the project of critical, transdisciplinary, heterodox and polycentric urban studies.

Notes

1. A project driven by often strange coalitions of multi-scale actors including place entrepreneurs and boosters as well as the transnational capitalist class.
2. This reading is based in particular on a very selective, almost entirely non-political science reading of the literature by Delphine Ancien (2011). See the work by Brenner, Keil and others on the subject.
3. For example Keil (1998) and Erie (2004) for Los Angeles.

Bibliography

Aalbers, M., E. Engelen and A. Glasmacher (2011) 'Mortgage Securitization and the State: "Cognitive Closure" in the Netherlands.' *Environment and Planning A* 43 (8): 1179–1795.

Abelson, P. (1993) 'Housing in Australia.' *Australian Planner* 31(2): 79–85.

Abu-Lughod, J. L. (1989) *Before European Hegemony: The World System AD 1250–1350.* Oxford: Oxford University Press.

Acuto, M. (2010) 'Global Cities: Gorillas in Our Midst.' *Alternatives* 35 (4): 425–448.

———(2011) 'Finding the Global City An Analytical Journey Through the "Invisible College".' *Urban Studies* 48 (14): 2953–2973.

———(2013a) *Global Cities, Governance and Diplomacy: The Urban Link.* London: Routledge.

———(2013b) 'City Leadership in Global Governance.' *Global Governance* 19 (3): 481–498.

———(2013c) 'World Politics by Other Means?' *The Hague Journal of Diplomacy* 8 (4): 287–311.

Adam, R. (2012) *The Globalisation of Modern Architecture.* Newcastle-upon-Tyne: Cambridge Scholars Publishing.

Agamben, G. (1998) *Homo Sacer: Sovereign Power and Bare Life.* Stanford: Stanford University Press.

———(2005) *State of Exception.* Chicago: University of Chicago Press.

Aglietta, M. (2000) [1976] *A Theory of Capitalist Regulation: The US Experience,* 2nd edition. London and New York: Verso.

Agnew, J. (1987) *Place and Politics: The Geographical Mediation of State and Society.* Boston MA: Allen and Unwin.

Alexander, N. (2011) *Ciaran Carson: Space, Place, Writing.* Liverpool: Liverpool University Press.

Alexander, N. and D. Cooper (eds.) (2013) *Poetry and Geography: Space and Place in Postwar Poetry.* Liverpool: Liverpool University Press.

Alderson, A. and J. Beckfield (2004) 'Power and Position in the World City System.' *American Journal of Sociology* 109 (4): 811–851.

———(2007) 'Power and Position in the World City System, 1981–2000.' In: P. Taylor, B. Derudder, P. Saey and F. Witlox (eds.), *Cities in Globalization: Practices, Policies, and Theories,* pp. 21–36. London: Routledge.

Alderson, A., J. Beckfield and J. Sprague-Jones (2010) 'Inter-City Relations and Globalization: The Evolution of the Global Urban Hierarchy, 1981–2007.' *Urban Studies* 47 (9): 1899–1923.

Allen, J. (2010) 'Powerful City Networks: More than Connections, Less than Domination and Control.' *Urban Studies* 47 (13): 2895–2911.

Al Sayyad, N. and M. Massoumi (2012) 'The Future of the City: Religious Fundamentalisms in the City: Reflections on the Arab Spring.' *Journal of International Affairs* 65 (2): 31–43.

Amen, M., N. J. Toly, P. L. McCarney and K. Segbers (eds.) (2011) *Cities and Global Governance.* Farnham: Ashgate.

Amin, A. and S. Graham (1997) 'The Ordinary City.' *Transactions of the Institute of British Geographers* 22 (4): 411–429.

Amin A. and N.Thrift (2002) *Cities: Reimagining the Urban.* London: Polity.

Ancien, D. (2011) 'Global City Theory and the New Urban Politics Twenty Years On: The Case for a Geohistorical Materialist Approach to the (New) Urban Politics of Global Cities.' *Urban Studies* 48 (12): 2473–2493.

Ansari, J. (2004) 'Time for a New Approach in India.' *Habitat Debate* 10 (4): 15.

Arias, E. D (2006) *Drugs and Democracy in Rio de Janeiro: Trafficking, Social Networks and Public Security.* Chapel Hill: University of North Carolina Press.

Arrighi, G. (1994) *The Long Twentieth Century: Money, Power, and the Origins of Our Times.* London and New York: Verso.

Ashworth, G. J. and H. Voogd (1990) *Selling the City: Marketing Approaches in Public Sector Urban Planning.* London: Belhaven.

Assembléia Legislativa do Estado do Rio de Janeiro (ALERJ). (2009) *Relatório Final da Comissão Parlamentar de Inquérito Destinada a Investigar a Ação de Milícias no Âmbito do Estado do Rio de Janeiro (Final Report of the Parliamentary Commission of Inquiry into the Actions of Militias in the Area of the State of Rio de Janeiro).* Rio de Janeiro: ALERJ.

Astarita, T. (2005) *Between Salt Water and Holy Water: A History of Southern Italy.* New York: Norton.

Australian Bureau of Statistics. (2011) *Housing Occupancy and Costs, 2009–10.* Cat. 4130.0. Canberra: ABS.

———(2012) *House Price Indexes: Eight Capital Cities.* Cat. 6416.0. Canberra: ABS.

Bain, J. (2007) *A Financial Tale of Two Cities.* Sydney: UNSW Press.

Bairoch, P. (1988) *Cities and Development: From the Dawn of History to the Present,* trans Christopher Brader. Chicago: Chicago University Press.

Ball, M. and D. Sunderland (2006) *An Economic History of London 1800–1914.* London: Routledge.

Barangaroo Delivery Authority. (2010) *Barangaroo Newsletter, August 2010.* Sydney: Barangaroo Delivery Authority.

Bassens, D., B. Derudder and F. Witlox (2010a) 'Searching for the Mecca of Finance: Islamic Financial Services and the World City Network.' *Area* 42 (1): 35–46.

———(2010b) 'The Making and Breaking of Dubai: The End of a City-State.' *Political Geography* 29 (6): 299–301.

———(2012) ' "Gatekeepers" of Islamic Financial Circuits: Analyzing Urban Geographies of the Global Shari'a Elite.' *Entrepreneurship and Regional Development* 24 (5–6): 337–355.

Baum, S., M. Haynes, Y. V. Gellecum and J. H. Han (2006) 'Advantage and Disadvantage across Australia's Extended Metropolitan Regions: A Typology of Socioeconomic Outcomes.' *Urban Studies* 43 (9): 1549–1579.

Bayliss, D. (2007) 'The Rise of the Creative City: Culture and Creativity in Copenhagen.' *European Planning Studies* 15 (7): 889–903.

Beall, J. and S. Fox (2009) *Cities and Development.* London and New York: Routledge.

Beauregard, R. A. and A. Haila (2000) 'The Unavoidable Continuity of the City.' In: P. Marcuse and R. Van Kempen (eds.), *Globalising Cities,* pp. 22–37. London: Basil Blackwell.

Beaverstock, J. V. (1996) 'Migration, Knowledge and Social Interaction: Expatriate Labour within Investment Banks.' *Area* 28 (4): 459–470.

———(2002) 'Transnational Elites in Global Cities: British Expatriates in Singapore's Financial District.' *Geoforum* 32 (4): 525–538.

———(2011) 'German Cities in the World City Network. Some Observations.' *Raumforschung und Raumordnung* 69 (1): 13–18.

Beaverstock, J. V., M. Hoyler, K. Pain and P. Taylor (2005) 'Demystifying the Euro in European Financial Centre Relations: London and Frankfurt, 2000–2001.' *Journal of Contemporary European Studies* 12 (1): 143–157.

Beaverstock, J. V., R. G. Smith and P. J. Taylor (1999) 'A Roster of World Cities.' *Cities* 16 (6): 445–458.

———(2000) 'World-City Network: A New Metageography?' *Annals of the Association of American Geographers* 90 (1): 123–134.

———(2003) 'The Global Capacity of a World City: A Relational Study of London.' In: E. Kofman and G. Youngs (eds.) *Globalization: Theory and Practice – Second Edition.* London and New York: Continuum.

Beavon, K. S. O. (2005) 'Changes in the Ordering of Johannesburg's Spatial Domain, 1990–2002.' In: S. Raiser and K. Volkmann (eds.), *Emerging Patterns of the Global City Region.* Berlin: Osteuropa Instituts der Freien Universität Berlin.

Beck, U. (2002) 'The Terrorist Threat: World Risk Society Revisited.' *Theory, Culture and Society* 19 (1): 39–55.

Behrendt, S. (2008) *When Money Talks: Arab Sovereign Wealth Funds in the Global Public Policy Discourse. Carnegie Papers from Carnegie Middle East Centre,* 12. Washington, DC: Carnegie Endowment for International Peace.

Benedictow, O. J. (2004) *The Black Death, 1346–1353: The Complete History.* Woodbridge, Suffolk: Boydell Press.

Benjamin, S. (2008) 'Occupancy Urbanism: Radicalizing Politics and Economy Beyond Policy and Programmes.' *International Journal of Urban and Regional Research* 32 (3): 719–729.

Bennett, C. J. and H. D. Haggerty (2011) *Security Games: Surveillance and Control at Mega-events.* London and New York: Routledge.

Bennett, C. J. and D. Lyon (eds.) (2008) *Playing the Identity Card: Surveillance, Security and Identification Regimes in Global Perspective.* London: Routledge.

Benton-Short L., M. D. Price and S. Friedman (2005) 'Globalization from Below: The Ranking of Global Immigrant Cities.' *International Journal of Urban and Regional Research* 29 (4): 945–959.

Berry, B. J. L. and A. R. Pred (1961) *Central Place Studies: A Bibliography of Theory and Applications.* Philadelphia Regional Science Research Institute.

Birmingham, J. (1999) *Leviathan: The Unauthorised Biography of Sydney.* Sydney: Knopf.

Bourdieu, P. (1985) 'Social Space and the Genesis of Groups.' *Theory and Society* 14 (4): 723–744.

Bouteliger, S. (2012) *Global Cities and Networks for Global Environmental Governance.* London: Routledge.

Boxer, C. R. (1965) The Dutch Seaborne Empire, 1600–1800, London: Hutchison.

Boyer, R. and Y. Saillard (eds.) (2002) [1995] *Régulation Theory: The State of the Art.* London and New York: Routledge.

Boyle, J. (2012) 'Dar es Salaam: Africa's next megacity?' *BBC News* 31 July 2012.

Bowling, B. (1999) 'The Rise and Fall of New York Murder: Zero Tolerance or Crack's Decline?' *British Journal of Criminology* 39 (4): 531–554.

Bracken, L. J. and E. A. Oughton (2006) ' "What Do You Mean?" The Importance of Language in Developing Interdisciplinary Research.' *Transactions of the Institute of British Geographers* 31 (3): 371–382.

Bradbury, M. (1998) *The Atlas of Literature.* London: Stewart, Tabori & Chang.

Braudel, F. (1973) *The Mediterranean and the Mediterranean World in the Age of Phillip II.* London: Collins.

———(1982) *The Weels of Commerce.* London: Collins.

———(1983) *On History,* trans. by S. Matthews. Chicago: University of Chicago Press.

————(1984) *The Perspective of the World.* London: Collins.

Brenner, N. (1998) 'Global Cities, Glocal States: Global City Formation and State Territorial Restructuring in Contemporary Europe.' *Review of International Political Economy* 5 (1): 1–37.

Brenner, N. and R. Keil (eds.) (2006) *The Global Cities Reader.* Abindon: Routledge.

————(2011) 'From Global Cities to Globalized Urbanization.' In: R. LeGates and F. Stout (eds.), *The City Reader*, 5th ed. London: Routledge.

Brenner, N. and C. Schmid (2012) 'Planetary Urbanization.' In: M. Gandy (ed.), *Urban Constellations*, pp. 10–13. Berlin: Jovis.

Brenner, N., J. Peck and N. Theodore (2010) 'After Neoliberalization?' *Globalizations* 7 (3): 327–345.

Bridge, G. and S. Watson (eds.) (2002) *A Companion to the City.* Oxford: Wiley-Blackwell.

Brown, A., J. O'Connor and S. Cohen (2000) 'Local Music Policies within a Global Music Industry: Cultural Quarters in Manchester and Sheffield.' *Geoforum* 31 (4): 437–451.

Brown, E., B. Derudder, C. Parnreiter, W. Pelupessy, P. J. Taylor and F. Witlox (2010) 'World City Networks and Global Commodity Chains: Towards a World-Systems' Integration.' *Global Networks* 10 (1): 12–34.

Brown, W. (2010) *Walled States, Waning Sovereignty.* New York: Zone.

Bryant, N. (2012) 'What's Better than the Sydney Opera House?' *The Global Mail* 6 November 2012.

Bulkeley, H. and M. Betsill (2003) *Cities and Climate Change: Urban Sustainability and Global Environmental Governance.* London: Routledge.

Bunnell, T. and A. Maringanti (2010) 'Practising Urban and Regional Research beyond Metrocentricity.' *International Journal of Urban and Regional Research* 34 (2): 415–420.

Bunnell, T. and J. D. Sidaway (2012) 'Preface.' In: X. Chen and A. Kanna (eds.), *Rethinking Global Urbanism.* New York: Routlegde.

Bureau of Infrastructure, Transport and Regional Economics. (2012) *International Airline Activity 2011: Statistical Report.* Canberra: Department of Infrastructure and Transport.

Buzan, B. (1999) ' "Change and Insecurity" Reconsidered.' *Contemporary Security Policy* 20 (3): 1–17.

Caldeira, T. (2001) *City of Walls: Crime, Segregation, and Citizenship in São Paulo.* Berkeley CA: University of California Press.

Cairns, S. and J. M. Jacobs (2008) 'The Modern Touch: Interior Design and Modernisation in Post-Independence Singapore.' *Environment and Planning A* 40 (3): 572–595.

Cannon, M. (1986) *The Land Boomers.* Melbourne: Lloyd O'Neill.

Cardoso, B. V. (2012) 'The Paradox of Caught-in-the-Act Surveillance Scenes: Dilemmas of police Video Surveillance in Rio de Janeiro.' *Surveillance & Society* 10 (1): 51–64.

Castells, M. (1972) *La question urbaine.* Paris: Maspero.

————(1983) *The City and the Grassroots.* Los Angeles: University of California Press.

————(1996) *The Rise of the Network Society.* Oxford: Blackwell.

Chandler T. (1987) *Four Thousand Years of Urban Growth: An Historical Census.* Lampeter: St. David's University Press.

Chase Dunn, C. (1985) 'The System of World Cities, 800 A.D.–1975.' In: M. Timberlake (ed.), *Urbanization in the World-Economy*, pp. 269–292. Orlando: Academic Press.

Chattaraj, S. (2012) 'The Making of a World-Class City.' *The Hindu Business Lind* 28 August 2012.

Choi, J. H., G. A. Barnett and B. S. Chon (2006) 'Comparing World City Networks: A Network Analysis of Internet Backbone and Air Transport Intercity Linkages.' *Global Networks* 6 (1): 81–99.

Chomsky, N. (1967) 'The Responsibility of Intellectuals.' *The New York Review of Books* 8 (3): 23 February.

Chosen, M. and M. Korach (2010) *Jerusalem: Facts and Trends 2009/2010.* Jerusalem: Jerusalem Institute for Israel Studies.

Christophers, B (2008) 'The BBC, the Creative Class, and Neoliberal Urbanism in the North of England.' *Environment and Planning A* 40 (10): 2313–2329.

Ciccolella, P. and I. Mignaqui (2002) 'Buenos Aires: Sociospatial Impacts of the Development of Global City Functions.' In: S. Sassen (ed.), *Global Networks: Linked Cities.* London: Routledge.

City of Sydney. (2008) *Sustainable Sydney 2030: The Vision.* Sydney: Council of the City of Sydney.

City of Sydney. (2010) *Barangaroo Concept Plan Modification MP06_0162 Mod 4. Submission to the NSW Department of Planning.* Sydney: Council of the City of Sydney.

Clark, G. and D. Wojcík (2007) *The Geography of Finance: Corporate Governance in the Global Market Place.* Oxford: Oxford University Press.

Clark, G. L., A. Monk, A. Dixon, L. W. Pauly, J. Faulconbridge, H. W. C. Yeung and S. Behrendt (2010) 'Symposium: Sovereign Fund Capitalism.' *Environment and Planning A* 42 (9): 2271–2291.

Coaffee, J. and D. Murakami Wood (2006) 'Security is Coming Home: Rethinking Scale and Constructing Resilience in the Global Urban Response to Terrorist Risk.' *International Relations* 20 (4): 503–517.

Coaffee, J., D. Murakami Wood and P. Rogers (2008) *The Everyday Resilience of the City: How Cities Respond to Terrorism and Disaster.* Basingstoke: Palgrave Macmillan.

Coaffee, J. and P. Rogers (2008) 'Reputational Risk and Resiliency: The Branding of Security in Place-Making.' *Place Branding and Public Diplomacy* 4 (3): 205–217.

Cohen, J. E. (2007) 'Cyberspace as/and Space.' *Columbia Law Review* 107 (1): 210–256.

Cohen, R. (1981) 'The New International Division of Labor, Multinational Corporations and Urban Hierarchy.' In: Michael Dear and Allen J. Scott (eds.), *Urbanization and Urban Planning in Capitalist Society*, pp. 287–315. New York: Methuen & Co. Ltd.

Cox, K. (1998) 'Spaces of Dependence, Spaces of Engagement and the Politics of Scale.' *Political Geography* 17 (1): 1–23.

Craig, J. A. (1975) *Population Density and Concentration in Great Britain 1931, 1951 and 1961.* London: HMSO.

Crang, M. (1996) 'Envisioning Urban Histories: Bristol as palimpsest, Postcards, and Snapshots.' *Environment & Planning A* 28 (3): 429–452.

———(1998) *Cultural Geography.* London: Routledge.

———(2000) 'Public Space, Urban Space and Electronic Space: Would the Real City Please Stand Up?' *Urban Studies* 37 (2): 301–317.

———(2001) 'Rhythms of the City: Temporalised Space and Motion.' In: J. Mayand and N. Thrift (eds.), *Timespace Geographies of Temporality*, pp. 187–207. London: Routledge.

Crang, M. and S. Graham (2007) 'Sentient Cities: Ambient Intelligence and the Politics of Urban Space.' *Information, Communication & Society* 10 (6): 789–817.

Crang, M., T. Crosbie and S. D. N. Graham (2007) 'Technology, Timespace and the Remediation of Neighbourhood Life.' *Environment and Planning A* 39 (10): 2405–2422.

Crawford, A. (2002) *Crime and Insecurity: The Governance of Safety in Europe*. Devon: Willan.

Curtis, M. (2009) *Orientalism and Islam: European Thinkers on Oriental Despotism in the Middle East and India*. Cambridge: Cambridge University Press.

Curtis, S. (2011) 'Global Cities and the Transformation of the International System.' *Review of International Studies* 37 (4): 1923–1947.

Daly, M. and P. Malone (1996) 'Sydney: The Economic and Political Roots of Darling Harbour.' In: P. Malone (ed.), *City, Capital and Water*, pp. 90–108. London: Routledge.

Daskalaki, M and O. Mould (2013) 'Beyond Urban Subcultures: Urban Subversions and Rhizomic Social Formations.' *International Journal of Urban and Regional Research* 37 (1): 1–18.

Datta, K., C. McIlwaine, J. Herbert, Y. Evans, J. May and J. Wills (2012) 'Global Workers for Global Cities: Low Paid Migrant Labour in London.' In: B. Derudder, M. Hoyler, P. Taylor and F. Witlox (eds.), *International Handbook of Globalization and World Cities*, pp. 390–397. Cheltenham: Edward Elgar.

Davidson, B. (1987) 'Agriculture.' In: W. Vamplew (ed.), *Australians: Historical Statistics*. Broadway, NSW: Fairfax, Syme and Weldon.

Davis, M. and D. B. Monk (eds.) (2007) *Evil Paradises: Dreamworlds of Neoliberalism*. New York: New Press.

De Certeau, M. (1984) *The Practice of Everyday Life*, transl. by S. F. Randall, Berkeley: University of California Press.

Degan, M and M. García (2012) 'The Transformation of the "Barcelona Model": An Analysis of Culture, Urban Regeneration and Governance.' *International Journal of Urban and Regional Research* 36 (5): 1022–1038.

De Menezes, C. (2012) 'Morte de PM em UPP devolve medo e tensão ao Complexo do Alemão.'('Death of a Military Police Officer from a UPP takes Place in the Midst of Tension in the Complexo do Alemão') *Jornal do Brasil* 24 July 2012.

Dennis, A. (2012) 'Build Locally, Think Globally.' *The Australian* 2 November 2012.

Derudder, B. (2006) 'On Conceptual Confusion in Empirical Analyses of a Transnational Urban Network.' Urban Studies 43 (11): 2027–2046.

Derudder, B., M. Hoyler, P. J. Taylor and F. Witlox (eds.) (2012) *International Handbook of Globalization and World Cities*. Cheltenham: Edward Elgar.

de Souza, A. e A. Silva (2006) 'From Cyber to Hybrid.' *Space and Culture* 9 (3): 261–278.

de Vries, J. (1984) *European Population, 1500–1800*. London: Methuen.

Dick, H. and P. J. Rimmer (2003) *Cities, Transport and Communications: The Integration of Southeast Asia since 1850*. London: Palgrave Macmillan.

Dillon, M. and L. Lobo-Guerrero (2008) 'Biopolitics of Security in the 21st Century: An Introduction.' *Review of International Studies* 34 (2): 265–292.

Dodge, M. and Kitchin, M. (2005) 'Code and the Transduction of Space.' *Annals of the Association of American Geographers* 95 (1): 162–180.

Donald, J. (2002) 'The Immaterial City: Representation, Imagination, and Media.' In: G. Bridge and S. Watson (eds.), *A Companion to the City*. Oxford: Wiley-Blackwell.

Dong, S. (2000) *Shanghai: The Rise and Fall of a Decadent City*. New York: HarperCollins.

Dovey, K. (1996) *Tall Towers and Short-Sighted Cities*. Tirra Lirra: Winter.

———(1999) *Framing Places: Mediating Power in Built Form*. London: Routledge.

Drabble, M. (1980) *A Writer's Britain: Landscape in Literature*. London: Thames and Hudson.

Dunning J. (1971) *The Mulitnational Enterprise*. London: Allen & Unwin.

Echanove, M.and R. Srivastava (2011) 'Urban Journal: The Vanishing Public of the "World Class City".' *The Wall Street Journal: India Realtime* 29 March 2011.

Economic Times. (2012) 'Why "Smart City" Rio is a Role Model for Indian Cities.' *Economic Times* 12 October 2012.

Eng, T. S.and V. R. Savage (1985) 'Singapore Landscape: A Historical Overview of Housing Change.' *Singapore Journal of Tropical Geography* 6 (1): 48–63.

Engelen, E., I. Ertürk, J. Froud, S. Johal, A. Leaver, M. Moran, A. Nilsson and K. Williams (2011) After the Great Complacence: Financial Crisis and the Politics of Reform. Oxford: Oxford University Press.

Engelen, E., I. Erturk, J. Froud, A. Leaver and K. Williams (2010) 'Reconceptualizing Financial Innovation: Frame, Conjuncture and Bricolage.' *Economy and Society* 39 (1): 33–63.

Ericson, R. V. (2007) *Crime in an Insecure World*. Cambridge: Polity Press.

Erie, S. P. (2004) *Globalizing L.A. Trade, Infrastructure, and Regional Development*. Stanford: Stanford University Press.

Evans, G. (2005) 'Measure for Measure: Evaluating the Evidence of Culture's Contribution to Regeneration.' *Urban Studies* 42 (5/6): 959–984.

———(2009) 'Creative Cities, Creative Spaces and Urban Policy.' *Urban Studies* 46 (5/6): 1003–1040.

Fainstein, S. (2001) *The City Builders: Property Development in New York and London, 1980–2000*. Lawrence: University Press of Kansas.

Fainstein, S., I. Gordon and M. Harloe (eds.) (1992) *Divided Cities: New York & London in the Contemporary World*. Oxford: Blackwell.

Faulconbridge, J. R. (2004) 'London and Frankfurt in Europe's Evolving Financial Centre Network.' *Area* 36 (1): 235–244.

———(2006) 'Stretching Tacit Knowledge beyond a Local Fix? Global Spaces of learning in Advertising Professional Service Firms.' *Journal of Economic Geography* 6 (4) 517–540.

———(2008) 'Managing the Transnational Law Firm: A Relational Analysis of Professional Systems, Embedded Actors, and Time – Space-Sensitive Governance.' *Economic Geography* 84 (1): 185–210.

Falconer, D. (2010) *Sydney*. Sydney: University of New South Wales Press.

Fenby, J. (2012) *Tiger Head: Snake Tails: China Today, How It Got There and Where It Is Heading*. London: Simon & Shuster.

Fischer, B. (2008) *A Poverty of Rights: Citizenship and Inequality in Twentieth-Century Rio de Janeiro*. Stanford CA: Stanford University Press.

Florida, R. (2002) *The Rise of the Creative Class: And How it's Transforming Work, Leisure, Community and Everyday Life*. New York: Basic Books.

———(2005) *Cities and the Creative Class*. New York: Basic Books.

Forêt, P. (2008) 'The Silk Road Network.' In: P. Forêt and A. Kaplony (eds.), *The Journey of Maps and Images on the Silk Road*. Leiden and Boston: Brill.

Foucault, M. (1977) *Discipline and Punish: The Birth of the Prison*. London: Penguin.

———(2007) *Security, Territory, Population: Lectures at the College de France 1977–1978*. New York: Picador.

Frank, A. G. (1969) *Latin America: Underdevelopment or Revolution: Essays on the Development of Underdevelopment and the Immediate Enemy*. New York: Monthly Review Press.

French, S., A. Leyshon and T. Wainwright (2011) 'Financializing Space, Spacing Financialization.' *Progress in Human Geography* 35 (6): 798–819.

Friedmann J. (1986) 'The World City Hypothesis.' *Development and Change* 17 (1): 69–83.

———(1995) 'Where We Stand: A Decade of World City Research.' In: Paul L. Knox and Peter J. Taylor (eds.), *World Cities in a World-System*, pp. 21–47. Cambridge: Cambridge University Press.

Friedmann J. and G. Wolff (1982) 'World City Formation: An Agenda for Research and Action.' *International Journal of Urban and Regional Research* 6 (3) 309–344.

Frodeman, R., J. T. Klein and C. Mitcham (eds.) (2010) *The Oxford Handbook of Interdisciplinarity*. Oxford: Oxford University Press.

Froud, J., S. Johal, A. Leaver, and K. Williams (2006) *Financialization and Strategy: Narrative and Numbers*. Oxford and New York: Routledge.

Fröbel, F., J. Heinrichs and O. Kreye (1977) *Die neue internationale Arbeitsteilung. Strukturelle Arbeitslosigkeit in den Industrieländern und die Industrialisierung der Entwicklungsländer*. Hamburg: Rororo Rowohlt.

Fujita, K. (2003) 'Neo-industrial Tokyo: Urban Development and Globalisation in Japan's State-centred Developmental Capitalism.' *Urban Studies* 40 (2): 249–281.

Gaffney, C. (2010) 'Mega-Events and Socio-Spatial Dynamics in Rio de Janeiro, 1919–2016.' *Journal of Latin American Geography* 9 (1): 7–29.

Galdo, E. (2011) 'Representante do Ministério de Segurança da Argentina visita favelas cariocas pacificadas.' ('Represenative of Argentina's Ministry of Security visits Rio's pacified favelas') *O Globo* 20 October 2011.

Garland, D. (2001) *The Culture of Control: Crime and Social Order in Contemporary Society*. Chicago: University of Chicago Press.

Geddes, P. (1915) *Cities in Evolution*. London: Williams and Norgate.

Gerber, J. S. (1992) *The Jews of Spain: A History of the Sephardic Experience*. New York: Free Press.

Gibson, K. D. and R. J. Horvath (1983) 'Global Capital and the Restructuring Crisis in Australian Manufacturing.' *Economic Geography* 59 (1): 178–194.

Giffinger, R., G. Haindlmaier and H. Kramar (2011) 'The Role of Rankings in Growing City Competition.' *Urban Research & Practice* 3 (3): 299–312.

Gilchrist, P. and B. Wheaton (2011) 'Lifestyle Sports, Public Policy and Youth Engagement: Examining the Emergence of Parkour.' *International Journal of Sport Policy and Politics* 3 (1): 109–131.

Glaeser, E. (2010) *The Triumph of the City*. London: Penguin.

Glancey, J. (1998) 'Urban Bullies.' *The Guardian*, 14 December 1998.

Glendenning, M. (2004) *The Last Icons: Architecture beyond Modernism*. Glasgow: Graven Images.

Glenny, M. (2012) 'Rio: The Fight for the Favelas.' *Financial Times*, 2 November 2012.

Global Networks. (2010) 'Special Issue: World City Networks and Global Commodity Chains.' *Global Networks* 10 (1): 1–163.

Globo.com. (2009) 'Governo do Rio contrata ex-prefeito de Nova York para ajudar na segurança.' ('Governor of Rio Contracts the Ex-Mayor of New York to Advise on Security') 3 December 2009.

Goh, R. (2003) 'Things to a Void: Utopian Discourse, Communality and Constructed Interstices in Singapore Public Housing.' In: R. B. Goh and B. S. Yeoh (eds.), *Theorizing the Southeast Asian City as Text*, pp. 51–75. Singapore: World Scientific.

———(2001) 'Ideologies of "Upgrading" in Singapore Public Housing: Post-Modern Style, Globalisation and Class Construction in the Built Environment.' *Urban Studies* 38 (9): 1589–1604.

Gold, J. R. and S. V. Ward (eds.) (1994) *Place Promotion*. New York: Wiley.

Goldsmith, B. and T. O'Regan (2003) *Cinema Cities, Media Cities: The Contemporary International Studio Complex*. Sydney: Australian Film Commission.

Gomez, M. V. and S. Gonzalez (2001) 'A Reply to Beatriz Plaza's "The Guggenheim-Bilbao Museum Effect".' *International Journal of Urban and Regional Research* 25 (4): 898–900

Gordon, J. (2007) 'Letting the Genie Out: Local Government and UNCED.' *Environmental Politics* 2 (4): 137–155.

Goss, J. (1995) 'We Know Who You Are and We Know Where You Live: The Instrumental Rationality of Geodemographic Systems.' *Economic Geography* 71 (1): 171–198.

Grabar, H. (2012) 'Why Has Scandinavia's Biggest Development Project Abandoned its Master Plan?' *Atlantic Cities*, available at http://www.theatlanticcities.com/design/2012/08/why-has-scandinavias-biggest-development-project-abandoned-its-master-plan/3120/

Graham, M. (2010) 'Neogeography and the Palimpsests of Place.' *Tijdschrift voor Economische en Sociale Geografie* 101(4): 422–436.

Graham, M. (2011) 'Wiki Space: Palimpsests and the Politics of Exclusion.' In: Lovink, G. and N. Tkacz (eds.), *Critical Point of View: A Wikipedia Reader*, pp. 269–282. Amsterdam: Institute of Network Cultures.

———(2012) 'Big Data and the End of Theory?' *The Guardian* 9 March 2012.

Graham, M., S. Hale and M. Stephens. (2011) *Geographies of the World's Knowledge*. London: Convoco! Edition.

———(2010) *Cities Under Siege: The New Military Urbanism*. London: Verso.

Graham, S. and S. Marvin (2001) *Splintering Urbanism*. London: Routledge.

Graham, M. and M. Zook (2013) 'Augmented Realities and Uneven Geographies: Exploring the Geo-linguistic Contours of the Web.' *Environment and Planning A* 45 (1): 77–99.

———(2011) 'Visualizing Global Cyberscapes: Mapping User Generated Placemarks.' *Journal of Urban Technology* 18 (1): 115–132.

Graham, M., M. Zook and A. Boulton (2012) 'Augmented Reality in the Urban Environment.' *Transactions of the Institute of British Geographers*. Online First.

Graham, S. (2002) 'Communication Grids: Cities and Infrastructure.' In: Saskia Sassen (ed.), *Global Networks, Linked Cities*, pp. 71–91. Routledge, London.

———(2010) Cities Under Siege: The New Military Urbanism. London: Verso.

Graham, S.and S Marvin. (1996) *Telecommunications and the City: Electronic Spaces, Urban Places*. New York: Routledge

———(2001) Splintering Urbanism. London: Routledge.

Greene, J. A. (1999) 'Zero Tolerance: A Case Study of Police Policies and Practices in New York City.' *Crime & Delinquency* 45 (2): 171–187.

Grubbauer, M. (2011) *Die vorgestellte Stadt. Globale Büroarchitektur, Stadtmarketing und politischer Wandel in Wien*. Bielefeld: Transcript.

G1 (2012) 'Operação do Bope no Morro do São Carlos tem três detidos, diz PM.' ('The BOPE operation in the Morro do São Carlos has resulted in three arrests, say the PM'), *Globo TV G1* news, 27 February 2012, available at: http://g1.globo.

com/rio-de-janeiro/noticia/2012/02/operacao-do-bope-no-morro-do-sao-carlos-tem-tres-detidos-diz-pm.html

Haila, A. (2000) 'Real Estate in Global Cities: Singapore and Hong Kong as Property States.' *Urban Studies* 38 (12): 2241–2256.

Hall, P. (1966) *The World Cities*. London: Weidenfeld and Nicolson.

——(1998) *Cities in Civilization: Culture, Innovation, and Urban Order*. London: Weidenfeld and Nicolson.

Hamnett, C. (1994) 'Social Polarisation in Global Cities: Theory and Evidence.' *Urban Studies* 31 (3): 401–424.

——(2012) 'Urban Social Polarization.' In: B. Derdudder, M. Hoyler, P. Taylor and F. Witlox (eds.) *International Handbook of Globalization and World Cities*, pp. 361–368. Cheltenham: Edward Elgar.

Hansen, A. L., H. Andersen and E. Clark (2001) 'Creative Copenhagen: Globalization, Urban Governance and Social Change.' *European Planning Studies* 9 (7): 851–869.

Hanssens, H., B. Derudder and F. Witlox (2012) 'Managing Organizational and Geographical Complexity: The "Positionality" of Advanced Producer Services in the Globalizing Economies of Metropolitan Regions.' *Erdkunde* 66: 45–55.

Harrison, P., A. Todes and V. Watson (2008) *Planning and Transformation: Learning from the Post-Apartheid Experience*. London: Routledge.

Harvey, D. (1973) *Social Justice and the City*. London: Edward Arnold.

——(1978) 'The Urban Process Under Capitalism: A Framework for Analysis.' *International Journal of Urban and Regional Research* 2 (1–4): 101–131.

——(1981) 'The Spatial Fix – Hegel, Von Thünen, and Marx.' *Antipode* 13 (3): 1–12.

——(1982) *The Limits to Capital*. Chicago: University of Chicago Press.

——(1989a) *The Condition of Postmodernity*. Oxford: Blackwell.

——(1989b) 'From Managerialism to Entrepreneurialism: The Transformation in Urban Governance in Late Capitalism.' *Geografiska Annaler: Series B, Human Geography* 71 (1): 3–17.

——(2001) 'Globalization and the "Spatial Fix".' *Geographische Revue* 2: 23–30.

——(2003a) 'The Right to the City.' *International Journal of Urban and Regional Research* 27 (4): 939–994.

——(2003b) 'The City as a Body Politic.' In: J. Schneider and I. Susser (eds.), *Wounded Cities: Destruction and Reconstruction in a Globalized World*, pp. 25–45. New York: Berg.

——(2005) *A Brief History of Neoliberalism*. Oxford: Oxford University Press.

Hebbert, M. (1998) *London: More by Fortune Than Design*. New York: Wiley.

Heenan, D. (1977) 'Global Cities of Tomorrow.' *Harvard Business Review*, 19 (3).

Hegglund, J. (2012) *World Views: Metageographies of Modernist Fiction*. Oxford: Oxford University Press.

Hill, R. and J. W. Kim (2000) 'Global Cities and Developmental States: New York, Tokyo and Seoul.' *Urban Studies* 37 (12): 2167–2195.

Hillier, J. and G. Searle (1995) 'Rien ne va Plus: Fast Track Development and Public Participation in Pyrmont-Ultimo, Sydney.' *Sydney Vision: UTS Papers in Planning* 3. Sydney: Planning Program, Faculty of Design, Architecture and Building, University of Technology, Sydney.

Hobbs, H. (1994) *City Hall Goes Abroad*. Ann Harbor: University of Michigan.

Hocking, B. (1993) *Localizing Foreign Policy*. New York: St. Martin's Press.

——(1999) 'Patrolling the "Frontier": Globalization, Localization and the "Actorness" of Non-Central Governments.' *Regional & Federal Studies* 9 (1): 17–39.

Holder, R. (1970) *The Bank of New South Wales: A History, Volume 1, 1817–1893.* Sydney: Angus and Robertson.

Holston, J. (2008) *Insurgent Citizenship: Disjunctions of Democracy and Modernity in Brazil.* Princeton: Princeton University Press.

Hones, S. (2008) 'Text as It Happens: Literary Geography.' *Geography Compass* 2 (5): 1301–1317.

———(2011) 'Literary Geography: The Novel as a Spatial Event.' In: S. Daniels and D. DeLyser (eds.), *Envisioning Landscapes, Making Worlds: Geography and the Humanities,* pp. 247–255. London: Routledge.

Hoyler, M. and K. Pain (2002) 'London and Frankfurt as World Cities: Changing Local-Global Relations.' In: A. Mayr, M. Meurer and J. Vogt (eds.), *Stadt und Region: Dynamik von Lebenswelten, Tagungsbericht und wissenschaftliche Abhandlungen,* pp. 76–87. Leipzig: Deutsche Gesellschaft für Geographie.

Hsu, H. L. (2010) *Geography and the Production of Space in Nineteenth-Century American Literature.* Cambridge: Cambridge University Press.

Hugo, G. J. (2006) 'Immigration Responses to Global Change in Asia: A Review.' *Geographical Research* 44 (2): 155–172.

Hymer, S. (1972) 'The Mulitnational Corporation and the Law of Uneven Development.' In: J. Bhagwati (ed.), *Economics and World Order,* pp. 113–140. New York: Free Press.

Infrastructure NSW. (2012) *State Infrastructure Strategy.* Sydney: Infrastructure NSW.

Isin, E. (2003) 'Historical Sociology of the City.' In: G.Delanty and E. Isin (eds.), *Handbook of Historical Sociology,* pp. 312–325. London: Sage.

Jacobs, J. (1969) *The Death and Life of Great American Cities.* London: Vintage.

Jacobs, W. and P. V. Hall (2007) 'What Conditions Supply Chain Strategies of Ports? The Case of Dubai.' *GeoJournal* 68 (4): 327–342.

Jencks, C. (2005) *The Iconic Building: The Power of Enigma.* London: Frances Lincoln.

Jenkins, P. and P. Wilkinson (2002) 'Assessing the Growing Impact of the Global Economy on Urban Development in Southern African Cities.' *Cities* 19 (1): 33–47.

Johannisson, B. (1990) *Organizing for Local Economic Development: On Firm and Context Dynamics.* Paper presented to the *30th European Conference RAS,* 28–31 August, Istanbul.

Jones, A. (2002) 'The "Global City" Misconceived: The Myth of "Global Management" in Transnational Service Firms.' *Geoforum* 33 (2): 335–350.

Jones, A. B. (2004) 'Challenging the Seductions of the Bilbao Guggenheim.' *International Journal of Iberian Studies* 16 (3): 159–165.

Jones, M. (2009) 'Phase Space: Geography, Relational Thinking, and Beyond.' *Progress in Human Geography* 33 (4): 487–506.

Jones, T. and T. Newburn (2002) 'Learning from Uncle Sam? Exploring US Influences on British Crime Control Policy.' *Governance* 15 (1): 97–119.

Jopson, D. and G. Ryle (2004) 'Grand Plan to Transform Suburbs into a New North Sydney.' *Sydney Morning Herald* 8 November 2004.

Kearns, A. and R. Paddison (2000) 'New Challenges for Urban Governance.' *Urban Studies* 37 (5–6): 845–850.

Keighren, I. M. (2006) 'Bringing Geography to the Book: Charting the Reception of Influences of Geogrpahic Environment.' *Transactions of the Institute of British Geographers* 31 (4): 525–540.

Keil, R. (1998) *Los Angeles: Globalization, Urbanization and Social Struggles.* Chichester: Wiley.

——(2011) 'Transnational Urban Political Ecology: Health, Environment and Infrastructure in the Unbounded City.' In: G. Bridge and S. Watson (eds.), *The New Companion to the City*. 2nd ed. Oxford: Wiley-Blackwell.

Kembrey, M. (2012) 'Overseas Students "Starved".' *Sydney Morning Herald* 29 October.

King, A. D. (1990) *Global Cities: Post-Imperialism and the Internationalization of London*. London: Routledge.

——(2004) *Spaces of Global Cultures*. New York: Routledge.

Kitchen, F. W. (1934) 'The Development of Secondary Industries in Victoria.' In: A. Pratt (ed.), *The National Handbook of Australia's Industries*. Melbourne: Specialty Press.

Knowles, R. (2012) 'Transit Oriented Development in Copenhagen, Denmark: From the Finger Plan to Ørestad.' *Journal of Transport Geography* 22 (1): 251–261.

Koonings, K. and D. Kruijt (eds.) (2007) *Fractured Cities: Social Exclusion, Urban Violence and Contested Spaces in Latin America*. London: Zed Books.

Korff, R. (1987) 'The World City Hypothesis: A Critique.' *Development and Change* 18 (3): 483–493.

Kotkin, J. (2005) *The City: A Global History*. New York: Modern Library.

Köhler, B. and M. Wissen (2003) 'Glocalizing Protest: Urban Conflicts and the Global Social Movements.' *International Journal of Urban and Regional Research* 27 (4): 942–951.

Kozloff, N. (2012) 'Is Brazil the Next Cop on the Beat in Africa? The Pentagon Seems to Hope So.' *Al-Jazeera* 10 June 2012.

Kramer, R. (2010) 'Painting with Permission: Legal Graffiti in New York City.' *Ethnography* 11 (2): 235–253.

Krätke, S. (2003) 'Global Media Cities in a Worldwide Urban Network.' *European Planning Studies* 11 (6): 605–628.

Lam, S. K., A. Uduwage, Z. Dong, S. Sen, D. R. Musicant and L. Terveen (2011) 'WP: Clubhouse?: An Exploration of Wikipedia's Gender Imbalance.' In: WikiSym'11, Proceedings of the 7th International Symposium on Wikis and Open Collaboration, pp. 1–10. New York, NY: ACM.

Lam Wo-Lap, W. (1999) *The Era of Jiang Zemin*. Singapore: Prentice Hall.

——(2006) *Chinese Politics in the Hu Jintao Era: New Leaders, New Challenges*. Armonk, NY: M.E. Sharpe.

Landers, J. (1993) Death and the Metropolis: Studies in the Demographic History of London, 1670–1830. Cambridge: Cambridge University Press.

Landry, C. (2000) *The Creative City: A Toolkit for Urban Innovators*. London: Earthscan.

Lai, K. P.-Y. (2006) ' "Imagineering" Asian Emerging Markets: Financial Knowledge Networks in the Fund Management Industry.' *Geoforum* 37 (4): 627–642.

——(2012) 'Differentiated Markets: Shanghai, Beijing and Hong Kong in China's Financial Centre Network.' *Urban Studies* 49 (6): 1275–1296.

Larner, W. and N. Laurie (2010) 'Travelling Technocrats, Embodied Knowledges: Globalising Privatisation in Telecoms and Water.' *Geoforum* 41 (2): 218–226.

Lash, S. and J. Urry (1994) *Economies of Signs and Space*. London: Sage.

Lawrence, A. (1999) *The Curse Bites: Skyscraper Index Strikes*. Property Report, Dresdner Kleinwort Benson Research (3 March).

Lees, L. (2001) 'Towards a Critical Geography of Architecture: The Case of an Ersatz Colosseum.' *Ecumene* 8 (1): 51–86.

Lee, R. (2002) 'Nice Maps, Shame about the Theory? Thinking Geographically about the Economic.' *Progress in Human Geography* 26 (3): 333–355.

————(2006) 'The Ordinary Economy: Tangled up in Values and Geography.' *Transactions of the Institute of British Geographers* 31 (4): 413–432.

Le Galès, P. (2002) *European Cities: Social Conflicts and Governance.* New York: Oxford University Press.

Lemanski, C. (2007) 'Global Cities in the South: Deepening Social and Spatial Polarisation in Cape Town.' *Cities* 24 (6): 448–461.

Ley, D. (2004) 'Transnational Spaces of Everyday Lives.' *Transactions of the Institute of British Geographers* 29 (2): 151–164.

Leyshon, A. and N. Thrift (1997) *Money Space: Geographies of Monetary Transformation.* London: Routledge.

Lipschutz, R. (1992) 'Reconstructing World Politics.' *Millennium* 21 (3): 389–420.

Livingstone, D. L. (2005) 'Science, Text and Space: Thoughts on the Geography of Reading.' *Transactions of the Institute of British Geographers* 30 (4): 391–401.

Lizieri, C. (2012) 'Global Cities, Office Markets, and Capital Flows.' In: P. J. Taylor, P. Ni, B. Derudder, M. Hoyler, J. Huang and F. Witlox (eds.), *Global Urban Analysis: A Survey of Cities in Globalization*, pp. 162–176. London: Earthscan.

Machimura, T. (1992): 'The Urban Restructuring Process in the 1980s: Transforming Tokyo into a World City.' *International Journal of Urban and Regional Research* 16 (1): 114–129.

Machor, J. L. (1993) *Readers in History: Nineteenth-century American Literature and the Contexts of Response.* Baltimore: Johns Hopkins University Press.

Maddison, A. (1998) 'Intensive and Extensive Growth in Imperial China.' In: *Chinese Economic Growth in the Long Run.* Paris: OECD Development Centre.

Magnusson, W. (2011) *Politics of Urbanism: Seeing Like a City.* London: Routledge.

Majoor, S. (2008) 'Progressive Planning Ideals in a Neo-Liberal Context: The Case of Ørestad Copenhagen.' *International Planning Studies* 13 (2): 101–117.

Malecki, E. J. (2002) 'The Economic Geography of the Internet's Infrastructure.' *Economic Geography* 78 (4): 399–424.

Marcuse, P. (2009) 'From Critical Urban Theory to the Right to the City.' *City* 12 (2–3): 195–197.

Markusen, A. (2006) 'Urban Development and the Politics of a Creative Class: Evidence from a Study of Artists.' *Environment and Planning A* 38 (10): 1921–1940.

Massey, D. (1992) 'Politics and Space/Time.' *New Left Review* 196: 65–84.

————(1994) *Space, Place and Gender.* London: Polity Press.

————(1999) 'On Space and the City.' In: D. Massey, J. Allen and S. Pile (eds.), *City Worlds*, pp. 151–166. London: Routledge/Open University.

————(2005) *For Space.* Thousand Oaks, CA: Sage.

————(2007) *World City.* Cambridge: Polity Press.

Massey, D., P. Quintas and D. Wield (1992) *High-Tech Fantasies: Science Parks in Society, Science and Space.* London: Routledge.

Matsumoto, H. (2004) 'International Urban Systems and Air Passenger and Cargo Flows: Some Calculations.' *Journal of Air Transport Management* 10 (1): 241–249.

Mbembé, J-A. (2003) 'Necropolitics.' trans. L. Meintjes, *Public Culture* 15 (1): 11–40.

McCann, C. (2009) *Let The Great World Spin.* London: Random House.

McCann, E. (2004) 'Urban Political Economy Beyond the "Global City".' *Urban Studies* 41 (12): 2315–2333.

————(2011) 'Urban Policy Mobilities and Global Circuits of Knowledge: Toward a Research Agenda.' *Annals of the Association of American Geographers* 101 (1): 107–130.

McCarthy, J. (2005) 'Cultural Quarters and Regeneration: The Case of Wolverhampton.' *Planning, Practice & Research* 20 (3): 297–311.

McGee, T. G. (1971) *The Urbanisation in the Third World: Explanations in Search of Theories*. London: G Bell and Sons.

———(2002) 'Reconstructing The Southeast Asian City in as Era of Volatile Globalization.' In: T. Bunnell, L. Drummond and K. C. Ho (eds.), *Critical Reflections on the City in Southeast Asia*, pp. 31–53. Singapore: Times Academic Press.

McEwan, C. (2009) *Postcolonialism and Development*. London: Routledge.

McNeill, D. (2005) 'In Search of the Global Architect: The Case of Norman Foster (and Partners).' *International Journal of Urban and Regional Research* 29 (3): 501–515.

———(2009) *The Global Architect: Firms,Fame and Urban Form*. New York: Routledge.

Melissen, J. and R. van der Pluijm (2007) *City Diplomacy: The Expanding Role of Cities in International Politics*. The Hague: Netherlands Institute of International Relations, Clingendael.

Meyer, D. R. (1991): 'The Formation of a Global Financial Center: London and its Intermediaries.' In: Resat, K. (ed.), *Cities in the World System*, pp. 97–106. New York: Greenwood Press.

Miles, S. and R. Paddison (2005) 'Introduction: The Rise and Rise of Culture-Led Urban Regeneration.' *Urban Studies* 42 (5/6): 833–839.

Minami, R. (1994) *The Economic Development of Japan: A Quantitative Study*, 2nd edition. London: Macmillan.

Miraftab, F. (2012) 'Colonial Present: Legacies of the Past in Contemporary Practices in Cape Town, South Africa.' *Journal of Planning History* 11 (4): 283–307.

Mitchell, B. R. (2007a) *International Historical Statistics: Africa, Asia & Oceania, 1750–2005*, 5th ed. Basingstoke: Palgrave Macmillan.

———(2007b) *International Historical Statistics: Europe, 1750–2005*, 6th ed. Basingstoke: Palgrave Macmillan.

Modelski, G. (2003) *World Cities, –3000 to 2000*. Washington, DC: Faros 2000.

Moeller, K. (2009) 'Police Crackdown on Christiania in Copenhagen.' *Crime, Law and Social Change* 52 (2): 337–345.

———. (1992) *A Phoenix in the Ashes: The Rise and Fall of the Koch Coalition in New York City Politics*. Princeton: Princeton University Press.

Mollenkopf, J. and M. Castells (1991) *Dual City. Restructuring New York*. New York: Russell Sage Foundation.

Moncada, E. (2009) 'Toward Democratic Policing in Colombia? Institutional Accountability through Lateral Reform.' *Comparative Politics* 41 (4): 431–449.

Montgomery, J. (2007) *The New Wealth of Cities*. Aldershot: Ashgate.

Montgomery, M. R., R. Stern, B. Cohen and H. E. Reed (eds.) (2004) *Cities Transformed: Demographic Change and its Implications in the Developing World*. London: Earthscan.

Moore, M. and L. Prain (2009) *Yarn Bombing: The Art of Crochet and Knit Graffiti*. Vancouver: Arsenal Pulp Press.

Moreno-Dodson, B. (2005) *Reducing Poverty on a Global Scale: Learning and Innovating Development*. Washington, DC: World Bank Publications.

Moretti, F. (1999) *Atlas of the European Novel, 1800–1900*. London: Verso.

Morris, I. (2010a) *Why the West Rules, For Now*. New York: Farrar, Straus and Giroux.

———(2010b) *Social Development e-book*. Stanford University. ianmorris.org/docs/social-development.pdf (accessed 23 June 2012).

Mould, O (2009) 'Parkour, the City, the Event.' *Environment and Planning D: Society and Space* 27 (4): 738–750.

Mullings, B., M. Werner and L. Peake (2010) 'Fear and Loathing in Haiti: Race and Politics of Humanitarian Dispossession.' *ACME: An International E-Journal for Critical Geographies* 9 (3): 282–300.

Mumford, L. (1961) *The City in History.* New York: Harcourt Brace.

Mundoreal. (2011) 'New Study Good News For Prazeres; Positive Step For Laboriaux.' Mundoreal.org http://1mundoreal.org/new-study-provides-hope-for-laboriaux

Murakami Wood, D. (2009) 'The Surveillance Society: Questions of History, Place and Culture.' *European Journal of Criminology* 6 (2): 179–194.

——(2011a) 'Cameras in Context: A Comparison of the Place of Video Surveillance in Japan and Brazil.' In: A. Doyle, R. Lippert and D. Lyon (eds.), *Eyes Everywhere: The Global Spread of Video Surveillance.* London: Routledge.

——(2011b) 'Surveillance.' In: P. Taylor, B. Derudder, M. Hoyler and F. Witlox (eds.), *International Handbook of Globalization and World Cities.* Cheltenham: Edward Elgar.

Murakami Wood, D. and R. Firmino (2009) 'Empowerment or Repression? Opening up Identification and Surveillance in Brazil though a Case of "Identification Fraud".' *Identity in the Information Society* 2 (3): 297–317.

Murphey, R. (1953) *Shanghai: Key to Modern China.* Cambridge: Harvard University Press.

National Housing Supply Council. (2010) *2nd State of Supply Report.* Canberra: Australian Government.

NBSC, (2011) *China Statistical Yearbook.* Compiled by National Bureau of Statistics in China. Beijing: China Statistics Press.

Neal, Z. P. (2010) 'Refining the Air Traffic Approach to City Networks.' *Urban Studies* 47 (12): 2195–2215.

——(2013) 'Brute Force and Sorting Processes: Two Perspectives on World City Network Formation.' *Urban Studies,* available online first: http://usj.sagepub.com/content/early/2012/09/23/0042098012460733.full.pdf+html

——(2014) Validity in World City Network Measurements. Tijdschrift voor Sociale en Economische Geografie, in press.

Newman, P. and A. Thornley (2011) *Planning World Cities,* 2nd edition. Basingstoke: Palgrave.

New South Wales Government. (2005) *City of Cities: A Plan for Sydney's Future.* Sydney: NSW Government.

——(2012) *Draft NSW Long Term Transport Master Plan.* Sydney: NSW Government.

Nicholls W. (2009) 'Place, Networks, Space: Theorizing the Geographies of Social Movements.' *Transactions of the Institute of British Geographers* 34 (1): 78–93.

Njoh, A. (2003) *Planning in Contemporary Africa: The State, Town Planning and Society in Cameroon.* Aldershot: Ashgate.

Ni, P. (2012) *The Global Urban Competitiveness Report 2011.* Cheltenham: Edward Elgar.

Norris, C. (2012) 'The Success of Failure: Accounting For the Global Growth of CCTV.' In: K. Ball, K. D. Haggerty and D. Lyon (eds.), *Routledge Handbook of Surveillance Studies.* London: Routledge.

Novick, A. (2003) 'Foreign Hires: French Experts and the Urbanism of Buenos Aires.' In: J. Nasr and M. Volait (eds.), *Urbanism Imported or Exported? Native Aspirations and Foreign Plans 1907–32.* Chichester: Wiley-Academy.

Nyland, C., H. Forbes-Mewett, S. Marginson, G. Ramia, E. Sawir and S. Smith (2007) International Students – A Segregated and Vulnerable Workforce, *Department of Management Working Paper* 24/07, Monash University.

O'Connell, J. F. (2006) 'The Changing Dynamics of the Arab Gulf Based Airlines and an Investigation into the Strategies that are Making Emirates into a Global Challenger.' *World Review of Intermodal Transportation Research* 1 (1): 94–114.

OECD (2001) *OECD Economic Surveys: Australia.* Paris: OECD.

Olds, K. and H. W. C. Yeung (2004) 'Pathways to Global City Formation: A View from the Developmental City-State of Singapore.' *Review of International Political Economy* 11 (3): 489–521.

Omahe, K. (1990) *The Borderless World*. New York: Harper Business.

Öncü, A. and P. Weyland (eds.) (1997) *Space, Culture and Power: New Identities in Globalizing Cities*. London: Zed Books.

O'Neill, P. and B. Fagan (2006) 'Geographical Takes on Three Decades of Economic Reform in Australia.' *Geographical Research* 44 (2): 204–219.

Ooi, G. L. and T. T. Tan (1992) 'The Social Significance of Public Spaces in Public Housing Estates.' In: B. H. Chua and N. Edwards (eds.), *Public Space: Design, Use and Management*, pp. 69–81. Singapore: NUS Press.

Parisier, E. (2011) *The Filter Bubble*. New York: Viking.

Parnreiter. (2010) 'Global Cities in Global Commodity Chains: Exploring the Role of Mexico City in the Geography of Global Economic Governance.' *Global Networks* 10 (1): 35–53.

———(2012) 'More than an Ordinary City: The Role of Mexico City in Global Commodity Chains.' In: B. Derudder, M. Hoyler, P. J. Taylor and F. Witlox (eds.), *International Handbook of Globalization and World Cities*, pp. 437–446. Cheltenham: Edward Elgar.

———(2013) Scrutinizing management and governance functions of APSFs in global cities. The case of Hamburg. mimeo.

Parnreiter, C., K. Fischer and K. Imhof (2010) 'Global Cities and the Governance of Commodity Chains: A Case Study from Latin America.' In: P. van Lindert and O. Verkoren (eds.), *Decentralized Development in Latin America. Experiences in Local Governance Local Development*, pp. 49–68. New York: Springer.

Parnreiter, C., C. Haferburg and J. O. ßenbrügge (2013) 'Shifting Corporate Geographies in Global Cities of the South: The Cases of Mexico City and Johannesburg.' *DIE ERDE* 144 (1): 41–62.

Patty, A. (2012) Overseas Students to Get Discounted Public Transport, *Sydney Morning Herald*, 30 October, http://www.smh.com.au/nsw/overseas-students-to-get-discounted-public-transport-20121029-28fkv.html, Accessed 30 October 2012.

Paul, D. (2004) 'World Cities as Hegemonic Projects: The Politics of Global Imagineering in Montreal.' *Political Geography* 23 (3): 571–596.

Peck, J. (2005) 'Struggling with the Creative Class.' *International Journal of Urban and Regional Research* 29 (4): 740–770.

———(2010) *Constructions of Neoliberal Reason*. Oxford: Oxford University Press.

———(2011) 'Recreative City: Amsterdam, Vehicular Ideas and the Adaptive Spaces of Creativity Policy.' *International Journal of Urban and Regional Research* 36 (3): 462–485.

Pe-Pua, R. (1996) *Astronaut Families and Their Children*. Canberra: Australian Government Publishing Service.

Perlman, J. (2009) *Favela: Four Decades of Living on the Edge in Rio de Janeiro*. New York: Oxford University Press.

Pevsner, N. (1957) London: The Cities of London and Westminster. Harmondsworth: Penguin.

Phillips, T. (2010) 'Rio Slum Dwellers Face Forced Eviction after Landslides: Mayor Signs Decree Permitting Forced Removal of Residents in high-Risk Areas, with Two Slums Set to be Permanently Removed.' *The Guardian* 11 April 2010, http://www.guardian.co.uk/world/2010/apr/11/rio-brazil-slum-forced-evictions.

Pickles, J. (2004) *A History of Spaces*. London: Routledge.

Pierce. J, D., G. Martin and J. T. Murphy (2011) 'Relational Place-Making: The Networked Politics of Place.' *Transactions of the Institute of British Geographers* 36 (1): 54–70.

Pike, A. and J. Pollard (2010) 'Economic Geographies of Financialization.' *Economic Geography* 86 (1): 29–51.

Pile, S. (2002) 'Sleepwalking in the Modern City: Walter Benjamin and Sigmund Freud.' In: G. Bridge and S. Watson (eds.), *A Companion to the City*. Oxford: Wiley-Blackwell.

Pinder, D. (2005) *Visions of the City*. Edinburgh: Edinburgh University Press.

Plaza, B., M. Tironi and S. Haarich (2009) 'Bilbao's Art Scene and the "Guggenheim effect" Revisited.' *European Planning Studies* 17 (11): 1711–1729.

Pollard, J. and M. Samers (2007) 'Islamic Banking and Finance: postcolonial Political Economy and the Decentring of Economic Geography.' *Transactions of the Institute of British Geographers* 32 (3): 313–330.

Pratt, A. (2008) 'Creative Cities: The Cultural Industries and the Creative Class.' *Geografiska Annaler: Series B, Human Geography* 90 (2): 107–117.

Preziuso, M. (2010) 'Mapping the Lived – Imagined Caribbean: Postcolonial Geographies in the Literature of the "Diasporic" Caribbean.' *Journal of Intercultural Studies* 31 (2): 145–160.

Purcell, M. (2002) 'Politics in Global Cities: Los Angeles Charter Reform and the New Social Movements.' *Environment and Planning A* 34 (1): 23–42.

Rabach, E. and E. M. Kim (1994) 'Where is the Chain in Commodity Chains? The Service Sector Nexus.' In: G. Gereffi and M. Korzeniewicz (eds.), *Commodity Chains and Global Capitalism*, pp. 123–143. Westport: Praeger.

Rimmer, P. J. (1998): 'Transport and Telecommunications among World Cities.' In: F. C. Lo and Y. M. Yeung (eds.), *Globalization and the World of Large Cities*, pp. 433–470. Tokyo: United Nations University Press.

Rimmer, P. J. and H. Dick (2009) The City in Southeast Asia: Patterns, Processes and Policy. Singapore: NUS Press.

Roberts, D. (2008) *Human Insecurity: Global Structures of Violence*. London: Zed Books.

Robinson, J. (2002) 'Global and World cities: A View from Off the Map.' *International Journal of Urban and Regional Research* 26 (3): 531–554.

———(2006) *Ordinary Cities: Between Modernity and Development*. New York: Routledge.

Roller, Z. (2012) 'Niterói Crime Wave Linked to Rio UPPs.' *The Rio Times* 17 April 2012, http://riotimesonline.com/brazil-news/rio-politics/niteroi-crime-wave-linked-to-rio-upps/

Rossi, E. and P. J. Taylor (2005) 'Banking Networks across Brazilian Cities: Interlocking Cities within and Bbeyond Brazil.' *Cities* 22 (5): 381–93.

———(2006) 'Gateway Cities in Economic Globalization: How Banks are Using Brazilian Cities.' *Tijdschrift voor Economische en Sociale Geografie* 97 (5): 515–534.

Rowe, W. (2009) *China's Last Empire: The Great Qing*. Cambridge, MA: Harvard University Press.

Roy, A. (2009) 'The 21st-Century Metropolis: New Geographies of Theory.' *Regional Studies* 43 (6): 819–830.

———(2011a) 'Slumdog Cities: Rethinking Subaltern Urbanism.' *International Journal of Urban and Regional Research* 35 (2): 223–238.

———(2011b) 'Urbanisms, Worlding Practices and the Theory of Planning.' *Planning Theory* 10 (1): 6–15.

———(2011c) 'Commentary: Placing Planning in the World – Transnationalism as Practice and Critique.' *Journal of Planning Education and Research* 31 (4): 406–415.

Rozenblat, C. and D. Pumain (2007) 'Firm Linkages, Innovation and the Evolution of Urban Systems.' In: P. J. Taylor, B. Derudder, P. Saey and F. Witlox (eds.), *Cities in Globalisation*, pp. 130–156. London: Routledge.

Rybczynski, W. (2002) 'The Bilbao Effect.' *The Atlantic Monthly* 290 (2): 138–142.

Said, E. (1975) 'The World, the Text, the Critic.' *The Bulletin of the Midwest Modern Language Association* 8 (2): 1–23.

Saitō, S. (1984) 'Urban Population during Edo Period.' *Chiiki Kaihatsu* 9 (1): 48–63.

Samers, M. (2002) 'Immigration and the Global City Hypothesis: Towards an Alternative Research Agenda.' *International Journal of Urban and Regional Research* 26 (2): 389–403.

Sassen, S. (1988) *The Mobility of Labor and Capital.* Cambridge: Cambridge University Press.

———(1991) *The Global City: New York, London, Tokyo.* Princeton: Princeton University Press.

———(1995) 'On Concentration and Centrality in the Global City.' In: P. L. Knox and P. J. Taylor (eds.), *World Cities in a World-System*, pp. 63–78. Cambridge: Cambridge University Press.

———(1996) 'The New Centrality.' In: W.S. Saunders (ed.), Reflections on Architectural Practices in the *Nineties*, pp. 206–218. Princeton: Princeton University Press.

———(1998) *Globalization and Its Discontents.* New York: New Press.

———(2001) *The Global City: New York, London, Tokyo*, 2nd edition. Princeton: Princeton University Press.

———(2002) Introduction. Locating cities on global circuits. In: Saskia Sassen (ed): Global Networks, Linked Cities. Routledge, London, 1–36.

———(2006) *Cities in a World Economy*, 4th edition. Thousand Oaks: Sage.

———(2007) *A Sociology of Globalization.* New York: W.W. Norton.

———(2010a) 'A Savage Sorting of Winners and Losers: Contemporary Versions of Primitive Accumulation.' *Globalizations* 7 (1): 23–50.

———(2010b) 'Global Inter-City networks and Commodity Chains: Any Intersections?' *Global Networks* 10 (1): 150–163.

Satterthwaite, D. (2009) 'Editorial: What Role for Mayors in Good City Governance?' *Environment & Urbanization* 21 (1): 3–17.

Saulwick, J. (2011) 'No Rail Plans for Barangaroo's Commuters.' *Sydney Morning Herald* 16 June.

Saunders, A. (2010) 'Literary Geography: Reforging the Connections.' *Progress in Human Geography* 34 (4): 1–17.

Saunders, W. S. (ed.). (2005) *Commodification and Spectacle in Architecture.* Minneapolis: University of Minnesota Press.

Saville, S. (2008) 'Playing with Fear: Parkour and the Mobility of Emotion.' *Social and Cultural Geography* 9 (4): 891–914.

Sayer, A. (2002) *Method in Social Science: A Realist Approach.* London: Routledge.

Searle, G. (1996) *Sydney as a Global City.* Sydney: Department of Urban Affairs and Planning and Department of State and Regional Development.

———(2002) 'Uncertain Legacy: Sydney's Olympic Stadiums.' *European Planning Studies* 10 (7): 845–860.

———(2008) 'Conflicts in Precinct Development.' In: B. Hayllar, T. Griffin and D. Edwards (eds.), *City Spaces – Tourist Places: Urban Tourism Precincts*, pp. 205–224. London: Elsevier.

———(2012) 'The Long Term Urban Impacts of the Sydney Olympic Games.' *Australian Planner* 49 (3): 195–202.

Searle, G. and M. Bounds (1999) 'State Powers, State Land and Competition for Global Entertainment: The Case of Sydney.' *International Journal of Urban and Regional Research* 23 (1): 165–172.

Searle, G. and R. Bunker (2010) 'Metropolitan Strategic Planning: An Australian Paradigm?' *Planning Theory* 9 (3): 163–180.

Searle, G. and P. Filion (2011) 'Planning Context and Urban Intensification Outcomes: Sydney versus Toronto.' *Urban Studies* 48 (7): 1419–1438.

Schottenhammer, A. (2007) 'The East Asian Maritime World 1400–1800: Its Fabrics of Power and Dynamics of Exchanges – China and Her Neighbours.' In: A. Schottenhammer (ed.), *East Asian Maritime History*, pp. 1–87. Wisebaden: Otto Harrassowitz Verlag.

Schumpeter, J. A. (1934) *The Theory of Economic Development.* New York: Oxford University Press.

———(1942) *Capitalism, Socialism and Democracy.* New York: Harper and Brothers.

Schweickart, P. P. and E. A. Flynn (2004) 'Introduction.' In: P. P. Schweickart and E. A. Flynn (eds.), Reading Sites: Social Difference and Reader Response, pp. 1–38. New York: Modern Language Association.

Scott, A. J. (1997) 'The Cultural Economy of Cities.' *International Journal of Urban and Regional Research* 21 (2): 323–339.

———(ed.) (2001) *Global City-Regions: Trends, Theory, Policy.* Oxford: Oxford University Press.

———(2006) 'Creative Cities: Conceptual Issues and Policy questions.' *Journal of Urban Affairs* 28 (1): 1–17.

Secord, J. A. (2000) *Victorian Sensation.* Chicago: University of Chicago Press.

Seyock, B. (2005) 'Pirates and Traders on Tsushima Island During the late 14th to Early 16th Centuries: As Seen from Historical and Archaeological Perspectives.' In: A. Schottenhammer (ed.), *Trade and Transfer Across the East Asian 'Mediterranean,'* pp. 91–124. Wisebaden: Otto Harrassowitz Verlag.

Shann, E. O. G. (1933) 'Economic and Political Development, 1885–1900.' In: E. Scott (ed.), *The Cambridge History of the British Empire*, Vol. VII, Part 1, *Australia.* Cambridge: Cambridge University Press.

Sharp, J. P. (1996) 'Locating Imaginary Homelands: Literature, Geography, and Salman Rushdie.' *GeoJournal* 38 (1): 119–127

———(2000) 'Towards a Critical Analysis of Fictive Geographies.' *Area* 32 (3): 327–334.

Sharpe, S. (2012) 'The Aesthetics of Urban Movement: Habits, Mobility, and Resistance.' *Geographical Research*, early view: http://onlinelibrary.wiley.com/doi/10.1111/j.1745-5871.2012.00781.x/abstract

Shatkin, G. (2007) 'Global Cities of the South: Emerging Perspectives on Growth and Inequality.' *Cities* 24 (1): 1–15.

———(2008) 'The City and the Bottom Line: Urban Megaprojects and the Privatization of Planning in Southeast Asia.' *Environment and Planning A* 40 (2): 383–401.

———(2011) 'Coping with Actually Existing Urbanisms: The Real Politics of Planning in the Global Era.' *Planning Theory* 10 (1): 79–87.

Shen, W. (2010) 'Globalizing Shanghai: International Migration and the Global City.' Working paper no. 2010/79, Tokyo: World Institute for Development Economics Research.

Short, J. R., Y. Kim, M. Kuus and H. Wells (1996) 'The Dirty Little Secret of World Cities Research: Data Problems in Comparative Analysis.' *International Journal of Urban and Regional Research* 20 (4): 697–717.

Sidaway, J. D. and J. R. Bryson (2002) 'Constructing Knowledges of "Emerging Markets": UK-Based Investment Managers and their Overseas Connections.' *Environment and Planning A* 34 (3): 401–416.

Sidaway, J. D. and M. Pryke (2000) 'The Strange Geographies of "Emerging Markets".' *Transactions of the Institute of British Geographers* 25 (2): 187–201.

Sim, L. L., S. M. Yu and S. S. Han. (2003) 'Public Housing and Ethnic Integration in Singapore.' *Habitat International* 27 (2): 293–307.

Skinner, G. (1964) 'Marketing and Social Structure in Rural China, Part 1.' *Journal of Asian Studies* 24 (1): 3–44.

——(1965a) 'Marketing and Social Structure in Rural China, Part 2.' *Journal of Asian Studies* 24 (2): 195–228.

——(1965b) 'Marketing and Social Structure in Rural China, Part 3.' *Journal of Asian Studies* 24 (3): 363–399.

Sklair, L. (2005) 'The Transnational Capitalist Class and Contemporary Architecture in Globalizing Cities.' *International Journal of Urban and Regional Research* 29 (3): 485–500.

——(2006) 'Iconic Architecture and Capitalist Globalization.' *City* 10 (1): 21–47.

Smith, D. A. (2003) 'Rediscovering Cities and Urbanization in the 21st Century World-System.' In: W.A. Dunaway (ed.), *Emerging Issues in the 21st Century World-System, Vol. II*, pp. 111–129. Westport: Praeger.

Smith, D. A. and M. F. Timberlake (1995) 'Conceptualising and Mapping the Structure of the World System's City System.' *Urban Studies* 32 (2): 287–302.

——(2001) 'World City Networks and Hierarchies 1977–1997: An Empirical Analysis of Global Air Travel Links.' *American Behavioural Scientist* 44 (10): 1656–1678.

Smith, M. P. (1998) 'The Global City-Whose Social Construct is it Anyway?: A Comment on White.' *Urban Affairs Review* 33 (4): 482–488.

——(2001) *Transnational Urbanism: Locating Globalization*. Oxford: Blackwell.

Smith, M. P. and J. R. Feagin (eds.) (1987) *The Capitalist City: Global Restructuring and Community Politics*. Oxford: Blackwell.

Smith, N. (1990) *Uneven Development: Nature, Capital and the Production of Space*. 2nd Edition. Oxford: Blackwell.

Smith, R.G. (2003) 'World City Actor-Networks.' *Progress in Human Geography* 27 (1): 25–44.

——(2011) 'Beyond the Global City Concept: Globalization and World City Research network.' *GaWC Research Bulletin 390*, http://www.lboro.ac.uk/gawc/rb/rb390.html

Smith, R. G. and M. A. Doel (2011) 'Questioning the Theoretical Basis of Current Global-City Research: Structures, Networks and Actor-Networks.' *International Journal of Urban and Regional Research* 35 (1): 24–39.

Spiller Gibbons Swan Pty Ltd & National Institute for Economic and Industry Research. (2000) *South West Urban System Economic Study – Future Perth*. Unpublished Report Prepared for the Western Australian Planning Commission. Perth: WAPC.

Standing, G. (2011) *The Precariat: The New Dangerous Class*. New York: Bloomsbury.

Steering Committee. (2012) *Joint Study on Aviation Capacity in the Sydney Region*. Canberra: Australian Government and NSW Government.

Sudjic, D. (1993) *The 100 Mile City*. London: Flamingo.

———(2005) *The Edifice Complex*. London: Penguin.

Sumiya, M. and K. Taira (eds.) (1979) *An Outline of Japanese Economic History 1603–1940*. Tokyo: University of Tokyo Press.

Swyngedouw, E. (1997) 'Neither Global nor Local: Glocalization and the Politics of Scale.' In: K. Cox (ed.), *Spaces of Globalization: Reasserting the Power of The Local*, pp. 137–166. London: Guilford Press.

———(2000) 'Authoritarian Governance, Power, and the Politics of Rescaling.' *Environment and Planning D* 18 (1): 63–76.

Taylor, M. and N. Thrift (1981) 'The Changing Spatial Concentration of Large Company Ownership and Control in Australia 1953–1978.' *Australian Geographer* 15 (2): 98–105.

Taylor, P. J. (1997) 'Hierarchical Tendencies amongst World Cities: A Global Research Proposal.' *Cities* 14 (6): 323–332.

———(2000) 'World Cities and Territorial States under Conditions of Contemporary Globalization.' *Political Geography* 19 (1): 5–32.

———(2001) 'Specification of the World City Network.' *Geographical Analysis* 33 (1): 181–194.

———(2004a) 'The New Geography of Global Civil Society: NGO's in the World City Network.' *Globalizations* 1 (2): 265–277.

———(2004b) *World City Network: A Global Urban Analysis*. London: Routledge.

———(2011) 'Advanced Producer Service Centres in the World Economy.' In: P. J. Taylor, P. Ni, B. Derudder, M. Hoyler, J. Huang and F. Witlox (eds.) *Global Urban Analysis: A Survey of Cities in Globalization*, pp. 22–39. London: Earthscan.

———(2013) *Extraordinary Cities*. Cheltenham: Edward Elgar.

Taylor, P. J., J. V. Beaverstock, B. Derudder, J. Faulconbridge, J. Harrison, M. Hoyler, K. Pain and F. Witlox (eds.) (2013) *Global Cities*. London: Routledge.

Taylor, P. J., B. Derudder, P. Saey and F. Witlox (eds.) (2007) *Cities in Globalization: Theories, Policies, Practices*. London: Routledge.

Taylor, P. J., B. Derudder, M. Hoyler and P. Ni (2013) New Regional Geographies of the World as Practised by Leading Advanced Producer Service Firms in 2010. Transactions, Institute of British Geographers, 38(3), 497–511.

Taylor, P. J., P. Ni, B. Derudder, M. Hoyler, J. Huang and F. Witlox (2011) *Global Urban Analysis: A Survey of Cities in Globalization*. London: Earthscan.

Teo, P. and S. Huang (1996) 'A Sense of Place in Public Housing: A Case Study of Pasir Ris, Singapore.' *Habitat International* 20 (2): 307–325.

Thacker, A. (2005) 'The Idea of a Critical Literary Geography.' *New Formations* 57: 56–73.

———(2003) *Moving Through Modernity*. Manchester: Manchester University Press.

Therborn, G. (2011) 'End of a Paradigm: The Current Crisis and the Idea of Stateless Cities.' *Environment and Planning A* 43 (2): 272–285.

Thornton, M. (2005) 'Skycrapers and Business Cycles.' *The Quarterly Journal of Austrian Economics* 8 (1): 51–74.

Thrift, N. (2003) 'Space: The Fundamental Stuff of Human Geography.' In: S. L. Holloway, S. P. Rice and G. Valentine (eds.), *Key Concepts in Geography*, pp. 95–107. London: Sage.

Timberlake, M. (1985) 'The World-System Perspective and Urbanization.' In: M. Timberlake (ed.), *Urbanization in the World-Economy*, pp. 3–22. Orlando: Academic Press.

Timberlake, M., M. R. Sanderson, X. Ma, B. Derudder, J. Winitzky and F. Witlox (2012) 'Testing a Global City Hypothesis: An Assessment of Polarization across US Cities.' *City & Community* 11 (1): 74–93.

Townsend, A. M. (2001) 'Network Cities and the Global Structure of the Internet.' *American Behavioral Scientist* 44 (10): 1697–1716.

Tranos, E. (2011) 'The Topology and the Emerging Urban Geographies of the Internet Backbone and Aviation Networks in Europe: A Comparative Study.' *Environment and Planning A* 43 (2): 378–392.

Travers, T. (2004) *The Politics of London: Governing the Ungovernable City.* Basingstoke: Palgrave.

Trounstine, J. (2009) 'All Politics Is Local: The Reemergence of the Study of City Politics.' *Perspectives on Politics* 7 (3): 611–618.

United Cities and Local Governments. (2010) *Local Leaders Preparing for the Future of our Cities.* Barcelona: UCLG.

US Department of Commerce. (1930) *Census of Population and Housing: 1930 Census, Metropolitan Districts Population and Area.* Washington, DC: United States Census Bureau.

van der Waal, J. (2012) 'Foreign Direct Investment and International Migration to Dutch Cities.' *Urban Studies*, early view. DOI: 10.1177/0042098012452326.

Verhetsel, A. and S. Sel (2009) 'World Maritime Cities: From which Cities do Container Shipping Companies Make Decisions?' *Transport Policy* 16 (2): 240–250.

Verne, J. (1872) *Le tour du monde en quatre-vingts jours* [Around the World in Eighty Days]. Paris: Le Temps.

Vind, I. and N. Fold (2010) 'City Networks and Commodity Chains: Identifying Global Flows and Local Connections in Ho Chi Minh City.' *Global Networks* 10 (1): 54–74.

Wacquant, L. (2008) *Urban Outcasts: A Comparative Sociology of Advanced Marginality.* Cambridge: Polity.

Wall, R. S. (2009) 'The Relative Importance of Randstad Cities within Comparative Worldwide Corporate Networks.' *Tijdschrift voor Economische en Sociale Geografie* 100 (2): 250–259.

Wall, R. S. and G. A. van der Knaap (2011) 'Sectoral Differentiation and Network Structure within Contemporary Worldwide Corporate Networks.' *Economic Geography* 87 (3): 267–308.

Wallenstein, I. M. (1974) The Modern World System: Capitalist Agriculture and the Origins of the European World Economy in the Sixteenth Century. New York: Academic Press.

———(1989) *World System III: The Second Era of Great Expansion of the Capitalist World-Economy, 1730s–1840s.* San Diego: Academic Press.

———(2000) 'Globalization or the Age of Transition? A Long-Term View of the Trajectory of the World-System.' *International Sociology* 15 (2): 249–265.

Wainwright, T. (2009) 'Laying the Foundations for a Crisis: Mapping the Historico-Geographical Construction of Residential Mortgage Backed Securitization in the UK.' *International Journal of Urban and Regional Research* 33 (2): 372–378.

Watson, A. and M. Hoyler (2010) 'Media Centres in the World Economy.' In: P. J. Taylor, P. Ni, B. Derudder, M. Hoyler, J. Huang and F. Witlox (eds.), *Global Urban Analysis: A Survey of Cities in Globalization*, pp. 40–47. Earthscan, London.

Watson, V. (2002) *Change and Continuity in Spatial Planning: Metropolitan Planning in Cape Town under Political Transition.* London: Routledge.

Weisburd, D., O. Shalev and M. Amir (2002) 'Community Policing in Israel: Resistance and Change.' *Policing: An International Journal of Police Strategies & Management* 25 (1): 80–109.

Weiser, M. (1991) 'The Computer for the 21st Century.' *Scientific American* 265 (3): 94–104.

West, A. (2010) 'Second Harbour Crossing – or Chaos.' *Sydney Morning Herald* 31 May.

Whyte, S. and C. Lucas (2013) "Restaurants" Dirty Secret Revealed.' *Sydney Morning Herald* 26 January.

Williams, R. (1985) *Keywords: A Vocabulary of Culture and Society.* Waukegan: Fontana Press.

Wimmer A. and N. Glick Schiller (2002) 'Methodological Nationalism and Beyond: Nation – State Building, Migration and the Social Sciences.' *Global Networks* 2 (4): 301–334.

Wittfogel, K. A. (1957) *Oriental Despotism; A Comparative Study of Total Power.* New Haven: Yale University Press.

Wolstein, B. (1987) 'Anxiety and the Psychic Center of the Psychoanalytic Self.' *Contemporary Psychoanalysis* 23 (4): 631–665.

Wójcik, D. (2011) 'The Dark Side of NY-LON: Financial Centres and the Global Financial Crisis.' *University of Oxford* Working Papers in Employment, Work and Finance, nos. 11–12, Oxford.

Wood, F. (1998) *No Dogs and Not May Chinese: Treaty Port Life in China, 1843–1943.* London: John Murray.

Wright, J. K. (1947) *'Terrae Incognitae*: The Place of Imagination in Geography.' *Annals of the Association of American Geographers* 37 (1): 1–15.

Xu, B. and F. Milthorpe (2010) 'Analysis of Journey to Work Travel Patterns in Sydney.' *Australasian Transport Research Forum Proceedings*, Sydney.

Yates, J. (2001) 'The Rhetoric and Reality of Housing Choice: The Role of Urban Consolidation.' *Urban Policy and Research* 19 (4): 491–527.

Yates, J., B. Randolph and D. Holloway (2006) 'Housing Affordability, Occupation and Location in Australian Cities and Regions.' *AHURI Final Report* No. 91. Melbourne: Australian Housing and Urban Research Institute.

Yeoh, B. S. A. (1999) 'Global/Globalizing Cities.' *Progress in Human Geography* 23 (4): 607–616.

———(2005) 'The Global Cultural City? Spatial Imagineering and Politics in the (Multi)cultural Marketplaces of South-east Asia.' *Urban Studies* 42 (5–6): 945–958.

Zanotti, L. (2010) 'Cacophonies of Aid, Failed State Building and NGOs in Haiti: Setting the Stage for Disaster, Envisioning the Future.' *Third World Quarterly* 31 (5): 755–771.

Zook, M. and M. Graham (2007a) 'Mapping DigiPlace: Geocoded Internet Data and the Representation of Place.' *Environment and Planning B: Planning and Design* 34 (3): 466–482.

———(2007b) 'The Creative Reconstruction of the Internet: Google and the Privatization of Cyberspace and DigiPlace.' *Geoforum* 38 (6): 1322–1343.

———(2007c) 'From Cyberspace to DigiPlace: Visibility in an Age of Information and Mobility.' In: H. Miller (ed.), *Societies and Cities in the Age of Instant Access*, pp. 231–244. London: Springer.

Zukin, S. (1992) 'The City as a Landscape of Power: London and New York as Global Financial Capitals.' In: L. Budd and S. Whimster (eds.), *Global Finance and Urban Living. A Study of Metropolitan Change*, pp. 195–233. London: Routledge.

Index

Note: The letters 'f', 'n' and 't' following locators refer to figures, notes and tables respectively

technocratic model, 195
technological revolution, 76
Tel Aviv, 3
telecommunications, 10, 34, 76, 85
Temple Mount, 132
temporal fix, 53–5, 61
tenement slums, 73
Teo, P., 167
terracotta warriors, 65
text-based interactions, 103
Thacker, A., 106, 115n5
Therborn, G., 25
Third World urbanization, 75
Thornley, A., 173, 174, 176, 183, 187
Thornton, M., 61n3
Thrift, N., 52, 103, 120, 203
Tigris River, 67
Timberlake, M. F., 21, 23, 34, 35
time-space compression, 81–7
  global city mall, 86f
  mid-nineteenth century
    representation, 84f
Tokyo, 21, 24–5, 34, 37, 49, 71, 73–5,
  79–80, 101, 123, 142
  city-by-firm matrix, 37t
  command-and-control function, 49
  connectivity, 25
  Dyad connectivity, 37t
  economic power, 24
  growth, 73
  infrastructure, 74
  IWCNM approach, 34
  Olympics (1964), 75
  population, 73, 75, 79, 123
  refugees, 79
  rivalry with Beijing, 71
  skilled professionals, 80
tolerance-testing eclecticism, 224
Toronto, 22
tourism, 164, 204
Tourism Research Australia, 206
Tower of London, 162
Townsend, A. M., 24
Tranos, E., 35
transatlantic trade, 72–3
transit-led mega-development, 150
transnational capitalist class, 159–60
travelling technocrats, 197
Travers, T., 181
Trounstine, J., 171

UNDP, 194
UNESCO World Heritage List, 220
uneven landscapes, 211
UN Framework Convention on Climate
  Change, 179
United Nations Environment
  Programme, 179
United Overseas Bank Plaza, 165
UPP model, 199
URA, *see* Urban Redevelopment
  Authority
urban age, 222
urban agglomeration, 166
urban analysis, 27, 186
urban civilizations, 83, 91
urban development model, 58
urban exploration, 12, 148
urban governance, 177
Urban Immigrant Index, 22
urban inhabitants, 126, 129
urban interventions, 93–4
urbanism, 5, 8, 50, 87, 93–4, 99, 145,
  165, 169, 182–4, 230, 236
  actually existing, 88, 93, 96, 100
  American model, 93
  nature of, 94
  occupancy, 88, 94, 96, 100
  politics of, 236
  subaltern, 86
  sustainable, 182–4
urbanization
  planetary, 222, 235
  spectacular, 55
urban mega-projects, 94
urban necropolitics, 190
urban pattern, 73, 75, 85
urban political economy, 16
urban racial segregation, 97
Urban Redevelopment Authority, 166
urban securitization, 199
urban splintering, 127
urban studies approach, 20–3
urban subcultures, 12, 146–7, 153
Urry, J., 191
US-Australian partnership, 208

van der Knaap, G. A., 35
van der Pluijm, R., 175, 176
varnbombing, 147

Printed and bound in the United States of America